There have been many attempts to refute objections to the factual, historical resurrection of Jesus Christ since these first gained prominence in the 18th-century, so-called Enlightenment. Ross Hickling offers a new analysis, relying especially on the canons of evidence applicable to factual determinations in general. His book should be read by skeptics, if only to discourage them from repeating Richard Carrier's errors. Christian apologists should also study Hickling's book carefully, thereby increasing the sophistication of their defense of the key piece of miracle evidence in support of the truth of the Christian religion.

> **Dr. John Warwick Montgomery**, Ph.D., D.Théol., LL.D., Professor Emeritus of Law and Humanities, University of Bedfordshire, England/UK; Professor-at-Large, 1517: The Legacy Project, Irvine, CA, USA; Director, International Academy of Apologetics, Evangelism and Human Rights, Strasbourg, France

This book should find a place on the shelf of every Christian apologist. Hickling is not only a fine scholar whose writing is pithy and easy to understand, he comes to the task as an experienced criminal investigator. It's about time the exaggerated claims of an atheist "scholar" were put under the microscope of the laws of evidence with respect to documents and eyewitness testimony. Hickling does this superbly proving the reliability of the gospel narratives and the admissibility of the resurrection evidence. He also tackles and refutes the alleged dependence upon pagan dying and rising god myths. A succinct apologetic that truly will aid those committed to defending and advocating the claims of the risen Christ.

> **Dr. Ross Clifford**, A.M., Principal, Morling Theological College, Sydney, Aus., Author of *John Warwick Montgomery's Legal Apologetic: An Apologetic for All Seasons* and *Leading Lawyer's Case for the Resurrection*.

Because of his experience in handling evidence throughout his career, Hickling's insight into evidentiary principles coming from long established federal criminal rules of evidence/jury instructions is of great use as he brings it to bear on a prominent skeptic's claims against the resurrection. After mining Carrier's views from his writings, Hickling compares them with pertinent scholarly material and the aforementioned evidentiary principles. In his apologetic refutations of Carrier's objections, Hickling deals, in a meaningful way, with important questions in the ongoing resurrection debate to include:

- 'Did the disciples hallucinate the risen Jesus Christ?'
- 'Was the resurrection of Jesus Christ developed from pre-existing pagan myths?'
- 'Do the resurrection accounts in the various Gospels contradict each other?'

It was a privilege to experience the precision of Hickling's scholarly research as it progressed through its various stages. I sincerely recommend it.

Dr. Henk G. Stoker, Ph.D., School of Theology, North-West University, Potchefstroom, South Africa

This remarkably thorough volume makes an invaluable contribution to legal apologetics by taking on a contemporary challenger to the resurrection of Jesus Christ and applying the federal rules of evidence in a trial court setting to a host of objections. The result, while stunning, has a long and prestigious pedigree of those who have also applied the common law rules of evidence to the central factual claim of Christianity and vindicated that claim that God was indeed "in Christ Jesus reconciling the world unto Himself" as is verified by the resurrection (see works by Simon Greenleaf, Sir Norman Anderson, and John Warwick Montgomery). Ross Hickling's work is sure to become a classic in the long line of works establishing the facticity of the resurrection as presented by the reliable testimony of a 'cloud of witnesses.'

Dr. Craig Parton, J.D., Trial Lawyer and Partner with Price, Postel & Parma LLP of Santa Barbara, California and former Chairman of the Litigation Section of the Santa Barbara County Bar Association, Author of *The Defense Never Rests* and *Religion on Trial.*

Richard Carrier has raised some common criticisms against the historical case for the resurrection of Jesus: Did the apostles hallucinate? Was the resurrection borrowed from pagan myths? Do contradictions discount the reliability of the Gospels? In this book "An evidentiary analysis of doctor Richard Carrier's objections to the resurrection of Jesus Christ", Ross Hickling responds to each of these critiques with careful research based upon the Federal Rules of Evidence. Hickling has done a tremendous amount of research and has helped advance the case for the resurrection.

> **Dr. Sean McDowell**, Ph.D., Associate Professor of Apologetics, Biola University, Author or co-author of over 18 books including *Evidence that Demands A Verdict*.

Virtually every scholar in the world in the relevant fields rejects the hypothesis that Jesus never existed. According to Richard Carrier, the leading proponent of that hypothesis, there are only eight scholars in the world holding this view. And that's including himself! Nevertheless, that has not stopped Internet bloggers from propagating it. In this book, Ross Hickling provides a unique approach to addressing Carrier's arguments. Combining historical scholarship with his expertise as a former law enforcement investigator, Hickling carefully dissects Carrier's arguments and reveals their weaknesses.

> **Dr. Michael R. Licona**, Ph.D., Associate Professor of Theology, Houston Baptist University.

If we could bring Richard Carrier's famously sceptical view of Jesus' resurrection into a lawcourt, what would the verdict on its plausibility be? In this helpful book Ross Hickling does three things: he enables us to listen carefully and critically to the case presented by Carrier and others; he presents the counterarguments from a wide range of other scholars, and finally as someone who is experienced in legal matters he suggests how we should weigh the evidence in a fair-minded and rigorous way.

> **Dr. David Wenham**, M.A., Ph.D., Trinity College, Bristol, U.K.

Anyone can concoct theories that assert the New Testament writers were mistaken about the Resurrection of Jesus. However, it's another thing completely to provide evidence for your concocted theory. Ross Hickling devastates the theories of skeptical scholar Richard Carrier by revealing how devoid of evidence — and accepted rules of evidence — Carrier's positions are. Hickling not only exposes Carriers errors, but answers Carrier's objections with evidence that affirms the historicity of the New Testament documents and the Resurrection of Christ. Highly recommended!

> **Dr. Frank Turek**, Ph.D., President, Cross-Examined.org, Charlotte, NC, Author of four books to include *Stealing from God: Why Atheists Need God to Make their Case* and *I Don't Have Enough Faith to be an Atheist*.

Dr. Richard Carrier has been one of the more vocal of the recent parade of skeptics calling into question the historicity of the resurrection of Jesus Christ. Dr. Ross Hickling has done a great service to the Christian community in amassing an astounding amount of data surrounding this most important event of history. Assessing this data not only with his skills as a researcher but also as a retired senior inspector with the U.S. Marshals Service, Dr. Hickling applies the Federal Rules of Evidence to deftly refute Carrier's skepticism, showing that there can be no reasonable doubt that Jesus Christ was indeed raised from the dead.

> **Dr. Richard G. Howe**, Ph.D., Emeritus Professor of Philosophy and Apologetics, Southern Evangelical Seminary, Past President, International Society of Christian Apologetics

S. Ross Hickling

An Evidentiary Analysis of Doctor Richard Carrier's Objections to the Resurrection of Jesus Christ

Christliche Philosophie heute – Christian Philosophy Today – Quomodo Philosophia Christianorum Hodie Estimatur

Volume 20

Vol. 1: John Warwick Montgomery. Tractatus Logico-Theologicus.

Vol. 2: John W. Montgomery. Hat die Weltgeschichte einen Sinn? Geschichtsphilosophien auf dem Prüfstand.

Vol. 3: John W. Montgomery. Jésus: La raison rejoint l'histoire.

Vol. 4: Horst Waldemar Beck. Marken dieses Äons: Wissenschaftskritische und theologische Diagnosen.

Vol. 5: Ross Clifford. John Warwick Montgomery's Legal Apologetic: An Apologetic for All Seasons.

Vol. 6: Thomas K. Johnson. Natural Law Ethics: An Evangelical Proposal.

Vol. 7: Lydia Jaeger. Wissenschaft ohne Gott? Zum Verhältnis zwischen christlichem Glauben und Wissenschaft.

Vol. 8: Herman Bavinck. Christliche Weltanschauung. hrsg. von Thomas K. Johnson und Ron Kubsch.

Vol. 9: John W. Montgomery. La Mort de Dieu: Exposé et critique du plus récent mouvement théologique en Amérique: Réimpression de l'édition 1971.

Vol. 10: David Andersen. Martin Luther – The Problem of Faith and Reason: A Reexamination in Light of the Epistemological and Christological Issues.

Vol. 11: Wim Rietkerk. In dubio: Handbuch für Zweifler.

Vol. 12: Patrick Werder: Wenig niedriger als Gott: Der Mensch als Person von der Antike bis zur Gegenwart.

Vol. 13: John Warwick Montgomery: Christ As Centre and Circumference: Essays Theological, Cultural and Polemic.

Vol. 14: Lydia Jaeger. Als Mensch in Gottes Welt: Im Licht der Schöpfung leben.

Vol. 15: Frederik Herzberg. Theo-Logik: Über den Beitrag des Jansenismus zur formalen Methode in Theologie und Religionsphilosophie.

Vol. 16: Hanniel Strebel. Eine Theologie des Lernens: Systematisch-theologische Beiträge aus dem Werk von Herman Bavinck.

Vol. 17: John Warwick Montgomery. Fighting the Good Fight – A Life in Defense of the Faith.

Vol. 18: Henry Hock Guan Teh. Principles of the Law of Evidence and Rationality Applied in the Johannine Christology: An Argument for the Legal Evidential Apologetics.

Vol. 19: John Warwick Montgomery. Defending the Gospel in Legal Style – Essays on Legal Apologetics & the Justification of Classical Christian Faith.

S. Ross Hickling

An Evidentiary Analysis of Doctor Richard Carrier's Objections to the Resurrection of Jesus Christ

WIPF & STOCK · Eugene, Oregon

Wipf and Stock Publishers
199 W 8th Ave, Suite 3
Eugene, OR 97401

An Evidentiary Analysis of Doctor Richard Carrier's Objections
to the Resurrection of Jesus Christ
By Hickling, S. Ross
Copyright©2018 Verlag für Kultur und Wissenschaft
ISBN 13: 978-1-5326-6313-0
Publication date 7/11/2018
Previously published by Verlag für Kultur und Wissenschaft, 2018

Contents

Introduction 17

Abstract 19

Acknowledgments 21

Abbreviations 22

Dedications 23

Chapter One
Introduction 25

Chapter Two
Objection One: The Resurrection Narratives Contradict Each Other 33

Chapter Three
Objection Two: The Gospel Accounts of the Resurrection of Jesus
Were Influenced by Pagan Myths 115

Chapter Four
Objection Three: The Disciples Hallucinated the Risen Jesus Christ 219

Chapter Five
Summary, Findings, and Conclusion 327

Bibliography 357

Contents (detailed)

Introduction 17

Abstract 19

Acknowledgments 21

Abbreviations 22

Dedications 23

Chapter One
Introduction 25
   1.1 Background and problem statement 25
       1.1.1 Background 25
       1.1.2 Problem statement 26
   1.2 Research questions 27
   1.3 Aim and objectives 28
       1.3.1 Aim 28
       1.3.2 Objectives 28
   1.4 Central theoretical argument 29
   1.5 Research methodology 29
   1.6 Concept clarification 30

Chapter Two
Objection One: The Resurrection Narratives Contradict Each Other 33
   2.1 Introduction 33
   2.2 Carrier's examination of the Gospel witnesses 34
       2.2.1 Contradiction: In general, the Gospel narratives contradict each other 34
       2.2.2 Contradiction: Number and activity of angels at the tomb .. 37
       2.2.3 Different women and their activities at the tomb 38
       2.2.4 Contradiction: Resurrection appearances 41
       2.2.5 Contradiction: Timing of the removal of the stone 42
   2.3 Cross-examination of Carrier's contention by Christian scholars 43

Contents (detailed) 11

- 2.3.1 Cross-examination: In general, the narratives are contradictory 43
- 2.3.2 Cross-examination: Number and activity of angels at the tomb 48
- 2.3.3 Cross-examination: Different women and their activities at the tomb 53
- 2.3.4 Cross-examination: Resurrection appearances 56
- 2.3.5 Cross-examination: Timing of the removal of the stone.....61
- 2.4 Evidence of similarity in the resurrection narratives...................64
  - 2.4.1 Evidence of similarity: Prominence of the women as witnesses...64
  - 2.4.2 Evidence of similarity: Doubting disciples.........................69
  - 2.4.3 Evidence of similarity: Joseph of Arimathea 73
- 2.5 Explanation of accepted principles of evidence...........................75
  - 2.5.1 Historical background of the *FRE* 75
  - 2.5.2 Accepted principles of evidence: Rules 102 and 401 78
  - 2.5.3 Accepted principle of evidence: Rule 104(b) 79
  - 2.5.4 Accepted principle of evidence: Rule 602 80
  - 2.5.5 Accepted principle of evidence: Rule 607 80
  - 2.5.6 Accepted principle of evidence: Rule 610 81
  - 2.5.7 Accepted principles of evidence: Rules 802 and 803 81
- 2.6 Federal jury instructions: Evaluation of the evidence 82
  - 2.6.1 Purpose and history of federal jury instructions 82
  - 2.6.2 Accepted principles of evidence: Direct and circumstantial evidence..84
  - 2.6.3 Accepted principle of evidence: Judging the credibility of witnesses 85
  - 2.6.4 Accepted principle of evidence: Weighing the evidence 86
- 2.7 Embellishment v. contradiction: Joseph of Arimathea....................87
- 2.8 Evidentiary analysis: Carrier's contention by accepted principles of evidence..91
  - 2.8.1 Evidentiary analysis: Carrier's view of evidence 91
  - 2.8.2 Evidentiary analysis: Carrier's contention in light of accepted principles of evidence 92
  - 2.8.3 Evidentiary analysis: Rebuttal evidence to Carrier's contention 97
  - 2.8.4 Evidentiary analysis: The testimony of John by accepted principles of evidence 102

2.8.5 Evidentiary analysis: The four evangelists as known persons with known sources..................105
2.9 Summary..................113

Chapter Three
Objection Two: The Gospel Accounts of the Resurrection of Jesus Were Influenced by Pagan Myths 115

3.1 Introduction 115
3.2 Carrier's claim: Christian resurrection influenced by mystery/pagan cults..................117
    3.2.1 Similarities between the resurrection of Jesus Christ and mystery religions: In general..................117
    3.2.2 Correlations between the resurrection of Jesus Christ and the myth of Osiris..................119
    3.2.3 Correlations between the resurrection of Jesus Christ and the myth of Inanna..................123
    3.2.4 Parallels between the resurrection of Jesus Christ and the myth of Romulus..................126
    3.2.5 Correlations between the resurrection of Jesus Christ and the myth of Zalmoxis..................131
3.3 Exposition of pagan/mythical literature..................135
    3.3.1 Exposition of the myth of Osiris..................135
    3.3.2 Exposition of the myth of Inanna..................147
    3.3.3 Exposition of the legend of Romulus and Remus 157
    3.3.4 Exposition of the legend of Zalmoxis 164
3.4 Cross-examination of Carrier by scholarly literature 171
    3.4.1 Cross-examination: The resurrection of Jesus Christ coming from mystery religions 171
    3.4.2 Cross-examination: Resurrection of Jesus Christ coming from Osiris/Inanna..................177
    3.4.3 Cross-Examination: Resurrection of Jesus Christ from Romulus..................179
    3.4.4 Cross-examination: Resurrection of Jesus Christ coming from Zalmoxis..................181
    3.4.5 Cross-examination: Christian baptism coming from pagan religions..................181
    3.4.6 Cross-examination: Carrier's thesis based upon a logical fallacy..................184

3.5 Evidence against Carrier's claim: New Testament scriptures reference Jewish soteriology and eschatology 186

3.6 Evidence against Carrier's claim: Paul's emphasis on the resurrection comes from the Old Testament..........................194

3.7 Evidence against Carrier's claim: Paul and idolatry 198

3.8 Evidence against Carrier's claim: The Old Testament and idolatry 200

3.9 Evidentiary analysis: Carrier's contention in light of accepted principles of evidence...204
   3.9.1 Mystery religions: In general 204
   3.9.2 Christian baptism influenced by pagan baptism 205
   3.9.3 Paul Influenced by the mystery cults 205
   3.9.4 Osiris...206
   3.9.5 Inanna/Ishtar...209
   3.9.6 Romulus 212
   3.9.7 Zalmoxis...215
   3.9.8 New Testament writers influenced by pagan mystery cults .216

3.10 Summary 217

Chapter Four
Objection Three: The Disciples Hallucinated the Risen Jesus Christ 219

4.1 Introduction 219

4.2 Carrier's Claim: PRA were hallucinations..220
   4.2.1 PRA: Hypnagogic/Hypnopompic hallucinations 220
   4.2.2 PRA: Bereavement/Grief hallucinations 223
   4.2.3 PRA: Schizophrenic hallucinations 225
   4.2.4 PRA: Hallucination caused by guilt 226
   4.2.5 PRA: Hallucinations from fatigue/seizures 227

4.3 Exposition of scholarly literature on hallucinations........................228
   4.3.1 Hypnagogic/Hypnopompic hallucinations 228
   4.3.2 Schizophrenic hallucinations 234
   4.3.3 Bereavement/Grief hallucinations 240
   4.3.4 Seizure related hallucinations 245
   4.3.5 Charles Bonnet syndrome 250
   4.3.6 Drug induced hallucinations 253
   4.3.7 Post-traumatic stress disorder related hallucinations 256
   4.3.8 Fatigue/Deprivation and guilt related hallucinations........258
   4.3.9 Conclusion: Exposition of scholarly literature on hallucinations 260

4.4 Cross-examination of Carrier's "hallucinating disciples" by scholarly literature 260
    4.4.1 Cross-examination: The disciples were hallucinating: In general 261
    4.4.2 Cross-examination: Schizophrenic hallucination 269
    4.4.3 Cross-examination: Bereavement hallucinations 270
    4.4.4 Cross-examination: PTSD hallucinations 275
    4.4.5 Cross-examination: Fatigue/Deprivation/Guilt hallucinations 276

4.5 Carrier's redirect examination 278
    4.5.1 Redirect examination: Countering "group hallucinations" cross-examination 278
    4.5.2 Redirect examination: Disciples were expecting to encounter the risen Jesus Christ 280

4.6 Recross-examination of Carrier 280
    4.6.1 Group hallucinations 281
    4.6.2 Disciples expected to see the risen Jesus Christ 283

4.7 Evidence against Carrier's hallucinating disciples 285
    4.7.1 Evidence against the hallucination hypothesis: PRA in bodily form 286
    4.7.2 Evidence against the hallucination hypothesis: The eyewitnesses of the PRA experience martyrdom 293
    4.7.3 Evidence against Carrier's hallucinating disciples: The conversions of James and Saul 302
    4.7.4 Evidence Against the hallucination hypothesis: The empty tomb in conjunction with the PRA of Jesus Christ .304

4.8 Evidentiary Analysis: Carrier's Contention in Light of Accepted Principles of Evidence 308
    4.8.1 Evidentiary Analysis: Disciples Were Hallucinating: In General 308
    4.8.2 Evidentiary analysis: PRA as hypnagogic/hypnopompic hallucinations 309
    4.8.3 Evidentiary analysis: PRA as schizophrenic hallucinations/"happy schizotypal" 311
    4.8.4 Evidentiary analysis: PRA as bereavement hallucinations 314
    4.8.5 Evidentiary analysis: PRA as seizure related hallucinations 316

Contents (detailed)

- 4.8.6 Evidentiary analysis: PRA as hallucinations caused by fatigue/deprivation 317
- 4.8.7 Evidentiary analysis: PRA as guilt hallucinations 318
- 4.8.8 Evidentiary analysis: PRA from other forms of hallucinations 319
- 4.8.9 Evidentiary analysis: PRA were bodily in nature 320
- 4.8.10 Evidentiary analysis: Disciples martyrdom as circumstantial evidence for PRA 322
- 4.8.11 Evidentiary analysis: Conversions of James and Saul as circumstantial evidence 322
- 4.8.12 Evidentiary analysis: The PRA of Jesus Christ corroborated by the empty tomb 323
- 4.9 Summary 324

Chapter Five
Summary, Findings, and Conclusion 327

- 5.1 Summary 327
  - 5.1.1 Summary: Accepted principles of evidence 327
  - 5.1.2 Summary: Carrier's contentions 329
  - 5.1.3 Summary: New Testament resurrection accounts are contradictory 329
  - 5.1.4 Summary: Antecedent dying/rising gods and Jesus Christ 333
  - 5.1.5 Summary: The disciples hallucinated the risen Jesus Christ 341
- 5.2 Evidentiary findings 349
  - 5.2.1 Evidentiary findings: Contradictory resurrection narratives 349
  - 5.2.2 Evidentiary findings: Antecedent dying/rising gods and Jesus Christ 351
  - 5.2.3 Evidentiary findings: The disciples hallucinated the risen Jesus Christ 352
- 5.3 Research limitations 354
- 5.4 Recommendations 355

Bibliography 357

Introduction

How can we know with any confidence about anything that has transpired in the past whether it be two minutes or two millennia ago? Police officers responding to crimes that have just been committed have the daunting challenge of gathering as much evidence as they can in a small amount of time in order to bring a perpetrator to justice before the case grows cold. Similarly, investigators of various sorts attempt to make sense of evidence that may be very old. When assessing the evidence on any given topic regardless of its age, there are germane questions that should be answered: 1) Is the evidence relevant to the matter under examination? 2) Are the data being put forth as evidence in accord with recognized forms of evidence? 3) In addition to the various forms of evidence, are the data being used as evidence supported by other long established evidentiary principles?

A number of years back, when going through seminary while still employed as a criminal investigator, I became familiar with the work of several skeptical authors who engaged in strong rhetoric arguing against the existence of the "god of Christian theism." It seemed that rather than a fair-minded assessment of this issue, they were more interested in presenting the worst portrait of who they believed Christians were in the past and are today. As they presented their arguments against Christian theism, it was hard to look at the actual case they were presenting because it was difficult to separate fact from the fiery language employed. In addition to these skeptical authors, there were several atheist writers who began to call into question the very existence of Jesus Christ as a historical person. They were no longer saying that the disciples were merely mistaken about the identity of Jesus Christ. Rather, they claimed that Jesus Christ was a mythical figure. One of these "mythicists," Dr. Richard Carrier, has offered various theories about early Christians and how they became to believe that Jesus Christ was the resurrected Son of God. Moreover, he utilizes various arguments to discredit the New Testament versions of the resurrection narratives. Should Christians consider Carrier's critiques on the origins of Christianity? I believe that they should consider them because as Paul states, "if Christ has not been raised, your faith is futile; you are still in your sins (1 Cor. 15:17)." Thus it is an important matter for the Christian community to deal with Carrier's claims and determine whether any of them are supported by good evidence. Because, if there is convincing evidence that the resurrection of Jesus Christ was a fraud or a myth, then serious Christians should reconsider their devotion to Jesus Christ.

As I first began to read Carrier's claims, I was curious what evidence he was using to support his positions. Was he utilizing relevant evidence? Did he have historical testimony backing up his claims against the resurrection of Jesus Christ? Even though Carrier is a talented writer with a bright mind, it was clear to me that his "evidence" was wanting the more I read on. Armed with a knowledge of basic principles of investigation from my years of law enforcement experience, I began to mine accepted principled of evidence from widely used documents from the criminal justice system here in the United States which were derived from centuries old English common law principles. Yes, I had used these principles when investigating crimes and had observed them in use on many occasions when judges and juries were handling evidence given them. After engaging in scholarly research, it was clear to me that Carrier was not familiar with these long established evidentiary principles as he was not using them in his material. Even as the New Testament makes historical claims about the life, ministry, death, and resurrection of Jesus Christ, so does Carrier. Thus, if Dr. Carrier is making historical claims that the resurrection of Jesus Christ did not occur, then, his claims should be supported by the aforementioned accepted principles of evidence if they are to be taken seriously.

For those of you who are scholarly investigators of one sort or another, I encourage you to read Dr. Carrier's positions and give them serious consideration. I have many excerpts from Carrier's writings contained within this volume and would encourage you to peruse them here. I would also encourage you to sift through the various evidentiary principles contained within this volume to see if Carrier has supported his claims with accepted principles of evidence. I would submit to you that in spite of his considerable talents as a writer and an internet blogger, it appears that what he uses as evidence for his positions are not supported by these principles.

Even as I mentioned above the increased rhetoric employed in recent years, I trust that you will find this volume lacking in incendiary language. I do not believe that maligning someone's character is a way to prove anything. Not that I am opposed to anyone writing or speaking clearly and forcefully about their positions as I have advocated strongly for my position in these pages. Regardless of your opinion on this topic, it is my hope that you will consider the material within this volume in respect to whether its conclusions are supported by evidence. If Dr. Carrier's claims are not supported by evidence then this should lead an investigator to seriously consider the resurrection of Jesus Christ as a historical event that occurred in space and time with all of its attendant implications for humanity both personally and culturally.

S. Ross Hickling, Kernersville, North Carolina, U.S.A.

Abstract

This study examines the writings of a prominent atheist scholar, Doctor Richard Carrier, Ph.D., regarding his view of the resurrection narratives of Jesus Christ as described in the New Testament. In his writings, Carrier questions the veridicality of these resurrection accounts. The main goal of this research project is to distill accepted principles of evidence from established legal precepts in order to determine if Carrier's views utilize these accepted principles of evidence. Three of Carrier's contentions against the resurrection of Jesus Christ are analyzed by comparing them with the aforementioned evidentiary precepts coming from the Anglo-American/common law tradition. This tradition includes rules/regulations governing the treatment of evidence in legal proceedings that have been in use since the eighteenth century and have long since been accepted in the modern era by countries that employ the Anglo-American common law jurisprudence system. These principles are codified and in use today in the *Federal Rules of Evidence* and also contained within federal pattern jury instructions both which are used in courts throughout the United States of America. The *Federal Rules of Evidence* govern the use of evidence in criminal trials and pattern jury instructions are given to jurors in order to educate them on how to interpret evidence they receive for and against criminal defendants. In addition to this analysis, relevant scholarly material to include Christian apologetic literature, and relevant passages of the New Testament are examined to determine if Carrier's claims regarding the resurrection of Jesus Christ are in accord with the aforementioned accepted principles of evidence.

Key Words: resurrection, Jesus Christ, Richard Carrier, evidence, analysis, contradiction, comparison, dying and rising gods, hallucination

Acknowledgments

In the development of this thesis, on many occasions, I found myself hearkening back to my past career as a criminal investigator. I remembered my law enforcement partners with whom I worked with, and who mentored me as I progressed through the various stages of my career. Working with these partners gave me a good foundation upon which to investigate the claims set out in my thesis. I also reflected on relationships and experiences with other colleagues who were part of the extended "court family." In my time investigating crimes, producing prisoners to court appearances, tracking down fugitives, and working to further the administration of justice, I came into contact with many prosecutors, judges, defense attorneys, and other officers of the court who shaped my experiences with evidence. Throughout my career, prosecutors would partner with me in presenting cases showing me the strengths and weaknesses of the evidence in a particular case I was working. I also befriended able defense attorneys as they worked on behalf of their clients in court. After their hearings concluded, we would discuss the different aspects of these cases to include the strengths and weaknesses of the evidence. I also had the privilege of working with and observing experienced judges as they made their legal findings on the bench. On occasion, I would have the opportunity to speak with them when in their chambers or in passing. In these experiences and interactions, not only did I make many friends, but I also learned much about evidence and investigation. I am truly privileged to have worked with so many outstanding individuals of good will from the law enforcement community and from the extended court family. It would take too much space to list them all here individually but know that I am greatly appreciative for their friendship, their insights, and their work that is indirectly reflected in these pages.

I would also like to acknowledge the work of several Christian legal thinkers, who through their scholarship, have contributed in blazing the path taken in this thesis. In particular, I would like to thank Dr. Ross Clifford, Principal of Morling College in Sydney, Australia, for his work and insights in applying legal principles to the study of Christian apologetics. His work in this area is insightful, yet easy to understand. I would also like to thank Dr. John W. Montgomery for his lifetime career in Christian apologetics, law, and theology. His work in Christian apologetics from a legal perspective has given great clarity to many complex arguments arrayed against core Christian tenets. His scholarship has greatly benefitted not only this research project, but also the Christian community at large. I would be remiss if I did not mention my father, Harley Hickling, under whose leadership I was introduced to Jesus Christ and who also launched me in a lifetime of intellectual endeavor. Finally, I would also like to thank Professor Doctor Henk G. Stoker, my research supervisor, for his support of this project throughout its development to its completion. Not only am I thankful for his guidance, time, and energies, but also I am very grateful for his patience as I worked through this project. Moreover, I am very appreciative for his patronage, for his enthusiasm, for his many suggestions, and for allowing me to study under his tutelage.

Abbreviations

ADC	After Death Communication
CBS	Charles Bonnet Syndrome
FPJI	federal pattern jury instructions
FRE	Federal Rules of Evidence
NDE	Near Death Experience
NRSV	New Revised Standard Version
NIV	New International Version
PRA	Post-resurrection appearance(s)
PBHE	Post Bereavement Hallucination Experience
VH	Visual Hallucinations
PTSD	Post Traumatic Stress Disorder

Dedications

This scholastic endeavor is dedicated to those family members who sacrificed so much:

To Andrea, the love of my life, this project would have never started without your endless support, prayers, and encouragement. Thank you for always being so patient and understanding.

To Ryan and Rachel, thank you for your patience and sacrifice through the years. Oftentimes, instead of being with you, I was researching and writing. I pray that you find satisfaction in that through your sacrifice, you supported me.

To Jesus Christ, I know that I would not be at this juncture if it were not for your guidance, sustenance, and provision in so many ways. Thank you from the bottom of my heart.

Chapter One

Introduction

1.1 Background and problem statement

1.1.1 Background

Dr. Richard Carrier is a prominent atheist scholar who has authored seven books and is included as an author of chapters in other volumes.[1] In these writings, Carrier questions the veracity of core Christian tenets. Several of his recent titles include *Why I Am Not a Christian: Four Conclusive Reasons to Reject Faith* (Philosophy Press, 2011), *On the Historicity of Jesus: Why We Might Have Reason to Doubt* (Sheffield Press, 2014b), and *Hitler, Homer, Bible, Christ* (Philosophy Press, 2014a). In addition to his publications, Carrier is listed on several Internet sites as being on lists of the most prominent atheists in the world (SuperScholar) (Thebestschools.org). Not only is Carrier gaining increasing notoriety in print, he also has a sizeable presence on the Internet as well. This presence can be seen on his own website (Carrier:2016), and also on *The Secular Web* (The secular web, Date of access: 30 Oct. 2014) where over thirty of his articles are posted that deal with anti-Christian and anti-theist views. In addition to his increasing popularity amongst atheists and skeptics in print and on the Internet, Carrier has also debated noted Christian apologists such as Dr. William Lane Craig (March 18, 2009) and Dr. Mike Licona (February 11, 2010) in the recent past. It is because of Carrier's continuous and growing presence in various forms of media that his views need to be examined from a Christian apologetic position as he questions the very foundations of Christian theology, doctrine, and practice.

I first became acquainted with Carrier's positions on the resurrection of Jesus Christ as recorded in the New Testament when I was a student at a seminary and was studying the resurrection of Jesus Christ from an apologetic perspective. When I began to examine Carrier's contentions related to this topic, it appeared that many of them were not buttressed by relevant evidence. Rather, much of what he wrote regarding his objec-

---

[1] This information is listed on the Amazon website under "Richard Carrier's Books" (Amazon.com, Date of access: 3 January 2017).

tions to the resurrection of Jesus Christ seemed to be based on his opinion or his reliance upon data that did not have a nexus or connection to the particular issue that he was discussing. Because of my experience with the criminal justice system as a criminal investigator who developed evidence to support criminal prosecutions against my own defendants, I was interested to know what Carrier was using as evidence to back his positions. Upon conducting further inquiry regarding his positions, I did not find data that would qualify as good evidence to support his assertions about the resurrection of Jesus Christ.

Because of the proliferation of atheist critiques against Christianity that are in the media and on the internet that question the validity of core Christian tenets of faith such as the resurrection of Jesus Christ, and because Carrier is one of the major spokesmen for these views, I believe that it is imperative for Christian scholars to engage with atheist scholars, such as Carrier, from an evidentiary perspective.[2] Ultimately, if atheist perspectives regarding the resurrection are founded upon solid evidence, it will not be logical for the orthodox Christian community to continue to assert that the resurrection of Jesus Christ was an actual historical event. Conversely, if the resurrection of Jesus Christ is based on good evidence, then Christian scholars should expose the weakness of these skeptical positions for the good of those who are seeking the truth on this central Christian tenet. It is my opinion that this research project will be invaluable to aid those who seek the truth about whether the Gospel accounts of the resurrection of Jesus Christ can be relied upon.

1.1.2 Problem statement

To determine whether the claims of Dr. Richard Carrier, regarding the resurrection of Jesus Christ, are supported by accepted principles of evidence coming from the Anglo-American common law tradition (specifically, the *FRE* and FPJI), whether the data that Carrier utilizes is in accord

---

[2] In recent years, there have been several best selling books by atheists that denigrate Christianity. Some books of this type that made it to the New York Times Best Sellers list (Hawes Publications, Date of access: 28 Oct. 2014) are *God is not Great: How Religion Poisons Everything* (Hitchens, 2007), *The God Delusion* (Dawkins, 2006), and *The End of Faith* (Harris, 2009). In addition to these books, there are several Internet sites that are repositories for anti-Christian literature. One of these sites, *The Secular Web*, is where many articles written by atheist authors are stored and where Dr. Richard Carrier has posted approximately thirty articles that dispute the veracity of Christianity (The secular web. Date of access: 29 Oct. 2014).

with relevant scholarly literature, and whether the data that Carrier uses is in accord with the relevant parts of the New Testament resurrection accounts.

1.2 Research questions

The research will focus on three questions about three widely publicized claims of Dr. Richard Carrier regarding the resurrection of Jesus Christ:

1) Does Carrier's assertion that the Gospel accounts of the resurrection of Jesus Christ contradict each other (Carrier, 2010:301-302) comport with relevant New Testament passages of scripture regarding the resurrection of Jesus Christ, accepted evidentiary principles of the Anglo-American common law tradition (as included within the *FRE* and the *FPJI*), and relevant scholarly literature?
2) Does Carrier's assertion that the resurrection of Jesus Christ was fabricated from earlier mythical and religious stories (Carrier, 2014b:77-78) comport with the relevant New Testament passages of scripture regarding the resurrection of Jesus Christ, accepted evidentiary principles of the Anglo-American common law tradition (as included within the *FRE* and the *FPJI*), and relevant scholarly literature?
3) Does Carrier's assertion that the post-resurrection experiences of Jesus Christ as recorded in the New Testament were based on hallucinations/visionary experiences (Carrier, 2005a:ch.5)[3] comport with the relevant New Testament passages of scripture regarding the resurrection of Jesus Christ, accepted evidentiary principles of the Anglo-American common law tradition (as included within the *FRE* and the *FPJI*), and relevant scholarly literature?

---

[3] The chapter, and not the page number, is cited because there are no page numbers available in the kindle edition of this book. This form of citation will be utilized hereafter when there are no page numbers present in the kindle edition of a book.

1.3 Aim and objectives

1.3.1 Aim

The primary aim of this research project is to expand Christian apologetics by conducting an evaluation of the claims of Dr. Richard Carrier regarding the resurrection of Jesus Christ, as recorded in the New Testament in order to determine whether they are supported by accepted principles of evidence[4] coming from the Anglo-American common law perspective (as included within the *FRE* and the *FPJI*); whether they comport with the Gospel resurrection narratives themselves; whether they are supported by related scholarly material.

1.3.2 Objectives

1) Examine Carrier's assertion that the accounts of the resurrection contradict each other by comparing it to accepted principles of the Anglo-American evidentiary perspective (as included within the *FRE* and the *FPJI*), relevant passages of scripture from the New Testament, and relevant scholarly literature in order to determine if Carrier's assertion comports with the aforementioned literature.
2) Examine Carrier's assertion that the Gospel accounts of the resurrection of Jesus Christ are fabricated from earlier mythical, religious stories by comparing it to accepted principles of the Anglo-American evidentiary perspective (as included within the *FRE* and the *FPJI*), relevant passages of scripture from the New Testament, and relevant scholarly material in order to determine if Carrier's assertion comports with the aforementioned literature.
3) Examine Carrier's assertion that the post-resurrection experiences of Jesus Christ, as recorded in the New Testament, were merely visions/hallucinations by comparing it with accepted principles of

---

[4] Utilizing accepted principles of evidence to analyze literature is not a novel concept. There are many authors who analyze the New Testament resurrection accounts by these principles. Examples of lawyers who utilize accepted principles of evidence in this project are Ross Clifford, John Montgomery, Val Grieve, Simon Greenleaf, Norman Griffith, Ken Handley, Joseph Sagebeer, and Don Gutteridge, Jr. In addition to these jurists who use these principles, accepted historiographical principles are also in accord with these principles as well (e.g. corroboration, eyewitness testimony, impeachment of historical witnesses, relevance, circumstantial evidence, etc.; cf. section 2.8.3-David Schum and Allen Johnson).

the Anglo-American evidentiary perspective (as included within the *FRE* and the FPJI), relevant passages of scripture from the New Testament, and relevant scholarly literature in order to determine if Carrier's assertion comports with the aforementioned literature.

1.4 Central theoretical argument

The central theoretical argument of this study is that Carrier's attacks on the resurrection narratives, as recorded in the New Testament, are not in accord with accepted principles of Anglo-American evidence (as included within the *FRE* and the FPJI), not in accord with relevant scholarly material, and not in accord with the New Testament resurrection narratives themselves.

1.5 Research methodology

This study will not emphasize a particular theological tradition as the research focuses on an analysis of literature from an evidentiary perspective. However, this study will be completed from an orthodox Christian perspective. This research project will utilize a comparative methodology where writings of Carrier will be analyzed and compared to Anglo-American standards of evidence, relevant scholarly literature treating specific contentions that Carrier has lodged, and relevant New Testament passages. Moreover, relevant Christian apologetic literature will also be surveyed to aid in the research of Carrier's objections.[5] The aforementioned research will include assimilating the data, comparing the data, writing drafts of my findings, and submitting the drafts to my research supervisor.

In setting forth an interpretive framework for analyzing the literature utilized in this thesis, the religious and mythical literature are not examined to determine the religious meaning of the texts, but for comparative purposes only.[6] For instance, accounts of mythical and religious figures will be examined to obtain information on the origins and other particu-

---

[5] Examples of Christian apologetic literature dealing with the issues Carrier raises in his three assertions regarding the resurrection of Jesus Christ are: (Johnson, 2001), (Torrey, 1922), (Perrin, 2009).

[6] Examples of mythical/religious literature that are compared with Dr. Richard Carrier's assertion that the resurrection narratives of Jesus Christ were fabricated from earlier mythical/religious stories are: (Eliade, 1972), (Wolkstein & Kramer, 1983).

lar details of their respective traditions. Thus, the analysis of this literature is not to determine the supremacy of one view over another.

In particular, the following methods are used to answer the various research questions:

1) In order to study and evaluate the positions of Doctor Richard Carrier regarding the resurrection of Jesus Christ, his contentions are researched and compared with accepted evidentiary principles from the Anglo-American common law tradition (as included within the *FRE* and the FPJI) (Langbein, 1996), (Mauet, T & Wolfson, W.D., 2009), (Cornell University Law School, Federal rules of evidence), (U.S. Court of Appeals, fifth circuit library system, 2012).
2) In order to study and evaluate the positions of Carrier regarding the resurrection of Jesus Christ, these contentions are researched and compared with relevant scholarly literature (Wolkstein and Kramer, 1983) (Eliade, 1972) (Sacks, 2012).
3) In order to study and evaluate the positions of Carrier regarding the resurrection of Jesus Christ, these contentions are researched and compared to relevant New Testament scripture to see if the different Gospel accounts of the resurrection of Jesus Christ contradict each other.
4) In order to study and evaluate the positions of Carrier on the resurrection of Jesus Christ, relevant Christian apologetic literature (Montgomery, 1983) is examined to see if they are probative in determining if Carrier's contentions cohere with the above-mentioned Anglo-American/common law literature, relevant scholarly literature, and relevant New Testament passages.

1.6 Concept clarification

The phrase *evidentiary analysis* in the title refers to examining the claims of Carrier regarding the resurrection of Jesus Christ with accepted principles of evidence from the Anglo-American common law tradition. These traditions are codified in the *FRE* and are included within the FPJI. The *FRE* are in use in the United States of America and govern the admissibility and introduction of evidence in criminal hearings and are in place to guard against the introduction of improper evidence in criminal hearings. FPJI are in place to instruct jurors as to how to properly interpret the evidence that they receive during criminal trials.

In regard to the phrase *resurrection of Jesus Christ,* as stated in the title of the thesis, these words refer to the bodily resurrection of Jesus Christ that is described in the Gospel accounts of the Holy Bible and that is also included within the confessions and creeds of the orthodox Christian church at large.

Chapter Two

Objection One: The Resurrection Narratives Contradict Each Other

2.1 Introduction

Doctor Richard Carrier's objection that the Gospel accounts of the resurrection of Jesus Christ contradict each other is woven into his polemic against the validity of the resurrection along with his other objections and appears throughout his writings.[7] Thus, there are no books, chapters, or sections in Carrier's writings that are titled "Contradictions Within the New Testament Resurrection Narratives." In lodging this objection, Carrier claims that the resurrection accounts not only contradict each other generally, but also in specific ways as well.

The first literature analysis will be of Carrier's "contradictory resurrection narratives" contention. Carrier draws his conclusions from analyzing the various passages of the resurrection of Jesus Christ presented by the four evangelists. In these conclusions, Carrier criticizes the various elements of the resurrection narratives to include the appearances of the risen Jesus Christ, the number and activity of the angels at the tomb of Jesus Christ, the different women and their activity at the tomb, the timing of the removal of the stone, and the accounts of the burial of Jesus Christ featuring Joseph of Arimathea. Carrier (2010:302) reasons that discrepant testimony in these accounts creates a contradiction between the four evangelists. Moreover in some instances, Carrier (2005b:ch. 9) observes contradictions between groups of evangelists. For instance, Mark and Matthew may be in agreement on a certain element whereas Luke and John may have another perspective or may not treat the element at all. When Carrier (2005b:ch. 9) observes this, he claims that a contradiction or embellishment has occurred.

---

[7] An example of this intermingling of objections is found in Carrier's *The Christian Delusion: Why Faith Fails,* (2010:303). Carrier writes, "The existence of improbabilities, contradictions, propaganda, evident fictions, forgeries and interpolations, and legendary embellishments in them has been exhaustively discussed in the modern literature, and most scholars agree the Gospels contain a goodly amount of these things."

After examining the perspective contained within Carrier's writings, the literature of Christian scholars/apologists who have researched related topics will be presented in order to "cross-examine" Carrier's contention. After this cross-examination has been completed, then a literature analysis will be conducted in order to determine if there is evidence of similarity among the Gospel resurrection narratives. If there is evidence of similarity in the resurrection narratives, then this similarity aids in rebutting Carrier's contention of "contradictory resurrection narratives." After these analyses have been conducted, a brief history of Anglo-American evidence rules culminating in the formation of the *FRE* and FPJI will be presented. This historical summary provides a foundation for the purpose of these two documents in the administration of justice and the relevance for use in this study. The Anglo-American system of justice has its roots in English common law and the aforementioned rules of evidence and jury instructions have been developed to prevent the acceptance of deficient evidence and to ensure that the trier of fact treats both parties equitably in legal proceedings. After this historical summary, a review of the relevant *FRE* and FPJI relating to contradictory testimony will be presented.

Another contention that Carrier (2005a:ch. 5) frequently makes is that the resurrection narratives contain embellishments (2.7). After conducting the aforementioned analyses, Carrier's position that the resurrection narratives of the four evangelists contain embellishments will be distilled from his literature in order to ascertain whether this claim works against his other claim that the narratives are contradictory (2.2.1). In addition to the aforementioned analyses, the *FRE* and FPJI will also be applied to Carrier's "examination" to determine if he is utilizing and interpreting accepted principles of evidence in his analysis of the resurrection narratives. The aforementioned analyses reveal that Carrier does not utilize accepted principles of evidence when he concludes that the resurrection narratives are contradictory.

2.2   Carrier's examination of the Gospel witnesses

2.2.1   Contradiction: In general, the Gospel narratives contradict each other

In presenting Carrier's examination and critique of the Gospels, the sources for his material were gathered from his printed books, from his electronic books, from his articles that are in included on "The Secular

Objection One: The Resurrection Narratives Contradict Each Other

Web" internet site, and from his personal internet website (www.richard carrier.info). Carrier's writings will be presented by starting with his most general objections and then analyzing his more detailed objections. After presenting this material, summary comments will be included. Following the explication of Carrier's perspective on the resurrection narratives, a "cross-examination" of Carrier's material will be conducted by the literature of Christian apologists (2.3). In addition to the cross-examination by Christian apologists, an analysis of Carrier's material by accepted principles of evidence will follow (2.8). Additionally, Carrier's general perspective on the Gospel narratives is relevant to his objection regarding the resurrection narratives as these narratives are obviously contained within the Gospels.

In his comments on the Gospel resurrection narratives, Carrier offers his overall skepticism about the Gospel narratives and claims that the narratives contradict each other. In his chapter, "Why the resurrection is unbelievable" (Carrier, 2010) which is contained within *The Christian Delusion: Why Faith Fails,* Carrier (2010:302) states:

> We can't even establish that the four Gospels are independent, since Luke and Matthew clearly copied extensively from Mark (often verbatim), and what they changed or added often doesn't agree between them or is outright contradictory (Carrier, 2010:301-302).
>
> (Mark seems not to have known), they have Jesus saying these things in completely different times and places, as if their sources really didn't know when or where Jesus said them, so they each had to make something up. John, meanwhile, contradicts the other three, more even than they contradict each other, and in the most fundamental ways.

In these excerpts from his writings, Carrier intermingles his objections regarding the authenticity of the various Gospels. He first brings out his skepticism that the four Gospels are independent works as he is troubled by similar material that the three Synoptic Gospels share together. Secondly, he charges the Gospels with contradiction, then next with outright fabrication. Lastly, Carrier brings forward a second charge of contradiction between John and the Synoptic Gospels. Even in this first quotation from Carrier, a logical conundrum begins for him in that he first complains about the similarity of the Gospels and then discusses the contradictions (2.7). In the same chapter as the above reference from Carrier (2010:294), he writes more about the contradictory nature of the Gospels:

> Worse, we don't even know for sure who Matthew is, or when exactly he wrote, or where, or who his sources were — except we know he copied

Mark almost verbatim, and then embellished his story with fantastic details like these. But we don't know who Mark is, either, or when or where he wrote or who his sources were. Even so, he never heard of any of this stuff either. Nor do we know who Luke or John were, or when or where they wrote, or who any of their sources were. The authors of John (and yes, that's plural) claim they got their information from some anonymous disciple (John 21:24 and 19:35) who is never clearly named and nowhere mentioned in any other Gospel, yet it's generally agreed that "John" wrote last of all — well after the other three Gospels were already circulating — and that "his" entire story fundamentally contradicts the others in countless details. And yet his authors hadn't heard of any of Matthew's marvels either. Just read the resurrection accounts yourself, the ones Christians are supposed to believe.

In this polemic against the Gospels, Carrier has the contradiction between John and the other Synoptic Gospels as a centerpiece but then introduces the proposition of the unknown authors as additional evidence against the authenticity of the New Testament. In addition, he speaks of the embellishments of Mark's accounts by Matthew. In similarity to the previous quotation, Carrier claims both contradiction and a form of similarity (embellishment). Does holding both views simultaneously weaken his claims? Carrier claiming both "fundamental" contradictions and embellishments at the same time will be explored in more detail (2.7). Moreover, the "unknown" authors and sources claim of Carrier will also be examined (2.8.5). Included below, Carrier again makes several charges against the Gospels (Carrier, 2006b:7.3):

> And Luke must surely have known there were conflicting claims, yet he never tells us about them, but instead just narrates his account as if everything were indisputable, never once telling us how or why he chose one version or detail and left out others. For example, though Luke copies Mark, he never tells us he did, much less for which material, and he changes what Mark said in some places. This entails either that Luke is fabricating, or preferring some other source that contradicted Mark. So why don't we hear of this other source? Or why Luke preferred it? Likewise, it is impossible to believe that Luke "closely followed everything" and yet had never heard of the alternative nativity account presented in Matthew (unless, of course, Matthew wrote after Luke and made it all up).

In this multi-pronged attack on the Gospels, Carrier asserts that there were not only "conflicting claims" but also accuses Luke of either inventing some material or drawing from a source that conflicts with Mark's Gospel. Moreover, when Carrier mentions that Luke borrowed from Mark and does not share the source of his material *contra* Mark, Carrier observes a problem. Furthermore, Carrier asserts that Luke was not privy to the alternative nativity report. Also in this passage, Carrier offers that the Gospels are not identical in the information they present. The writings of the Christian apologists (2.3) as well as a further analysis of Carrier's writings by accepted principles of evidence (2.8) will be used to determine whether Carrier's theses are founded upon accepted principles of evidence.

2.2.2 Contradiction: Number and activity of angels at the tomb

Comparing the angel reports of Mark with Matthew, Carrier (2010:295) writes, "Except in Matthew the young man sitting inside the tomb has become an angel descending from heaven, causing an earthquake and paralyzing some guards that Mark has no idea were ever there." Regarding the difference in the report of the angels in Mark as compared to Luke, Carrier opines, "these are still details not mentioned by Mark. Likewise, the one boy has been multiplied into two men, but who 'suddenly appear in dazzling apparel' (24:4). This is an obvious embellishment" (Carrier, 2005a:ch. 5). Regarding the difference in the report of angels at the empty tomb by Mark, Matthew, and John, Carrier (Carrier, 2006e) complains about the reported differences of the angels:

> The one young man of Mark, which became a flying angel in Matthew, in this account has suddenly become *two* men, this time not merely in white, but in dazzling raiment...Finally along comes John, perhaps after another decade or more. Now the legend has grown full flower, and instead of one boy, or two men, or one angel, now we have *two angels* at the empty tomb.

Carrier now observes differing details with the reports of the angel(s) at the tomb. In addition, he reports that the differences among the angel accounts point to legendary development. In pointing out the differences in the accounts, he does not give an outline of the similarity of these accounts but just the differences. In order to compare and contrast the views of Carrier with Christian scholars, an analysis of the writings of Christian apologists and accepted principles of evidence will be offered to cross-examine Carrier's assertion that the differences in the angelic visitations at the tomb are contradictions (2.3.2)

Another quotation from Carrier's material about the "angel reports" is probative in the discussion on contradictions. Carrier (2014b:760n) notes the similarities between the Lucan and the Johannine versions of the angel stories: "In fact John repeats several elements from Luke: that there were two angels instead of one (John 20:11-12), which only women saw." These noted similarities go against his overall theme of contradicting Gospel accounts and his specific contention that the Gospel resurrection narratives contradict each other. As with the other material from Carrier regarding the angel reports, analysis by Christian apologists/scholars and by accepted principles of evidence will be offered regarding similarities between the resurrection narratives and the angel reports contained within them (2.3.2).

2.2.3 Different women and their activities at the tomb

Another way that Carrier observes contradiction in the resurrection narratives is in the identification and functions of the women who traveled to the tomb. As noted before, opinions of Carrier on this topic are spread throughout various articles and books and are not treated as a unit. Rather, they are intermeshed with other complaints against the resurrection narratives. In the following two quotations, Carrier takes Matthew to task for altering Mark's resurrection narrative and for the variance of other details between the resurrection narratives:

> An additional reason to reject Matthew's story is that it contradicts all other accounts and is illogical: if the tomb was sealed until the angel came and moved the stone before the women and the guards, how did Jesus leave the tomb undetected? Did he teleport? For he wasn't in the tomb: it was already empty. Even if we want to imagine that he did teleport, all the other Gospels record that the stone had already been moved when the women arrived (Mark 16:4, Luke 24:2, John 20:1) (Carrier:2006f).
>
> Mark tells a simple story about a Sanhedrist burying Jesus, women going to the tomb and finding it open, meeting a single boy in white, then running off. But by the time we get to Matthew, Joseph has become a "disciple of Jesus" (27:57) who buried Jesus "in his own new tomb" (27:60); the boy has become an angel descending from heaven ...the women experience a "massive earthquake" and watch the angel descend and open the tomb (28:2); guards have been added to the story (27:62-66; 28:4, 11-15); and the women run off but now get to meet Jesus, even touch him (28:9). There can be no doubt that we are looking at extensive legendary embellishment upon what began as a much more mundane story...Of course, the appearance to Mary does not seem consistent with Mark, is not corroborated by Paul, and is internally superfluous, since Jesus merely repeats the instructions that Mary was already in the process of following. So it may be a didactic

invention...while the other three Gospel accounts entail their absence: the tomb is already open when the women first arrive, and they approach and enter without any challenge or opposition by guards, and naturally none are mentioned (cf. Mark 16:4, Luke 24:2, John 20:1, and surrounding rounding material) (Carrier, 2005a:ch.5).

Then in Matthew a report is given (similar to what was later added to Mark), where, contrary to the angel's announcement, Jesus immediately meets the women that attended to his grave and repeats what the angel said. Matthew is careful to add a hint that this was a physical Jesus, having the women grovel and grab his feet as he speaks (Carrier:2006e).

And it is most suspicious that the other gospel accounts omit any mention of a guard, even when Mary visits the tomb (compare Matthew 28:1-15 with Mark 16:1-8, Luke 24:1-12, and John 20:1-9)...This skeptical charge would then inspire the addition of guards, which would also require a story of bribery to explain why there are no guards around who could vouch for the resurrection, as well as the invention of an earthquake and angelic intervention to explain why the guards would not interfere with Mary, since, now that he has placed guards on the scene, Matthew has to invent some bizarre reason for their cowering before a woman, a strange story appearing in no other accounts of Mary's visit to the tomb. (Carrier, 2006f).

Carrier describes what are variances in the accounts with the women at the tomb where Jesus Christ had been laid with particular emphasis on Matthew's account. Even as he mentions some variances in these narratives, he loses sight of the fact that there are many similarities between these accounts (heavenly messengers, supernatural events, etc.). The reaction of the Christian apologists that some of these details can be "harmonized" will be considered and an analysis of accepted principles of evidence will be completed in order to understand why each witness reports their observations from differing perspectives. Furthermore, defining what a contradiction is will be probative in determining if these accounts are contradictory (2.7).

Included below are several quotations from Carrier (2005a:ch. 5) regarding the resurrection narratives in Mark:

> But it may be that the role of the "women" here is an invention of Mark, a mere act of reversing expectation, but then later authors were compelled to retain or rework it. The Gospel authors had to relate this tradition to the empty tomb once it was invented by Mark, but the fact that every single Gospel connects the two in an entirely different way is evidence that they are fabricating, not preserving any common truth...

In these passages, Carrier identifies the role of the women in the Markan resurrection narrative as inventions or fabrications and that the other authors "had" to adopt Mark's invention as their own. Relevant to Carrier's argument and what is important to consider are the different types of evidence that have been brought out in the relevant FPJI as well as accepted principles of evidence coming from the FRE (2.6 and 2.5). Does Carrier utilize any of these accepted principles of evidence when he offers his various persepctives?

Included below is a snippet of material from Carrier (2014b:669) that casts doubt on Luke because of his independent mention of Peter receiving the message of the women:

> No prior Gospel, nor Paul, had ever heard of the peculiar and convenient details that suddenly make their first appearance in Luke, such as that Peter double checked the women's claim that the tomb was empty and handled the burial shroud (Lk. 24.11-12).

Additionally, Carrier (2005a:ch. 5) makes another brief comment about Luke's narrative account differing from Mark's: "The women don't get to meet Jesus this time, but we do get a tale now of Peter going to check the tomb and confirming that it is empty (24:12), also something not mentioned by Mark." Carrier casts doubt on the Lucan account by noting that it is the first time in the resurrection narratives that the women advise the disciples with Peter responding himself to verify the report of the empty tomb. Again, as in previous "contradictions" noted by him, Carrier observes that two sources are not identically reporting every detail of the resurrection narrative.

A key consideration of this research project is to investigate whether differences perceived by Carrier within the Gospel resurrection accounts can be utilized to impeach the Gospel writers. As will be reported in a later section of this study (2.6.3), generally, witnesses frequently report the same event differently because they will view the event from their own perspectives. Furthermore, John's resurrection narrative has made a similar report excepting that John's rendition, on this particular event, includes himself along with Peter going to the tomb to verify the report of Mary (not the "women") (John 20:1-10). Another theme to be brought out by the Christian apologists is that one account not including a detail from another account does not necessarily mean that the author did not know about the account.

In the quotation below, Carrier (2005a:ch. 5) lists inconsistencies that he observes in John's Gospel in contrast to the other Gospels:

Objection One: The Resurrection Narratives Contradict Each Other

> ...only one woman (Mary) goes to find the tomb empty (20:1), but as in Luke, she tells Peter, who goes to see for himself, this time with another disciple (20:3-8).... Of course, the appearance to Mary does not seem consistent with Mark, is not corroborated by Paul, and is internally superfluous, since Jesus merely repeats the instructions that Mary was already in the process of following. So it may be a didactic invention...Mary gets to meet Jesus and possibly touch him (20:16-17).

In this passage from the Johannine resurrection narrative, Carrier finds conflicts between the Lucan and Johannine renditions of Mary's notification of Peter and Peter's response to the tomb. He observes that only Mary is mentioned as finding the tomb and notes that in the Johannine version, John is present with Peter when he visits the tomb. Moreover, the fact that John did not mention certain details in his narrative will be analyzed by utilizing the writing of Christian apologists. Similarly, it is important to investigate the accounts of this event written by the other evangelists. If they do not list John or Mary, does this necessarily mean that they did not know of these details? Furthermore, if they did not know of these details (cf. 2.3.1), does contradiction logically follow if a source is not acquainted with every detail (cf. 2.6.3)?

In addition to this quotation, Carrier (2014b:760n) offers another criticism: "In fact John repeats several elements from Luke: that there were two angels instead of one (John 20:11-12), which only women saw; that Mary reported the empty tomb to the disciples (and wasn't believed)...." Although he mentions the difference of John being present in the Johannine account, he also mentions agreement between Luke and John as far as the number of angels that were at the tomb and of Mary's report to the disciples. Again, a comparison of similarities with varying (not contradictory) accounts will be analyzed by the writings of the Christian apologists (2.3) as well as consulting accepted principles of evidence (2.8).

2.2.4 Contradiction: Resurrection appearances

In Carrier's analysis of the differences of the resurrection appearances, he observes both contradictions and embellishments. Carrier notes that there is a fundamental difference between the Luke-John appearance tradition and the Mark-Matthew appearance tradition. However, even though he notes the difference in the above appearance traditions, Carrier also notes that the appearance traditions begin after Mark and that the difference in traditions is between Matthew's appearance and that of the Luke-John appearance:

After Mark, there arose essentially two different appearance traditions: that found in Matthew, and that found in Luke and John. Luke and John both place the first appearances in or around Jerusalem, and not in Galilee. This is strange, since the only reference Mark makes to the appearances is that they will take place in Galilee, and Matthew accordingly places the most central appearance event exactly there. The fact that Luke and John fundamentally contradict the tradition of Matthew and Mark argues against the authenticity of the tradition they preserve... Matthew even places the focal experience outdoors, whereas John (and possibly Luke) places it indoors, another fundamental discrepancy (Carrier, 2005a:ch. 5).

Luke makes a point of noting that they still don't believe him, so Jesus asks for and eats a fish to further prove his point. This story becomes enormously embellished and even more overtly polemical once John gets his hands on it...and its own content betrays it as deliberate propaganda (Luke 24:37; Acts 1:3; John 20:25, 29, 31). Add the fact that Matthew and Mark also know nothing of the event and all the evidence adduced above against the authenticity of the John appearance tradition, and there remains little credibility. (Carrier, 2005a:ch. 5).

Then, maybe a little later still, Luke appears, and suddenly what was a vague and perhaps symbolic allusion to an ascension in Mark has now become a bodily appearance, complete with a dramatic reenactment of Peter rushing to the tomb and seeing the empty death shroud for himself (Carrier:2006e).

Carrier notes that there are two sets of Gospels that have similar appearance traditions. Does this observation by Carrier work against his objections of contradicting Gospels and resurrection narratives? Does the fact that Matthew (28:9) reports the initial appearance of Jesus in Jerusalem to the women who have just left the empty tomb in keeping with the above stated objections? Furthermore, does the PRA of Jesus in Jerusalem weaken Carrier's theory of contradiction as Matthew, Luke, and John all catalog appearances of Jesus Christ in Jerusalem? What about Carrier's mention that Matthew and Mark have no accounts of Jesus eating food *contra* Luke and John? Does this observation by Carrier support his objection of contradiction? More detailed analysis on the topic of the alleged contradictory appearance traditions is included in the literature of the Christian apologists (2.3.4.).

2.2.5 Contradiction: Timing of the removal of the stone

Carrier (2006f) observes contradiction between Matthew and the other three Gospels authors as he notes that Matthew's version of the women

Objection One: The Resurrection Narratives Contradict Each Other

arriving at the tomb of Jesus Christ is different than the other three evangelists:

> An additional reason to reject Matthew's story is that it contradicts all other accounts and is illogical: if the tomb was sealed until the angel came and moved the stone before the women and the guards, how did Jesus leave the tomb undetected? Did he teleport? For he wasn't in the tomb: it was already empty. Even if we want to imagine that he did teleport, all the other Gospels record that the stone had already been moved when the women arrived (Mark 16:4, Luke 24:2, John 20:1). Thus, Matthew's account is contradicted three times, even by an earlier source (Mark), and does not make a lot of sense. That is further grounds for rejecting it: for Matthew alone must have the angel open the tomb when the women are present in order to silence the guards that he alone has put there. Thus, if his account of the opening is false, the reason for that account--the guards--is likely also false.

In Carrier's above quotation, he asserts that the stone being rolled away after the women arrive at the tomb in Matthew's account contradicts the other evangelists. He also attributes bad intentions to Matthew for formulating his narrative in the manner that he did. He then concludes that the entire account of the women coming to the tomb must be false because the opening of the tomb was false. Further discussion of this topic will be included in (2.3.5).

2.3 Cross-examination of Carrier's contention by Christian scholars

2.3.1 Cross-examination: In general, the narratives are contradictory

In contrast to Carrier's view of contradictory resurrection narratives, theologians Gerd Theissen and Annette Merz (1998:495) first describe how Hermann Reimarus used contradictions among the evangelists in order to "deny their historicity" by attributing the differences in them to the disciples not doing a very good job of covering up the theft of the body of Jesus by writing their narratives. They contrast this with the theological research of today where there is a different view on the differences and similarities of the resurrection narratives by way of "three comparable units." In these units, Theissen & Merz identify the tomb accounts as having a high degree of similarity. In relation to the appearance narratives, because of the evidence of diversity of the appearance accounts from a literary viewpoint demonstrating different sources and because of the clear agreements observed between the accounts, they submit that it is possible to infer a real event behind these accounts.

In discussing the discrepancies within the four accounts of the resurrection, R.A. Torrey[8] (1922:144) notes that there is a harmony in the accounts of the resurrection but that the harmony is not apparent when reading superficially and only can be discovered when reading the accounts on a deeper level and dealing with the seeming discrepancies. Moreover, Torrey discusses the diversity of the resurrection accounts that are given by several independent witnesses and that this testimony increases the weight of the evidence to almost certainty when these witnesses all assent to similar facts. He further posits that even though the Easter stories are told in different ways, the seemingly contradictory narratives demonstrate that their writing has not been coached.

In illustrating his points, Torrey (1922:145) writes that if there were four accounts of a battle by those who had participated in the prosecution of it, there would be some portions of these accounts that would agree and other accounts that would be obviously independent of the other accounts. If we were to analyze all four of these accounts together, we would see that there would be "striking indications" that the accounts were derived from the eyewitnesses. This would be borne out by the general outline of the battle being similar yet there being divergence in the small details. We would be compelled after looking at these accounts to aver that these were actual reports of the battle.

Regarding the charge of inconsistencies in the Gospel reports of the resurrection of Jesus Christ, William Milligan (1917:56) asserts that, in general, two people will not see the same situation in the same way. If they are to be true to themselves, a person's testimony must of necessity be different than the account of someone else, as each person will naturally perceive the same event differently. He also notes that the role of an impartial judge is to clear up the ambiguities between witnesses and to determine the facts from this investigation. Moreover, Milligan offers that this principle is "fully applicable to the Scriptures." In noting the applicability of this principle, Milligan (1917:57) observes that statements that are without doubt, contradictory, should be rejected. However,

---

[8] R.A. Torrey was a noted theologian who was a prolific writer, and itinerant speaker. He was the superintendent of the Chicago Bible Institute between 1899-1904. Torrey would also become the first academic dean of the Bible Institute of Los Angeles (Biola) in 1912 (Sanders, 2015).

"where the main point is admitted by every witness, slighter differences are not only perfectly consistent with its truth, but are of the utmost importance for establishing it."

Supplementing his aforementioned principle of judging truthful testimony, Milligan (1917:57) offers that in crafting their Gospels, the evangelists would not be interested in only relaying objective facts as they received them. Rather, they would interpret these facts in light of what importance they held to each writer and the value these facts held for the writer's audience.[9] As the evangelists selected what they wrote, they would be careful not to veer away from "historical truthfulness."

Relating his perspective to the charge of contradictions within the Gospel narratives, Jack O'Connell (2010:148) submits that some contradictions observed in the Gospel narratives are not important enough to raise doubts about the accuracy of the accounts. In supporting his perspective, O'Connell demonstrates that there were many different reports about Wilt Chamberlain's one-hundred point performance in a record setting NBA basketball match. Even though there were many different written accounts of his scoring feat, there was never any doubt that Chamberlain actually scored one hundred points.[10] O'Connell also shares the results of an investigation into the 1881 lynching of the "McDonald Boys" where one account listed the men were hung from a railroad crossing whereas another account stated that they were hung on a pine tree. These different accounts of the lynching appeared to be irreconcilable until the in-

---

[9] Regarding the Gospel evangelists and the perspective they held about the Resurrection of Jesus Christ, Larry Hurtado (2013:52) writes, "Unquestionably, the four Evangelists all wrote from the standpoint of post-Easter faith, and for them all, as well as their intended readers, Jesus was the exalted Messiah, Lord, and Son of God. Their narratives were all prompted and shaped by this faith-standpoint. But, equally, they were concerned to underscore a direct link with the human figure of their narratives. This is reflected in the quasi-biographical literary genre that they all followed (albeit in varying ways). In short, these Gospels demonstrate how the conviction that Jesus has been resurrected, personally and bodily, had a profound effect in generating and maintaining a strong interest in Jesus' historic ministry."

[10] O'Connell (2010:148) offers these specific discrepant accounts of Chamberlain's record setting game to support his point: "Chamberlain claims he had ten assists that game, while the official score reveals he had only two. Some accounts have Chamberlain scoring his 100th point on a lay up, while others say it was a dunk. When Chamberlain scored his 100th point, the crowd rushed onto the court, but some accounts say the game was called at this point, while others claim that the crowd was cleared and the game resumed. Minor contradictions such as these do not cast doubt on the essential accuracy of the story."

vestigators discovered original photographs showing the men hung in both locations.

Regarding the mistaken perceptions of some readers and those who oppose the authenticity of the Gospel narratives, Dr. Edward Robinson (1993:10) offers that they "take it for granted that each Evangelist would naturally present an account of all the circumstances accompanying and following our Lord's resurrection." Robinson avers that doing this throws up "insurmountable obstacles" for harmonizing the narratives. Moreover, Robinson asserts that those opposed to Christianity exploit the impossibility of witnesses to perfectly match details, and press their objections that the Gospels are unreliable due to conflicting accounts.

In addition to Robinson, Richard Swinburne (2003:148) submits that the differences in the resurrection accounts can be understood by knowing that the authors were doing "'a little theologizing' (putting his own gloss on a common historical core), or having a source whose memory was not totally accurate. The differences are certainly not substantial enough to cast doubt on the basic story" (Swinburne, 2003:148). In similarity to Swinburne, Michael Licona (2010:593-95) regards the differences in the resurrection narratives to be more along the lines of the individual perspective of the author. Moreover in the resurrection narratives, he recognizes an emphasis not on the particulars, but on the "historical core in the narratives."

Regarding the presence of discrepancy as well as agreement in the resurrection narratives, Simon Greenleaf[11] offers that there is enough discrepancy in them to demonstrate that "there could have been no previous concert among them" but their agreement reveals "they were independent narrators of the same great transaction, as the events actually occurred" (Greenleaf, 1984:32-33). Greenleaf further submits that the discrepancies between the various accounts do not negate these similar yet differing accounts. If the stories were exactly the same, then there would be doubt as to their authenticity because their credibility would be questioned because of the uniformity of the testimony.

Norman Geisler (2007:657-58) submits that there are some parts of the narratives that do not fit together well. Furthermore, Geisler continues that this "should be expected of authentic testimony from independent witnesses. Were the accounts perfectly harmonious on the surface, there

---

[11] Simon Greenleaf (1783-1853) became Royall Professor of Law at Harvard University in 1833 and wrote *A Treatise on the Law of Evidence* "which became a standard authoritative text in nineteenth century American jurisprudence" (Philip Johnson, 2008:7).

would be suspicion of collusion." He further offers that some confusion at an "intense and bewildering moment" would be expected from a credible account from a personal perspective.

In their analysis of the charge of contradiction leveled against the Gospels by critics, Timothy and Lydia McGrew (2009:597) notice that skeptical scholars use the absence of total uniformity among the Gospel authors as grounds to deem them as unreliable. The McGrews (2009:597) offer Hermann Samuel Reimarus as an example of one who pointed to "various discrepancies, real or imagined, in the telling of the same story and to conclude that the texts contradict each other and therefore are untrustworthy at best and worthless at worst."[12] In addition to skeptical scholars employing minor differences in the Gospels as grounds to claim contradiction, the McGrews (2009:598) also observe that oftentimes these scholars cry "foul" when any of the four evangelists do not mention an episode included in another Gospel:

> The number of alleged discrepancies in the Gospels is greatly exaggerated by a free use of the *argumentum ex silentio*: if an author does not mention some piece of information, it is too often assumed that he was unaware of it or even that he positively believed the contrary. Such arguments from silence are pervasive in New Testament scholarship, but they are tenuous at best.

McGrew and McGrew (2009:598) also utilize the perspective of noted jurist Thomas Starkie to show that unless the differences in testimony of two witnesses are "too prominent and striking a [sic] nature to be ascribed to mere, inadvertence, inattention, or defect of memory," these differences are not important.

Another similarity in the resurrection narratives noted by Derek Tidball (2006:172) is the verbiage that is utilized by the Gospel evangelists as they transition from the events of the Passion of Jesus to Easter Day. As Passion Week unfolds, Jesus speaks to the disciples and shares how he must die and then be raised to life "on the third day" (Matt. 16:21; 17:23; 20:19; 27:64; Lk. 9:22; 13:32; 18:33; 24:21, 46). However, when the events of the resurrection begin to unfold on Easter Sunday, the evangelists no

---

[12] The McGrews (2009: 598) offer the differing estimates of various authors when they give their accounts of the army of Xerxes as it readied for its invasion to Greece. The McGrews also provide the example of a discrepancy in the number of troops assembled at the battle of Pharsalia where the estimate of Florus varies from the estimate of Caesar by 150,000 men. In both cases, there is no doubt among historians that these battles were prosecuted.

longer refer to the resurrection as occurring "on the third day." Rather on Easter morning, the evangelists refer to the events of the resurrection as occurring on "the first day of the week" (John 20:1; Matt. 28:1; Mk. 16:2; Lk. 24:1).

Regarding this change in phrasing of Easter day, Tidball (2006:172) cites D.A. Carson who believes that the switch in phrases is due to "the desire of the evangelists to present the resurrection of Jesus as the beginning of something new." Tidball (2006:172) also paraphrases the perspective of N.T. Wright on this subject when he writes, "This day of the week is the marker of a new beginning. Just as the first creation began on the first day of the week, so Jesus initiates the new creation through his conquering death and coming back to life again on the first day of another week." The observations of Tidball, Carson, and Wright identify another similarity in the four evangelists in the new way of referring to Easter day as the day begins.

In their comments about contradictions within the resurrection narratives, there is one major theme that is picked up by all of these scholars. In their writings, they observe that differences or seeming contradictions along with the similarities within the narratives actually support their veracity.[13] Moreover, a prominent theme also touched upon in this section is that much of what appears to be differences in the narratives are attributable to the particular emphasis of each evangelist.

2.3.2 Cross-examination: Number and activity of angels at the tomb

In responding to Carrier's contention of contradiction in the report of the angels by the evangelists, Christian apologists and theologians sound similar themes in their writings on the topic. Geisler and Turek (2004:284) assert that the mention of angels in the Gospel accounts of the Resurrection of Jesus Christ is not contradictory when Matthew mentions one and John mentions two. Matthew's account does not say that there was *only* one angel at the tomb. Moreover, they recognize the reality of diverse reports of similar events when they write, "Two independent eyewit-

---

[13] On this topic, Hugo Grotius (2010:Bk. III, Sect. VIII) notes, "It is objected by some, that the sense of these books is sometimes very different: but whoever fairly examines this matter will find, that, on the contrary, this is an addition to the other arguments for the authority of these books; that in those places which contain any thing of moment, whether in doctrine or history, there is every where such a manifest agreement, as is not to be found in any other writers of any sect, whether they be Jews, or Greek philosophers, or physicians, or Roman lawyers."

nesses rarely see all the same details and will never describe an event in exactly the same words" (Geisler & Turek:284). "In Fact, when a judge hears two witnesses giving exactly the same testimony, what does that judge rightly assume? Collusion-the witnesses got together beforehand to make their stories agree."

Regarding the message of the angels at the tomb, Norman Anderson (1973:145) points out that "the substance of what the angels are recorded as having said, in each of the Gospels, may well be supplementary rather than contradictory; for the sum of all their recorded statements would represent only an exceedingly short communication." Anderson cites William Temple regarding the position of the angels at the tomb. In treating these differences between Mark's angels, Temple states that the Markan account did not necessarily have the angel inside the tomb. Rather, the angel could have been sitting on the right side of the exterior of the tomb (Anderson, 1973:144).

In his examination of the report of the angels in the resurrection narratives, Simon Greenleaf (1984:539) is of the opinion that there is no discrepancy between the accounts of Mark, Luke, and John (that has the tomb already open) with the angels of the Matthean narrative which emphasizes the activity of the angel as being contemporaneous with that of the arrival of the women at the tomb. Greenleaf notes that in the Matthean version of this story, the angel had already moved from outside of the tomb to the inside of the tomb with the women who were inside. The angel merely points out where the body of Christ had lain inside the tomb. Greenleaf comes to this conclusion by the implication (v. 8) that the women had exited the tomb.

Greenleaf (1984:539-540) also observes that this is similar to the scenario reported in Mark 16:6 where the angel discusses with the women details about the interior of the tomb regarding Jesus' absence from it. Concerning the angels at the tomb, Greenleaf avers that the differences between the number of angels between the four evangelists is due to the fact that the Markan witness focused mainly on one angel whereas the other evangelists described the scene more completely than the Mark's source. Moreover, Greenleaf notes there is no use of exclusive language in any of the verbiage (e.g. Mark does not state that there was *only* one angel).

Expanding on Greenleaf's opinion that Mark's one angel does not create a contradiction with the two angels of other evangelists, Alfred Plummer (Cited by Lilley, 1940:108) writes, "where out of two or more, one only is spokesman, he is necessarily remembered and "It is an exaggeration to call such differences discrepancies." In commenting on Matthew's angel whose appearance was "like lightning" and signified the "presence of divine power," E. Carson Brisson (2011:73) also observes that the apparel of the angels described in Mark and Luke "befits and reflects" their positions as heavenly messengers. Even though the descriptions of the angels in these Gospels are not identical, Brisson observes that it is obvious from their impressive appearance that they all are heavenly envoys and that their role as heavenly messengers signals "the dawn of a long-awaited eschatological age" (Matt 24:27; Luke 2:22-38; 17:24).

In his assessment of the angelic reports of the evangelists, Gerald O'Collins (1987(a):122) offers a similar perspective as the aforementioned Christian scholars. As far as the identities of the angels in the different narratives, O'Collins observes, "Exegetes agree that Mark's 'young man' is to be understood as an angel."[14] Likewise Luke's 'two men in brilliant clothes' are angelic beings." In addition to his perspective on the identities of the "men" observed in the Gospel accounts, O'Collins also reports commonalities with the evangelists' tomb accounts as all of the Gospels include angelic elements in them.

Also, O'Collins (1987(a):122) supports his contention that "successive embellishment hardly fits the movement from Mark to John," when he writes, "John's two angels do not announce Jesus' resurrection but rather act as guards of honor who courteously question Mary about the reason for her distress" (John 20:13). In continuing his apologetic theme to this end, O'Collins notes that "John's angels do not develop the message of Mark's angel" then concludes that "'Differences' rather than 'embellishments' describe better the various ways the four evangelists handle the angelic tradition in their Easter narratives...that there are no 'remarkable discrepancies' regarding the tomb stories." O'Collins continues that often the four evangelists do not agree on the secondary details of the resurrection, mainly regarding the women and the angels. However, he notes that there is no question that "the four evangelists, Mark (followed by Matthew and Luke) and John, agree on the primary datum" (O'Collins, 1987(a):123).

---

[14] Susan Miller is one such scholar who affirms that Mark's "young man" is actually an angel. Miller (2004:80) writes, "The young man acts as a mediatory figure sent from the heavenly realm, who appears to be waiting for the women in order to give them the news of the resurrection...The supernatural appearance of the man is indicated by the reference to his white clothes (cf. 9.3; Rev. 7.9, 13-14) and he is described as sitting on the right...The place on the right is associated with the place of honour and it recalls the prophecy of Jesus at his trial that the Son of Man will appear sitting on the right hand of power (14.62)."

Regarding Mark's mention of the angels at the tomb, John Wenham (1992:85) succinctly observes that the "young man" is an angel as the experience of him evokes "awe and fear" from the women who subsequently flee from the tomb. Similarly in Luke's version of the events, there are two men who appear, and have a dazzling appearance that inspires fear in the women and the women describe having a vision of angels later (Wenham, 1992:85-86). Wenham concludes from Mark and Luke that these are descriptions of angels and not just ordinary men. Regarding the differing number reported by the evangelists, Wenham (1992:87) explains:

> It should be said once and for all that the mention by one evangelist of two angels and by another of one does not constitute a contradiction or discrepancy. If there were two, there was one. When learned critics make heavy weather about the accuracy of such accounts, they lack common sense. Contradiction would only be created if the writer who mentioned the one should go on to say that there was only one.

In similarity with the writings of the other Christian scholars on this topic, Wenham notices that critics do not use their best judgment when making this pronouncement and that there is a significant difference between mentioning the actions of one with saying there is only one angel acting alone.

In addition to Wenham, Guy Williams (2013:280) also asserts that the "young man" mentioned in Mark 16 is an angel. He notes that there are other references of angels being described as young men in literature in the proximate era of the writing of Mark. Williams points to the book of 2 Maccabees 3:26, 27 and to Josephus' *Antiquities* as using the term "young man" to refer to beings who are surely angelic. Further proof that Williams offers for his assertion comes from the reaction of the women themselves:

> The source of the women's alarm evidently is the "young man" himself, and it is likely that Mark understood that fear would be a natural response to a convincing angelophany. It could be that Mark is observing a literary convention, but it also seems to have been common opinion that genuine angelic revelations should be terrifying. We can see examples of this typical response to angels in the fear inspired by the Seraphim of Isaiah 6 or the 'mighty dread' of the shepherds of Luke 2…listeners and readers [of Mark's resurrection account in Mark 16] know that they can rely upon what has been heard because of the authentic reaction of those who heard it.

In like fashion as the other noted Christian authors, Elmer Parsons (1967:43) submits that even though there are subtle differences among the angelic revelations, "He is not here, He is risen" resounds through all three gospels' angelic announcements. Regarding his thoughts on the report of the angels at the tomb by each evangelist and the difference in the numbers of angels, Parsons submits that several different groups of women would help explain the different cast of angels that were encountered on Easter morning. About Mark's one angel, Parsons offers the perspective of Arnold Lunn (cited by Parsons, 1967:43) who wrote, "If Joanna saw two angels, and Mary, in the language of the law courts, was only prepared to swear to one. There would be no necessary contradiction between the two accounts."

In reference to this group (the women) reporting about the angels as noted by the evangelists, Parsons (1967:43) believes that the minor differences would "tend to accentuate" rather than to take away from the truthfulness of the accounts. Summarizing Parson's position on the report of the angels, Parsons not only observes that the diversity in the reports of the angels as a strength but also adds that the original sources to the evangelists who were groups of people reporting to other groups of people strengthens the evidence for the accounts.

Giving his take on the number of angels at the tomb, Gary Habermas (2012a:35-36) reports that Matthew and Mark only report one angel present at the tomb and that Luke and John report two angels there. Habermas also mentions there are three trips to the tomb mentioned by John and two trips taken to the tomb described by Luke. In mentioning this information, Habermas points out that angels were not mentioned in John's Gospel as being present during all of the trips. Therefore, there is a possibility that there were other angels that John and Luke chose not to mention. So, if there were alternately sometimes angels and then not angels present at the tomb, perhaps there were other angels present that were not mentioned.

In analyzing the speeches of the angels in the resurrection narratives, Wright (2003:641) offers that Matthew's angel recites a long speech that is similar to Mark and Luke but yet fuller. Even though the resurrection narrative of Matthew is similar to that of Mark and Luke, he recognizes the independence of Matthew's chronicle with his own distinct elements and verbiage manifested. This counters Carrier's contradiction claim in that even though these accounts are different, there are similar themes as well. Moreover, the "distinct" character of Matthew's resurrection guards is evidence against Carrier's accusation of embellishment.

2.3.3 Cross-examination: Different women and their activities at the tomb

In their interpretation of the response of the women to the empty tomb, Christian apologists and theologians have several different ways of accounting for the seeming differences in the resurrection narratives. Richard Bauckham (s.a.:12) notes that Mark has the same three women at the tomb that observed the cross. In Matthew's report of the women at the tomb, Salome is not mentioned with the two Marys. In like fashion as Matthew, Luke also omits Salome but replaces her with Joanna who is unique to Luke's account. However, Luke keeps the two Marys as witnesses to the empty tomb. Bauckham believes that the mention of Joanna in Luke's account demonstrates that Luke's report of the women responding to the tomb originates from its own unique tradition. In reference to the different accounts in the Gospels regarding the activity of the women at the tomb Bauckham (s.a.:12) explains his perspective on the sources of these Gospel narratives:

> If, as I have suggested and allowing for the evangelists' freedom as storytellers, the stories of the women are substantially as the women themselves told them, then we must regard the differences between the stories as irreducible. We cannot go behind them to a supposedly original version. Nor can we dispense with the angels and reconstruct a less mythologically laden event. These are the stories as doubtless different women told them.

In his apologetic discourse on the women at the tomb, Bauckham emphasizes the diversity of the witnesses in each account as well as the diversity in sources for the testimony of the women at the tomb.

Frank Morison (1993:74) relates that John emphasizes Mary Magdalene but that he phrases Mary's excited utterance as "and *we* know not where they have laid him." Morison wishes that John would have been more complete with this passage yet the use of *we* does imply that she was attended by other women as is included in the other three Gospel accounts. So the accounts of the women at the tomb are similar and do not contradict each other. Although all of the Gospels do not discuss the problem of rolling the stone away as in Mark, Morison shares that all of the Gospels do note that the missing body of Jesus was a shock to the women (Morison, 1993:76-77).

In similar fashion as Morison, Zane Hodges (1966:309) also observes a unity in the empty tomb testimony of the female witnesses:

> It will be seen from what has been said that there are no insuperable difficulties to harmonization of the women's role in the resurrection narratives, so long as the evangelists are allowed to pass over unnoticed those facts which did not serve their purpose...But, in fact, writing for circles where the living voice of tradition was still to be heard, the gospel authors had no need to be compendious.

Hodges posits that each evangelist had his particular thematic interest and would not list every detail of the events of the empty tomb account unless it was relevant to his purpose.

In relaying the account of the first appearance of Jesus by Mary Magdalene, John Wenham (1992:90-91) suggests that John, even though he was aware of the other women who were at the tomb, chose to describe the immediate notification from Mary that had a profound impact on him personally. In like fashion as Morison, Wenham supports his proposition about John knowing about the other women at the tomb by pointing to the fact that Mary stated "we do not know where they have laid him" and by inferring that Mary would not have traveled alone "while it was still dark."

In regard to the first appearance of Jesus Christ to Mary Magdalene, Simon Greenleaf observes another aspect of her testimony. Greenleaf (1984:540-41) believes that Mary Magdalene must have been quartered in a different part of the city than the other women. At first, she observes the tomb empty by herself and makes her report to Peter and John who are not with the other disciples.

Greenleaf (1984:540-41) further offers that she goes back to the tomb and encounters the angels as well as Jesus himself. As the other women are transiting from the location to tell the disciples the news about the empty tomb and the angels, they see Jesus wholly apart from Mary and make their announcement to the other disciples. Jesus tells them not to be afraid and to tell all of the disciples to go to Galilee where he will meet them. So, according to Mark they left in fear but Greenleaf points out that Jesus allays their fears and gives them further instruction to tell the disciples to meet him in Galilee. This interchange is included only in Matthew but Matthew augments Mark's account of the frightened flight of the women from the tomb.

Writing on the witness list shared by the Gospels, E. Robinson (1993:15) opines, "The first three Evangelists accord then in respect to the two Marys, but no further; while John differs from them all. Is there here a real discrepancy?" In like manner as Frank Morison and John Wenham, Robinson notices that John implies through his writing that there were other witnesses in addition to Mary Magdalene. But he also observes that Matthew, only speaking of the two Marys, does not preclude the existence of others (Robinson, 1993:14-15).

Succinctly summarizing his views on the topic of the female resurrection witnesses, Gary Habermas (2012a:35) reports that every Gospel includes Mary Magdalene, and that Mary, Jesus' mother, went to the tomb, that Mark adds an additional witness (Salome) and that Luke adds an additional witness (Joanna). Habermas writes that there is no contradiction in these varied Gospel accounts of the women at the tomb because of the usage of grammar (e.g. accounts do not use phrases such as "only two" or "not Salome"). Equally as brief, William Lane Craig (cited by Strobel, 2003:48) posits that no Gospel claims to give a "complete list." Rather, "They all include Mary Magdalene and other women, so there was probably a gaggle of these early disciples that included those who were named and probably a couple of others, I think that it would be pedantic to say that's a contradiction."

Vincent Taylor (cited by Bryan 2011:167-168) recognizes in the different resurrection narratives that they "reflect a desire to connect to the death, burial, and resurrection of Jesus with accredited witnesses," nevertheless, "they cannot be regarded as inventions, for otherwise they would have agreed more closely." Bryan further reasons that Matthew and Luke would have no motive to bother with Mark's list unless it was for the purposes of establishing "accredited witnesses." With this in mind, all of the "centres" of Palestinian Christianity would recognize the prime female witness, Mary Magdalene. However, the local women who were a part of the company of women who traveled to the tomb, like Mary Magdalene, would be mentioned in their own "centre" as witnesses along with Mary Magdalene.

It is by use of this schema that Taylor (cited by Bryan, 2011:168) asserts the different witness lists of the evangelists came to be. Because of these "centres," Matthew's community would not have included Salome, Luke (Caesarean centre) would keep Joanna and Susanna on his list, and Mark (Jerusalem centre) would include a second Mary as well as Salome. In addition to Taylor, Richard Bauckham (cited by Bryan, 2011:168) notes "The scrupulous care with which the Gospels present the women as witnesses. The Evangelists were careful to name precisely the women who were well known to them as witnesses to these crucial events in the origins of the Christians movement."

2.3.4 Cross-examination: Resurrection appearances

Regarding the cross-examination of Carrier's claims of contradictory resurrection narratives, Christian scholars share similar sentiments regarding how the evangelists treat the resurrection appearances. Even though there are differences observed in the appearance reports, the following scholars are comfortable with these differences and also note similarities among them. Merrill Tenney (1963:125) shares that the Synoptic accounts (Matt. 28:1-10; Mark 16:1-8; Luke 24:1-11) are in accord generally with one another regarding the resurrection narratives even though there are differences in some of the details. In speaking of the appearances of Jesus to the women, Tenney states that the accounts bear out that women hurriedly left the tomb and that, according to Matthew, the women encounter Jesus Himself. Moreover, Tenney (1963:133) observes that none of the Gospel writers had an odd or artificial version of the events such as exaggerations of His abilities or powers, or any violence or posturing. These descriptions are brief and treat his appearances as an ordinary part of His character.

Regarding charges of discrepancies and legendary development in the appearance reports, William Lane Craig (cited by Josh McDowell, 1999:249) submits that during the lifetime of the apostles, it would have been hard for any sort of fabricated appearance stories to begin and then persist through the lives of the apostles. Continuing on this topic Craig avers, "Discrepancies in secondary details could exist, and the theology of the Evangelists could affect the traditions, but the basic traditions themselves could not have been legendary." About Luke's compression of the resurrection narrative in one day, N.T. Wright opines, "We should not suppose that we have caught him out in some terrible historical oversight (Wright 2003:649)." Similarly, Wright (2003:643) believes that the small discrepancies between the historical accounts should not be interpreted as a reason to doubt the evidence that the resurrection occurred. Rather, it should work the other way as all four accounts would be the same if there was a concerted effort by the church to fool people into believing a fraudulent story.

In reference to his opinion regarding whether the appearance reports of the evangelists were contradictory, Fausto Salvoni (1961:96) emphasizes the divergence in theological perspectives but also the unanimity of the evangelists who describe the resurrected Jesus Christ. Salvoni submits that the Gospel writers used the material from the eyewitnesses that "they thought well suited to their purposes." Moreover Salvoni submits, "They especially preferred to lay emphasis on the twelve (we do not know why they did not emphasize the appearance to Peter), remembering the women as the first intermediaries between Jesus and the twelve." In discussing the aspect of the two different locations of the resurrection appearances reported by the Gospel authors, Salvoni believes that some critical commentators want to label either those who set the appearances in Galilee or those who locate in Jerusalem as historically wrong. Salvoni recognizes that the Johannine report of the appearances unifies the locations of the reports as this version mentions that Jesus Christ appeared in both areas.

Regarding his stance on the physical body of Jesus mentioned in three of the four evangelists, William Lane Craig (1989:66-67) submits, "Every resurrection appearance narrated in the gospels is a physical, bodily appearance." Craig is impressed by this agreement when he considers that the resurrection narratives "were originally more or less separate, independent stories, which the different evangelists collected and arranged." Moreover, he posits that all of the individual traditions list Jesus Christ as physically appearing to a number of different witnesses. Furthermore, Craig observes that the testimony of the witnesses to the physicality of the risen Jesus Christ and the lack of "visionary experiences" adds significant weight to the historical credibility of the resurrection narratives. Concluding his thought on this aspect of the appearance reports, Craig offers, "Incredible as it may seem, the evidence for the physical, bodily appearances of Christ after his death is quite strong and cannot, it seems, be plausibly rejected on historical grounds."

In further commenting on the appearance reports of the risen Jesus Christ, William Lane Craig (2006:6) also emphasizes the independent traditions that undergird these reports. He explains that the source for the appearance report of Peter is Luke and Paul. Also, Craig mentions that Luke, John, and Paul attest to the appearance report of the twelve, and that Matthew and John attest to the appearance report of the women. In these independent attestations, Craig observes strong evidence for their veracity. Moreover, critical scholar Gerd Ludemann (Cited by Craig, 2006:6) avers, "It may be taken as historically certain that Peter and the disciples had experiences after Jesus' death in which Jesus appeared to them as the risen Christ."[15]

---

[15] Even though Ludemann shares this opinion, he believes the disciples were not experiencing Jesus in the flesh after his death. Donald H. Hermann (2014:79) shares that Ludemann "is a strong proponent of the subjective vision theory and has identified such mental processes as involving 'stimulus,' 'religious intoxication,' and 'enthusiasm' as likely producing the visions seen by Peter, as well as

Regarding the meaning of the differences along with the similarities in the evangelists' resurrection narratives, James D.G. Dunn sees a steady core even as the reports diverge. Dunn (2003:865) observes that there has been a merging of the traditions to some extent. However, he notes that Luke is the one account that only mentions one locale for appearances of the Risen Jesus Christ. In noticing the unity amongst the diversity, he notes a core that includes the appearances and that the core "remains consistent, despite and through all the diversity." Dunn continues, "Here too, evidently, so long as the key point was being made through all various performances, the degree of divergence was not regarded as serious." Dunn (2003:866) also asserts that in addition to the empty tomb, the appearances go back to the origin of the "traditioning process" and that some of these appearances "were very personal in character and gave the tradition the character of personal testimony." In concert with the theme of Dunn, John Johnson (2004:142) points out that most conservative scholars grant that there are discrepancies among the four gospel resurrection appearance narratives, but they are not concerned with whether they all tell an identical story. Rather, they are concerned with the appearances themselves.

In commenting on his view of the alleged contradictions among the appearance narratives, Norman Anderson (1973:109) draws from his experience as a lawyer when he discusses this allegation. He states that witnesses to the same event will give what appear at the start to be inconsistent testimony about an event but then upon analysis, the accounts only diverge in minor details and Anderson sees this as strength rather than a weakness of the resurrection narratives.

In specifically commenting on the location of the appearance narratives, Anderson (1973:137) observes that many readers of the Gospels miss the fact that Matthew records appearances both in Jerusalem and Galilee. Additionally Anderson points out that even though Luke's appearance report only mentions appearances of Jesus in Jerusalem on one day, many critics lose sight of the fact that Luke authored Acts and that he wrote that Jesus was observed in bodily form for forty days after his resurrection. In addition to his observations of the location and duration of the risen Jesus Christ, Anderson (1973:134,138) also comments on the alleged problem of imperfect matching of appearance accounts:

---

those of others including Paul, which resulted in the conviction that Jesus was alive, although nothing had actually happened to the dead Jesus himself" (Ludemann, G. 1994, The resurrection of Jesus: History, experience, theology. Translated by John Bowden. Minneapolis: Fortress Press. pp.106-107, 174- 175, 180).

It may be suggested, therefore, that the evangelists felt free to concentrate on Galilee or Jerusalem, as the case may be-whether for literary, theological or other reasons- just because it was well-known that the risen Lord appeared in both...It is important to realize in this context that these alleged discrepancies and contradictions may indeed, at least at first sight, constitute a problem for one whose primary preoccupation is the precise accuracy of the biblical records, but not for one whose immediate concern is the strength of the evidence.

In his analysis of the appearance reports, Anderson observes that the data coming from these reports are strong evidence for their veracity. However, even though the evidence is strong, there are no problems with an evangelist offering the different locations for the resurrection appearances in that all of the authors knew that these appearances occurred in both areas. With this knowledge of both appearance traditions, an evangelist could either use one or both settings for his purposes.

After discussing the New Testament as a reliable source, John W. Montgomery (1986:154) sees the general reliability of the New Testament as a factor in considering the claims of the details of the resurrection to include the PRA which all describe the raised body of Jesus Christ. In addition to this claim of historical reliability for the appearance reports, Montgomery addresses the matter of the type of evidence needed to prove the claim of the physical resurrection of the body of Jesus Christ from the dead and quotes Thomas Sherlock. Thomas Sherlock (cited by Montgomery, 1986:154) asserts that even in the situation of a "fantastic claim" the evidence needed for proving this claim would not need to rise to the level of extraordinary.[16]

Writing about the differences within the resurrection narratives, several "juridical" apologists offer their opinions. About evidence for the resurrection appearances of Jesus Christ, Val Grieve (1991:74) explains that the best evidence is direct evidence and regarding evidence for the resurrection, the best evidence would come from the witnesses who had

---

[16] Sherlock (1729:62) opines, "But wou'd [sic] you say, this Case [sic] excluded all human Testimony; and that Men [sic] could not possibly discern, whether one with whom they conversed familiarly, was alive or no? Upon what ground cou'd [sic] you say this? A man rising from the grave is an Object [sic] of Sense [sic], and can give the same evidence of his being alive, as any other Man [sic], in the World [sic] can give. So that a resurrection consider'd [sic] only as a Fact to be proved by Evidence [sic], is a plain Case [sic]; it requires no greater Ability [sic] in the Witnesses [sic], than that they be able to distinguish between a man dead, and a Man [sic] alive: A Point, in which I believe every Man [sic] living thinks himself a Judge [sic]."

encountered the risen Jesus Christ (Grieve, 1991:62). Moreover, Grieve shares that the more corroboration there is on a given point, the more certain the evidence appears. He then mentions that Jesus appeared twelve different times to over 500 people and that the evidence was mostly firsthand and not hearsay evidence.

Approving of the divergence of the details of the appearance narratives, Joseph Sagebeer (1988:132) submits that not only is their veracity enhanced by these differences but he also advises that the opposite circumstance where "narratives of the appearances that agree accurately in immaterial detail upon contested points are always suggestive of collusion, if not fabrication" would detract from their truthfulness.[17] On the overwhelming experience of the witnesses of the risen Jesus Christ, Chuck Colson (1996:69) submits, "Nothing less as a witness as awesome as the resurrected Christ could have caused those men to maintain to their dying whispers that Jesus is alive and Lord." Agreeing with Grieve and Sagebeer, Norman Anderson (1985:150) stresses the importance of looking at all of the evidence within the resurrection narratives as a whole and then posits that it is important that all of "the different strands of information included within them cohere with each other."

In his analysis of the appearance reports, O'Collins (1988:64) notices that Mark's resurrection narrative was augmented by Matthew's appearance report which functioned as a link between the empty tomb in Mark and the appearance to the eleven in Galilee. Moreover, the appearance reports of Luke and John are also related in that their reports of the appearances of Jesus Christ (and the proclamation of the angel at the empty tomb) are both set in Jerusalem and take place on the same date and time. Matthew and John utilize the same appearance of Jesus (to the women) in Jerusalem to emphasize different important themes to the nascent church. O'Collins (1988:64-65) observes commonality in Matthew's appearance with John's as well as Luke's Jerusalem appearance as all three make use of the same appearance to the women in Jerusalem.

However, Matthew and John use the appearance to the women as an intermediate link from the empty tomb to the appearance of the risen Jesus Christ to the disciples in Galilee. Furthermore, O'Collins (1988:65)

---

[17] On this topic, Justice Ken Handley (1999:14) further explains, "Courts expect that evidence given by honest and reliable witnesses will agree in substance but differ in detail, and they view with suspicion witnesses who give the same evidence word for word. This always suggests that they have put their heads together to make up their story. The gospels are four substantially independent accounts of the events which agree in substance, but differ in detail, and they pass this test."

notices that Matthew uses the appearance of Jesus as a commission to ministry whereas John utilizes the appearance to affirm the identity of Jesus Christ as the risen Son of God in order to strengthen those whose faith had been weakened. These appearances of Jesus Christ noted by Matthew, Luke, and John demonstrate that each author utilizes the testimony regarding the same event for different purposes while still remaining faithful to the core details. This feature strengthens the reliability of these appearance narratives in their divergence in themes yet similarity in testimony.

In similarity to O'Collins, R.L. Bruckberger (1965:411) observes that any recalling or retelling of the "secondary facts carries with it a margin of hypothesis and personal choice." Additionally, Bruckberger notes that the resurrection narratives seem somewhat "disordered and difficult to harmonize." He uses the example of the inconsistent reports of the assassination of President Kennedy as an example to illustrate the fact that when something happens that is "amazing, sudden, and brutal," the reports of what happened will conflict and seem to be confused in details. According to Bruckberger, the only thing that most of these reports agreed upon was that President Kennedy had died. Even though the details are different, the core story of the appearance reports remains the same.

2.3.5 Cross-examination: Timing of the removal of the stone

In responding to Carrier's accusation of contradiction in regard to the timing of the removal of the stone from the tomb, Christian scholars do not go into great detail or type many pages on the issue. As Carrier contended, there is a question about whether the stone was rolled away before "the women" arrived at the tomb or whether their arrival was after the tomb was already open. In similarity to the Christian scholars, Carrier does not include much on this topic in his writings as well. Sharing his perspective on this issue, Merrill Tenney (1963:111) notes that all of the Gospel accounts record that by the time the women arrived at the tomb the stone had already been rolled away (Matthew 28:2; Mark 16:3; Luke 24:2; and John 20:1). Moreover, Tenney (1963:111) demonstrates the Gospels all report that:

> 1) Jesus was buried in a tomb hollowed out of limestone rock 2) a large circular stone was rolled in front of it 3) the women realized that if they were to complete their sad errand somebody would have to open the door of the

tomb; 4) they did not expect to find it open; and 5) when they did, the discovery was a distinct shock to them.

In similarity to Tenney, Samuel Chandler (cited by McDowell, 1999:232) writes, "The witnesses here all agree, that when the women came, *they found the stone rolled or taken away*. The women could not do it, the stone being too large for them to move." Furthermore, McDowell (1999:67) notes, "All the Gospels mentioned the removal of the stone." In their opinion of the "Matthean tomb opening" account, both Tenney and McDowell believe that the tomb was already open when the women arrive and that the stone would have been a problem for the women to move by themselves without assistance.

In his thoughts on the stone movement at the tomb, Frank Morison (1993:147-152) calls the stone that blocked the entrance to the tomb "the one silent and infallible witness in the case." In the symbolism of naming the stone as a witness, Morison emphasizes that the presence and movement of the stone reveals many things about the story of the empty tomb. Moreover, Morison avers that the size of the stone was described as both "exceeding great" (Mark) and that it was "a great stone" (Matthew). Therefore, the women would have to figure out how they would move the stone in order to gain access to the tomb. The ruminating of the women about the size of the stone points to the fact that the movement of the stone was an issue that was of concern to them. This concern of the women in the resurrection narratives lends credence to the significance of its movement.

In contrast to Carrier, Morison, in like manner as McDowell and Tenney, avers that the tomb was open when the women approached the tomb and that this fact has important historical ramifications. To the end of investigating who may have moved the stone, Morison discounts various theories of how the tomb became empty other than supernatural agency by showing that the circumstances before and after the crucifixion of Jesus Christ would have negated the discovery of any natural method of body removal.

In his perspective on the movement of the stone, D.J. Gutteridge (1975:38) focuses on the importance of the size of the burial stone as well as the unanimity of the witnesses to the empty tomb. Gutteridge refers to the words of the women who were in route to the tomb when they ask among themselves, "Who will roll away the stone for us from the entrance of the tomb (Mark 16:3)?" but then he observes their surprise when they arrive and find the tomb empty. Moreover, Gutteridge also notes that each of the four evangelists report that the stone had already been rolled away.

However, Gutteridge (1975:44) notes that there is a theory involving the stone that is allegedly derived from Mark and comes from an interpretation of Mark 16:6 put forth by Kirsopp Lake. Lake (cited by Gutteridge, 1975:44) posits that the young man at the tomb was a man who happened to be near the tomb and was trying to let the women know of the true location of where the body of Jesus was actually laid.[18] Embarrassed or frightened by their error, the women fled from the tomb. In comparing Carrier's position on this topic to Lake's theory, Carrier is not served by Lake's theory as Carrier contends that the Matthean account of the discovery of the empty tomb was false to begin with.[19] Also, Gutteridge (1975:45) quickly dismisses Lake's contention by observing that it does not take into account the witnesses who also observed the empty tomb and the grave clothes. In agreement with Gutteridge and the aforementioned Christian scholars on the unanimity of the arrival of the women at the tomb and their discovery of it being open and empty, Norman Anderson (1973:124) posits, "A number of different women visited the tomb, found the stone rolled away, saw the empty space where the body had lain, were told by one or more angelic messengers that he had risen, and were given messages for his disciples."

Concerning the arrival of the women at the tomb and the timing of the movement of the stone, Simon Greenleaf (1984:539) is of the opinion that apparent differences between the accounts of Mark, Luke, and John with the Matthean account are reconcilable. Additionally, he posits that the movement of the stone from the entrance of the tomb was contemporaneous with the arrival of the women at the tomb in the Matthean account. However, in the Matthean version of this story, Greenleaf points out that the angel moved from outside the tomb to the inside of the tomb with the women who were inside. The angel merely pointed out where the body of Christ had lain inside the tomb. Greenleaf's concern is that the description of the location of Matthew's angel is unclear and appears

---

[18] Lake (1907:250-53) writes, "The women came in the early morning to a tomb which they thought was the one in which they had seen the Lord buried. They expected to find a closed tomb, but they found an open one; and a young man...guessed their errand, tried to tell them that they had made a mistake in the place, 'He is not here,' said he, 'See the place where they laid him' and probably pointed to the next tomb. But the women were frightened at the detection of their errand and fled."

[19] See Section 2.2.5 that discusses Carrier's view that the Matthean account of the discovery of the empty tomb is false.

to differ from the other accounts if Matthew's angel is positioned outside of the tomb. Greenleaf comes to his conclusion that Matthew's angel was inside by the implication that the women had exited the tomb after they had conversed with the angel who was inside the tomb with them (Mat. 28:8). Greenleaf also observes that this is similar to the scenario reported in Mark 16:6. Even though Carrier argues for differences among the evangelists regarding the timing of the movement of the stone, the aforementioned Christian scholars agree that the stone was moved either before or contemporaneously with the arrival of the women at the tomb.

2.4 Evidence of similarity in the resurrection narratives

2.4.1 Evidence of similarity: Prominence of the women as witnesses

In moving from cross-examining Carrier's contention of contradiction in the resurrection narratives to a direct examination[20] of them (the narratives), similarities in the various narratives count as rebuttal evidence[21] against Carrier's argument. One such theme that emerges from the resurrection narratives is the prominence of the female witnesses to the events surrounding the resurrection of Jesus Christ. Moreover, the literature of Christian scholars is replete with the recognition of their eminence. In addition to their central role, their fearful demeanor is also noted in the resurrection narratives.

Supporting the centrality of the women witnesses in the resurrection narratives, Gerald O'Collins (2009:100) submits, "The Gospel stories of one or more women finding Jesus' tomb to be mysteriously open and empty contain a reliable historical core...the central place of women in the empty tomb stories speaks for their historical reliability." He then goes on to

---

[20] Margaret Stopp (1999:162) defines direct examination: "On direct examination, the party who calls the witness to the stand to testify asks questions to elicit a response that reflects the witness's knowledge of issues related to the litigated matter. The questions require responsive narrations from the witness." In this study, the literature review of Christian scholars "directly examines" the testimony of the women contained within the resurrection narratives of the four evangelists.

[21] Evidence offered to counteract (rebut) other evidence in a case. There are some restrictions on the admissibility of evidence in rebuttal, e.g. if it relates to a collateral question, such as the credibility of a witness (Gooch, G. & Williams, M., 2007).

describe the activity of the women witnesses to the empty tomb and the risen Jesus. After further discussing details of their foundational testimony, O'Collins adds that women witnesses were not considered to be valid witnesses in the time frame of the resurrection events and that if these reports were merely legends, then they would have had male witnesses instead. Gerald O'Collins also affirms Perkins' assessment of the women witnesses as they relate to the male apostolic witness of Peter *et al*.[22] Moreover, O'Collins (1987b:645) submits that the women and in particular, Mary Magdalene, were either the first or among the first witnesses to the appearances of the risen Jesus Christ and that because of this they should be afforded a lead role in the witness list of the evangelists.[23]

In similarity to the observations of O'Collins, Pheme Perkins (1992:36) observes that the empty tomb reports of the women are similar throughout the evangelists' narratives. Perkins submits, "The accounts in Matthew and Luke modify their Markan source material to suit their individual narrative perspectives. They concur in affirming that the women did report to the disciples what had happened at the tomb." Perkins further identifies that the women's report being confirmed by Peter *et al* in Luke (24:12, 22-24) may very well be a pre-Lucan tradition as this confirmatory search of the tomb by Peter is also mentioned in John (20:3-10). Perkins also notes that the testimony of Mary Magdalene about the empty tomb is believed by some scholars to be from "the most primitive layer of tradition" and also notes that this evangelist writes from his own theological perspective.

Jake O'Connell (2012:129) also emphasizes the importance of Mary Magdalene as a witness. After explaining the primacy of Mary Magdalene as a resurrection witness, O'Connell offers a solution to the apparent "contradiction" between the synoptic evangelists who center on the women's activity at the tomb of Jesus and John's Gospel that focuses on

---

[22] Pheme Perkins (cited in O'Collins, 1987(b):646) avers, "The women were (1) the primary messengers who were commanded to announce the resurrection, and (2) among those commissioned to witness. In addition, Mary Magdalene was considered equal to a (male) disciple as a witness for the resurrection".

[23] O'Collins (2012:276) also points out that "all four Easter narratives found in the Gospels feature Mary Magdalene at the discovery of the empty tomb, and always name her in first place, whether she has two other women as companions (Mk. 16:1-8), only one woman companion (Mt. 28:1-10), more than two other women companions (Lk. 24:1-11), or seemingly goes alone and returns alone to the tomb (Jn 20:1-2, 11-18). O'Collins underscores the importance of the women as witnesses to the resurrection by showing the primacy of Mary as the first witness to the risen Jesus Christ.

the activity of Mary Magdalene on Easter Day and her report of the empty tomb to John. O'Connell asks the question, Why would John write his account of Easter morning differently than the other evangelists? In reply to his own question, O'Connell (2012:129-130) states, "Matthew, Mark, and Luke keep their focus on the major event (the appearance of the angel) without 'bothering' to relate Mary's departure to tell Peter and John about the empty tomb and their subsequent return." In reference to John, O'Connell offers that "Mary's departure" and subsequent inspection of the tomb by Peter and John were of more interest to John than the appearance of the angels to the women because John was an eyewitness to the empty tomb. O'Connell concludes that there is no contradiction between the Synoptic Gospels and John's Gospel regarding these events involving the "women" and Mary Magdalene.[24]

In her assessment of the female witnesses within the resurrection narratives, Claudia Setzer (1997:264) also observes similarities in the evangelists. Setzer sees not only the theme of the women's "fear and bewilderment" but also notes that "all three Synoptic resurrection narratives contain some reference to Jesus' previous relationship with the women, whether in their following, their serving him, or his predictions to them." Furthermore, Setzer (1997:268) postulates that there is a contrast in the prominence of the women in the resurrection narratives of the Gospels in comparison with the lack of their mention in the rest of the Gospel narratives. On the one hand the women are essential to the resurrection narratives in witnessing the death, burial, and resurrection of Jesus. However, on the other hand it seems that the evangelists "soft-pedal" the prominence of the women as resurrection witnesses.

William Lane Craig (1997a:251-252) offers some circumstantial evidence in his writings on the female witnesses and their testimony noted in the four evangelists. Of the witnesses, Craig avers that the accounts of the empty tomb are contained within each of the resurrection narratives of the four evangelists. This is of relevance to the discussion of the women female witnesses as if it were not for the testimony of the women that was related to the disciples, then the disciples would not have responded to the tomb to confirm the report of the women. Thus, if the disciples had not responded to the women's report of the empty tomb to investigate,

---

[24] Regarding the seeming divergence in these accounts of Easter morning between the synoptic evangelists and John, O'Connell (2012:130) asserts, "It turns out, that though the other women knew Jesus was raised when they left the tomb, Mary Magdalene did not know this, because she had left the tomb before the appearance of the angel."

then the public would not have received the resurrection report of the empty tomb and resurrection faith would not have flourished like it did in the early church. Therefore, the female testimony is foundational to the resurrection faith that took hold of the early Christian church as a result of the Gospel message of the empty tomb.

In discussing the seeming failure of the women to proclaim the report of the empty tomb to the disciples (Mark 16:8), Carrier uses this to claim contradiction in the resurrection narratives as the other evangelists have the women reporting the empty tomb to the male disciples (Mary to "the beloved disciple").[25] In contrast to Carrier's view, William Lane Craig (2008:368) mentions that interpreting the Markan women, as they fled the tomb, as permanent silence is absurd. He further opines that Mark meant that the women were in silence as they "fled to the disciples" as Matthew and Luke have interpreted him in their accounts. Furthermore, Zane Hodges (1966:305n) also submits that the silence of the women in Mark did not necessitate total silence and observes that Mark similarly includes the account of the leper where the leper was instructed by Jesus to tell no one. Even though the passage also describes that he was supposed to inform the priest about the miracle wrought upon him, the passage indicates that he is to tell no one else (Mark 1:44).[26]

In his perspective on the topic of the silence of the Markan women, N.T. Wright (2002:47) offers that the complete ending of Mark included more than what is contained within the final chapter and that the complete ending is lost. He believes that Mark wrote what he did about the silence of the angels in order to counter the idea that the female witness-

---

[25] Carrier (2005b:ch. 9) believes that the women telling no one the story of the empty tomb (Mark 16:8) is to be taken literally and is the reason that it had not been heard before. Carrier asserts: "Isn't it obvious that the claim that the women 'said nothing to anyone for they were afraid' functions to explain to the reader why nothing of this had been heard of before? In other words, it is a late tradition after all, and not just because 1 Corinthians 15 lacks it" and then states that Matthew, Luke, and the author of the Markan appendix ignored Mark 16:8. In his view, Carrier precludes the existence of independent sources for each evangelist that would govern their decision for their texts. Moreover, it is not known which ending of Mark the other evangelists had access to.

[26] If the "young man" in Mark (16:8) told the women to report to the disciples what they had seen and heard, then the fact that they told no one makes sense as it is in keeping with the instruction of the "young man" as the "young man" instructed the women to tell the disciples and not other persons who they may encounter on their journey to the disciples. So implicit in the instruction of the angels to go and tell the disciples is also the tacit proviso not to tell anyone else other than the disciples.

es would need to tell every person that they encountered after witnessing the miraculous events at the empty tomb. Some scholars say that the women not informing everyone leads them to conclude that they did not see something as miraculous as what is described in the final chapter of Mark. Wright succinctly replies to this charge by paraphrasing Mark's words: "Certainly not, replies Mark: the reason they said nothing to anyone (16:8) (until, we presume, they got to the disciples) is because they were scared stiff." In addition to Wright's perspective, Norman Anderson (1973:145) adds that the Markan account of the women saying nothing to anyone about the empty tomb would only last the duration of the trip back to the disciples and upon returning would proclaim what they had witnessed there.

In reference to the Markan female witnesses fleeing in fear, Greenleaf (1984:540-541) points out that Jesus allays their fears and gives them further instruction to tell the disciples to meet him in Galilee (Matt. 28:9-10). This interchange is included only in Matthew but Matthew augments Mark's account of the frightened flight of the women from the tomb. Greenleaf also mentions that Luke adds the women returning to the disciples and the disciples not believing their report about seeing Jesus. Greenleaf offers that this very well could be the reason (disbelief of disciples) why this interlude (Matthean encounter of Jesus by the women while on the way to the disciples) is not included in the other three Gospel accounts. The augmentation of Mark's fleeing and silent witnesses by Matthew provides another possible reason regarding why Mark's witnesses started out from the tomb with the intention of not speaking but then are described as informing the disciples in the narratives of the other evangelists.[27] Moreover, David Wenham (1973:32) treats Matthew and Luke's renditions of the women fleeing the tomb as augmentations of the Markan text.[28]

---

[27] In this discussion, the independence of the evangelists with their different sources of information must not be forgotten. On the strength of the evidence coming from varied independent sources, Thomas Chalmers (1816:108) writes, "But the great strength of the evidence lies in that effulgence of testimony, which enlightens this history at its commencement-in the number of its original witnesses-in the distinct and independent records they left behind them, and in the undoubted faith they bore among the numerous societies which they instituted."

[28] "Luke, however, sides with Matthew against Mark, since he has 'and returning from the tomb they announced all these things to the eleven and to all the rest.' There are differences between Matthew and Luke, and it is possible to hold that

Additionally, Michael Licona (2010:347) observes that the women fleeing from the tomb and telling no one about what they saw was due to their encounter and mission given to them by the angel. This encounter provided a reason for the women to "be on their best behavior and amazement had gripped them, and they said nothing to anyone on their way to tell the disciples the news. For they had a reverential fear as a result of the revelation that kept them laser focused on their assigned task." In similarity to Hodges, Licona also offers Mark 1:44 (Jesus and the healing of the leper) as evidence that Mark did not intend to communicate total and complete silence about what the women had seen at the tomb of Jesus.

Adding her perspective on the women of Mark chapter sixteen who remain silent as they flee the tomb in fear, Susan Miller (2004:82) asserts the women who encounter the "young man" at the tomb "do not recognize the significance of Jesus' identity as the Son of God, nor do they understand that his death and resurrection have inaugurated a new age." In addition to their inability to recognize the risen Jesus Christ, Miller (2004:89) also observes the humanity of the women as they wrestle with what they saw and the natural inclination of humans to doubt and fear. However, she also adds that the women are key in that "the future mission depends upon the women's proclamation" and that they are essential in bringing "continuity to Jesus's mission in the time between the resurrection and the Parousia." In similarity to the inevitability of the women's testimony espoused by Miller, Christine Joynes (2011:19) affirms that the "impact of reading Mark chapter 16 in the light of the other Gospels illustrates a typical approach to Mark's concluding emphasis on silence, namely the assumption that the women did not really remain silent." Even though the Women of Mark sixteen flee in silence, they will eventually fulfill their duty to notify the disciples of the Risen Jesus Christ. If they had not done so then how would the disciples have ever been alerted to the empty tomb of Jesus Christ?

2.4.2 Evidence of similarity: Doubting disciples

In addition to the prominent roles of the women as witnesses another concordant theme of the resurrection narratives is the doubt registered by the disciples that Jesus had been raised from the dead. Regarding the closing paragraph of Matthew, N.T. Wright (2003:643) observes that the

---

the editors of Matthew and Luke supplemented Mark in a similar way" (Wenham, 1973:32).

mention of the phrase "but some doubted" (v. 17) is actually the "strongest mark of authenticity" in this closing paragraph, as someone who is making up a story would not add this phrase. Wright (2003:644) also identifies similarities in the accounts of doubting disciples in Luke and John even though John's description of the actions of Jesus go a long way to allay these doubts while Matthew leaves the tension in his account. In regard to the doubting disciples, Licona (2010:360) asserts that Matthew and Mark describe scenarios where the disciples both believe and doubt at the same time (Matthew 14:30-31- Peter walking on the water with Jesus but then sinking; Mark 9:24- a man exclaims to Jesus "I believe, help my unbelief")."

Joseph Plevnik (1987:798) also describes the struggles of the disciples in their coming to faith and submits that no matter how good the ability of one to perceive the events of the resurrection of Jesus Christ, there can still be no faith without connecting these events to the death and burial of Jesus Christ. Furthermore, Plevnik (1987:800-801) contemplates the reasons behind the doubt of the disciples described in Matthew 28:17 when they experience the glorified Jesus Christ. He asks the questions regarding this doubt: 1) Was it because Jesus was not recognized? 2) Was the appearance of Jesus not glorious of enough to engender belief? 3) Was it because he appeared in different forms? 4) Was it as a result of listening to the word of God? Plevnik (1987:802) then describes instances of doubt in Luke's Gospel with the activity of the women at the tomb, their interaction with the angels, and then their journey to notify the disciples. After giving their testimony to the male disciples, the disciples respond to their report in total disbelief. Plevnik asserts that they could not accept the proposition that Jesus arose from the dead in spite of the testimony from the women because they could not accept that Jesus Christ had risen from the dead.

Plevnik (1987:802) also mentions Cleopas and the other disciple who received the report of the risen Jesus Christ from the women and who still did not believe the women's testimony about experiencing the risen Jesus Christ (Luke 24:20-23). Plevnik (1987:805-806) further accedes that the death of Jesus was an obstacle to Mary Magdalene in the Gospel of John. Mary Magdalene (20:15-17) did not really grasp that Jesus had arisen even as she physically touched him and most people are familiar with the experience of "Doubting Thomas (20:24-28)" who would not believe that Jesus died unless he physically experienced him. Throughout the resurrection narratives the followers of Jesus could not accept that Jesus had risen from the dead. Even the "Beloved Disciple" did not believe in the resurrection of Jesus until he was confronted with the evidence of the

Objection One: The Resurrection Narratives Contradict Each Other

empty tomb (20:8). Plevnik's survey of the doubt of the disciples reveals that throughout the resurrection narratives of the evangelists, the disciples register nagging doubt and then belief that Jesus Christ was raised from the dead.

David Norman observes undertones of doubt between both the female witnesses to the empty tomb and the male disciples who later also witness the empty tomb as well as the risen Jesus Christ. Norman (2008:800) offers that the women who flee the tomb in Mark's account are disbelieving of what they just experienced at the tomb. He then points to the encounter of the women fleeing the tomb in Matthew and asserts that before they encounter Jesus, they were in disbelief until meeting him. Again in Matthew, Norman (2008:801) mentions the mountain top experience of the disciples with the glorified Jesus where "some of them doubted" (Mat. 28:17) and is puzzled over their non-belief in this setting. However, he comes to the conclusion that it was not that they did not recognize Jesus here but that it was a matter of "insufficient faith" as they grappled with their imperfect grasp and preconceived notions of who God/Jesus were.

In Luke, Norman (2008:801-802) asserts that the problem of the disciples is again a problem of lack of faith being evidenced in both Luke 24:3 with the women not comprehending or believing that Jesus had been raised in their search of the tomb. Moreover, this lack of faith is also observed in Luke 24:16-26 where Cleopas and the other disciple do not recognize or believe the report of the women (v. 22) that Jesus had been raised. In John's Gospel, "Jesus rises to a new state. As Thomas is John's foil to prove Jesus' divinity, Mary acts as the vehicle that establishes Jesus' glorified state as creation's new reality" (Norman, 2008:803).

Gerald O'Collins (1987(a):120) also lists the doubt of the disciples as spanning the Gospel resurrection narratives. O'Collins notes that when some of the disciples saw Jesus, they still remained doubtful but that these doubts dissipated when Jesus himself came up and commissioned them (Matt. 28:17-20). O'Collins also lists the Lucan Emmaus Road appearance and shows that the doubt slowly gave way to belief even as the disciples broke bread with Jesus himself (Luke 24:13-35). Additionally in John's Gospel (John 20:13-16), O'Collins observes that even though Mary first turned around physically in the direction of Jesus, she then "turned to" Jesus Christ and recognized him as Lord after Jesus called her by name. O'Collins submits, "This second turning fairly clearly indicates Mary's spiritual collaboration in the meeting."

As James Dunn (2003:859) recognizes a motif of a *failure to recognize Jesus* among the disciples, he also recognizes a matching "note of doubt and disbelief" among them as well. He mentions that he observes this in the appearances of Jesus in Jerusalem to the eleven (Luke 24:41), to the eleven disciples whom Jesus appeared to in Galilee, and also to Thomas (John 20:24-29). He also notes that even though Thomas' doubt was carefully removed in John, Matthew never removes the doubt of the Galilean eleven. Even though these authors identify different instances of doubting in the accounts of the evangelists, both list evidence for their positions that come from three of the four evangelists.

In her article entitled "Written That You May Believe," Kelli O'Brien (2005:299) discusses the doubt and misunderstanding in John's Gospel. O'Brien describes the journey of Mary Magdalene, the Disciple Thomas, and the Disciple John to faith in the resurrected Jesus Christ. In her survey of these three prominent characters of the fourth evangelist, O'Brien observes Magdalene and Thomas, grappling with the reality of the resurrection. O'Brien also points out that the disciple John, although portrayed by many New Testament commentators as the ideal disciple, also struggles with fully understanding the events of Easter:

> But the author has also demonstrated that, for the Beloved Disciple as for the others, authentic discipleship is not easy. It does not come whole, in an instant. Discipleship involves mistakes. It involves the overcoming of the darkness of the world, the blindness with which we were born. Becoming a full authentic disciple is a process from which no one, not even the Beloved Disciple, is exempted.

Even as the events of Easter unfold, O'Brien (2005:297) points out that John "believes" (20:9) even though John and Peter still do not "understand from Scripture that Jesus had to rise from the dead" (20:10). Even after all of the activity at the tomb, O'Brien notes that John just packs up, goes home, and that the reader, Mary Magdalene, and Peter have "learned nothing from the Beloved Disciple's insights." Not only do Mary and Thomas struggle, but also so does the Beloved Disciple.

In his writings on this topic, Ulrich Wilckens (1978:50) also observes doubt in the resurrection narratives with the exception of Mark. Luke's chronicle describes that the disciples believed that they had seen a ghost, that they are frightened (Luke 24:37), and that Jesus Christ had to convince them otherwise (v. 39). Even after speaking face to face with the Risen Jesus Christ, they were still not convinced. In his efforts to convince the disciples of his physical body, Jesus eats fish in front of them (v. 42). Of the Johannine emphasis on Jesus proving his identity, Wilckens writes, "In the tradition before John, however, the risen Christ appears in order to overcome his disciples' doubts as to his identity and in order to give them proof that he really is physically their Master, the Crucified One." In Matthew's account, Wilckens observes only marginal mention of the doubts of the disciples whereas in Luke, "the issue of identity dominates the centre [sic] of the scene."

Furthermore, Wilckens (1978:53) observes that in John, the theme of doubt grows stronger until the climax of the story of Christ's appearance. After the disciples are unencumbered of their doubt, then the commission of the disciples follows in both Luke 24:44-49 and John 20:21-33. In spite of the lingering doubt of the disciples, Matthew (Mat. 28:18-20) also has the disciples being commissioned by the risen Jesus Christ (Wilckens, 1978:53). In similarity to the other aforementioned authors, Wilckens observes the doubt of the disciples spanning three of the four resurrection narratives.

2.4.3 Evidence of similarity: Joseph of Arimathea

The burial of Jesus is a relevant matter when discussing the veracity of the resurrection as the witnesses of the burial verify that a known person laid Jesus in the tomb and that other listed witnesses watched this occur. Regarding the burial of Jesus, John Wenham (1992:64) states that the four evangelists all list Joseph of Arimathea as the person who arranged his burial. In addition to Joseph's involvement with the burial, Matthew and Mark mention that Mary Magdalene and "the other Mary" were sitting nearby the sepulcher where he was laid (Mark 15:40-41; Matt. 27:55-56). Luke (23:55-56) also mentions the women at the tomb of Jesus even though he does not name them specifically. Although Luke is less specific in one sense in not naming the women who were at the tomb, he is more specific about what the women actually observed (how the body was positioned) when they followed Joseph into the tomb. John refers only to the activities of Joseph and Nicodemus with no mention of the women's presence (John 19:38-40). Not mentioning the women in the account of the burial is no discrepancy as John's account merely emphasizes the activity of the men and not the women. Apparently John did not feel that it was important to mention the women at this juncture.

> William Lyons (2004:38-39), commenting on the burial of Jesus and Joseph of Arimathea, notices that "most exegetes" assert that the other three evangelists complement the Markan burial narrative and his description of Joseph of Arimathea. W.F. Albright and C.S. Mann (Cited by Lyons, 2004:39) write that "each evangelist provides 'additional information' when describing the burial of Jesus and proceed to incorporate the details accordingly."

Lyons continues that these commentators make the assumption that there is a genuine tradition that is apportioned between the four resurrection narratives in the Gospel texts. Because of this belief in the reliability of the traditions, these commentators "have no qualms about grafting the numerous details available onto Mark's account" and this harmonization by the commentator "recreates the original."

In affirming the historical nature of Joseph of Arimathea, a number of Christian scholars share their thoughts. On the believability of Joseph as a real person, Raymond Brown (1994:240) states:

> That the burial was done by Joseph of Arimathea is very probable, since a Christian fictional creation...of a Jewish Sanhedrist who does what is right is almost inexplicable, granted the hostility in early Christian writings toward the Jewish authorities responsible for the death of Jesus.

In addition to Brown, Paul Gwynn (2000:8) offers that Arimathea is a locale that has no real historical significance outside of the Bible that one would expect in an "apologetically inspired legend." Because of this, William Lane Craig submits that this tradition has "the ring of truth."[29] Joining in with Gwynne and Brown, Samuel Abogunrin (1981:56-57) notes the different language used by the different evangelists regarding Joseph of Arimathea's efforts to take the body of Jesus down from the cross.[30] Although there is some difference in the wording of the passages among Mark and John in Joseph's actions to take charge of the body of Jesus, Abogunrin sees no contradiction as the difference in wording regards different contextual concerns of each evangelist.

Joining in the affirmation of the burial of Jesus by Joseph of Arimathea, Pierre Benoit (cited by Smith, 2006:161-162) asserts there is no doubt that he was a historical person. Benoit avers, "Where except in life did they find this Joseph of Arimathea who is named nowhere else? This

---

[29] Craig, 1997b:256-257
[30] "In Mark 15:46 and Luke 23:53 Joseph of Arimathea took the body. But in Acts 13:29 Jesus' enemies took the body and laid him in a tomb. In John 19:38 Joseph took the body 'away' but in Mark 15:46 he took the body 'down'...As regards Acts 13:29, Paul is only giving a summary of what happened by the use of the indefinite pronoun 'they' for those who took part in the arrest, trial, crucifixion and burial. This cannot therefore be said to contradict the gospel records. Moreover the 'away' of John 19:38 is referring to the request to take away the body of Jesus by Joseph and the 'down' of Mark 15:46 is referring to the action of Joseph after Pilate had granted his request. Therefore no contradiction appears to exist here" (Abogunrin, 1981:56-57).

personage is a precious historical datum, which imposed itself on all the Evangelists and which by itself guarantees the burial of Jesus." Regarding the historicity of Joseph of Arimathea, Rudolph Bultmann (cited by Smith, 2006:161) concludes, after examining Mk. 15:42-47, that "the historical notice does not give the impression of legend. It would be difficult to show that it was introduced afterwards in view of the story of Easter."

William Lane Craig (cited by Strobel, 2003:37) echoes the sentiment of the aforementioned scholars in noting the presence of Joseph of Arimathea in the narratives of all four evangelists. Furthermore, Craig offers the early date of the writing of Mark as a reason against the idea that Joseph of Arimathea was merely a legendary character. Responding to the questioning of Lee Strobel on the issue of a prominent Pharisee who voted to have Jesus killed being involved in the burial of Jesus, Craig observes that there is mention in Luke that Joseph did not cast his vote, as he was not present when the vote was taken. Furthermore, Craig (cited by Strobel, 2003:38) offers that Joseph is not the type of legendary character that would be created by the evangelists for several different reasons.[31] One further point that Craig (Cited by Strobel, 2003:38) makes about the possibility of a legendary Joseph is that there would be other accounts of the burial of Jesus in the historical record but there are no other "competent" traditions that can be found.

2.5 Explanation of accepted principles of evidence

2.5.1 Historical background of the *FRE*

Margaret Stopp (1999:1-2) explains the origins of Western law when she shares that very early in Western history, trial by ordeal was the norm where the aim of adversaries was to outlast each other as they were exposed to the elements. This contest turned into limited battle during the reign of William the Conqueror in eleventh century England where favorable judgment would be awarded to the victor. In these "legal contests," when the litigants faced off against each other before the judge,

---

[31] Craig (cited by Strobel, 2003:37-38) reasons about a legendary Joseph that "Given the early Christian anger and bitterness toward the Jewish leaders who had instigated the crucifixion of Jesus," he said, "it's highly improbable that they would have invented one who did the right thing by giving Jesus an honorable burial-especially while all of Jesus' disciples deserted him! Besides, they wouldn't make up a special member of a specific group, whom people could check out for themselves and ask about this. So Joseph is undoubtedly a historical figure."

there were prescribed rules to follow. Stopp recognizes that as time has progressed, two litigants still battle before the judge today, albeit without weapons. Rather, they battle with attorneys who utilize evidence to best represent their client's interests.

John Langbein (1996: 1169-1170) shares that the precursor to the Anglo-American jury system came about in the twelfth century and that the laws of evidence were not part of this system until the sixteenth and seventeenth centuries. Langbein (2003:338-339) contrasts the Anglo-American system with the European or Continental system (utilized by other countries outside the sphere of Great Britain) that does not utilize the jury but has a judge to decide upon all legal matters and where the responsibility for seeking the truth is given to the court. In looking back at the role of the jury in Western history, Langbein offers that the shortcomings of the jury system needed the corrective measure of the rules of evidence. In developing his thesis, Langbein (1996:1170-1171) observes that the early English jury was investigative in nature. In the Medieval era, the jury only arrived in court after they determined the truth of the matter and only to render their judgment. Moreover, when the medieval jury was appointed, it was hoped that these jury members knew something about the matter in conflict so that they could render an informed judgment.

In its continuing metamorphosis and towards the end of the Middle Ages, the jury began to turn from one that investigated to "passive triers" (Langbein, 1996:1170-1171). It was at this time that the jury began to resemble the modern Anglo-American jury panel with its members no longer knowing about the matter under consideration. Rather, the jury members would be ignorant of the issue before the court. In this nascent form of trial procedure, the use of witnesses who came to court to testify and to inform the jury was a radical departure from its past investigative function.

In his survey on the history of the rules of evidence, Langbein (1996:1172) asserts that rules of evidence originated in the mid-eighteenth century and he discerns this from his analysis of court documents that are extant and from that time period. Upon examining Gilbert's treatise on *The Law of Evidence* (Gilbert:1754), Langbein observed the court proceedings of Dudley Wright, an eighteenth century judge whose court cases were listed and described in this volume. In addition to Ryder's court hearings, Gilbert also included within his treatises limited laws of evidence that were important in proceedings of that time. Of importance to Gilbert was the rule of best evidence that placed emphasis on the primacy of documentary evidence and caution against the admission

Objection One: The Resurrection Narratives Contradict Each Other 77

of hearsay evidence to the jury. Gilbert opined that hearsay evidence should not be allowed in court proceedings unless this evidence could be corroborated by other evidence (Langbein, 1996:1175). Although Gilbert cautioned against the use of hearsay, Langbein (1996:1176) observes that there was no formal rule established in that time frame. Langbein (1996:1181) recognizes in his analysis of Ryder's court transcripts that the law of modern evidence was really not in use, as the emphasis was on the scrutiny of documentary evidence with only scant attention being given to oral testimony or hearsay evidence. In noting only traces of evidence law, Langbein (1996:1194) classifies the state of evidence rules in Ryder's era as "pre-modern law."

John Henry Wigmore (1913:4-5) notes that evidentiary rulings were on the increase in England in the first quarter of the nineteenth century and that the increase was attributable to a rise in the publishing of court proceedings (Nisi Prius reports of Peake, Espinasse, and Campbell). This printing of court records was a new development that brought some "fixity" to court proceedings. In years prior to the new reporting, the precedence for rulings was contained only in the mind of the ruling judge who would make his decisions based on his memory of previous evidentiary findings. With the new recording of judicial findings, these rulings were no longer at the whim of a magistrate's memory. Rather, they were written, collected, and stored for future use by attorneys. In addition to the Nisi Prius reports, Wigmore observes that new published books centering on rules and practice ushered in a new system of evidence (e.g. Phillips, Starkie, and Greenleaf).

Wigmore (1913:6-7) also notes that in the mid to latter part of the nineteenth century, common law reform in England culminated in the passage of the *Common Law Procedures Acts* of 1852 and 1854. Moreover, Wigmore notices that progress in evidentiary reform was also being made in the United States even though this progress came later than it did in England. In his final comments on the state of the law of evidence in England, Wigmore writes that the *Judicature Act of 1875* and the *Rules of Court* (of 1883) brought about a time of rest. Wigmore characterizes these acts as being "harmonious with the present demands of justice" and that "no further detailed development is called for."

In the United States, Robert Mosteller (2005:524) reports that early attempts at evidentiary reform were mostly unsuccessful. An attempt was made by an organization named the "Commonwealth Fund" to implement evidentiary reform in the United States. This report focused on enhancing the power of the trial judge and limiting the influence of lawyers. In 1939, another push for evidence reform was made by the

American Law Institute that had as its purpose the establishment of a "model code of evidence" for the entire country. Mosteller writes that the failure of this venture was due to the fact that it gave too much discretion to trial judges and also because the man spearheading the effort was not a convincing salesman. Although, ostensibly, the "model code of evidence" initiative was a failure, it became the foundation for a successful evidence reform movement that culminated in the successful issuance of the *Uniform Evidence Rules* in 1953 and had limited success as it was only adopted in the states of New Jersey, Kansas, and Utah.

Mosteller (2005:526) identifies that the impetus for an organized and national set of rules in the United States came from the federal court system. The beginning of this new push for a uniform code of evidentiary principles began in 1963 and after years of wrangling, Congress enacted the *Federal Rules of Evidence* in 1975. Mosteller (2005:527) notes that even though there have been some changes to the rules of evidence, the rules have remained relatively stable since they were enacted in 1975.

2.5.2 Accepted principles of evidence: Rules 102 and 401

In defining the purpose for the *Federal Rules of Evidence*, rule 102 states that the purpose of the FRE is to "administer every proceeding fairly, eliminate unjustifiable expense and delay, and promote the development of evidence law, to the end of ascertaining the truth and securing a just determination" (Cornell University Law School, FRE 102). It is the first phrase of this rule that relates to the topic of this project. Does Carrier "fairly" treat the data of the Gospel resurrection narratives in accordance to the accepted principles contained within the FRE and FPJI?

FRE 401 simply states, "Evidence is relevant if (a) it has the tendency to make a fact more or less probable than it would be without the evidence; and (b) the fact is of consequence in determining the action"[32] (Cornell University School of Law: FRE 401). In his writings, Carrier utiliz-

---

[32] In its notes pertaining to FRE 401, the Advisory Committee on Proposed Rules had several comments that were pertinent to the discussion of relevant evidence as it relates to the present topic. Further explaining relevant evidence, the committee noted, "Relevancy is not an inherent characteristic of any item of evidence but exists only as a relation between an item of evidence and a matter properly provable in the case. Does the item of evidence tend to prove the matter sought to be proved?" Moreover the committee commented on 401b: "The rule uses the phrase 'fact that is of consequence to the determination of the action' to describe the kind of fact to which proof may be properly directed" (Cornell University School of Law, FRE 401).

Objection One: The Resurrection Narratives Contradict Each Other

es the resurrection narratives as evidence to make his objection of contradiction. These narratives are, of course, relevant evidence to his objection under analysis because they bear directly upon his objection. However, Carrier makes claims about the Gospel authors in order to discredit them. He states that it is not known who the Gospel authors really were and he also states that the sources that the evangelists used were unknown as well (2.2.1). He discredits the authors of the resurrection narratives in order to bolster his first objection regarding contradictory resurrection narratives. If Carrier's two claims are supported by relevant evidence or evidentiary facts, then they could also be considered as relevant evidence towards Carrier's objection because they would satisfy both parts of the rule. Thus, an important point to study is whether Carrier offers relevant evidence to buttress these two claims or whether he merely offers assertions as evidence to support his objections (2.8).

M.G. Graham and E.D. Ohlbaum discuss what an "intermediate" fact is in relation to Rule 401. They define an intermediate fact as one "arising by inference from an evidentiary fact while at the same time giving rise to an inference of an ultimate fact" (Graham & Ohlbaum, 1997:10n). The aforementioned claims of Carrier would be intermediate facts if they were supported by evidentiary facts. Does Carrier provide evidentiary facts or proof to support his intermediate "facts" ("unknown authors" and "unknown sources")? If not, then Carrier's claims do not rise to the level of being classified as intermediate facts.[33] Thus, if his two claims are unsupported by relevant evidence or evidentiary facts, then they do not make his objection "more or less probable." Furthermore, it would be probative to investigate whether there is relevant evidence to refute Carrier's objections. An examination of Carrier's aforementioned claims and evidence in opposition to his claims will be included in this chapter (2.8).

2.5.3 Accepted principle of evidence: Rule 104(b)

Rule 104b states, "Relevance That Depends on a Fact. When the relevance of evidence depends on whether a fact exists, proof must be introduced sufficient to support a finding that the fact does exist. The court may admit the proposed evidence on the condition that the proof be introduced

---

[33] In its notes on FRE 401, the Advisory Committee on Proposed Rules writes, "The fact to be proved may be ultimate, intermediate, or evidentiary; it matters not, so long as it is of consequence in the determination of the action" (Cornell University School of Law: FRE 401). Does Carrier supply facts based on evidence to support his claims?

later" (Cornell University Law School, *FRE* 104). In similarity to Rule 401, Rule 104(b) is germane to Carrier's objections under analysis because Carrier seeks to discredit the Gospel authors by making claims that he believes are supported by the evidence. A relevant point to discuss is if Carrier has evidence to support his views. Therefore, Rule 104(b) is relevant to this evidentiary analysis as it necessitates that any facts be supported by a sufficient amount of proof to establish that the fact exists.[34]

2.5.4 Accepted principle of evidence: Rule 602

Rule 602 states:

> A witness may testify to a matter only if evidence is introduced sufficient to support a finding that the witness has personal knowledge of the matter. Evidence to prove personal knowledge may consist of the witness's own testimony (Cornell University Law School, *FRE* 602).

This rule is germane to Carrier's "contradiction" objection under analysis. In his article, *Stephen Davis gets it wrong*, Carrier (2006a) calls into question the reliability of the Gospel witnesses. Rule 602 is relevant as there is evidence from a Gospel witness (John) that he has personal knowledge of the events leading up to and after the resurrection of Jesus Christ that rebuts Carrier's claim of unreliability. This particular matter will be treated in more detail in this chapter (2.8.4).

2.5.5 Accepted principle of evidence: Rule 607

Rule 607 states, "The credibility of a witness may be attacked by a party, including the party calling the witness" (Cornell University Law School, *FRE* 607). However, other rules of evidence provide guidelines by which the credibility of a witness may be impeached. In regard to impeaching a witness, M. Stopp (1999:164) shares four ways to properly accomplish this:

> 1) Offering evidence of the untruthful character of a witness (Rule 608); 2) offering evidence that the witness has been convicted of a crime 3) offering evidence of prior inconsistent statements 4) generally bringing out the in-

---

[34] "Once a sufficient foundation has been laid, the jury must consider such evidence, together with the opponent's contrary evidence" (Graham & Ohlbaum, 1997:57). When Carrier discredits the Gospel authors, is his evidence founded upon a sufficient standard of proof?

formation that the witness is biased or prejudiced, has an interest in the litigation, or has an improper motive for testifying.

In addition to these methods of impeachment offered by Stopp, T. Mauet and W.D. Wolfson (2009:359-62) offer three additional methods of impeachment: 1) contradictory facts (related to prior inconsistent statements); 2) conduct probative of untruthfulness FRE 608(a); 3) treatises (written statements) FRE 803(18). These standards of witness impeachment will be utilized to determine if Carrier properly impeaches the Gospel witnesses in his literature. This topic will be discussed in more detail later in the chapter (2.8.2).

2.5.6 Accepted principle of evidence: Rule 610

Rules 610 states, "Evidence of a witness's religious beliefs or opinions is not admissible to attack or support the witness's credibility" (Cornell University Law School, FRE 610). This rule is applicable to the current analysis as Carrier (2006e), in his article *Why i don't buy the resurrection*, asserts that the Gospel authors are religiously biased.[35] Rule 610 is relevant to this study as it relates to testimony coming from the Gospel witnesses.

2.5.7 Accepted principles of evidence: Rules 802 and 803

Rule 802 states that "Hearsay is not admissible unless any of the following provides otherwise: 1) a federal statue 2) these rules; or 3) other rules prescribed by the Supreme Court" (Cornell University Law School, FRE 802). In regard to other rules that permit the introduction of hearsay evidence, Rule 5.1 allows for hearsay evidence to be offered as evidence in a probable cause hearing before a federal magistrate. Additionally, Graham and Ohlbaum (1997:94) note that if opposing counsel in a case do not make a timely objection, the hearsay testimony will be admitted as evidence. Another example of when hearsay evidence has been admitted is when a judge is the trier of fact. In certain cases where the judge allows the hearsay evidence to be admitted as evidence, the judge remarks that he will "receive the evidence and consider the objection as going to its

---

[35] Regarding the Gospel authors, Carrier (2006e) writes, "However, I do not merely charge the Gospels with their obvious bias, but in some cases with an *overtly stated* propagandist mission, which is something much more damning than mere bias: some of the sources specifically state that their versions of events were written to convert people."

weight." Although hearsay evidence is not admissible as a rule, there are exceptions to where it will be admitted without invoking rule 803.

Rule 803 naturally follows Rule 802 and simply states, "The following are not excluded by the rule against hearsay, regardless of whether the declarant is available as a witness" (Cornell University Law School, FRE 803). There are many exclusions to the hearsay rule that are listed in Rule 803 but one exclusion that is relevant to the topic at hand is Rule 803(16) that lists an ancient document meeting certain criteria as being eligible to be considered excluded hearsay (Cornell University Law School, FRE 803).[36] This hearsay exclusion is relevant to Carrier's objection in that Carrier accuses the Gospel witnesses of unreliability. Thus, the Bible's qualification as an ancient document with all of its other credentials will be considered (2.8.3).

2.6 Federal jury instructions: Evaluation of the evidence

2.6.1 Purpose and history of federal jury instructions

In John Wigmore's (1913:1038-1039) *Select cases on the law of evidence,* he offers accounts of various trials in English and American history. These brief descriptions of trial proceedings focus on the relationship of the judge and jury. In a proceeding that occurred in seventeenth century England, Wigmore supplies several descriptions of a discussion between a judge and a jury about their roles in the trial process. In one case, the judge and the defendant debate as to whether the jury should decide matters of law in addition to its duty to be judges of the fact. This demonstrates the dramatic shift from the judge/jury relationship of yore where the jury held preeminence over the judge to the modern relationship where the courtroom duties are divided equitably.

---

[36] *FRE* 803(16) permits statements that are in a document that has been in existence for twenty years or more where the authenticity of the document is unquestioned (Cornell University Law School, *FRE* 803). Graham and Ohlbaum (1997:174) further explain that the "authenticity of an ancient document is established pursuant to FRE 901b(8), by showing that (a) its condition creates no suspicion concerning its authenticity, (b) it was in a place where it would be likely if authentic, and (c) it has been in existence 20 years or more at the time it was offered." There are several "legal" or "juridical" apologists, to include John W. Montgomery, who assert that the Bible is just such a document that would qualify as an excluded exception under this hearsay provision.

Objection One: The Resurrection Narratives Contradict Each Other

In another case mentioned within Wigmore's (1913:1039-1042) aforementioned book, a nineteenth century Massachusetts case is described where the judge instructed the jury that he was to be the arbiter in matters pertaining to law. However, the judge clearly instructed the jury that they were responsible to return the verdict. These early recordings of trial proceedings reveal that jury instructions have been used for centuries and that the relationship of the jury with the judge has morphed through the centuries. Furthermore, John Langbein (1996:1196) describes that even though jury instructions were in use in the court of Dudley Ryder in the 18th century, there is not a clear history of jury instructions available.

Concerning the recent history of jury instructions in the United States, Lester Orfield (1945:544) writes that the *Federal Rules of Criminal Procedure* were drafted by an advisory committee and finally printed in January of 1945 after a review from the Supreme Court, the Attorney General's office, and finally from Congress. Within these rules, Orfield explains that Rule 30 provides for the instructing of the jury by the judge after counsel for the parties have had an opportunity to consult with the judge pertaining the content of these instructions. J. Alexander Tanford (1990:91-94) describes the general composition of the instructions that are given to the jury before they render their verdict. These instructions explicate the role of the jury as well as explain pertinent substantive and procedural law. Moreover, they also demonstrate how the jury should organize their deliberations as well as how the court should instruct the jury as to how they should evaluate the evidence that has been admitted during the trial.

An example of pattern jury instructions that are provided by the U.S. Court of Appeals for use by federal judges to instruct juries are FPJI from the U.S. Court of Appeals, Fifth Circuit Library System (2012). In these preliminary instructions the jury is charged with being the judge of the facts of the case. Specifically regarding evidence, these preliminary instructions list what types of evidence they will hear, that certain items are not evidence and should not be considered, and the forms of evidence that the jurors will encounter during the trial. Moreover, these preliminary instructions charge the jury with rendering its decision by weighing the evidence. FPJI are pertinent to this research project because of their use and because they are a reliable and time-tested guide that assists juries in how to interpret evidence.

2.6.2 Accepted principles of evidence: Direct and circumstantial evidence

Included in the U.S. Court of Appeals for the Sixth Circuit[37] (2014) FPJI, general instruction 1.06 deals with instructing the jury on the meaning of direct and circumstantial evidence. Direct evidence is defined as "simply evidence like the testimony of an eyewitness which, if you believe it, directly proves a fact." If a witness testified that he saw it raining outside, and you believed him, that would be direct evidence that it was raining" (U.S. Court of Appeals for the Sixth Circuit, 2014:Section 1.06). Circumstantial is defined as "simply a chain of circumstances that indirectly proves a fact. If someone walked into the courtroom wearing a raincoat covered with drops of water and carrying a wet umbrella, that would be circumstantial evidence from which you could conclude that it was raining" (U.S. Court of Appeals for the Sixth Circuit, 2014:Section 1.06).

This instruction is relevant to Carrier's objections under analysis because Carrier's main premise of his first objection is that the resurrection narratives are contradictory both generally and in specific instances as well. This instruction assists in identifying whether the resurrection narratives are supported by historical direct or circumstantial evidence. If different forms of evidence can be observed in the resurrection narratives, then an evidentiary evaluation can be performed to determine the strength and quality of the evidence contained therein. Regarding a form of direct evidence, eyewitness testimony, Jay Grenig et al. (2000:145 of pocket part supplement) includes an instruction that lists criteria for determining the validity of eyewitness testimony. These criteria will also be probative in determining the strength of any eyewitness accounts included within the resurrection narratives.[38]

---

[37] The Sixth Circuit encompasses the states of Kentucky, Michigan, Ohio, and Tennessee.

[38] Regarding weighing eyewitness testimony given at trial and instructing the jury on how to consider this evidence, Grenig et al. (2000:145) published, "You may consider, in that regard, such matters as the length of time the witness had to observe the person in question, the prevailing conditions at that time in terms of visibility or distance and the like, and whether the witness had known or observed the person at earlier times."

2.6.3 Accepted principle of evidence: Judging the credibility of witnesses

Contained within the FPJI of the United States Court of Appeals for the Sixth Circuit (2014), Section 1.07 contains an instruction that suggests certain criteria by which jurors can judge the credibility of a witness. The general instruction on the credibility of witnesses is included below:

> (1) Another part of your job as jurors is to decide how credible or believable each witness was...It is up to you to decide if a witness's testimony was believable, and how much weight you think it deserves. You are free to believe everything that a witness said, or only part of it, or none of it at all. But you should act reasonably and carefully in making these decisions. (2) Let me suggest some things for you to consider in evaluating each witness's testimony.

The instruction continues with specific criteria that jurors should consider when receiving testimony from a witness. Among the criteria are: 1) the ability of the witness to "clearly see or hear the events (sometimes an honest witness may not have been able to see or hear what was happening, and may make a mistake)" 2) "Did the witness seem able to accurately remember what happened?" 3) Did the witness have "any bias, or prejudice, or reason for testifying that might cause them to lie or to slant the testimony in favor of one side or the other" [39] 4) If the witness's statement was inconsistent, does this make the testimony less believable? (If so, was the inconsistency about something important; did it seem like an innocent mistake or was it deliberate?) 5) "Was the witness's testimony supported or contradicted by other evidence that you found believable? If you believe that a witness's testimony was contradicted by other evidence, remember that people sometimes forget things, and that even two honest people who witness the same event may not describe it exactly the same way[40]" (United States Court of Appeals for the Sixth Circuit, 2014:1.07).

---

[39] "Interest exists where a witness's relationship to a party or the lawsuit is such that he stands to gain or lose, usually financially, from a particular outcome to the case; A witness can be examined about any matters that are relevant to any gain that the witness would expect to receive" (Mauet, T. & Wolfson, W.D., 2009:373). Certainly, the Gospel authors did not have a financial interest that would cause them to be biased on the basis of financial gain.

[40] In addition to FRE 607 regarding the impeachment of a witness, jury instructions from the D.C. Circuit Court also instruct jurors regarding prior inconsistent statements they may notice during testimony of a witness: "The testimony of a

The aforementioned jury instruction is strongly applicable to Carrier's objection because his objection of "contradictory resurrection narratives" attacks the credibility of the Gospel witnesses (2.2). In this instruction, there are criteria given to assess the credibility of witnesses and to assess the credibility of the Gospel witnesses. In particular, criterion number five will be highlighted in more detail when we analyze Carrier's claims (2.8.2).

2.6.4 Accepted principle of evidence: Weighing the evidence

Contained within the pattern jury instructions of the United States Court of Appeals for the Sixth Circuit, Section 1.05 contains an instruction regarding "consideration of evidence" (United States Court of Appeals for the Sixth Circuit, 2014: Section 105). The topic of this instruction is regarding weighing the evidence that has been submitted to the jury. The instruction states:

> You should use your common sense in weighing the evidence. Consider it in light of your everyday experience with people and events, and give it whatever weight you believe it deserves. If your experience tells you that certain evidence reasonably leads to a conclusion, you are free to reach that conclusion.

This jury instruction is relevant to Carrier's objection of "contradictory resurrection narratives" because those who assess his claims or for that matter the claims offered by this author, should consider it in light of their own personal life experiences. If any information offered as evidence is found wanting or other information offered as evidence is convincing, in consideration of one's own personal experience, one should afford it the appropriate weight.[41]

---

witness may be discredited or, as we sometimes say, impeached by showing that he or she previously made statements which are different than or inconsistent with his or her testimony here in court" (Grenig *et al.*, 2000:414-15). This is relevant to our discussion of Carrier's objection because he often attempts to discredit the Gospel authors as a group with inconsistent or contradictory statements. Carrier's approach is improper as this principle applies to individual persons and not to groups of people.

[41] Supreme Court and Sixth Circuit cases indicate that jurors should consider the evidence in light of their own experiences, may give it whatever weight they believe it deserves, and may draw inferences from the evidence. Cf. Turner v. United States, 396 U.S. 398, 406-407 (1970) (the jury may consider its own store of

2.7 Embellishment v. contradiction: Joseph of Arimathea

Now that Carrier's position on contradictory resurrection narratives has been cross-examined and a survey of accepted principles of evidence has been completed, it is appropriate to examine his contention that there are embellishments in the resurrection narratives. This examination is appropriate as his perspective in this regard actually works against his "contradictory resurrection narratives" argument. In beginning an examination on this topic, a definition for the terms "contradiction" and "embellishment" will be offered. After the examination of the terms "embellish" and "contradiction," Carrier's examination of the resurrection narrative accounts of Joseph of Arimathea will be explicated and then cross-examined to determine if his theory of "embellished Gospel resurrection narratives" actually aids his "contradictory resurrection narratives" contention.

Merriam Webster (2015a) defines the term "contradiction" as:

1: act or an instance of contradicting
2:a: a proposition, statement, or phrase that asserts or implies both the truth and falsity of something b: a statement or phrase whose parts contradict each other <a round square is a *contradiction* in terms>
3:a: logical incongruity b: a situation in which inherent factors, actions, or propositions are inconsistent or contrary to one another.

From these definitions, it is clear that a contradiction occurs when there are two conflicting elements in a single proposition, statement, or phrase. In the second definition, a contradiction refers to a single statement or phrase whose parts are not in agreement with each other. In the third definition for contradiction (part a), a contradiction refers to a state where there is a divergence between two ideas or terms that cannot be reconciled. Additionally, the second part of the definition three demonstrates that for a contradiction to be present, the divergence in factors or ideas occurs within one entity.

---

knowledge, must assess for itself the probative force and the weight, if any, to be accorded the evidence, and is the sole judge of the facts and the inferences to be drawn therefrom) Committee Commentary 1.05 (current through April 1, 2013) (United States Court of Appeals for the Sixth Circuit, 2014:1.05). Weighing evidence by one's own personal experiences should be used as a criterion to assess Carrier's claims.

The *Cambridge Dictionaries Online* (Cambridge Dictionaries Online:2015) defines the term "contradiction" as:

The fact of something being the complete opposite of something else or very different from something else, so that one of them must be wrong: [Example:] *You say that you're good friends and yet you don't trust him. Isn't that a contradiction?*

In this definition of "contradiction," the explanation includes two "somethings" that conflict with each other. However, in the example listed above for this first definition, the contradicting elements come from the words of one person. The example provides two statements from one person where the person's latter spoken words are contrary with the former spoken words of the same person. A third set of definitions for the term "contradiction" comes from the Oxford Dictionaries (Oxford Dictionaries:2015):

1.1 A combination of statements, ideas, or features of a situation that are opposed to one another: *the proposed new system suffers from a set of internal contradictions*'
1.2 A person, thing, or situation in which inconsistent elements are present: 'the paradox of using force to overcome force is a real contradiction'

In the aforementioned definitions of the term "contradiction," all but one of these definitions has one set of data with inherent elements that are in opposition to one another. The exception to this comes from the first definition from the *Cambridge Dictionaries Online* where there are two sets of data that are inconsistent or contrary with one another. In that Carrier posits that the resurrection narratives are contradictory, he must show that there is no way in which the alleged four sets of contrary data coming from the four evangelists can be reconciled. However, if these four sets of data (testimony from the evangelists) come from different sources, then the data would not be of identical circumstances as each evangelist includes data of different circumstances from four different perspectives.

Therefore, merely observing differences in the resurrection narratives of the four evangelists does not rise to the standard of contradiction. As offered earlier, differences will naturally occur when there are different sources for the information (2.3.1). In order to rise to the standard of contradiction, one Gospel author would have to come up with an entirely different narrative of events where the elements from the resurrection account of one evangelist were totally inconsistent or contrary or incongruous with the resurrection narrative from another Gospel author.

In keeping with the aforementioned discussion regarding the definition of the term "contradiction," it is probative to offer a definition for the term "embellishment" as Carrier has offered that not only do the resurrection narratives contradict each other, but there are also embellishments present in them as well. Merriam Webster (2015b) defines "embellish" and "embellishment" as:

1) to make beautiful with ornamentation: decorate <a book *embellished* with illustrations>
2) to heighten the attractiveness of by adding decorative or fanciful details: enhance <*embellished* our account of the trip>
-em·bel·lish·ment *noun* act or process of embellishing
3) Something serving to embellish (Merriam Webster, 2015c)

In this definition of embellishment as it relates to the issue at hand, an embellishment of an original set of data by a second set of data would make the first set of data more appealing by adding ornamentation (definition 1) or by adding decorative or fanciful details (definition 2). What is immediately apparent is that there would be similarities between the first and second set of data, as the second set of data would merely modify the first set with ornamentation or even fanciful details. However, there would still be core data that the two sets would share.

Applying these two definitions to the current discussion, anytime that Carrier raises the accusation that the evangelists embellish the accounts of the other evangelists, he actually weakens his other contention that the accounts of the evangelists contradict each other as contradiction implies inconsistency, contrariness, or incongruity. Again, applying the definition of "embellishment" to the analysis of two sets of data demonstrates there is similarity between the accounts with the second account changed to be made more attractive. An example of an accusation of embellishment Carrier makes is observed with the accounts of Joseph of Arimathea in the resurrection narratives of the four evangelists. Included below are Carrier's (2005a:ch. 5) comments on the embellishments that he observes in the resurrection narratives of the four evangelists regarding Joseph of Arimathea:

> Mark tells a simple story about a Sanhedrist burying Jesus, women going to the tomb and finding it open, meeting a single boy in white, then running off. But by the time we get to Matthew, Joseph has become a "disciple of Jesus" (27:57) who buried Jesus "in his own new tomb" (27:60).

Luke, unaware of Matthew and less prone to the fabulous, also "embellished" the story received from Mark, though less excitingly. Joseph is only said to have been a swell guy who abstained from condemning Jesus (23:50-51), who buried Jesus in an empty tomb (not said to be his own; 23:53). But these are still details not mentioned by Mark... John borrows some of the embellishments of Luke, but makes the story entirely his own: Joseph is now a secret disciple (19:38), and again uses an unused tomb (not said to be his own; 19:41), but delivers an absurdly fabulous burial (19:39) (Carrier, 2005a:ch. 5).

There is also no motive for Joseph to weather such a storm, beyond what is obviously a legendary embellishment of the plain story in Mark: from merely a god-fearing man who doesn't even finish the burial (Mark 15:43, 16:1), Joseph becomes someone said to have actually abstained from condemning Jesus (but who still didn't finish the burial: Luke 23:50-51, 24:1), then he's a "disciple" of Jesus who gives a simple burial (Matt. 27:57-59), and finally, the transformation complete, he becomes a "secret disciple" who gives Jesus a king's burial defying all credulity (John 19:38-40). Surely Mark's account is closest to the truth here: This best explains why Mark and Luke agree that Joseph didn't finish the burial rites and therefore did not formally bury Jesus on Friday (Carrier, 2005c, ch. 10).

Even in Carrier's theory of embellishment, he establishes several similarities between the resurrection narratives against his own theory of contradiction (2.4). In his criticism of the Gospel accounts mentioning Joseph of Arimathea, Carrier confirms details about him. Without even reading the Gospel passages that include Joseph, from Carrier we know that he is a "Sanhedrist" who buried Jesus after his death and placed him in a tomb.

In contrast to Carrier's perspective, if one reads the burial accounts in the Bible in respect to Joseph of Arimathea, they are quite similar even though there are some minor differences. In all of the accounts Joseph is listed as a believer[42] (*contra* Carrier in this section) who laid Jesus in a tomb (Mark 15:46; Matt. 27:60; Luke 23:53; John 19:41-42), and who wrapped him in a cloth (Mark 15:46; Matt. 27:59; Luke 23:53; John 19:40). There are some differences in minor details such as the inclusion of Nicodemus (John 19:39) with Joseph as he wrapped Jesus in a linen cloth and anointed the body of Jesus with spiced ointments. But to characterize additions or differences such as these as legendary embellishments does not properly utilize the data coming from the various accounts of Joseph of

---

[42] In Mark and Luke, Joseph is listed as one who was "waiting for the kingdom of God" and in Matthew he is listed as a disciple of Jesus; In John, he is listed as a disciple but who was one secretly.

Objection One: The Resurrection Narratives Contradict Each Other 91

Arimathea in the resurrection narratives. Moreover, the confusion of Carrier on this topic foreshadows a problem that he will face when his views are compared with FRE 607 (and other related rules) (2.5.5, 2.8.2).

2.8 Evidentiary analysis: Carrier's contention by accepted principles of evidence

2.8.1 Evidentiary analysis: Carrier's view of evidence

In his chapter entitled, *The spiritual body of Christ and the legend of the empty tomb*, Carrier (2005a:ch.5) discusses Paul, the apostle, and the evidence he gives for the resurrection of Jesus Christ. As Carrier summarizes the evidence that Paul presents, he submits that Paul does not offer any evidence other than "scriptures and epiphanies."[43] Carrier (2005a:ch. 5, 233-234 fn.) cites 1 Corinthians 9:1 and 1 Corinthians 15 3-8 as support for this assertion and further states that Paul really has "no other evidence." In further discussing evidence regarding the four evangelists, Carrier (2005c:ch. 10) posits, "We cannot know what really happened, since we cannot be sure of the reliability of the Gospels and we have no other sources to work from, nor can we entirely trust our legal evidence." In this quotation, Carrier avers that there is no real, and valid legal evidence within the Gospel narratives. Responding to Stephen Davis on the evidentiary value of the Gospels when discussing differences and additions in them, Carrier (2006a) submits that because of the contradictions, embellishments, and fictionalized elements in them, it is more credible to believe that the differences are due to legendary development. He further opines that when the Gospels are compared to real histories of the same period, it will be obvious to see the differences between them.

In commenting on the unreliability of Luke as a historian, Carrier (2006b) not only criticizes Luke for his lack of inquisitiveness, but also censures him for not having any basis in knowing the source for Mark.

---

[43] Regarding Paul's evidence for the resurrection, Carrier (2005a:ch.5) asserts, "The purpose of Paul's list is to summarize all the evidence on which their faith in the resurrection of Christ rests, since he then uses the presumption of that faith as the linchpin in his following argument (as we saw earlier). We can therefore be assured that this is the best he had to offer by way of proving it. Yet all he mentions are scriptures and epiphanies. No physical evidence, no special testimony. Yet we already saw how priceless such evidence and testimony would have been for illustrating and demonstrating whatever he wanted to say about the nature of the resurrection. So its absence here is not a mark of assumption, brevity, or oversight. It indicates there is no other evidence."

Furthermore, he accuses Luke of not describing "the relative reliability" of his sources and does not show any interest in distinguishing between good and bad evidence. Moreover, Carrier (2006b) also takes Luke to task for not knowing of Matthew's version of the nativity story and offers the possibility that Matthew "Made it all up." In showing agreement with his previous information offered on the topic, Carrier further casts doubt on Matthew, Mark, and Luke when he offers that the sources for Luke's documents are not historical documents.[44]

In his assessment of John's Gospel, Carrier (2014b:696) is no more sanguine about his opinion of its veracity. He states that John's Gospel is an "elegant literary invention just as we saw in the early Gospels" and that John "employs the device of inventing his stories by creatively, and meaningfully rewriting stories (or adapting story ideas) from the Old Testament" (Carrier, 2014b:696). In summary, Carrier (2014b:703) avers that all of the Gospel narratives "are simply myths about Jesus and the gospel." In making these claims against the four evangelists, and in particular their resurrection narratives, does Carrier utilize accepted principles of evidence to support his claims? An examination of the evidence for the veracity of the evangelists will be conducted by surveying scholarly Christian literature and by comparing Carrier's claims to the aforementioned *FRE* and FPJI.

2.8.2 Evidentiary analysis: Carrier's contention in light of accepted principles of evidence

Upon completing an analysis of Carrier's contention of "contradictory resurrection narratives," generally, and comparing them with the *FRE* and FPJI, it is apparent that he does not utilize accepted principles of evidence in his examination of the evangelists. The most significant violation of the principles of the *FRE* is when he attempts to impeach the Gospel witnesses by way of contradictory statements. If Carrier were properly impeaching the evangelists by way of *FRE* Rule 607 (2.5.5), Carrier would have to impeach each *individual* evangelist by way of offering relevant evidence that each *individual* evangelist had made prior inconsistent

---

[44] Regarding the evidentiary value of Luke, Carrier asserts, "So once again, there is in fact no way to discern what if anything that Luke has added to Mark and Matthew has any historical basis or even a source. And its having a source would still not establish that it's historical; after all, his primary sources, Mark and Matthew, are not demonstrably historical, so why would any of his unknown sources be" (Carrier, 2014b)?

or contradictory statements about their testimony. In this way, Carrier could properly impeach the Gospel witnesses one by one. There is no record of Carrier doing this in all of his writings that have been surveyed except in the case where he attempts to impeach the author of the "Marcan appendix (long ending)" with the author of Mark's short ending (the "short ending" stops at Mk. 16:8).[45] However, if his assertion that the long ending is written by an author other than the author of Mark, then he still is not properly impeaching either author because in his analysis they are different authors.

With this limited proviso, in no other circumstance does he properly impeach the evangelists. Rather, he tries to impeach them corporately as a unit and that is not provided for in *FRE* Rule 607 that specifically limits the impeachment of a witness to an individual. Furthermore, Carrier has not offered evidence based on facts that are substantiated by proof (*FRE* Rule 104(b)) that the Gospel evangelists had untruthful character, that they were convicted of a crime, that they made prior inconsistent or contradictory statements that are wholly inconsistent with other statements that they subsequently made, and/or that there was evidence based on facts that the evangelists were biased, and/or had an improper interest or motive for testifying.

Regarding the FPJI pertaining to the credibility of witnesses, does Carrier offer any evidence that the resurrection narratives are inconsistent other than his own opinions (2.2.1)? Also, does Carrier offer any evidence to undergird his attack on the evangelists regarding their identity and sources (2.2.1)? Carrier has only offered his opinions in this instance. Therefore, Carrier's claim of contradictory resurrection narratives and unknown sources are not supported by *FRE* 104(b) and FRE 401 as Carrier has not offered facts that are based on proof for his opinions. Therefore, his opinions are not relevant evidence (FRE 401) because there is no proof to establish his opinions as facts (FRE 104(b)) (2.5.2 and 2.5.3).

---

[45] The wording in this sentence regarding the authorship of the Markan appendix (vv. 9-19) and the author of Mark are meant to reflect Carrier's position that there are two separate authors for these two sections of the book of Mark; the wording in this sentence is not intended to reflect the opinion of the author of this paper. Regarding the authorship of Mark and the "Markan appendix," Carrier offers, "If the author of the LE [long ending also referred to as the Markan appendix] were Mark, he would have added this exorcism story into the narrative of Jesus' ministry, and then alluded to it (if at all) when Mary Magdalene was first introduced in verse 15:40, or when she first appears in the concluding narrative *(in* verse 16:1)" (Carrier, 2014a:245).

Concerning *FRE* Rule 602, this rule is relevant regarding Carrier's contention of "unknown or unreliable evangelists." Does Carrier have a historical witness with personal knowledge that can refute the authorship of the evangelists that are affirmed by early church tradition? If Carrier has relevant evidence (401) that is based upon facts that are substantiated by proof (104 (b)), then he should submit these for consideration. If Carrier even had some form of hearsay evidence whether it is first-hand, second-hand, or third-hand, he should submit it for consideration. But again, his unsupported opinion should not carry any weight (2.6.4) at all if it is merely a bald assertion.

Regarding the FPJI on the credibility of a witness (1.07; 2.6.3), there are several of the criteria that are relevant to Carrier's contention of contradicting resurrection narratives. Regarding his charge of contradiction, did any of the evangelists have a bias that would cause them to "lie or to slant the testimony in favor of one side or another (criterion #3)"? Regarding criterion number three, the religious beliefs of the evangelists could not be used to discredit their testimony (*FRE* Rule 610; 2.5.6). Excluding any reasons based on their religious beliefs, Carrier offers no reasons as to why the disciples would lie in his literature. In reference to criterion number four concerning the prior inconsistent statements of witnesses in this jury instruction (1.07; 2.6.3), it would not apply to Carrier's contention. It does not apply because Carrier has not impeached the evangelists with their own prior inconsistent statements (to include the previously mentioned passage in Mark 16-cf. footnote 42).

Regarding criterion number five, this criterion is applicable to Carrier's contention. Does Carrier show that the testimony of the evangelists (a) was supported or (b) contradicted by other evidence? Specifically, Carrier should show that the testimony of the evangelists was contradicted with other "believable" evidence (2.6.3). Furthermore, the criterion notes that honest people "sometimes forget things," and that "even two honest people who witness the same event may not describe it exactly the same way" (2.6.3). Moreover as put forth by the Christian scholars, mere differences in the accounts would in no way suggest that the accounts are contradictory but they are merely from the personal perspective of the evangelist which is in keeping with criterion five of the federal pattern jury instruction on the credibility of the witnesses.

Specifically regarding Carrier's contention that the PRA reports of Jesus Christ contradict each other, *FRE* Rule 607 (and other related rules) also applies here in that to properly impeach the evangelists on this point, Carrier would have to show that each individual evangelist contradicted himself by way of a prior inconsistent or contradictory statement or fell afoul of any other criteria offered above (untruthfulness, etc.). However, Carrier does not offer any relevant evidence to support this.[46]

However, regarding the FPJI on the credibility of witnesses (2.6.3), an important consideration regarding criterion number five, part (b), is that in attacking the testimony of the evangelists regarding the presence of contradictions in the PRA of Jesus Christ, Carrier would need to demonstrate that the disciples are referencing the same event. As he has stated regarding these appearances (2.2.4), "Luke and John fundamentally contradict the tradition of Matthew and Mark." However, Mark merely states that Jesus Christ will appear to them in Galilee which testimony does not preclude that Jesus will appear to them in Jerusalem as well. Furthermore, Carrier minimizes the fact that Matthew has Jesus Christ appearing to the women in Jerusalem (Matt. 28:9), ignores the fact that Luke mentions that Jesus appeared to the disciples "over a period of forty days" in his subsequent book of Acts (1:3) (2.2.4), and that John mentions both locations for the appearances of Jesus (John 20:19-29, 21:1). Moreover, these appearances of the risen Jesus Christ that Carrier notes in the evangelists are not the same appearances. Therefore, inconsistency or contradiction should not be entertained as Carrier lists different appearances.

In regard to Carrier's contention of contradictory angelic narratives, again FRE Rule 607 would apply for the same reasons as noted above as there are four different perspectives that are offered and he should not try to impeach four witnesses at the same time. Relating to the federal pattern jury instruction on the credibility of witnesses, did Carrier demonstrate that the different witnesses were inconsistent or contradictory with that of the other witnesses?" As was shown in the cross-examination of Carrier's contention, the fact that one evangelist only mentions one angel whereas another evangelist mentions two does not entail an inconsistency or contradiction (2.3.2). Moreover, the evangelists describe the report of angelic activity at the tomb from their individual perspectives. Reporting from their own personal perspectives would naturally entail differences in their reports and these differences in description are wholly compatible with criterion five of the federal pattern jury instruction on the credibility of witnesses.

---

[46] Regarding the testimony contained in the four evangelists on the Resurrection of Jesus Christ, Richard Swinburne (cited by Glenn Siniscalchi, 2011:365) avers, "in the absence of counter-evidence . . . testimony ought to be believed. If someone says, 'I saw so-and-so happen,' we ought to believe that they saw so-and-so happen, unless we have a positive reason to suppose that they didn't."

Concerning the objection that the evangelists list different women and activity at the tomb, FRE 607 would also work against Carrier in this instance as he attempts to impeach four witnesses at once. The federal pattern jury instruction on credibility of witnesses would apply especially in relation to part criterion five part (b) as there are different combinations of women mentioned in the various narratives. However, as observed in the cross examination of this contention (2.3.1), actual scenarios of historical events were given as proof that there were differences in the accounts of eyewitnesses of the same events yet the core facts of the story remained intact.

Moreover, the literature coming from Christian scholars submitted that each evangelist reported from a personal perspective that was informed by different sources who were reporting the testimony of prominent female witnesses from their own geographical "centre" as well as listing the aspects of the account that were important to them. Upon considering these arguments, the alleged contradiction between witnesses does not hold up under scrutiny. As has been pointed out, the Gospel evangelists utilize different witnesses and the testimony of these witnesses will be colored by their personal perspectives (FPJI on weighing the evidence; 2.6.4.). Additionally, there are only several differences between the four lists offered by the evangelists so the variance is only a minor one (2.3).

Regarding the activity of the women at the tomb, the main difference among the evangelists would be in the Matthean account where there was a guard that was reported as well as different persons experiencing the risen Jesus Christ (women/Mary Magdalene). Moreover, there are the women who left the tomb and were reported to have initially told no one (Mark 16:8) whereas in the other narratives the women reported to the disciples what they had witnessed. In these accounts, the FPJI regarding the credibility of witnesses is germane as criterion number five would be satisfied as each evangelist had different sources of information. Moreover, each evangelist need not report every detail of the events they described. They only mentioned those details that were important to their personal and thematic purposes (2.3.3).

In reference to the timing of the removal of the stone, the differences in the movement of the stone are quite insignificant and do not need a full evidentiary explication. The Matthean account, as brought out in the cross-examination of Carrier's contention of contradiction, is described with a more immediate context and does not have an inconsistency. However, Carrier asserts that the women came before the stone was moved because of the activity of the earthquake and the reaction of the guards as the women approached the tomb (2.2.5). In that there is no *prima facie* inconsistency observed in the evangelists regarding the movement of the stone, FRE rule 607 would not apply. However, if Carrier's theory, that it was before the movement of the stone, is taken into account, the pattern jury instruction on the credibility of witnesses would be applicable because there would be an apparent discrepancy. However, the time period between "before the stone was moved" and then "after the stone was moved" could be trivially insignificant, literally even seconds or even fractions of a second. Thus, this may be Carrier's weakest contention of contradiction from an evidentiary standpoint because the probative value of his claim is so insignificant.

In section 2.6.4, the FPJI for "criteria to consider when weighing the evidence" is included from the U.S. Circuit Court of Appeals for the Sixth Circuit section 1.05. In evaluating the evidence presented to them, jurors should consider the evidence and reach their own conclusions based on their own experience from their daily lives. Certainly, the other jury instructions on the different forms of evidence as well as the credibility of witnesses are probative in assisting one in their goal of assigning weight to the evidence as well as the rules of evidence, in particular rules 401 and 104(b). In these accepted principles of evidence, there are guidelines that are useful to all who are trying to discern between two differing theories and these accepted principles of evidence have been utilized above in evaluating Carrier's evidence. In discussing the amount of weight (2.6.3) that should be attributed to Carrier's contention of contradiction in the resurrection narratives, what weight should his proposition be given? Based upon the above evidentiary analysis of Carrier's contention, it is submitted that little if any weight should be granted to his main contention for the reasons stated above.

2.8.3 Evidentiary analysis: Rebuttal evidence to Carrier's contention

As Carrier has contended that the resurrection narratives are contradictory in nature and as he has specifically cast doubt on the resurrection accounts of the Gospel evangelists, it is both relevant and probative to assess the quality of the evidence within these narratives by offering rebuttal evidence. However, as it is in the scope of this research project not to offer a full apologetic argument for the reliability of the New Testament, a limited defense of the reliability of the evidence for the resurrection narratives will be offered. This defense will concentrate on the witness testimony given, the forms of evidence that buttress this testimony, as well as principles of evidence supporting this testimony.

In being a proponent of the utilization of the Scriptures as admissible hearsay evidence under the Ancient Documents Rule[47] under the Common Law tradition, J.W. Montgomery observes that Simon Greenleaf (cited by Montgomery, 1986:139), "the greatest nineteenth-century authority on the law of evidence in the common-law-world," applied this hearsay rule exclusion to the gospels and averred that "the competence of the New Testament would be established in any rule of law" as it is "fair on its face" meaning that there is no internal evidence of tampering and that it has been "maintained in reasonable custody." Moreover, Montgomery observes the function of the hearsay rule (FRE 802; 2.5.7) "as a technical device to protect juries from secondhand evidence" as jurors are not trained legal professionals. Furthermore, Montgomery notes that with the progression of time the hearsay rule has "almost been swallowed up" and observes that the ancient documents rule allows for the introduction of the New Testament as competent evidence.[48]

In further describing the presence of hearsay information in the New Testament and thus for the resurrection narratives by extension, Montgomery (1975:88) gives a brief explanation of the hearsay rule (FRE 802) as prohibiting someone from testifying in a court hearing about "facts that they have not observed themselves." In contrast to this prohibition, Montgomery then offers that the witnesses to the accounts of the New Testament testified to what they sensed with their sight, hearing, and touch. Thus, the four evangelists were either reporting what they had seen themselves or what had been reported by those who were eyewitnesses themselves. Realizing the limits of hearsay evidence, F.W. Binder (1983:231) offers, "an exemption contained in an ancient document will not be excepted to the hearsay rule if it appears that the declarant would be incompetent to testify to the assertion if he were present in court."

In addition to his endorsement of the use of the Ancient Documents Rule, Montgomery (1969:81-82) also offers his sentiments regarding the testimony behind the resurrection narratives. Montgomery asserts that the claims regarding the resurrection of Jesus were written by either

---

[47] FRE 803(16); See Section 2.5.7 Accepted Principles of Evidence: FREs 802 and 803
[48] In addition to being in compliance with FRE 802, FRE 1004(a)(b) also applies as the original manuscripts of the resurrection narratives included within the New Testament need not be preserved in order to be admissible as evidence. Copies of the manuscripts of these narratives can be considered as evidence if the (a) originals have been lost/destroyed and also if (b) the original cannot be obtained by any available judicial process (Cornell University Law School, FRE 1004).

eyewitnesses or those who had heard the resurrection account from the eyewitnesses. Montgomery continues that the period of time was so short between the time of the writing of the resurrection narratives and the resurrection itself that there was not enough time for communal redaction to affect the accounts of the resurrection in the Gospels. Further strengthening his assertion, Montgomery (1969:82) submits, "If Jesus had failed to rise from the dead as He promised is there any real likelihood that His message would have become the basis of a church that eventually conquered the Roman world?" Regarding the evidence for the resurrection compared to evidence from the classical era, Montgomery further opines, "I never heard of any questioning of the events of the classical [era] as to their *per se* historicity despite the fact that these are based in much less data than the resurrection of Christ." Moreover, Montgomery (1969:106) states that if we do not accede that the resurrection of Jesus Christ is based upon solid evidence then "we are going to drop out not simply the resurrection but a tremendous portion of world history, which I don't think we're prepared to do."

In recognizing the reliability of the text of the Gospels, Ross Clifford (2004:70) describes the 'ancient document' hearsay exclusion rule as a useful and applicable principle of evidence regarding the gospels. In that Clifford's dissertation topic was J.W. Montgomery's utilization of this rule in his apologetic writings, he endorses Montgomery's use of this rule as a "most appropriate" way to show the evidential value of the gospels, and that the burden in attacking them should be placed on the "adverse party" (Clifford, 2004:70). Moreover, Clifford (2004:82) goes on to describe that first hand hearsay is "an assertion in a document that if the declarant appeared he would be able to testify to the truthfulness of that assertion" and then Clifford goes on to assert that the New Testament writers had this type of knowledge when they wrote their books.

In addition to J.W. Montgomery's assessment of the Ancient Documents Rule to validate the evidence coming from the Bible, Clifford (2004:85) mentions the research of Pamela Ewen regarding hearsay information and that she is a "legal apologist" who cites *FRE* 602 (2.5.4) in support of the normal legal requirement "that a witness giving testimony should have first-hand knowledge remains an important standard for determining the credibility, or the actual value, that the jury will give to that (gospel) testimony." Clifford agrees with Ewen that the courts have given some latitude in interpreting first-hand knowledge "to permit either a showing of first-hand knowledge or showing that circumstances were sufficient to support such a finding." In identifying these circumstances, the main criterion is that the circumstances should corroborate or confirm personal observation (the author had the opportunity to observe the events he is testifying to, etc.).[49]

Regarding documentary evidence, this flexibility is relevant to our topic at hand as it can be shown that the Gospel of John, in particular, was based on first hand observation and very likely the Gospel of Matthew as well. However, Clifford also notes the limitations of utilizing the New Testament as first hand hearsay evidence (or historical direct evidence) as some of the events that the New Testament authors describe are not events that they had witnessed themselves (e.g. the virgin birth accounts and the Gospel of Luke). Reinforcing the view of Clifford, A.M. Ramsey (1969:79) affirms the acceptance of the first hand hearsay evidence of the New Testament authors at a *"prima facie* level" and also that the New Testament "is a foundation for the credibility and the objectivity of the Christian message."

In continuing the theme of the reliability of the Gospel accounts, Ross Clifford and Philip Johnson (2012:80) assert that the accounts of Matthew and John were from an eyewitness perspective, that Mark wrote from what he had heard from Peter, and that Luke was careful in his investigation and checked things out with the eyewitnesses as well. This historical eyewitness testimony of John and Matthew of the Risen Jesus Christ and other related details is historical direct evidence as well as circumstantial evidence in accord with accepted principles of evidence.[50] Moreover, Clifford and Johnson offer Greenleaf's tests regarding the testimony of witnesses. They observe that there could be an issue regarding testimony to the resurrection of Jesus Christ as some may complain that it is beyond the experience of normal people. However, Clifford and Johnson (2012:80-81) state that if there is a God that is all-powerful, then the notion of the resurrection would be within the scope of the beliefs of people to testify from.

In addition to the aforementioned reliability of the Gospel narratives described by the above Christian scholars, a historian, David A. Schum (2003:11), offers evidentiary principles that are germane in assessing the quality of any historical evidence, in general. These principles support the above listed examination on the evidence listed within the resurrec-

---

[49] Pamela Ewen (1999, 36-37) further explains, "In a situation in which the evidence that the witness had an adequate opportunity to observe the facts is uncertain, the evidence will be admitted and the jury will decide the issue."

[50] cf. 2.5, FRE 401, relevant evidence; FRE 104(b), relevance that depends on a fact; rule; FRE 602, testimony from personal knowledge; FRE 803(16), ancient rules document-excepted hearsay in the Gospel records; In the specific case of John's Gospel this will be treated in more detail in this section.

tion narratives. In his chapter entitled "Evidences and Inferences in Past Events," Schum establishes the major credentials of evidence as being "relevance, credibility of the evidence, and inferential or probative force of evidence." In this process of analysis, Schum also emphasizes other qualities regarding the authenticity of historical testimony to include the chain of custody of the testimony, its accuracy, and its reliability. Moreover, Schum (2003:15-17) brings out the importance of whether the information comes from a primary source or whether it has been obtained from someone who heard it from someone else. Regarding historical evidence, it is said to be direct if the evidence goes from hypothesis to conclusion in one step as in credible, eyewitness testimony (Schum, 2003:18-21).

Not only does Schum discuss direct evidence, but offers that circumstantial evidence may only establish particular facts and often is combined with other forms of evidence to support the historical occurrence of an event. Schum (2003:22-24) also discusses recurrent evidence or more than one piece of evidence on a given point as being either divergent (contradictory) or harmonious (corroborative). Thus, recurrent evidence that supports a certain hypothesis is associated with the concept of corroborative evidence. As observed in 2.6.3, evidence is strengthened when two or more lines of evidence report the same thing about an event.[51] In confirmation of Schum, Doyle, *et al.* (2013:117) aver, "One of the first things any responsible investigator will look for in an eyewitness case is corroboration: some facts outside the eyewitness's own account which seems to confirm it." As has been seen throughout the analysis of the resurrection narratives, there is strong corroboration of the core facts of the resurrection (*contra* Carrier).

In summarizing Schum's perspective on historical evidence, he emphasizes that a body of historical evidence is often inconclusive, incomplete, dissonant, and that historical evidence can be ambiguous. Schum's analysis of evidence echoes the general principles of evidence gleaned from the FRE and FPJI. It also emphasizes the primacy of the observational aspect of evidence over opinion evidence as well as supports the concept of harmonious or corroborative evidence. Furthermore, Schum un-

---

[51] See in particular, criterion number five from the pattern jury instruction on "credibility of witnesses (2.6.3)" which applies to the evidence within the resurrection narratives of each evangelist; most of the elements of the resurrection narratives are either corroborated or augmented by the other evangelists. Moreover, many of the differences are on peripheral details and would be in keeping with criterion number four.

derstands that several witnesses of the same event will not report the exact same thing as they have observed the event from different perspectives (e.g. physical proximity, closeness of relationship, emotional impact, etc.) and that there will be gaps of evidence that are to be expected in any body of evidence.

Another historian, Allen Johnson (1965:90-148) emphasizes the importance of working to remove subjectivism from historical evidence, understands that one can never reach mathematical certainty from historical investigation, asserts the importance of examining the character of a historical witness, and endorses the importance of corroborative evidence. Moreover, he posits that two independent witnesses can testify about the same event but if these two witnesses testify to exactly the same circumstances, an observer may believe that collusion has occurred. In similarity to Schum, Johnson realizes that it is rare to have a set of facts where two witnesses agree on everything.

2.8.4 Evidentiary analysis: The testimony of John by accepted principles of evidence

In relation to the disciple John as a witness to the risen Jesus, Richard Bauckham (2006:390-399) demonstrates that John was in a unique position to be an excellent witness because of his close relationship to Jesus. In specifically discussing the reliability of John's account of the resurrection, Bauckham zeroes in on the continuity of John's testimony from the beginning until the end of the earthly ministry of Jesus. Bauckham speaks of the *inclusio* of eyewitness testimony that mentions "the beloved disciple" at the beginning of John's Gospel and then reintroduces him at the end of the account as well. Bauckham also observes this device is present in Mark and Luke as well. The use of this device bolsters the veracity of John's testimony as it shows a continuing relationship with Jesus. John's testimony is more than merely a recitation of a sequence of events. Rather, there is a strong bond between the author and Jesus that is evident throughout the book.

Additionally, Bauckham shows the involvement of John in the actual events themselves when he contrasts himself with the other characters. Bauckham also affirms the reliability of John's Gospel by demonstrating that John is present at key points with Jesus, has detailed recall of events and circumstances, and directly observes not only the death of Jesus but also the empty tomb/risen Jesus Christ. Affirming Bauckham's perspective, Dr. Louis Gottschalk (Cited by McDowell, 1981:28-29) is a historian, who avers that a witness's ability to "tell the truth" about a matter relates upon the nearness of the witness to the event observed. In addition to John meeting the criteria of Gottschalk, his testimony also conforms to the FPJI and in particular to the instruction regarding how the jury should weigh the testimony of the witness (2.6.4).

In addition to Bauckham's perspective on John, John's own testimony regarding the resurrection of Jesus Christ will be compared with the above-mentioned accepted principles of evidence (2.5 and 2.6). Again, this investigation is pertinent as Carrier has discredited the testimony of the four evangelists. In comparing John's testimony with Rule 401(a), John's evidence of seeing the empty tomb and the risen Jesus on several of occasions would make the conclusion that Jesus Christ rose from the dead "more probable" (cf. 2.5.2). Moreover, concerning Rule 401(b), John's testimony would be of consequence in determining that Jesus Christ was raised from the dead (2.5.2).

In regard to Rule 104(b) John's testimony must be based "on whether a fact exists (2.5.3)" to undergird his testimony and his testimony must contain proof that the fact exists. John's eyewitness testimony does establish the fact that the tomb of Jesus Christ was empty and that he had seen Jesus Christ alive on several occasions after he had observed the death of Jesus Christ by crucifixion. These two aspects of John's testimony satisfy the requirements of Rule 104(b).

In regard to FRE Rule 602 (2.5.4), John would need to testify from his own personal knowledge of seeing the empty tomb and Jesus Christ alive after he had seen Jesus executed. As shown above, John did testify that he observed the empty tomb of Jesus and that he observed Jesus Christ alive after he had been executed by means of crucifixion.[52] Therefore. John's testimony satisfies the requirement of FRE Rule 602.

Concerning FRE Rule 607 (and other related rules; 2.5.5), Carrier has offered no evidence that John has been untruthful in his past, that John was a convicted criminal, that John had made prior inconsistent statements about his observations of the risen Jesus Christ, and that John would gain anything from testifying falsely about the risen Jesus Christ. Therefore, Carrier presents no evidence to impeach John. In order for Carrier to impeach John, he would have to offer proof that John satisfied

---

[52] Regarding the personal knowledge requirement of FRE 602, Edward Imwinkelried (2015:28) writes, "To establish this element in convincing fashion, the proponent often elicits the witness's explanation of why the event is so memorable to the witness. For example, the proponent might elicit the witness's testimony that she remembers the event so clearly because the event is the one and only traffic accident she has ever personally witnessed." Certainly, the events of the resurrection of Jesus Christ would have been very memorable for John.

at least one of these elements and he has only made assertions without proof. As was observed in Rule 104(b), Carrier would be required to furnish a fact of John's bad character that would be based on proof or other evidence. Carrier offers no historical witness to "testify" against John. In regard to FRE 802 and 803(16) (2.5.7), it is contended that John's written testimony in the form of His Gospel should be recognized as admissible hearsay evidence under the hearsay exception listed in 803(16). Upon proving the authenticity of the document by proving its reliable transmission as well as providing evidence that John was the author, John's testimony meets the requirement for admissible hearsay (2.8.4).

In reference to the federal pattern jury instruction (2.6.2) dealing with direct and circumstantial evidence, John's testimony would be consistent with direct evidence if it "directly proved a fact." In that he is an eyewitness to the risen Jesus Christ and observed the empty tomb, John had direct evidence that the body of Jesus was no longer in the tomb and that he had seen Jesus Christ alive after his execution by crucifixion. Regarding circumstantial evidence, John's testimony would have to elicit proof that would indirectly prove a fact by a chain of circumstances (2.6.2). John testified that he had seen the tomb of Jesus to be empty and that he had seen Jesus alive on several occasions after he had observed the death of Jesus by crucifixion. In that he has testified to observing Jesus alive after dying and his tomb without the corpse of Jesus Christ laying in it, an inference can be drawn that Jesus Christ was raised from the dead. So, in the testimony of John, there is historical direct evidence that Jesus Christ was alive after his death and circumstantial evidence that Jesus Christ was raised from the dead, as he did not directly observe the resurrection event itself. Moreover, his testimony is included within a document that should be considered "first-hand hearsay (or historical direct evidence)," namely the Gospel that he has written.

In regard to the FPJI on the credibility of the evidence (2.6.3), in order to be deemed as rising to the level of credible testimony, John's testimony would need to meet the five criteria within this jury instruction. Thus, John must have been able to clearly see or hear the events he describes, have the ability to accurately remember what happened, must have been free of any bias or interest that would cause him to falsify his testimony (*FRE* Rule 610-religious affiliation cannot be a reason in itself to claim bias), and his testimony must not have been inconsistent to the extent that it made his testimony unbelievable. Moreover, John's testimony would be strengthened if it was supported by other evidence. As has been offered previously, other evidence has corroborated John's testimony. Moreover, differences in his testimony in relation to other evidence do not necessarily make John's testimony contradictory as borne out by the analysis of the terms contradiction and embellishment (2.7).

2.8.5 Evidentiary analysis: The four evangelists as known persons with known sources

2.8.5.1 Authorship of Mark

In opposition to the charge of "unknown sources or authors" that Carrier levels to support his claim of contradictory narratives, D.A. Carson and Douglas Moo (2005:172), aver that there are good reasons to believe that the Gospel of Mark is written by the one whose name is attached to that Gospel. The duo offers that this Gospel came to be attributed to Mark by the early Christian church around the timeframe of A.D. 125 when the Gospels were collected together as a unit. In assigning this date, Carson and Moo acknowledge that the actual date of attributing the authorship to Mark could be even earlier.

A prominent source that Carson and Moo (2005:173) use for their opinion is the mention of Mark by the early church leader Papias (circa A.D. 130) that is no longer extant but can be observed in the writings of other early church leaders such as Eusebius and Irenaeus.[53] Carson and Moo distill the statement of Papias and offer three important facts concerning Mark: 1) Mark wrote the gospel that, in Eusebius' day, was identified with his name. 2) Mark was not an eyewitness but obtained his information from Peter 3) Mark's gospel lacks 'order,' reflecting the occasional nature of Peter's preaching. In addition to the commentary on Papias from Carson and Moo, Richard Bauckham (cited by C. Evans, 2008:214) affirms the strength of the testimony of Papias as he heard from the eyewitnesses themselves and not those who were merely hearers of the eyewitnesses:

> What Papias thinks preferable to books is not oral tradition as such but access, while they are still alive, to those who were direct participants in the

---

[53] As included in the History of the Church, Bk. 3, Ch. 39, Papias describes the information that he received from the "Presbyter:" "When Mark became the interpreter of Peter, he wrote down accurately whatever he remembered though not in order, of the words and deeds of the Lord...Mark then made no mistake, but wrote things down as he remembered them; and he made it his concern to omit nothing that he had heard nor to falsify anything therein;" St. Papias was the Bishop of the Christian church at Hierapolis. (cf. Eusebius, s.a.(a), 1970:38-39).

historical events — in this case 'disciples of the Lord'...he is not speaking metaphorically of the 'voice' of oral tradition, as many scholars have supposed. He speaks quite literally of the voice of the informant — someone who has personal memories of the words and deeds of Jesus and who is still alive.

In addition to Papias, Carson and Moo (2005:173) submit that other early church leaders such as Justin Martyr, Tertullian, Origen, and Clement of Alexandria also attribute the identity of the second evangelist as Mark. Furthermore, the attribution of "John Mark" as the writer of the second Gospel is the only logical candidate for this position as he is a prominent figure and is mentioned in other Gospels. Moreover, further buttressing the claim of Markan authorship is that this position is uncontested by any early church leaders or rival theories of authorship that have been propounded.

In addition to these external evidences coming from outside of the New Testament, it is worthwhile mentioning several New Testament Scriptures that mention Mark a.k.a. "John Mark." In Colossians 4:10-18, Paul is giving his salutations as he ends his letter to the church at Colossae and mentions the greetings of other fellow Christians who are with him. In doing this, he mentions that Mark (v. 10) as well as Luke (v. 14), send their greetings. In similarity to the salutations in Colossians, Philemon 24 also lists Paul sending greetings from Mark and Luke to Philemon. This data coming from the New Testament is relevant regarding Carrier's charge of "unknown sources" against the evangelists. These passages are proof that Mark and Luke were acquainted with each other. Even though it cannot be proven from these verses that Luke received Mark's gospel from him, the fact that Mark was personally well acquainted with Luke can be proven. In that these evangelists were well acquainted with each other, this relationship would facilitate the passing of Mark's Gospel to Luke where Luke could utilize Mark as a source for his Gospel.

Moreover, The Apostle Paul recognizes both of these men as his aides in Christian ministry. Therefore this identification by Paul of two Gospel evangelists is good relevant evidence (401) based on a fact that can be proven (104(b)) that Luke and Mark are known persons, in contrast to Carrier's unsupported assertion to the contrary. Rather, they are established leaders in the early Christian church who knew each other. In pointing to evidence about the authorship of the Gospels by Jesus' disciples, Thomas Chalmers (1816:34-35) offers the second-century writings of Celsus that criticize the Gospels. In criticizing the Christian faith, Celsus, an enemy of the early Christian church, confirms that the disciples' of Jesus wrote two of the Gospels. Celsus criticizes Christianity yet he confirms authorship of two of the Gospels approximately one hundred years after they were published. Celsus takes it as a known fact of that time period that Jesus' disciples wrote two of the Gospels.

In addition to the aforementioned authors, Richard Bauckham (2009:21) describes the testimony of Peter included within Mark as an *inclusio*. In using this term, Bauckham shows that Peter's influence in Mark's Gospel was "pervasive" and extended from the beginning of the evangelist to the ending. Bauckham argues that the *inclusio* is "intended to indicate that Peter was the major eyewitness behind Mark's narrative." Bauckham's observation is further corroboration of Peter as the source for Mark's Gospel, *contra* Carrier's contention of unknown sources.

In the aforementioned evidence for the authorship of Mark and the source of Peter for Mark, there are many principles of evidence evinced. The evidence submitted is in accord with Rule 401 (2.5.2) as it is relevant evidence in that it makes the fact of Mark's authorship and Peter as the main Markan source more probable, and as it is in accord with Rule 104(b) as the aforementioned evidence (Celsus, early Christian church leaders, and Paul's witness of their relationship) is based upon facts that are supported by proof. Moreover, the evidence should be deemed credible in accord with the FPJI dealing with the credibility of evidence in criterion number five (2.6.3), as it is supported by other evidence. Moreover, this evidence should be granted much weight because it is well supported by several streams of evidence (*FPJI* Section 1.05- weighing the evidence).

2.8.5.2 Authorship of Matthew

In similarity to the Gospel of Mark, there is early church attestation of Matthew being the first evangelist. David Black and Thomas Lea (2003:132-33) submit that Eusebius again includes material from the no longer extant work of Papias regarding the identity of the first evangelist as Matthew.[54] Moreover, they also mention internal factors that they believe point to Matthew as the author to include mention of Jesus paying the temple tax (17:24-27), the mention of the disciple Matthew as a tax collector (9:9-13), and the organization of the text which they believe "re-

---

[54] As included in the History of the Church, Bk. 3, Ch. 39, Eusebius (s.a.(a):39) cites Papias: "In regard to Matthew, he says this: 'Matthew indeed composed the sayings in the Hebrew language; and each one interpreted them to the best of his ability."

flects the tidy mindset of one who could have been a tax collector." They also assert that it is the unanimous opinion of the early church that Matthew was the author of the first Gospel (Black & Lea, 2003:134).

In addition, F.F. Bruce offers the words of Irenaeus (cited by Bruce, 1988:174) through Eusebius, who offers his support for the authorship of the first Gospel to Matthew. Irenaeus states, "Matthew published among the Hebrews a gospel in writing also [i.e. in addition to the oral preaching] in their own speech, while Peter and Paul were preaching the gospel and founding the church in Rome." Moreover, Carson and Moo (2005:143-45) aver that not only Papias endorsed Matthew as the first evangelist, but the later church fathers did so as well.[55] In similarity to the supposed anonymity of Mark, Carson and Moo (2005:140) also posit that even though some have asserted that the Gospels, to include Matthew, were anonymous, there is no evidence that this is the case. They offer that, the first Gospel, had the phrase "according to Matthew" attached to it as early as A.D. 125 or even earlier. Martin Hengel (cited by Carson & Moo, 2005:140-41) states that the Gospels were read publicly in the early Christian churches as early as A.D. 100 and would be attributed to an author upon its reading. Hengel supports his conclusion from studying the distribution of books in this early era and the necessity of attributing authorship.

Additionally, it can be adduced that the evidence coming from the book of Matthew would be his eyewitness testimony of some of the events of the resurrection, and PRA of Jesus Christ. Also there is hearsay testimony from the other eyewitnesses of the resurrection events who Matthew would be acquainted with by virtue of his close relationship with Jesus Christ and the other apostles. Thus, the portions of his narrative where he was an eyewitness to the events would be evidence affirmed by *FRE* Rule 602 as he would have personal knowledge from his own observations. In his reporting of the observations of others, it is highly probable that this hearsay information is accurate as he obtained it directly from the witnesses themselves because of his close association with them.

As in the case of Mark, the evidence for Matthean authorship would be in accord with *FRE* Rule 401 and Rule 104(b) as it would tend to make Matthean authorship and knowledge of his sources more probable (relevance-FRE 401) and the evidence would be based on facts that are based on proof (rule 104(b)). Furthermore, the evidence for Matthean author-

---

[55] Carson and Moo (2005:145) list the later church fathers who endorse the authorship of Matthew as Irenaeus, Eusebius, Tertullian, Origen, and Jerome.

Objection One: The Resurrection Narratives Contradict Each Other

ship would be in line with the federal pattern jury instruction on credibility of witnesses as there are several streams of data that support Matthean authorship. Finally, the weight of the evidence is strong that Matthew is the author of the first Gospel and that the source for his information would be his own observations and reports from other eyewitnesses whom he knew by virtue of his position as an apostle of the early Christian church.[56] Also, by virtue of his position as a leader of the early Christian church, he may have known Luke and Mark as well. Also, the weight of the evidence for this conclusion is strengthened by corroboration from several lines of evidence coming from various sources.

2.8.5.3 Authorship of Luke

In relation to the Gospel of Luke, Black and Lea (2003:147) explain that Luke's Gospel has the support of the early Christian church fathers to include Tertullian, and Irenaeus.[57] F.F. Bruce (1988:154-55) observes that the writer of the so-called "Anti-Marcionite" prologues of the late second century endorsed Luke as the author of the third Gospel.[58] Furthermore, Luke is also endorsed as the third evangelist by the second-century Mura-

---

[56] Even though the scope of this project is limited to Richard Carrier's perspectives, it is still probative to note that a large number of scholars dispute that Matthew was the author of the first book of the New Testament citing textual difficulties and borrowing from Mark (Keener, 1999:38-41). However, even though Keener (1999:40) notes the aforementioned obstacles, he still supports Matthew as the author "with admitted uncertainty." Regarding Matthean authorship, Wenham and Walton (2001:224) discuss similar problems noted by Keener. In similarity with Keener, they aver that it is "perfectly possible" that Matthew may very well be the author of the first Gospel. A pertinent matter for any investigator to determine from an evidential perspective is whether there is evidence to impeach either the early documents or the historical witnesses that support Matthean authorship. If there is no impeachment of the sources supporting Matthean authorship, then the evidence should be accepted until it is successfully attacked. Moreover, is there good evidence to support any alternate theories? Even though it is perfectly acceptable to speculate about possible theories of authorship, conclusions should not be made upon mere conjecture (*contra* FRE 104b). Conversely, it must also be noted that a conclusion cannot be drawn with absolute certainty that Matthew was the author even though there are a number of accepted principles of evidence that support his authorship.

[57] Of Luke, Irenaeus (s.a.) states, "Luke, also the companion of Paul, set down in a book the Gospel preached by him."

[58] "Luke was a native of Syrian Antioch, a physician by profession, a disciple of the apostles. Later, he accompanied Paul until the latter's martyrdom...Luke wrote his Gospel in the region of Achaia." (Bruce, 1988:154).

torian fragment, a listing of the books acknowledged by the early Church as being part of the New Testament Canon of Scripture.[59]

In addition to these endorsements as stated above, Luke is also identified in Scripture in similarity to Mark. Again, as listed above, Mark and Luke are both associates of Paul which establishes that the two had a relationship that could have facilitated Mark sharing his Gospel with Luke (cf. Col. 4:14 and Phil. 24). Moreover, his relationship to Paul is corroborated by Colossians 4:14 as Paul refers to him as "his dear friend." Thus, in relation to the contention of unknown authors and unknown sources for the Gospels put forth by Carrier, this information is relevant evidence in support of Lucan authorship of the third Gospel as well as good information on the background relationship of why Luke would know Mark and use Mark as a source.

Moreover, the notes coming from the Anti-Marcionite prologues as well as the notes from the Muratorian fragment also give reasons for Paul being another source for his Gospel. Regarding external evidence for Lucan authorship of the third gospel, Carson and Moo (2005:205) offer that the oldest manuscript of the Gospel of Luke, the *Bodmer Papyrus XIV*, which is dated from between A.D. 175 to A.D. 225, attributes authorship to Luke as well. Other information about Luke coming from Carson and Moo (2005:204) is that in the Book of Acts, which is the second part of the Luke-Acts series, Luke uses the pronoun "we (e.g. Acts 16:11)" when referring to the journeys of Paul. This usage, according to Carson and Moo, demonstrates that the author was traveling with Paul. By virtue of this relationship, Luke would be in a good position to have Paul as a source for the details of his Gospel. Also, in Luke 1:12, Luke avers that the details of the accounts contained within his Gospel were "handed down to us by those who from the first were eyewitnesses and servants of the word."

Because of obtaining his information from the eyewitness accounts of others to include Paul, and the other eyewitnesses of the events of the

---

[59] Of Luke, the Muratorian Fragment states, "The third book of the Gospel is that according to Luke, the well-known physician, which, after the ascension of Christ, Luke wrote in his own name from what he had learned when Paul associated him with himself as a companion of his journey. Nor did he himself see the Lord in the flesh; but inasmuch as he was thus enabled to proceed, he began his account with the birth of John" (Anon., The Muratorian Fragment, s.a., Cited by Jurgens, 1970:107); The Muratorian fragment gets its name from its publisher (who published it in 1749), Lodovico Antonio Muratori, a "distinguished antiquarian and theologian in his day, from a codex copied in the seventh or eighth century at the monastery of Bobbio, in Lombardy, but later lodged in the Ambrosian Library, Milan..." (Bruce, 1988:158).

resurrection of Jesus Christ, Luke's Gospel can be considered relevant evidence in accord with Rule 401 and 104(b) as the evidence would tend to make Lucan authorship and knowledge of his sources more probable. Additionally, the aforementioned information is also based on facts supported by proof so Rule 104(b) would affirm it. In relation to the FPJI, the evidence for the Lucan authorship and for the sources for Luke are also supported by several streams of evidence (credibility of witnesses) and the weight of the evidence should be considered as strong because of this corroboration of evidence.

2.8.5.4 Authorship of John

From an evidentiary standpoint, the identity of John, the Son of Zebedee as the fourth evangelist also demonstrates affirmation from the early Church authors. Carson and Moo identify that the early Church leaders who endorse John as the author of the fourth Gospel are Irenaeus,[60] Clement of Alexandria,[61] and Tertullian. Moreover, the "Anti-Marcionite" prologues[62] and the "Muratorian Fragment"[63] also accord John as the author of the fourth Gospel as well. Black and Lea (2003:157) observe that there is internal evidence to the identification of the fourth evangelist as John and that it hinges on the use of the title "The Beloved Disciple."

---

[60] Of John, Irenaeus states, "John the disciple of the Lord, who leaned back on his breast, published the gospel while he was resident at Ephesus in Asia" (Carson & Moo, 2005:230).

[61] Of John, Clement of Alexandria states, "John, last of all, seeing that the plain facts had been clearly set forth in the Gospels, and being urged by his acquaintances, composed a spiritual Gospel under the divine inspiration of the Spirit" (Clement of Alexandria cited by Eusebius, s.a.(b), cited by Jurgens, 1970:188).

[62] Of John, the Anti-Marcionite prologue to Luke has a note contained within it which states, "Later still, the apostle John, one of the twelve, wrote the Apocalypse on the island of Patmos, and the gospel in Asia;" Of John, The Anti-Marcionite Prologue to John states, "The gospel of John was published and given to the churches by John while he was still in the body, as Papias of Hierapolis, John's dear disciple, has related in his five exoteric, that is his last books" (Bruce, 1988:154,156).

[63] Of John, the Muratorian Fragment states, "The fourth Gospel is by John, one of the disciples...It is no wonder then that John constantly returns to these things even in his Epistles, saying of himself, 'What we have seen with our eyes and have heard with our ears and what our hands have touched, these things have we written to you.' And thus he professes that he is not only an eyewitness but also the hearer, and moreover, also the writer of all the marvels of the Lord as they happened" (Anon., The Muratorian Fragment, Cited by Jurgens, 1970:107).

Black and Lea further affirm that by process of elimination from the list of the seven disciples that are included in chapter twenty-one of John, John the Apostle is the logical choice as the "Beloved Disciple." Moreover, Carson and Moo (2005:253), even though they describe a number of modern objections to Johannine scholarship, still affirm from their investigation of the evidence that John, the son of Zebedee, was the author of the fourth Gospel. In addition to the identity of John as the "Beloved Disciple," he also makes it clear that he has testified of these things and that he wrote them down as well (John 21:24). Therefore, he is an eyewitness to many of the accounts and was also in the position to query the other eyewitnesses regarding circumstances surrounding the resurrection of Jesus Christ by virtue of his position of leadership within the early Christian church.

In similarity to the other Gospels, there are several lines of intersecting evidence to include internal and external evidence that back the Apostle John as "The Beloved Disciple" and the "Fourth Evangelist." Because of this corroborative evidence coming from different sources, and because John was an eyewitness to a number of resurrection events, John's testimony would comport with *FRE* Rule 602 because he had personal knowledge of some of the events that he testified to in regard to the resurrection of Jesus Christ. Furthermore, the aforementioned evidence regarding the authorship of John would be in conformity with *FRE* Rule 401 as the evidence is relevant in determining whether it is more probable that the author of the fourth Gospel was John and whether we can determine who the sources for John may be, generally. Also, *FRE* Rule 104(b) applies because there are facts that are based on proof that support the assertion that John was the author of his Gospel.[64]

---

[64] Even though the scope of this paper is confined to the writings of Richard Carrier, it is useful to mention the ongoing debate regarding the authorship of the fourth Gospel. In similarity to the question of authorship for the first Gospel, there is no scholarly concensus on the writer of the fourth one (Keener, 2003:11-115). Keener provides from other scholars a number of alternate theories casting doubt on the traditional view of John, the son of Zebedee. One of these challenges includes a community or school influenced by John, son of Zebedee who authored the Gospel. Another rival theory has a different "John" who was also a disciple of the early Christian community and known as "the elder." Still others include a divergence in the writing styles of John's supposed works, internal inconsistencies, and signs of major redactions being accomplished. Even though Keener has considered these alternate theories, he supports the traditional position.

Moreover, the federal pattern jury instruction on the credibility of witnesses in regard to corroborative evidence is also evident in the aforementioned information supporting Johannine authorship. Because of the corroborative nature of the evidence, the weight of the evidence is strong that John, the "Beloved Disciple," is the author of the fourth Gospel and that he was an eyewitness to many of the resurrection events. One further proviso should be noted about the research in this section. This evidential analysis is not exhaustive and was not completed to demonstrate the vast number of opinions and theories regarding the authorship of the four Gospels. Rather, it was completed to demonstrate that there is good evidence based upon accepted principles of evidence to support that the authors and the sources of the four evangelists can be known, *contra* Carrier's position.

2.9 Summary

In conducting an evidentiary analysis of Carrier's first contention of "contradictory resurrection narratives," an exposition of Carrier's first objection to the resurrection narratives was completed and a cross-examination of his contention by the literature of Christian scholars ensued. In this cross-examination of Carrier's view by scholarly Christian literature, it was observed that differences among the evangelists are to be expected due to the independence of the sources and the personal perspective of each evangelist. Moreover, when the selected accounts were examined closely, it was shown that these accounts were not contradictory. Rather, they were supplementary. After these analyses were completed, a foundation was given for the history and development of the Anglo-American evidentiary perspective with its culmination in the *FRE*. Moreover, a similar and brief historical analysis was also completed regarding the FPJI and their relevance in explicating accepted principles of evidence.

After a cross-examination of Carrier's contention of "contradictory resurrection narratives" was conducted, positive evidence was given regarding the similarity of several aspects of the four resurrection accounts against Carrier's "contradictory resurrection narratives" contention. Moreover, Carrier's alternate contention of "embellished narratives" was also analyzed. In this analysis of his alternate contention, it was shown that this argument actually detracts from his "contradictory narratives" contention. Upon conducting an evidentiary analysis of Carrier's contention with accepted principles of evidence, it was found that his contention was not supported by the previously exposed *FRE* and FPJI. In contrast, an evidentiary analysis was completed on rebuttal evidence against Carrier's contention, to include the types of evidence from and the identities of the four evangelists. Moreover, an evidentiary analysis was also conducted on the testimony of the Apostle John. This examination revealed compliance with many of the aforementioned principles of evidence.

A final evidentiary examination was completed to determine whether Carrier's claim that "the Gospel authors and their sources are unknown" was founded upon accepted principles of evidence. This examination demonstrated that there is evidence that the evangelists and their sources were, in fact, known. Furthermore, this evidence, in addition to the rebuttal evidence, was analyzed and was found to be supported by accepted principles of evidence from the Anglo-American common law tradition as codified in the *FRE* and observed in the FPJI.

CHAPTER THREE

Objection Two: The Gospel Accounts of the Resurrection of Jesus Were Influenced by Pagan Myths

3.1 Introduction

Carrier writes extensively on the topic of the presumed influence of pagan myths on Christianity. According to his view, there are many pagan gods that preceded Christianity who have also arisen from the dead and because of the many similarities between them and Christianity, it is reasonable to conclude that Christianity developed the concept of a resurrected Jesus Christ from these antedated myths. Carrier has a long list of gods that he believes fits these criteria.[65] As this list is long, the focus of chapter three will be limited to Carrier's writings in relation to Osiris, Inanna/Ishtar, Romulus, and Zalmoxis. These four pagan gods have been chosen to analyze out of the many offered by Carrier because he makes frequent mention of them in his writings as prime examples of gods to whom Christianity is beholden. In similarity to chapter two, an analysis of Carrier's writings will be conducted in order to ascertain the facts he is relying upon. Also, brief summaries of these gods and the various beliefs or doctrines held by adherents of the gods will also be exposited and offered in order to ascertain whether Carrier accurately deals with the various mythical traditions.

After this analysis, a cross-examination will be conducted of the evidence that Carrier offers to support his assertions. This examination will be conducted in the light of writings from Christian and secular scholars alike. Moreover, Carrier's contentions regarding the influence of pagan religions upon Christianity will be analyzed by comparing them to the appropriate New Testament scriptures. A key question to investigate is whether there are any New Testament passages that indicate an influence from pagan myths or idols. In addition to comparing the selected

---

[65] Carrier has a long list of gods who fit the above description to include Zalmoxis, Osiris, Romulus, Inanna, Attis, Adonis, Orpheus, Dionysius, etc. (Carrier:2009; Carrier:2014b).

pagan myths with the New Testament, inquiries will be conducted to determine not only if there is any proof of pagan syncretism within Old Testament scriptures, but also if there is any accommodation of Old Testament Judaism to pagan religions at all? If Carrier can demonstrate that there is a legitimate link between the two, then he would have some evidence for his views in this regard.

In addition to the aforementioned analyses, another literature analysis will be employed to determine if Carrier utilizes principles coming from the aforementioned *FRE* or *FPJI* (2.5 and 2.6). Important areas of evidentiary inquiry include:

- Does Carrier present evidence founded upon accepted principles of evidence that there was a mingling or syncretism of pagan mythical beliefs with Judaism or early Christianity?
- Are there sources that Carrier utilizes to demonstrate the handoff of pagan mythical traditions to early Jews or Christians?
- Does Carrier provide any direct or indirect historical evidence to support his claims?
- Does Carrier provide any hearsay evidence to undergird his suppositions?
- Is Carrier's evidence corroborated by other sources that confirm a particular event where this syncretism occurred?

If Carrier's evidence is able to meet the above criteria, then he would have met the standards of accepted principles of evidence that are displayed through the *FRE* and *FPJI*. However, if he does not offer any of the aforementioned evidence, then his writings are not well supported by the aforementioned accepted principles of evidence.

Along with the aforementioned cross-examination of Carrier's contention, New Testament Scriptures and scholarly literature will also be offered that include positive evidence that the New Testament is framed by Judaism and not pagan mystery cults. Specifically, the writings of Paul will also be reviewed to see if he writes from the perspective of one affected by paganism or from a devout Jew turned Christian. The Pauline corpus will also be scanned regarding his writings on the resurrection to determine whether Paul's reference point is from pagan roots or whether he writes about the resurrection from a Jewish perspective. Moreover, the other Gospels and the other writers of the New Testament will be examined as well regarding the presence of evidence confirming or disconfirming pagan mythical influence.

3.2 Carrier's claim: Christian resurrection influenced by mystery/pagan cults

3.2.1 Similarities between the resurrection of Jesus Christ and mystery religions: In general

In his book, *Not the Impossible Faith: Why Christianity Didn't Need a Miracle to Succeed*, Carrier (2009) portrays the milieu in the era around the advent of Christ as being rife with stories of gods who arose from the dead. In the aforementioned book, Carrier is responding to the thesis of J.P. Holding regarding Holding's view that Christianity's origin and growth were so improbable during the era of the Roman Empire, that the resurrection of Jesus Christ must have been a true story. In refuting Holding, Carrier offers that the resurrection of Jesus Christ would not be improbable because there were many pagan gods preceding Christianity as well as during the era of the early Christian church who themselves had risen from the dead in similarity to Jesus Christ. In supporting this view, he observes in this same era that the theme of resurrected gods abounded in the mystery religions of the day. Regarding this belief Carrier (2009: ch. 3) writes, "Yet they could not stem the tide of elites and commoners who embraced all these diverse foreign religions all over the Roman Empire. As far as foreign cults go, Christianity had stepped into a seller's market."

Adding to the above information that resurrection of gods from the dead was a notion common in the religious milieu before and during the early Christian era, Carrier (2009:ch.3) offers many other mythical pagan figures as proof of this. Among the many examples he offers of pagan gods who rise from the dead are the gods Asclepius, Dionysius, the Roman legendary founder turned god, Romulus, the Egyptian god Osiris, Adonis, the Thracian god Zalmoxis, and Inanna/Ishtar. Moreover, on this topic of similarity between pagan systems of resurrection generally, Carrier writes, "Any differences there may have been between the many and varied pagan ideas of resurrection and what the Christians taught (which itself varied according to sect) were all minor points of metaphysical detail, not fundamental barriers to the idea of Jesus returning bodily from the dead. In further support of his belief in the ubiquity of dying and rising gods, Carrier shares, "The Zoroastrians believed this explicitly, and many of the Greeks and Romans did, too, in their conception of the divine body of gods and immortal heroes — and what the Christians were selling was essentially the very same thing." Carrier (2009:ch. 1) also provides data showing the commonality between some pagan gods and Jesus Christ:

> Both Osiris and Romulus were dismembered. So was Orpheus, and Bacchus before his own resurrection and ascension to heaven. And though Jesus is not dismembered, his clothes were (e.g. Mark 15: 24), and clothing was a common metaphor for the body in Jewish thought.

In this quotation, Carrier offers more examples of mythical gods (some who have already been mentioned by Carrier) who parallel Jesus Christ. In similarity to Jesus Christ they were dismembered physically even as Jesus clothes were "dismembered." Carrier submits that the "dismembering" of Jesus' clothes affirms that Jesus was physically dismembered before he was raised from the dead in similarity to the above-mentioned gods. Does Carrier's metaphorical comparison comport with accepted principles of evidence?

In responding to Bart Ehrman's challenge to his mythicist views of Jesus Christ, and supporting his views by comparing the resurrection of Jesus Christ to earlier pagan myths, Carrier (2013:ch. 2) explains:

> Even if the later Christian idea [referring to the resurrection of Jesus Christ] did not come from these pagan 'same-body' resurrection myths, a pagan body-exchange resurrection (returning to earth after their deaths in an immortal glorious resurrection body, as Romulus does, for example) combined with a Jewish resurrection of the flesh still gets you the version of dying-and-rising god that we meet with, for example, in the Gospel of John. But that's still just a variant of the same mytheme: a god who dies and is then celebrated as having risen again, in a more glorious body than he once had... So is it likewise for other gods, from Inanna and Zalmoxis to Hercules and Romulus, and many others besides.

In reference to the Christian rite of water baptism and its relationship to pre-existing pagan myths, Carrier (2013:ch. 2) also observes that pre-existing pagan cults utilized baptism as an initiatory rite and that this rite symbolically brought the devotee to identify with the death and resurrection of their god. Carrier asserts this perspective in response to Bart Ehrman (2012:28) who questioned the validity of Carrier's assertions between the pre-existence of water baptism in pagan cults before its establishment as a Christian rite. Ehrman offered his critique of Carrier's views because he disagrees with Carrier's assessment that Jesus Christ was a mythical figure and Carrier's attempt to utilize pagan baptism ceremonies as evidence for this view. In this regard, Carrier writes (2013:ch. 2):

Apuleius gives us a first person account of baptism in Isis cult, which he describes as a symbolic death and resurrection for the recipient, exactly as Paul describes Christian baptism in the New Testament (e.g., Romans 6: 4), a fact that surely undermines Ehrman's entire argument and makes the Mythicist case look significantly stronger.

Of merit to an investigation of whether the resurrection of Jesus Christ was developed from pagan myths would be to know whether Carrier's analysis of pagan myths is substantiated. Therefore, it will be probative to conduct an analysis of Carrier's views by examining the writings of other scholars who have conducted research in this area. Moreover, Carrier must answer certain evidentiary concerns regarding the information that he relies upon: Does Carrier utilize a historical source that can demonstrate the mixing of these diverse religions in influencing the resurrection of Jesus Christ? Does Carrier utilize data that is in accord with accepted principled of evidence? Is there a historical source that can demonstrate that a pagan god and its adherents utilized water baptism in similarity to Christianity? Answers to these key questions are needed in order to determine if what he puts forth can be confirmed by accepted principles of evidence. In order to ascertain whether Carrier has met these evidentiary standards, his writings on the supposed resurrections Osiris, Inanna, Romulus, and Zalmoxis will be further investigated to determine if there are any correlations with the resurrection of Jesus Christ.

3.2.2 Correlations between the resurrection of Jesus Christ and the myth of Osiris

In surveying Carrier's (2009:ch. 1) writings on the cult of Osiris, he points out that there are differences as well as similarities between the myth of Osiris and the resurrection of Jesus Christ. Even though he doesn't specifically mention these differences, he states that there are many similarities between the Osirian cult and the Christian faith which he believes support his perspective of a linkage between the two. On the existence of differences and similarities between the two belief systems, Carrier writes:

> Osiris was likewise murdered, dismembered, buried, then ascended to heaven to become "the Supreme Father of the Gods." Like the Inanna myth, the Osiris myth also contained curious yet inconclusive parallels with the Christ story. Although it's otherwise a very different tale, there are still a few similarities that might be too unusual to be coincidental:

both were "sealed" in their tomb or casket; both were killed by seventy-two conspirators; both rose on the third day after their death; and both resurrections took place during a full moon.

In this excerpt, Carrier only includes several instances of alleged similarity between the Osirian cult and the New Testament. Two of these pertain to general parallels between the passion of Jesus Christ and one parallel related to the resurrection of Jesus Christ. In that he offers several instances of general similarity between the two, he is using these general similarities to buttress his perspective on the resurrection of Jesus Christ. Specifically regarding the "seventy-two conspirators," Carrier (2009, ch. 1fn.) further adds more detail to this perceived correlation. He offers that there were seventy-one men who voted as members of the Sanhedrin to crucify Jesus and the other person who can be considered as a co-conspirator who killed Jesus was Judas.

In addition to more detail on the conspirators, Carrier also gives additional information related to the comparisons between the resurrections of Osiris and Jesus Christ.[66]:

> It is absurd to insist there is no parallel in concept here to what would later be claimed for Jesus. Jesus is clearly very much like Osiris: both die and both get raised in improved bodies and both end up living as lords in heaven (not on earth) (Carrier, 2014b:249)
>
> It is even further in support of this conclusion that pagan theology had a similar concept- the savior god Osiris was also called the Logos and the one through whom all was created and governed-thus demonstrating the notion was ubiquitous (and might even have been a common element of mystery religion) (Carrier, 2014b:280)
>
> But those Egyptians (not representing all Egyptians) will have believed Osiris rose from the dead by assuming a new body, and ascending to heaven therein, leaving the old one in its grave. And the first Christians probably believed the very same thing of Jesus, the empty tomb story evolving more than a generation later (Carrier, 2013:ch. 2).

---

[66] In regard to further detail on the similarities between the resurrections of Osiris and Jesus Christ (with both the resurrections of Osiris and Jesus occurring on the third day and during a full moon), Carrier offers, "Compare 1 Corinthians 15: 4, and in every story Jesus always dies on a Friday and rises on a Sunday (which is the third day, since in antiquity days were counted inclusively). Full moon: Plutarch, On Isis and Osiris 42.367e-f; all stories have Jesus dying on or within a day of the Passover, which always occurs during a full moon. See my discussion of these details in my online FAQ for The Empty Tomb (http://www.richardcarrier.info/SpiritualFAQ.html#osiris-parallel)." (Carrier,2009:ch. 1fn.)

Objection Two: The Gospel Accounts of the Resurrection of Jesus ...

In these quotations from Carrier, he continues noting similarities in various parts of the Osirian myth and the narratives of Jesus Christ. In the first excerpt, Carrier observes comparisons between the two in that both of them die physical deaths, are raised in physical bodies, and end up as gods who are exalted in the heavenly realm. In the second passage he draws comparisons to the notion that Osiris and Jesus Christ were "the Logos" and the ones who created all that exists in the universe. In the third quotation, Carrier is responding to objections from Bart Ehrman (2012:26) who disagrees with Carrier's mythicist perspective regarding Jesus Christ. In this excerpt, Carrier refers to similarities in both the death and resurrection of Osiris and Jesus Christ. He focuses on the corporality of the births of Osiris and Jesus Christ and continuing on to when they make the transition from death to life.

Regarding more detailed information on the similarity of the resurrection accounts of Osiris and Jesus Christ, Carrier (2014b:249) offers:

> As surveyed for element 14, Plutarch is explicit about the cosmic version of the Osiris myth: he says Osiris *actually* incarnates and actually dies (albeit in outerspace; but he dies, too, as Plutarch admits, also in the myth that places his death on earth at a single time in history) and is *actually* restored to life in a new supernatural body (just as Jesus was, as Paul thoroughly explains in 1 Cor. 15). Plutarch has this event repeated only annually (as was likely the case for Ishtar and Tammuz), but that's not a relevant difference, since syncretism with Jewish apocalypticism fully explains the replacement of a cyclical with a one-time resurrection (in fact the peculiarly Jewish logic of that modification is fully explained in Hebrews 9; see element 43, and Chapter 11).

In this quotation, Carrier draws from Plutarch in order to establish the details for the resurrection of Osiris. Carrier also points out metaphysical aspects of the existence of Osiris (according to Plutarch) in that Osiris takes bodily form, dies, is finally restored to life in a new supernatural body, and then comments how this was in similarity to the account of Jesus when he was restored to life. Moreover, Carrier offers that Osiris not only died in outer space, but also that he died in space and time on the earth. In addition to these metaphysical details, he offers Plutarch's perspective on the cyclical nature of the resurrection of Osiris that he states is in accord with the notion of resurrection according to Jewish apocalypticism and with the resurrection of Jesus. He justifies this particular comparison of the resurrection of Osiris with Christianity by offering that Jewish apocalypticism modified the Christian version of resurrection from a cyclical occurrence to a one-time event. Carrier justifies this stance by relying upon the epistle to the *Hebrews*.

In addition to these general comparisons as well as specific comparisons, another parallel between them that Carrier (2009: ch. 2) sees is that there are "theological" similarities between Osiris and Jesus Christ. Regarding this similarity between Osiris and Jesus Christ, Carrier posits:

> We know Egyptian afterlife-belief made the physical weight of sin a factor in deciding one's placement in the afterlife (one's soul was weighed against a feather by Ma'at, and too many sins made it weigh more, thus signaling your doom), and that baptism into the death and resurrection of Osiris washes away those sins (as we just saw) and thus lightens the soul to obtain the best place in heaven. It is hard to imagine how this does not entail that the death and resurrection of Osiris somehow procured salvation through remission of sins.

In this passage, Carrier alleges the Osirian mythology conveyed salvation to its adherents. He describes the weighing of deeds as the criteria for determining who received eternal life. In this description, Carrier not only uses the term "afterlife" but also mentions "heaven" as a synonym for the afterlife. Carrier further elucidates that as a result of baptism into Osiris, one obtains salvation through the remission of sins. It will be beneficial to examine this claim by Carrier in light of the scholarly literature on Osiris in order to ascertain how a devotee of Osiris obtained entrance into the netherworld.

In furtherance of the aforementioned line of reasoning, Carrier (2009:ch. 2) continues:

> One could perhaps get nitpicky as to what might be the exact theology of the process, but whatever the differences, the similarity remains: the death and resurrection of Osiris was clearly believed to make it possible for those ritually sharing in that death and resurrection through baptism to have their sins remitted. That belief predates Christianity.

In the above quotation, Carrier claims a thematic link of the mythical resurrection of Osiris with the resurrection of Jesus Christ by ostensibly showing that the ritual of baptism for both deities leads to the salvation of their respective devotees. Furthermore, he is sure to point out that the Osirian resurrection precedes the resurrection of Jesus Christ. Relevant questions that Carrier needs to contend with are: Does the Osirian literature from ancient Egypt as well as from Plutarch demonstrate that Osirian soteriology consisted of the forgiveness of sins by being baptized into the death and resurrection of Osiris? Can a mythical account of a pagan deity dying and rising again be fairly compared to the Christian concept of Jesus taking flesh in a human body in real space and time? Is the evidence coming from the Bible that Jesus existed in space and time as "God incarnate" germane to this discussion?

Further attempting to establish that the Osirian myth influenced Christianity, Carrier (2013: ch. 2) offers:

> Plenty of pre-Christian evidence already establishes that belief in the resurrection of Osiris long preceded that of Jesus anyway... For example, consider these descriptions of the resurrection of Osiris in the Pyramid Texts: "I have come to thee...that I may revivify thee, that I may assemble for thee thy bones, that I may collect for thee thy flesh, that I may assemble for thee thy dismembered limbs, for I am as Horus his avenger, I have smitten for thee him who smote thee... raise thyself up, king, Osiris; thou livest!" (1684a– 1685a and 1700 = Utterance 606; cf. also 670) "Raise thyself up; shake off thy dust; remove the dirt which is on thy face; loose thy bandages" (1363a–b = Utterance 553) "Osiris, collect thy bones; arrange thy limbs; shake off thy dust; untie thy bandages; the tomb is open for thee; the double doors of the coffin are undone for thee; the double doors of heaven are open for thee... thy soul is in thy body... raise thyself up!" (207b– 209a and 2010b– 2011a = Utterance 676).

Carrier shares a passage from the pyramid texts that shows how Horus, the son of Isis and Osiris, is involved with the resurrection of Osiris after he avenged his father's death by his uncle Seth. He also gives an exhortation for Osiris to raise himself up from the dead. However, Carrier must answer certain evidentiary concerns regarding the information that he relies upon: Is the involvement of Horus with the resurrection of Osiris paralleled in the New Testament regarding the circumstances surrounding the resurrection of Jesus Christ? Are there other ancient texts that give a different accounting of the resurrection of Osiris? Would the resurrection of Osiris back to life entail his "revivification" here on earth or was there a new metaphysical formulation for the newly revivified body?

3.2.3 Correlations between the resurrection of Jesus Christ and the myth of Inanna

In addition to Osiris, Carrier (2013:ch. 2) also draws parallels to the myth of Inanna from ancient Sumerian culture. Related specifically to the resurrection of Inanna, Carrier offers, "Likewise for Inanna: a clear-cut, death-and-resurrection tale for her exists on clay tablets inscribed a thousand years before Christianity (in which she dies and rises in hell, but departs from and returns to the world above all the same)." In this short quotation, Carrier avers that there is evidence that exists for Inanna's resurrection from the dead from antiquity. Moreover, he describes Inanna's resurrection as rising from the dead but then she rises to life in the realm of the dead. However, she is able to re-enter the realm of the living. Are there metaphysical differences with the resurrection of Inanna compared to that of Jesus Christ? An exposition of the accounts of Inanna would be helpful in this aspect of the investigation.

Carrier also discusses a similarity in the time span between the death and resurrection of Inanna and Jesus. Carrier (2009: Ch. 1) writes:

> Jesus also supposedly said he would be "three days and three nights" in the grave (Matthew 12: 40), while Inanna herself was dead for three days and three nights. Of course, we are told Jesus was not actually dead for three nights, only at most two, but it remains curious why there would be a tradition of his saying otherwise, a tradition matching that of Inanna".

In this description of the time span between the two, Carrier's aforementioned description of the circumstances reveal that Jesus would be in the grave for three days and three nights. Even though he describes that there was a difference in the number of nights between the account of Inanna and Jesus, a relevant avenue of investigation would be to study whether Inanna was placed in a grave or if some other arrangement was made for her after her death.

In addition to the similarities that Carrier (2009:ch.1) recognizes in the above referenced time spans, he also submits that there are similarities in their deaths, resurrections, and commemorative meals:

> After she is stripped naked and judgment is pronounced against her, Inanna is 'turned into a corpse' and 'the corpse was hung from a nail' and 'after three days and three nights' her assistants ask for her corpse and resurrect her, and 'Inanna arose' according to her plan, because she knew her father 'will surely bring me back to life', exactly as transpires. Indeed, there is a third parallel: Inanna's resurrection is secured by a ritual involving the divine 'food of life' and the divine 'water of life' The Eucharist is only a few steps away. If all those elements are removed from Christianity, it's hard to think what could possibly remain that makes Jesus' historicity at all likely.

In his exposition of the parallels between Jesus Christ and Inanna, Carrier describes Inanna after her demise and what was done to display the body. Probative questions would be to determine how Inanna was killed and

Objection Two: The Gospel Accounts of the Resurrection of Jesus ...

any metaphysical comparisons with Jesus. In addition to this matter, another pertinent matter of inquiry would be to determine what happened to both bodies after they died. Carrier also mentions the resurrection of Inanna that was procured by her assistants. Delving deeper in this circumstance would also be probative to determine if there were similarities in how the resurrection was effected.

Going from the specific similarities between Inanna and Jesus Christ to general comparisons between the two, Carrier (2009:ch. 1) writes:

> Insufficient evidence survives to ascertain whether this is the route from which Christianity *itself* derived, but with this text the evidence is undeniable that Christianity had merged its own myth with this pre-Christian dying and rising god concept very early and very thoroughly (Carrier, 2014:74)...Like the Inanna myth, the Osiris myth also contained curious yet inconclusive parallels with the Christ story.

In the aforementioned quotation, Carrier states that even if Christianity did not come directly from the Inanna myth, it is certain that Christianity became thoroughly enmeshed with that of the "dying and rising gods" that included the cult of Inanna. Even though Carrier gives this opinion of the relation between the two belief systems, he then offers a mixed review showing that there are similarities and differences. However, as mentioned above, Carrier offers many supposed correlations between Inanna and Jesus Christ.

Regarding another general comparison Carrier (2014:247) writes:

> The dying-and-rising son (sometimes daughter) of god 'mytheme' originated in the ancient Near East over a thousand years before Christianity...The earliest documented examples are the cult of Inanna and Dumuzi (also known as Ishtar and Tammuz)....

Carrier posits that the Inanna cult is the earliest version of the dying and rising gods paradigm coming forward from antiquity. He makes the point that the founding of the Inanna cult far precedes the advent of Christianity in actually being the first in the chain of dying and rising gods. In similarity with the Osiris cult, an inquiry into whether it is proper methodology to compare a mythical god to a historical person who has existed in space and time would be probative.

3.2.4 Parallels between the resurrection of Jesus Christ and the myth of Romulus

Not only does Carrier (2014:302) observe parallels between Osiris, Inanna, and Jesus Christ, but he also observes many parallels with the resurrection account of Jesus Christ and the Romulan legend of ancient Rome. In his exposition of these parallels, Carrier writes:

> The Christian conception of Jesus' death and resurrection appears to have been significantly influenced by the Roman conception of Romulus's death and resurrection. Even if we discounted that for any reason, the Romulus parallels definitely establish that all these components were already part of a recognized hero-type, and are therefore not surprising or unusual or unexpected. The story of Jesus would have looked familiar, not only in the same way all translation stories looked familiar even when different in many and profound ways, but also in the very specific way that among such tales it looked the most like the story of Romulus, which was publicly acted out in passion plays every year. And this was the national founding hero of the Roman Empire. What better god's tale to emulate or co-opt?

Carrier makes two claims above. He states that the story of Jesus Christ has definitely been influenced by the Romulan legend. But he also offers another possibility that if this is not the case, then it establishes his general thesis that the account of Jesus Christ in the New Testament has developed from earlier "dying and rising gods." He also offers the Romulan legend as being the most similar to that of Jesus Christ and evinces that the yearly plays in honor of Jesus Christ also are similar to the many festivals given in honor of Romulus.

In continuing to establish his thesis, Carrier looks specifically at the Gospel of Mark to include its resurrection account to underscore his point about the relationship between Romulus and Jesus Christ:

> It certainly seems as if Mark is fashioning Jesus into the new Romulus, with a new, superior message, establishing a new superior kingdom. This Romulan tale looks a lot like a skeletal model for the passion narrative; a great man, founder of a great kingdom, despite coming from lowly origins and of suspect parentage, is actually an incarnated son of god, but dies as a result of a conspiracy of the ruling council, then a darkness covers the land at his death and his body vanishes, at which those who followed him flee in fear (just like the Gospel women, Mk 16:8; and men, Mk 14.50-52), and like them too, we look for his body but are told he is not here, he has risen; and some doubt, but then the risen god 'appears' to select followers to deliver his gospel (Carrier, 2014b: ch. 4).

But we needn't rely on Plutarch, because for Romulus and Zalmoxis we undeniably have pre-Christian evidence that they actually die (on earth) and are actually raised from the dead (on earth) and physically visit their disciples (on earth) (Carrier, 2013:Ch. 2).

In these passages, Carrier sees many similarities between the mythical/legendary Romulus with the Jesus Christ of Mark's Gospel. In addition to these similarities that he observes, Carrier, responding to the criticism of Bart Ehrman regarding Carrier's linkage of mythical "dying and rising gods" with Jesus, discusses that there is pre-Christian evidence to support the similarities. Carrier's objective in this linkage of these "dying and rising gods" is to support his thesis that Jesus Christ is not a historical person but rather a mythical person.[67] Carrier further describes other details of the Romulan legend that he believes support the linkage of "dying and rising gods" to Jesus Christ:

As it happens, the founding myth of Rome, then famously known everywhere and celebrated in annual passion plays, is almost the exact same story: a man named Proculus (archaic Latin for 'Proclaimer' or 'He Who Proculus', thus not only again a fictional name designed for the story but essentially the same name as Cleopas) journeys by road from nearby Alba Longa to Rome, after the Roman people learn the corpse of Romulus has vanished; and on the way, the resurrected Romulus appears to him (*not* in disguise but this time in glorious form) and explains the secrets of the kingdom (literally: how to conquer and rule the world), then ascends into heaven (as Luke eventually has Jesus do as well), and Proculus recognizes who he was and goes on to proclaim what he was told (Carrier, 2014b:681).

In Plutarch's biography of Romulus, the founder of Rome, we are told he was the son of god, born of a virgin; an attempt is made to kill him as a baby, and he is saved, and raised by a poor family, becoming a lowly shepherd; then as a man he becomes beloved by the people, hailed as king, and killed by the conniving elite; then he rises from the dead, appears to a friend to tell the good news to his people, and ascends to heaven to rule from on high. Just like Jesus (Carrier, 2014b:91).

Another God who submitted to being murdered in order to triumph was the well-revered Roman national deity Romulus, whose death and resurrection was celebrated in annual public ceremonies in Rome since before Christian times (Carrier, 2009:ch. 1).

---

[67] On this point, Carrier (2014b:899) gives his assessment that Jesus Christ is a mythical character and that his study of earlier religious mythical gods provides evidence for this when he writes, "We need to consider all the evidence now from a new perspective. We need to see it in light of what the present study has shown to be the most likely account of the origin and early development of the Christian religion, which now fits the theory of minimal mythicism..."

In the above quotations, Carrier gives a general description regarding the life of the legendary Romulus and then makes a comparison with Jesus Christ. At this juncture, there are germane inquiries to make regarding Carrier's data that he offers: Are there any differences coming from various accounts of the Romulan legend that would differ from Carrier's rendition of it? Is the general synopsis given by Carrier the only version of the Romulan legend or are there other versions? Are there other aspects of the Romulan legend that do not comport with what Carrier has offered?

In the following quotation, Carrier (2009:ch. 1) gives more of these parallels between Romulus and Jesus Christ:

> Though again a very different story, the Romulan tale shared with Christ's at least the following elements: both were incarnated gods (Romulus descended from heaven to become human and die); both became incarnate in order to establish a kingdom on earth (for Romulus, the Roman Empire; for Christ, the Kingdom of God, i.e. the Church); there was a supernatural darkness at both their deaths (as in Mark 15: 33, etc.); both were killed by a conspiracy of the ruling powers (Christ, by the Jewish and Roman authorities; Romulus, by the first Roman senate); both corpses vanished when sought for (in the earliest and canonical Gospels Christ's tomb is found empty — no one sees him rise); both appear after their resurrection to a close follower on an important road (Proculus on the road to Alba Longa; Cleopas on the road to Emmaus)...

Carrier describes here specific elements of similarity even though he states that they are different stories. Upon reviewing more of Carrier's claims regarding the parallels between Romulus and Jesus Christ, more evidentiary analysis is needed: What are the differences that Carrier notices? Are these comparisons all factually correct? Are these correlations along with the differences enough to provide an inference that the Romulan legend influenced Christianity?

Carrier (2014:683) again observes differences between the two stories (Jesus Christ and Romulus) and now even uses these alleged differences to support his thesis. Noting differences on these occasions is in juxtaposition to his main strategy of observing supposed similarities between mythical gods and Jesus Christ:

> But the changes are the point. While Proculus receives his gospel on the road to Rome, the new story suggests all roads lead *from* Jerusalem: so while the old story suggests 'all roads lead to Rome', the new story suggests all roads lead *from* Jerusalem. While Romulus appears in awesome glory,

Objection Two: The Gospel Accounts of the Resurrection of Jesus ... 129

> befitting the awesome glory of Rome's dominion and the very visible empire he promises, Jesus appears in disguise, hidden, just as the kingdom he promises is hidden, and which, like Jesus, becomes visible (and thus knowable) only in the communion of believers. Luke has thus transvalued the Romans' founding myth: Unlike the Romans, *their* resurrected hero promises a *hidden* spiritual kingdom originating from Jerusalem on high.

In this quotation from Carrier, he emphasizes the dissimilarities between the Romulan legend and the Lucan account of Jesus Christ. Included in these differences is the awesome appearance of Romulus compared to the normal appearance of Jesus after he appeared to others after his resurrection. Another contrast Carrier observes is the centrality of Rome to the affairs of the entire world in the Romulan legend while Jesus Christ emphasizes that his new kingdom starts from Jerusalem and spreads out to the entire earth. A relevant matter to investigate is whether the aforementioned Lucan resurrection narrative provides actual useable evidence for Carrier's thesis of pre-existing "dying and rising gods."

Continuing on his theme of changes in the accounts of the resurrection as being necessary modifications that the disciples made, Carrier (2005a:ch. 5) offers another change that the Gospel authors made to the Romulan legend:

> I think I have made an adequate case that Luke and John (and possibly Matthew), want to establish Jesus as risen in the flesh, which entails eliminating the expected "glorious" enhancements to a divine appearance that we see in other epiphanies. Jesus looks normal because he has to. Anything else would undermine their belief in the nature of his risen body. But some signature of divinity had to be retained, so the Gospel authors resorted to the only standard motif left.

Above, Carrier provides a motive for the Synoptic evangelists to change an aspect of one Romulan characteristic, his epiphany. This is necessary in order for the Gospel authors to demonstrate that Jesus resurrected body was a normal human body in order to suit their needs. In response to his claim that the authors borrowed from the Romulan legend, does Carrier offer any evidence that this was in fact the case? Is he making his conclusion on his analysis of the text or does he have sources that verify the Gospel authors made these adjustments to the Romulan legend?

In the following quotation, Carrier (2014b:895) makes a conclusion about Jesus Christ from what he gleans from the evidence:

> And were he not the figure of a major world religion-if we were studying the Attis or Zalmoxis or Romulus cult instead-we would have treated Jesus that way from the start, knowing full well we need more than normal evidence to take him back out of the class of mythical persons and back into that of historical ones. Jesus can no longer be treated as just any person claimed to have existed. He's not. From the Epistles alone, but even more from the Gospels, we can tell that Jesus was, from the earliest recorded point in Christian history, a rapidly mythicized cosmic savior lord. That remains a fact even if he was a historical man. Yet that fact takes him out of the category of ordinary men, Jesus is simply not just like Pontius Pilate...There is so much more evidence for Jesus than for Pontius Pilate.

Here, Carrier opines that Jesus Christ is a mythical god and that more than normal evidence would be needed to transition him back to the status of a historical person. He then offers that the evidence for Jesus shows that he is more than just a regular person. Furthermore, he states that Jesus is much more than a regular historical person such as Pontius Pilate. The inference here is that Jesus is a mythical character with the possibility that even if he did exist the evidence shows that he was not a just a normal person, but a legend. Furthermore, in this quotation, Carrier states that more than normal evidence is needed to prove that Jesus was a historical person. What does Carrier mean when he states that "more than normal evidence" is needed to take him from being a mythical character to a historical person? Does the comparison that Carrier draws with Pontius Pilate aid him in proving his thesis that Jesus is not a historical person?

Carrier (2005a: ch. 5) goes into more detail about the Romulan legend concentrating on the end of his life on earth as well as his apotheosis:

> In Plutarch's biography of Romulus, the Founder of Rome, we are told about annual public ceremonies that were still being performed, which celebrated the day Romulus ascended to heaven. The sacred story told at this event went basically as follows: at the end of his life, amidst rumors he was murdered by a conspiracy of the Senate (and dismembered, just like the resurrected deities Osiris and Bacchus), a darkness covered the earth, thunder and wind struck, and Romulus vanished, leaving no part of his body or clothes behind; the people wanted to search for him but the Senate told them not to, "for he had been taken up to the gods"; most people then went away happy, hoping for good things from their new god, but "some doubted"; later, Proculus, a close friend of Romulus, reported that he met him "on the road," and asked him, "Why have you abandoned us?" to which Romulus replied that he had been a god all along, but had come down to earth to establish a great kingdom and now had to return to his

home in heaven; then Romulus told his friend to tell the Romans that if they are virtuous they will achieve a great empire.

Again Carrier briefly discusses the murder of Romulus as well as other circumstances that are similar to that of Jesus Christ and events around the end of his life. Are there other accounts of the demise of Romulus that differ from what Carrier shared? If so, would that lessen the impact of Carrier's thesis? Would the difference in the kingdom that Romulus had established and the one that Jesus Christ established be different? Would the nature of the Roman Empire that Romulus founded be in similarity to the kingdom that Jesus Christ established? Carrier further observes a borrowing from Romulus by Luke in his account of the encounter of two disciples on the road to Emmaus when he writes, "And Luke appears to have fabricated his Emmaus narrative (in Luke 24:13-34) to emulate the epiphany of Romulus, the mythical founder of Rome who — just like Jesus — was the Son of God incarnate, was born of a virgin..." and included other qualities the two shared that have already been mentioned above (Carrier, 2010:304). Carrier's direct claims about Luke's account of the Emmaus narrative confirm that he believes that there is borrowing from Romulus by Luke with his use of the road to Emmaus story.

In order to meet the objectives of this research project, the details of the Romulan legend will be studied in order to determine if Carrier's representations are in accord with the story of Romulus. Moreover, after examining the information, the representations made by Carrier as well as the information coming from the various accounts of Romulus will be analyzed to determine whether Carrier utilizes accepted principles of evidence when he reaches his conclusion about the nexus between Romulus and Jesus Christ.

3.2.5 Correlations between the resurrection of Jesus Christ and the myth of Zalmoxis

In similarity with the preceding examples of dying and rising gods, Carrier also offers the Thracian deity Zalmoxis as a mythical god who has parallels with Jesus Christ and who also preceded Jesus Christ in time. Carrier's source material is mainly the account of Zalmoxis coming from Herodotus. But he also mentions information coming from Plato as well. To this end, Carrier states:

> The more so as we can confirm several other examples of *clearly* pre-Christian dying-and-rising gods well known across the Roman Empire: the

savior cult of the resurrected Zalmoxis (of Thracian origin) is clearly attested in Herodotus centuries before Christianity (Carrier, 2014:249)

...for in Romulus and Zalmoxis we undeniably have pre-Christian evidence that they actually die (on earth) and are actually raised from the dead (on earth) and physically visit their disciples (on earth) (Carrier, 2013:ch. 2).

Then there is Herodotus, who was always a popular author and had been for centuries. He told of a Thracian religion that began with the physical resurrection of a man called Zalmoxis, who then started a cult in which it was taught that believers went to heaven when they died (Carrier, 2006b).

In these passages, Carrier makes the observation that Zalmoxis preceded Christianity and that there is evidence that Zalmoxis (and Romulus too) arose from the dead and was the savior God for the Thracians. He further refers to Herodotus to show that the Thracians believed that Zalmoxis did offer them immortality upon death. As a result of Carrier's stated views in regard to Zalmoxis, a relevant question to ask is "If the evidence that Carrier uses to support his conclusion in this regard based upon accepted principles of evidence?" Moreover, is there a good evidential foundation for the accounts from the Greeks regarding Zalmoixs?

Carrier (2006b) continues to offer information about Zalmoxis reported by Herodotus:

The Thracian god Zalmoxis (also called Salmoxis or Gebele'izis) was buried, resurrected and deified in his own lifetime, as described in the mid-5th-century B.C. by Herodotus (4.94-96), and also mentioned in Plato's Charmides (156d-158b) in the early-4th-century B.C. According to the hostile account of Herodotus' Greek informants, Zalmoxis buried himself alive, telling his followers he would be resurrected in three years, but he merely resided in a hidden dwelling all that time. His inevitable "resurrection" led to his deification, and a religion surrounding him (which preached heavenly immortality for believers) persisted for centuries.

Carrier proclaims that as a result of his dying, being buried, and rising from the dead, Zalmoxis was deified by his followers during his lifetime. However, Carrier also adds that Zalmoxis had deceived his followers into believing this. What must be considered is if there really is a close correlation between the circumstances surrounding the supposed apotheosis of Zalmoxis and the resurrection of Jesus Christ.

In the quotation below, Carrier (2009:ch. 3) expands on the departure, time spent in paradise, and reappearance of Zalmoxis:

> Though Herodotus also can't decide if Zalmoxis was ever a real person, this is the natural doubt of a rational Greek historian, who might suspect even the Getic account to be a mere myth that they nevertheless believe to be true. And what that was is fairly obvious: they believed their one and only god Zalmoxis had visited a group of their ancestors, then died, and then appeared risen from the dead as a proof of his teaching that believers would eternally live with him in paradise. The Thracian deity Zalmoxis was also anciently believed to have died and risen from the dead, procuring salvation for all who share in his cult (including a ritual eating and drinking), as attested by Herodotus in the fifth century bce, which also suggests an early mystery cult.

This passage shared by Carrier demonstrates that Herodotus was skeptical of the account that he received about Zalmoxis. Additional information about Zalmoxis is that Herodotus was unconvinced about the historicity of Zalmoxis and Carrier points out that even with questionable information, the Getae still believed that Zalmoxis was a god. Furthermore, Carrier shares that the soteriology of the cult of Zalmoxis included partaking in a ritual meal. In the following paragraph, Carrier (2013:ch. 2) discusses the merging of different influences on the resurrection of Jesus Christ:

> Insofar as even the first Christians — or certainly later ones — believed Jesus rose from the dead in the same body that died, that would be an element of syncretism with the Jewish belief in corpse reanimation (held by many but not all Jews), or even an adaptation of other pagan views of gods that experience the same kind of resurrection — most clearly, Zalmoxis and Inanna — and probably Inanna's consort Tammuz, i.e., Adonis.

Carrier states that the resurrection of Jesus Christ is a merging of several mythical pagan traditions to include Inanna, Zalmoxis and also the Jewish belief in the re-animation of the body. Once more, Carrier's statements in this regard need further investigation. Did the Jews believe that their future Messiah would die and resurrect from the dead? In similarity to the other aforementioned pagan mythical traditions, does Carrier offer evidence based on accepted principles of evidence for his position? Shown below are more parallels between the story of Zalmoxis and Jesus Christ:

> We must be consistent: claiming the disciples stole the body is as much a proof of a resurrection-belief as claiming Zalmoxis pretended to be dead. Again, none of this entails or implies that Christians "borrowed" from Zalmoxis cult the idea of an incarnated, dying, and rising god promising

eternal life through a sacred act of drinking at a meal. But it does entail that those elements of Christianity were not new, but had been elements of other cults long before (and possibly still in their day). In other words, there were already pagans who saw nothing wrong with believing their one and only God had come to earth and visited them, died, and appeared risen from the dead. These same pagans also had no trouble believing that sharing in a sacred meal could secure for them (and their descendants) an eternal life promised by their god (Carrier, 2009:ch. 3).

Carrier mentions again that there might not be a direct borrowing from the cult of Zalmoxis by the Christian faith. However, he continues to demonstrate the similarities between the two religious perspectives zeroing in on the sacred meal that the adherents of Zalmoxis partook of in order to receive the approval of Zalmoxis. Additionally another point that Carrier emphasizes is the ubiquitous nature of pagan belief in a god who died and resurrected with the inference drawn from his remarks that the Christian notion of the death and resurrection of Jesus would not be anything out of the ordinary for those living in the milieu before, during and after the timeframe of the "supposed" life and ministry of Jesus Christ.

In the quotation below, Carrier (2006f) offers his perspective about a possible pass down of the Zalmoxis myth to Jesus Christ or one of his followers:

> It is interesting to note that the Zalmoxis story may have been heard by Jesus or a colleague and inspired the idea of a similar plan. It is even possible that this plan failed, and that Jesus died even though he expected to survive by deceit, at which his colleagues might have tried to salvage the plan by hiding the body.

Carrier offers the possibility that Jesus Christ or his followers may have conducted a plan of deceit similar to what Zalmoxis may have perpetrated in order to fool his followers into believing that he died or may have died during the execution of the fraudulent scheme. Does Carrier utilize any relevant evidence from accepted principles of evidence to buttress his assertions? As in the exposition of Carrier of other pagan/mythical gods, relevant areas of investigation regarding the correlation between Jesus and Zalmoxis are to determine whether the facts Carrier utilizes are in accord with accepted principles of evidence and whether these facts are supported by the scholarly literature about the cult of Zalmoxis.

3.3 Exposition of pagan/mythical literature

3.3.1 Exposition of the myth of Osiris

In expositing the Myth of Osiris, a literature survey will be conducted to determine the nature and details surrounding the origins of the Osirian myth to include its central characters and other important facets of this ancient, pagan religion. Information developed from the survey include his birth, death, and resurrection. Also relevant to this investigation are the details of the related gods of Egypt who interacted with Osiris. In addition to making the aforementioned inquiries into pertinent literature on the subject, it is also probative to bring out metaphysical and soteriological aspects of ancient Egyptian religious belief.

Jan Assman (2005:10-11) provides a look into the perspective of ancient Egyptians in relation to life and death. He advises that the Egyptians were well acquainted with the realm of the dead that was described as a dreary and desolate place. But they were also familiar with another realm known as "Elysium" where people who were saved from the realm of death resided. However, Assman also notes the primacy of remaining present here on earth even as portrayed in the elaborate tombs that they constructed for themselves. Assman asserts that these opulent tombs were important to assure their posterity in the future, another very important aspect of ancient Egyptian culture. On this perspective to mix both an emphasis on life and death at the same time, Assman (2005:12-13) writes:

> The Egyptians did not do life and death as we do. For them, life and death were quantifiable entities: one could be more or less alive and also more or less dead or subject to death." This also caused the Egyptians to be active in investing in their future by constructing their eternal homes before they left (their tombs).

In addition to this observed integration of death and life together, Assman (2005:17) also observes that there was not a total acceptance of death nor was there a repression of it either. An accurate portrayal would be to say that it was "integrated in the warp and woof of their daily lives." Continuing on a related theme, Assman (2005:18) offers that the mummies, coffins, and pyramids were a rejection of life going beyond death. "For the Egyptians, the 'counter images' that they constructed were an 'impetus' or a call to action against the notion of death. Even though they could not defeat death, they could, at minimum, handle death" (Assman, 2005:19).

> In the ancient Egyptian formulation of a human, J.P. Allen (2005:8) shares from the pyramid texts that the body is composed of essentially three parts, the *ka*, the *ba*, and the *akh* upon death. The role of the ancient funerary texts as well as the *Pyramid Texts* was to allow for a qualified person to be transformed into an *akh*. Allen explains that the *ka* is the life force that distinguishes a living being from a dead one.[68] In addition to the *ka*, the *ba* can be compared to the Western idea of the soul or someone's personality and is unique to each person. In relation to becoming an *akh*, that is able to exist eternally, Allen (2005:7-8) writes:
>
> Two forces played a key role in this transition, incorporated by the Egyptians in two gods, the Sun [Re] and Osiris. The Sun was the original and daily source of all life: his appearance at the creation and at every sunrise thereafter made life possible in the world...The themes of daily death and rebirth were closely associated with the Egyptian formulation of the afterlife. In similarity to the daily path of the Sun, the *ba* of every person passes through the night or death and then is reanimated with the sunrise. This daily reinvigoration was made possible by the meeting of Osiris with the Sun in the night and the result of this meeting in the netherworld corresponded with the "*ba*" of each person being merged with his or her mummified corpse. This reunion causes a person to become an *akh* or someone who is capable of "renewed life."[69]

---

[68] "Ultimately the body was the receptacle for the soul and not reverenced because of itself. The body and the statue performed basically the same function, but within different contexts: the body, preserved within its wrappings and coffin deep within the tomb; the statue in the chapel above to receive the offerings for the continuance of the *ka* which moved from the body to the statue" (Morkot, 2010:52-53).

[69] Speaking of Ra [Re] in relation to Osiris, Assman writes, "The nightly journey of the sun as a *descensus ad inferos* brought the sun god into constellations with the inhabitants of the netherworld, the transfigured dead. His light, in particular his speech, awoke them from the sleep of death and allowed them to participate in the life giving order that emanated from his course. But in this, the god himself experienced the form of existence of the transfigured dead and set an example for them by overcoming death. For in the depths of the night and the netherworld-and this was the most mysterious constellation of all-he united with Osiris, the son with the deceased father, the *ba* with the corpse, and from this union, he received the strength for a fresh life cycle (Assman, 2001:185); "An Egyptian did not die individually. Rather an Egyptian died as a part of a constellation of others who went before him. Also, the dead will live on in the lives of those who come after him " (Assman, 2005:409).

Objection Two: The Gospel Accounts of the Resurrection of Jesus ...

The importance of the sun god Re and his nightly journey that causes him to come into union with Osiris who remains in the netherworld as a catalyst for Re, is observed in these passages as being the key to the renewal for each *ba* in order to maintain *akh* status each day.[70] Allen also explains another reason for the necessity of this nightly journey of renewal. He states that this resurrection ritual was used to release the *ba* from the mummified corpse of the individual. Allen also mentions that the recitation of certain incantations or spells would assist the *ba* in navigating "potential pitfalls" in order that it could be "reunited with the gods" (Allen, 2005:8). So, the continued animation of the believer in the nether world was as a result of Osiris working in tandem with the sun every day.

Another important aspect that Assman (2001:185) brings out is that the ancient Egyptians believed their kings were an embodiment not of Horus but upon death the embodiment of Osiris:

> What spread at first, already at the end of the Old Kingdom, was the specifically royal concept of a life after death: that the king as "deceased father" became Osiris after death and assumed rule over the netherworld and that the king possessed an immortal soul-called *ba* in Egyptian- that survived of its own accord independently of his integration into the community, ascending to the sky and entering the world of the gods.

Thus, on every occasion of the death of a pharaoh, there would be a succession of the prior Osiris as the newly deceased pharaoh would take the place of the pharaoh who had preceded him in death.

Regarding the cosmology of the ancient Egyptians, Allen (2005:9) offers:

> The ancient Egyptians believed that the daily path of the Sun was a journey completed by boat and believed that the world as we know it was finite in nature and limited by land and sky. The land and sky were personified by the god Geb and the goddess Nut. In addition to being associated with the sky, the goddess Nut was also known by the Egyptians to be the mother of

---

[70] Taylor also describes the ancient Egyptian state of existence known as *akh*: "The sun god Ra and Osiris were constantly being rejuvenated on a daily basis. By close association and identification with them, the decedent could trust that he would receive endless rebirths too. *Neheh* was the term used for this cyclical eternity that could be observed in the daily movements of the sun and the various seasons experienced each year. The concept of *djet* was a linear eternity of unchanging existence. This existence was in the tomb of the deceased where they were constantly fed and provided for by the power coming from the mortuary cult and the magical texts" (Taylor,2001:31).

the Sun as well. At night the sun [Re] would travel in the Nightboat through the realm beneath the earth known as Duat.[71]

As described above, Egyptian mythology had a pantheism of sorts, as actual parts of the heavens (namely the sun) were known to be a god (e.g. Re/Ra/Atum as the sun). In addition to this basic description of the Egyptian cosmology, it was also the belief that the mummy chamber not only gave the structure that contained the mummy, but that this structure also symbolized various aspects of Egyptian religion. The structure of this chamber itself symbolized the rebirth of the decedent who is contained within his casket (the casket symbolizing being contained within the womb of the mother god, Nut). The casket and mummy is contained within the lower burial chamber, and ascends upwards through the corridors and exits the pyramid. So, in the structure of the pyramid itself in addition to the mummified corpse within the casket, a metaphysical display of the nightly ritual of resurrection is displayed (Allen, 2005:9).

E.A.W. Budge (2002:xxiii-xxv) offers additional insight into the Egyptian pantheon of Gods. Budge believes that Osiris originated in Africa and specifically, in Upper Egypt. Moreover, the author does not know the meaning of the name of Osiris, even though the name "Seat-maker" is mentioned in the pyramid texts as a suggested name. Budge offers that the Osirian cult replaced the cult of "ancestral spirits" which was believed to be pervasive in ancient Nile Valley culture. However, in adopting the new Osirian Cult, the Egyptians gained one who was the Divine ancestor to all. The priests of Osiris instructed the Egyptians that only through Osiris would an individual be able to become immortal and be able to access the Osirian kingdom.

Regarding the Egyptian pantheon of gods, the ultimate deity, "Neter," created animals as well as greater gods and lesser gods. Neter was self-existent, eternal, and omnipotent. Upon creating two of the greater gods, Neter formed a trinity with Shu and Tefnut. Two other gods, Keb [also known as Geb] and Nut then conceived Osiris, as well as other offspring to include Isis, Seth, and Nephthys who were all born with regular human bodies even though they were gods/goddesses. Osiris was born white and

---

[71] Allen continues his explanation of the resurrection cycle by offering, "After uniting with Osiris in the Duat in the fifth hour of the night, the Sun would then continue its voyage through the Akhet and then eventually becoming visible again in the Eastern hemisphere. In this process of union with Osiris, the Sun was capable of having independent life. In this myth Osiris is observed to be not only within the life-giving womb of his mother, Nut, but also within the confines of the Duat" (Allen, 2005:9).

viewed as the personification of good and Set (or Seth) was born a darker color and was viewed as the personification of evil (Budge, 2002:xxvii-xxviii).[72]

In addition to introducing some of the Egyptian pantheon, Budge also offers that the cult of Osiris engaged in human sacrifice. Budge (2002:200) offers several instances from the ancient Egyptian texts to give foundation to his view:

> The Egyptian texts contain many proofs that the overthrow of the original enemies of Osiris by Horus was accompanied by great slaughter, that their bodies were presented to him as sacrifices, and that, at the burial of the God-man Osiris, human beings were, and their bodies placed in his tomb. Thus, in chapter XVIII of the Book of the Dead, we read of the great battle which took place at night, when all Sebau friends were taken prisoners, and then butchered by order of Osiris…Originally, that is to say, when Osiris was buried, the earth was broken up with the implement, but it was then turned over and over and mixed with the blood of the victims who had been sacrificed to Osiris.

In the myth of Osiris, human sacrifice is part of his history and it is noted that there were many human sacrifice victims. In these passages cited by Budge, Osiris is observed acting in the role of a conquering, brutal king. Not only were the dead victims placed in his tomb as offerings but so were living ones as well.

Rosalie David (1998:28-29) provides further insight into the Osirian myth. She shares the account of how Osiris died and then came back to life. First, Seth murdered his brother Osiris. Isis then found the dismembered body parts of Osiris and magically re-assembled them. However, before Osiris was slain, she had become pregnant with his son. After the birth of Horus, Isis secretly raised her son amongst the marshes of the Egyptian Delta. Upon Horus becoming a man, he sought to avenge the death of his father by fighting Seth. The matter was brought before a

---

[72] Taylor shares a slightly different perspective on the genesis of the universe: "From a 'primeval watery chaos (Nun) there emerged a mound of earth on which appeared the god Atum.' 'Atum created first atmosphere and moisture (the god Shu and the goddess Tefnut), and they in turn produced the god Geb (earth) and the goddess Nut (sky).' The offspring of this pair were the gods Osiris and Seth, and the goddess Isis and Nephthys" (Taylor, 2001:25); Another important observation Taylor makes is that not only was Osiris capable of conferring *akh* upon people, but so were other Egyptian gods as well to include Nut, Isis, and Horus. Also, all of the above referenced gods were referred to as *akh* as well (Taylor,2001:31-32).

council of the gods who issued their judgment against Seth. The council reinstated King Osiris to life. However, instead of reigning over the realm of the living, he now ruled the region of the underworld. Horus remained among the living and became associated with the living king of Egypt. There are some who suggest that Osiris was the name of an actual pre-dynastic ruler who came from Asia and settled his people in the region of the Delta. Another theory mentioned for Osiris is that he may have begun as a local fertility god.

Taylor (2001:25, 27) shares a summary of Plutarch's version of the resurrection of Osiris. After Osiris had been betrayed, dismembered, and scattered about Egypt, Isis and Nephthys retrieved and reassembled the body of Osiris. However, they were not able to find his phallus. After putting the body of Osiris back together again, the god Anubis mummified the corpse.[73] Subsequent to this mummification, Isis and Nephthys were able to resurrect Osiris from the dead. Upon being brought back to life, Osiris was named king of the underworld and Horus, the son of Osiris who had avenged his murder at the hands of his uncle Seth, became the king of Egypt.[74]

Other details regarding the death of Osiris are that his brother Typhon (Seth) wrought these acts of violence upon Osiris because it was revealed that Osiris had sexual intercourse with his other sister Nephthys who also his brother Typhon's (seth's) wife. However, according to the myth the facts would bear out that Osiris had made love to Nephthys thinking that he was making love to Isis, his wife. Typhon (Seth) then launched a conspiracy where he deceived Osiris to lay down in a casket.

---

[73] Death was associated with dismemberment in the embalming process of the mummy. This is symbolized by the dismemberment of Osiris. The dismembered corpse is a "starting point for action." The embalming process took seventy days and prepared the decedent for eternal life. In addition to the transformation of the physical body of the decedent, there were also religious liturgies that purified the person in order that they would be able to cross the lake (David,1998: 31-33).

[74] Mark Smith Offers more details regarding the Osirian family: "At the age of 28 the god was murdered by his brother, Seth (Quack 2004: 330-331). According to some sources, the killer justified his act with the claim that he had acted in self-defense (Mathieu 1998: 71-78). According to others, he took retribution because Osiris had engaged in an illicit affair with his wife, Nephthys (Spiegelberg 1902: 21 and pl. 95, lines 12-15; Von Lieven 2006: 141-150). The offspring of this adulterous union was Anubis, who is sometimes called the eldest son of Osiris (Smith 2005: 203). A few texts say the god also had a daughter or daughters, without indicating who their mother was, by one of whom he fathered additional sons (Meeks, 2006: 21-23, 49-50, 104, 151)" (Smith, 2008:2).

When he was able to lure Osiris to the casket, Typhon along with his seventy-two co-conspirators, nailed the casket shut and placed the casket in the sea with the result being the death of Osiris. Isis learns of the plot and eventually finds the casket. On one occasion when Isis was not present with the body of Osiris, Typhon (Seth) finds the body, dismembers it cutting it into fourteen pieces, and scatters the pieces throughout Egypt. Isis is able to find the pieces and the body of Osiris is reassembled magically. However, the phallus is not located as a fish ate it. The phallus of Osiris was eventually magically recreated and attached to the body of Osiris (Plutarch, 2012:8-10).[75]

As demonstrated by the above narrative, one component that is present in the Osirian myth is the centrality of sexual imagery in pivotal points of the action of the story. In the very beginning one of the versions of the creation of the universe begins with an act of magical masturbation.

Regarding the origin of the universe in the Egyptian formulation, Kathlyn Cooney (2010:227) writes:

> Atum was the first known creator-god in the Egyptian pantheon, but he was also a solar deity, and the daily cycle of the sun can be seen as a sexualized male creation through union with the sky-goddess Nut (Allen, 1988:5-6; Assman, 2005:172-74)...When the sun set in the west, Atum entered the mouth of the sky-goddess Nut, whose body was thought to contain the *duat*, or "netherworld." This essentially planted the seed of conception and Atum's reborn self within his own mother (fig. 3).

Cooney (2010:227) further describes the presence of sexual acts in one version of the resurrection of Osiris:

> Another creator-god, Osiris, was thought to have the same potentiality for resurrection. After his murder and dismemberment by his brother Seth, his consort and sister Isis reassembled him. Osiris was then able to re-create himself through a sexual act with himself, the same act of masturbation used by Atum at the first moment of creation. Isis provided sexual excitement, but it was Osiris who essentially raised himself from the dead (fig. 4). Isis created the enclosure for Osiris's rebirth — his mummy wrappings — and she acted as the vessel for the conception of their son, Horus.

---

[75] Cf. (Budge:1934, 121-22) "When Isis discovered the phallus of Osiris that had been cut off, the god Thoth, the greatest of all magicians and the mind and tongue of the god Ra, assisted her by reattaching the phallus of Osiris and causing it to function normally even when he was dead."

Another version of this story has Isis taking the form of a bird and mounting the magically restored phallus of Osiris. Regarding this sexual act, Hare (1999:120) writes, "At this point, Isis becomes a small bird, a kite, and flies up to mount the phallus.[76] She thereby receives the semen of the dead god and conceives his son Horus, who, as the instantiation of divine kingship in the human world, enables the beginning of 'real history'".[77]

Here in these passages are graphic depictions of sexual acts (Atum and Nut) that are foundational to the Osirian myth. The sexual relationship between Isis and Osiris is also foundational to the revivification of Osiris after his death. Even as they are together in the womb of their mother Nut, this sexual relationship begins between brother and sister. Referring to Isis and Osiris within the womb, Mark Smith (2008:1) shares, "He married his younger sister Isis, with whom he had initiated a sexual relationship while both were still in their mother's womb..." In addition to Smith, Plutarch (2010:6) shares that "Isis and Osiris were enamored with each other and consorted together in the womb." So, even at the very beginning of Osiris's life *in utero,* the centrality of sexual activity is observed.

In regard to the prominent use of the phallus in the Osirian myth, Hare (1999:22) observes that even though the phallus is celebrated throughout Egyptian mythology, the Osirian cult is unique in that the phallus is linked to death. Not only is Osiris portrayed as weak in that he becomes a victim, but he is also later portrayed as overcoming death. This revived strength is observed as Osiris ejaculates his identity into the living king via a "keening bird." This process is reversed when the living king of Egypt dies and "becomes Osiris." Upon the death of a sitting King of Egypt, the new king who replaces the deceased king becomes the new Horus. The primacy of the phallus is also observed in the above reference to Isis when she mounts the phallus of Osiris. Hare further discusses the "obsessive concern" of the Egyptians with "phallocentrism" as the phallus is the instrument and symbol for paternal authority (Hare,1999:235).

In addition to the possibility that Osiris was a real king who met an early demise, David (1998:105-106) states that Osiris was resurrected as a

---

[76] "As 'resurrectress' of her brother-husband, Isis could be held responsible for both aspects of impregnation in a most miraculous way, for she could characterize herself as a woman who turned herself into a male" cf. (Witt, 1971:44).

[77] In the following quotation, Renggli (2002:224) analyzes a diagram taken from an ancient Egyptian drawing: "The bent body of the father *Osiris* lies in the drop of semen...Out of his body emerges his falcon-headed son *Horus.* The father resurrects as a fetus in his wife's womb."

dead god and has always been represented as residing in the realm of the dead as king of that region.[78] He also wears a long white cloak, wears the insignia of Egypt and also dons the royal crown of Egypt as well. Osiris was also known as the god of vegetation and rebirth. In his role as the god of vegetation and rebirth, his death and resurrection are observed annually in the cycles of the agricultural year. This was observed when the land would suffer from drought and then subsequently inundated by the waters of the Nile River.[79] The resurrection of Osiris was symbolized in this death and rebirth of the vegetation cycle. In addition to David's information on the linkage to Osiris and the vegetation cycles, Tom Hare (1999:15) also gives the yearly flooding of the banks of the Nile River as an example of the Egyptians belief that the death of Osiris by drowning, magically imparted fertility to Egypt through the yearly cycle.

Regarding the theology of the early Egyptians Mark Smith (2009:6) asserts that the concepts of revivification and justification are closely related:

> In obtaining justice against Seth, Osiris regains full life, since his death was an injustice. By his justification, he gains total mastery over death. As Osiris was restored to life and declared to be free of wrongdoing, so all who died hoped to be revived and justified, as a result of the ceremonies of mummification and the performance of the requisite mortuary rituals.

The hope of the devotee of the Osirian cult was to be able to obtain justice in like fashion as Osiris had received justice when he was abused and murdered by his brother. In addition to the hope of eternal life by reliance upon Osiris and his reception of justice, an assessment of the character of the decedent was also a part of these rituals and was believed to

---

[78] Plutarch (2012:8) shares of Osiris: "... the king could be seen as the embodiment of various gods, notably Horus, the young son born from its predecessor which had died the previous night. This predecessor was Osiris, a god who can be thought of as the photographic negative of the sun god: a being who had ruled on earth, been put to death by machinations of evil and disruptive forces, and who passed into a new life as the light below earth, ruler and judge of the dead who are in the Underworld."

[79] "Osiris revives in the underworld when his son, Horus, avenges his death. That this turn of events corresponds to natural fertility has been inferred from texts and iconography associating Osiris with the sprouting of grain. Iconography likewise shows grain sprouting from the coffin of Osiris, as he is to awaken to new life thanks to the rays of the sun above. It has been often claimed that the story of the struggle between Osiris and Seth identifies the former with the fertility of the Nile and the valley which the river inundated" (Smith, 1998:271).

be a precursor to the tribunal in the afterlife. A good assessment of one's life was also important as it determined how the decedent would integrate into the society of the underworld.[80]

Thus, from the viewpoint of Smith, the reception of justice from a devotee was not in the death and rising of Osiris because of the blood or sacrifice of Osiris itself. Nor was justice hoped for because of the relationship of the adherent with Osiris and gaining leverage to enter the netherworld because of identifying with Osiris in his sufferings. Nor did the adherent hope for resurrection from the dead based on joining with Osiris in death and then joining him in his resurrection. Rather, the reception of eternal life by a follower of Osiris was based upon the fact that Osiris received justice from the tribunal of gods after he had been put to death.[81] Therefore, the follower of Osiris could be confident that the tribunal of gods would deal with him favorably when he died. Of course, the nightly revivification cycle was important to the individual with the role of Osiris being central in it. But it was not the grounds by which the individual adherent gained entry in to "life after life."

In addition to these observations, Smith (1998:271) also explains the aspect of Osiris as a funerary deity:

> Indeed, Osiris has been understood fundamentally as a funerary deity. What may be helpful to note at this juncture is the observation of Frazer and many Egyptologists that the "mythology" of Osiris was influenced by Egyptian mortuary cult. Griffiths notes at many points the conceptual relations between the presentation of Osiris and royal funerary practices and beliefs. He argues that it 'is in the royal funerary rites that the cult of Osiris achieves an early ascendancy.' Of particular interest is Griffiths' view that the 'Osiris myth ... grew out of the royal funerary ceremonial'.

It is the funerary aspect of the cult of Osiris that causes it to flourish. The assurance of security after physical death contributes to the overall growth and popularity of the movement.

---

[80] "In this capacity he also became the model of human endeavors and virtues, judging each and every individual at the moment of death and also demanding an accounting of human behavior and attitudes. This role distinguishes Osiris, particularly in view of the normal religious or moral concepts governing other nations on the early stages of human development" (Bunson, 2012:313-14).

[81] Rosalie David (1998:110) describes how the cult of Osiris taught that when a person dies: "they are immediately brought before a tribunal or board to determine the fate of the decedent. The tribunal consisted of forty-two judges in similarity to the gods who judged Osiris and then voted to raise him from death to king of the realm of the dead."

In continuation of the theme of Osirian soteriology, Joshua Roberson (2015:20) brings out the importance of spells:

> The spells reinforced this affirmation through constant identification of the deceased king with Osiris, the god whose death and resurrection functioned as an additional template for salvation alongside the concept of solar rebirth. Ultimately, every part of the body was imbued through magic with the divine properties and immortality of Egypt's most powerful gods (Roberson, 2015:20)...When the spells assure us that the deceased individual is not, in fact, "dead" but "alive," we may infer that the former state represents the antithesis of the hoped-for divine transformation. Further, spell 93 reveals that the beings, known collectively as "the Dead," are possessed of "wrath" against those who have avoided their fate. In spell 524, they are trapped behind a "boundary," which does not hinder their deified counterparts, who are directed, in spell 666B, to avoid the canals that lead to their abode, which is both "dangerous" and "painful." Given these clues, it becomes clear that the "Dead" in such cases must connote some darker reality: Not merely death, but a terrible fate beyond death, which is to say, damnation.[82]

Not only is the solar rebirth cycle a way in which to obtain eternal security in the Osirian cult, but also those who were able to procure the right magical spells were able to appropriate eternity for themselves as well.[83]

In addition to the centrality of the funerary customs and the importance of magical spells, Roberson (2015:21) also describes the Osirian concept of divine judgment. From the *Books of the Dead* are provided descriptions of the process of this divine judgment. In spell 25, the newly dead individual goes before Osiris and other gods that are a part of the "divine tribunal" that is located in the "Hall of Two Truths." Located within this hall is a great balance that weighs a person's heart against the standard of "cosmic order," known as Ma'at. In various versions of this

---

[82] Roberson (2015:20) shares more about the centrality of spells procuring eternal life..."by the end of the First Intermediate Period (ca. 2190-2061 BCE) and into the Middle Kingdom (ca. 2061-1700 BCE), unambiguous textual evidence from private tomb walls and coffins — the so-called 'Coffin Texts' — demonstrate clearly that any Egyptian with financial means could obtain spells guaranteeing his or her divine status after death."

[83] Dunand and Zivie-Coche (2002:185-188) mention the use of not only pyramid texts and coffin texts, but they also mention the writing of the Book of the Dead which was on papyrus scrolls that were inserted into the coffin of the deceased: "His or her name would be placed within the coffin as insurance of his burial status with Osiris. This later form was of benefit to more people as it was more affordable for the common people of Egypt."

scenario, the jackal headed god Anubis tends the scales and is assisted by Horus manifesting a falcon head (Thoth, who has the head of an Ibis, is also known to assist Anubis). How did the life of the individual compare to this principle of "cosmic justice"? According to the book of the dead:

If the lifetime of the deceased contributed to the maintenance of order, the heart would strike a balance with *Ma'at*. A successful judgment came with the verdict "true of voice," transmission into the blessed afterlife, and entry into the company of the gods. Ownership of a Book of the Dead effectively guaranteed this outcome (Roberson, 2015:21).

If the individual's heart was judged not to have achieved Ma'at, the execution was swift. As the *Book of the Dead* describes, a demon monster quickly consumes the transgressor. The Osirian formulation of damnation is included in the *Books of the Underworld*. In these books the description of the residence of the damned is a place of fire, torture, suffering and is in similarity to descriptions of hell coming from Christianity and Islam. However, unlike the eternal punishment of those in the Christian formulation of hell, the damned in the Osirian myth would be totally and utterly destroyed (Roberson, 2015:22-23).

In discussing how the Egyptians believed they could "kill" the dead, Robert Morkot (2010:43) explains:

> Therefore, to kill the dead, the Egyptians needed to destroy the body — the mummy — so that the soul had no place to rest in. Equally important was to cut out the eyes, noses and mouths of their images so that they could not see, breathe or eat: and most importantly, to cut out their names, so that their souls could not find the images through which to partake of offerings.

This view is instructive regarding the metaphysical composition of the dead from the ancient Egyptian formulation. They only utilize their mummified corpse as a place to return to on occasion in order to receive sustenance from the offerings from those alive.

Within the Osirian myth, there are a variety of characters, concepts, and stories that are interwoven to form a multifaceted religious worldview/system. It is not just the main character, Osiris, who justifies the believer and guarantees them eternal life. Rather, it is a number of the gods of the Egyptian pantheon who work together in assuring that the adherent of Osiris makes the proper transition from life to the netherworld. Not only is the activity of these gods important in the securing of life after death, but also through use of magical spells is one afforded entry to eternal life. We also glean important knowledge about the metaphysical aspects of the departed dead as spirits and not as bodies. Rather, the mummified body is a place the disembodied spirit of the dead can return to in order to be reinvigorated. This also informs us as to the metaphysical composition of the King of the Realm of the Dead, Osiris, after his resurrection. Moreover, it is observed that Osiris arose not to life in the land of the living. Rather, he arose to life in the realm of the dead. In summation, determining the metaphysical composition of Osiris aids in understanding his revivification or resurrection from the dead.

3.3.2 Exposition of the myth of Inanna

In similarity to Osiris, an exposition will be conducted of scholarly literature related to Inanna (and other named deities believed to be forms of her in cultures other than her native Sumer) in order to be able to discern whether Carrier's claims regarding the parallels between the resurrection of Osiris and Jesus Christ are in accord with the related data. In similarity to the myth of Osiris, there are several key characters that are integral to the myth of Inanna. These characters will be identified and their roles described. Also, as mentioned above, as the cult of Inanna was known to have spread to cultures other than its native Sumerian milieu, there will be an inquiry into the spread of the Inanna cult through ancient history and a brief survey conducted to determine its impact on these other cultures.[84] In addition to these inquiries, a brief study will also be conducted regarding the religious, theological, and soteriological aspects of the Inanna cult with the objective of determining whether there are parallels between these aspects of the cult and orthodox Christianity.

Jane McIntosh (2005:212) introduces Inanna as being the daughter at different times to several gods. On occasion, she has been named as daughter of Enlil, Enki, or Nanna.[85] At the beginning of the universe, the

---

[84] In reference to the Akkadian form of Inanna, Ishtar, Benjamin Foster (1995:238) writes, "Ishtar, one of the most complex figures in Mesopotamian religion, is early attested as a goddess of warfare and as the morning and evening star. Partly through syncretism with the Sumerian goddess Inanna, she became as well a goddess of fertility, reproduction and love. She is often portrayed as harsh, capricious, and vindictive; fearless and joyful in the battle fray; urgent, ardent, and alluring as a lover, she was also associated with prostitution, sexual impersonation, self-mutilation, and homosexuality. Penitential and devotional literature tends to stress her valor and queenly tenderness."
[85] "The family tree of Inanna/Istar differs according to different traditions. She is variously the daughter of Anu or the daughter of Nanna/Sin and his wife Ningal;

gods (Enlil, Anu, and Enki) were dividing the various regions of the universe among them by casting lots. After the universe was divided among these three gods, the lesser deities known as Igigi were tasked with the maintenance of the earth while the aforementioned gods were in repose. In response to their exhausting work in keeping up with the demands of the earth, the Igigi revolted, began to set fires, and intimidated the god Enlil by surrounding his dwelling. As the spokesman for the burdened Igigi, Enki stated to the higher gods that people should be formed in order to take the labor of the earth from the Igigi (McIntosh, 2005:214).[86]

In relation to determining the personal traits of Inanna, Brigitte Groneberg (2009:322) gives a description of Inanna/Ishtar as the foremost goddess of those goddesses who were known to assist in royal ceremonies. Groneberg also describes her as the goddess of war, as well as the goddess of fertility. Groneberg further lists other attributes of Inanna/Ishtar:

> Her significance for the royal cult can hardly be overstated. It is she who bestowed sovereignty. This goddess not only controlled the fertility of plants and animals as well as humans, and thus was ultimately responsible for all wealth and offspring. But, in addition, she stabilized the king's power, allowing him to protect his realm also by destroying his enemies.

Groneberg (2009:323) provides more information about the origins of Inanna. She informs that the Inanna cult made a sudden entrance into history at the city of Uruk and lasted there in Uruk from the Old Babylonian period to the close of the first millennium BC. In addition to the city of Uruk, her cult also flourished in other areas to include ancient cities such as Kazullu, Babylon, and Ur as well as the more recent cities of Assur, Usbassu, and Borsippa. Adding to the description of Inanna by Groneberg, Westenholz (2009:332) adds that there are many different accounts as to the details of Inanna/Ishtar that seem to be in dispute. Also, there are many facets to Inanna/Ishtar that come from different writings about her. Concerning her appearance in mythology, she is the young maiden who Westenholz describes as "self-absorbed and materialistic, who holds out the promise of sweet delight to her beloved." However, in other writings

---

and sister of Utu/Samas (Abusch, 2000: 23); or else the daughter of Enki/Ea." (Heffron:2013).

[86] McIntosh (2005:214) continues, "The mother goddess, variously called Belet-ili, Mami, and Nintu in the poem, agreed to join Enki in creating humanity. One of the gods, possibly the ringleader of the revolt, was slain and his flesh and blood mixed with the clay from the Abzu, which Belet-ili formed into fourteen pieces. These were given to the fourteen womb goddesses, who after ten months gave birth to seven men and seven women."

from antiquity, she is also a rebellious teenager, a confronter of father figures, and a rival to her sister, Ereshkigal, who is the queen of the netherworld.

In the second millennium B.C., the cult of Inanna/Ishtar is established in most of the major cities of Sumer. In one city, there could be multiple forms of Inanna that are worshipped at the same time. In the second millennium, the term *istaratu* came into being as the common form for any goddess that referred to Inanna/Ishtar (Westenholz, 2009:339).

In reference to the Sumerian pantheon, Jean Bottero (1992:216) advises that there were up to two thousand gods most which were Sumerian in origin. The compositions of these gods were often changed as they acquired new attributes from other gods. One example Bottero uses, as an example is the merging of Inanna also known as Istar by the Semites with the deity associated with the planet Venus named Delebat. Even though Delebat had warlike qualities that were transferred to Inanna, Inanna still remained basically the same. Inanna retained the roles of the celestial Courtesan, the divine Prostitute, and the "patroness of free love." The prominence of Istar became so complete that by the second millennium and on, a form of the name Istar was used to describe any feminine deity in the common form. In reference to the pattern observed in the expanding influence of Inanna, Jane McIntosh (2005:208) informs that, "Inanna the Sumerian goddess of love, the morning and evening star, rain, thunder, and war, became synonymous with the Akkadian Ishtar and the Levantine goddess Astarte."

In addition to the information about Inanna and her expanding influence in other countries shared by McIntosh, Daniel Miller (2013:346n) also shares of this expansion as well. Miller explains that the origin of the Greek goddess Aphrodite, also known in Rome as Venus, was "mediated" through Astarte from her beginning. So, this trail of divine translatability begins with Inanna goes through Ishtar, then through Astarte with the next transfer of divine identity to Aphrodite/Venus. This situation can also be observed in other localities as well where there are goddesses for smaller areas that have taken on new names yet are derived from Inanna.

Moreover Robert O'Brien (1999:149) writes that Inanna, through the identity of Astarte, is observed in the pages of the Old Testament as well. In 1 Kings 11:5 (NRSV) is a description about how Solomon had followed Astarte the goddess of the Sidonians. Moreover, O'Brien (1999:145-46) also notices:

Both Astarte and Ascalon would have been familiar from the OT. In I Samuel 31:10 the Philistines put Saul's armor in the house of Astarte (called Ashtoreth in the Geneva Bible), and in Judges 14:19 Samson kills thirty men at Ascalon. We know that Ascalon was a cult center for Astarte, since a man from Ascalon wrote a votive inscription to the goddess at Delos.

O'Brien (1999:149,153) also detects other mentions of Astarte in the Old Testament in the form of Ashtoreth/Asherah:

> Although Solomon did not place an image of this goddess in his temple, a future king of Israel, Manasseh, would as evidenced in 2 Kings 21:17. Classical writers are not alone in associating Astarte with ritual prostitution; Old Testament prophets inveigh repeatedly against the male and female prostitution that they associate with the Astarte cult (see, for example, I Kings 14:24 and II Kings 23:7).

In their book, *Inanna queen of heaven: her stories and hymns from Sumer*, Diane Wolkstein and Samuel Kramer (1983:29-84) give a summary of several prominent stories from the life of Inanna. Relating these ancient stories from the life of Inanna gives a glimpse into her character, her abilities, as well as her limitations. The first summary is a brief synopsis of the courtship between Inanna and Dumuzi[87]:

> In a conversation with her brother, Utu the sun god, Inanna and Utu discuss who will be her husband and who will consummate the marriage on her "bridal sheet." Utu proclaims that it will be Dumuzi the shepherd. Inanna protests and states that it should not be a shepherd. Rather, the man who she will marry will be a farmer. Dumuzi then enters the action of the narrative and begins to answer Inanna's complaints about a shepherd husband. After discussing the matter with her mother, Inanna permits Dumuzi into the palace and their relationship begins as lovers and as a married couple. The courtship of Inanna by Dumuzi is recorded with their passionate and erotic conversation, and sexual intimacy (Wolkstein &Kramer,1983:29-49).[88]

---

[87] When Ishtar, not Inanna, is the goddess in the descent to the underworld, her husband is known as Tammuz instead of Dumuzi (Pinker,2005:96); The name Tammuz is observed in Ezekiel 8:14, 15; "Then he [the Lord] brought me to the entrance of the north gate of the house of the Lord, and I saw women sitting there, mourning the god Tammuz. "He said to me. Do you see this, son of man? You will see more things that are more detestable than this" (NIV).

[88] "In the Sumerian text, 'Inanna's Descent to the Underworld', the goddess only escapes death by supplying a substitute and she chooses her lover/husband Dumuzi who had failed to mourn her. She also decrees death and punishment to

In the action of the above story, a short summary of the romance of Inanna and Dumuzi is given in which its events quickly lead to a passionate sexual encounter and marriage.

In the paragraphs to follow, Inanna desires to attend a funeral in the netherworld and ends up in a deadly encounter with her sister, Ereshkigal, Queen of the netherworld. The following is a short summary that was derived from *The Descent of Inanna* (Wolkstein & Kramer, 1983:52-84):

Inanna descends to the gates of the underworld with her servant, Ninshubur in order to witness the funeral rites of her older sister's (Ereshkigal) husband, Gugalanna who has died. As she waits for entrance at the gate of the underworld, Neti (the gatekeeper) responds by stating that he will go to the queen, Erseshkigal, to see if Inanna will be permitted to enter the underworld. Upon speaking with Ereshkigal and gaining her permission, Neti allows Inanna to enter under conditions that she removes all of her royal clothing and jewels. As she goes through the seven gates of heavens, Inanna removes all of her clothing and other items until she stands naked and bowed low before her sister, Ereshkigal in the throne room of the underworld. Upon Inanna entering the throne room, the judges of the underworld, the Anunna, sentence Inanna to death. Subsequent to his judgment against Inanna, Ereshkigal strikes Inanna dead.[89] After her death, Inanna is hung from a hook on a wall.[90]

As instructed by Inanna, after Inanna had not returned to her home by the pre-appointed time, her servant, Ninshubur, mourns for Inanna by the ruins and then beats the drum for her in various places to include the houses of the gods. This activity had been pre-planned in the event that Inanna did not return home. Ninshubur also dresses in mourner's clothing. Ninshubur then nears the holy shrine and informs Enlil of the plight of Inanna who has not returned from the underworld. Ninshubur pleads with Enlil and Nanna who rebuff her attempts of intercession on behalf of Inanna.

---

the Gardener Shukalletuda, who raped her during a deep sleep (ETCSL 1.3.3) and condemns the slave girl, the 'Mother of Sin,' to death for having had sex with Dumuzi (Cohen 1988; Leick 1994, pp. 212-6)" (Leick, 2008:29).

[89] Dina Katz (2003:263-64) suggests that the offense committed by Inanna was that she wanted to usurp the throne of the netherworld held by her sister Ereshkigal. Katz also opines that Inanna was not a mortal being but a god and that her death revealed that she did not keep her divine status when she entered the netherworld as she ceased to exist.

[90] Victor Hurowitz (2003:156) offers that *The Descent of Inanna* could likely refer to damaged statues of Inanna being refurbished for use again. The breaking of the statue could occur by an enemy damaging it or by accident.

The faithful servant of Inanna then goes to the house of Enki and implores him to aid Inanna and Enki responds favorably to her. He creates the Kugarra and the Galatur who will give comfort to Ereshkigal and aid her in her turmoil. The creatures complete their mission to comfort Ereshkigal and then ask her for the body of Inanna. Ereshkigal gives them the body and the creatures sprinkle their life-giving materials on the corpse of Inanna with the result that she is re-enlivened in the underworld.[91] As she leaves the underworld, the Anunna, cause her to be escorted by two demons known as galla whose aim is to gain a substitute for Inanna.

As Inanna returns, the two galla look for the substitute for Inanna as she visits her friends and family. The galla attempt to take different family members of Inanna but Inanna tells them not to do this until she gets to Dumuzi, the king and her husband[92] who sits on his throne. At this point the galla seize upon Dumuzi who temporarily escapes from them. However, the galla, end up finding Dumuzi in the sheepfold of his sister, Geshtinanna. They strip Dumuzi of his royal vestments and then Dumuzi is "no more." In addition to this foundational tale of love, betrayal, death and revivification there are several other associated mythical stories with Inanna as one of the central characters.

In further analysis of the relationship of Dumuzi and Inanna, Karen Sonik (2012:388) discusses the metaphysical aspects of Dumuzi[d] in the background of *The Descent of Inanna*:

> As the spouse of Inanna, typically one of the highest order of gods, we might expect Dumuzi[d] to be of comparable rank and power and to be capable of independently escaping his ultimate unhappy fate. His actual status, however, is somewhat ambiguous as he straddles the boundary between mortal and divine. Further, even if he were as powerful as his daring

---

[91] Regarding the time span from the death of Inanna to her reanimation, Brian Metzger (1968: 22fn.) opines, "a careful examination of the epic (conveniently edited by J.B. Pritchard, Ancient Near Eastern Texts [Princeton 1950], pp. 52-57) indicates that it is 'after three days and three nights had passed' (line 169) that Ninshubur, perceiving that his mistress, Inanna, has not returned from the Nether World, proceeds to make the rounds of the gods, lamenting before each of them in accord with a formula which Inanna had previously given him...The time of the reanimation is not disclosed but doubtlessly the mythographer conceived it to be considerably later than the period of three days and three nights."

[92] Benjamin Foster (1995:78) notes regarding Dumuzi, "When Ishtar returns from the netherworld to find her lover dallying with harlots and not in mourning, in a fit of jealous passion she offers him to the netherworld in her stead."

spouse, even Inanna would not independently escape from the netherworld or from its wardens, the *galla*, forced as she is to fall back upon a ruse devised by Enki for her resurrection and, ultimately, also upon the provision of a substitute to take her place among the dead. Regardless of Dumuzid's divinity or lack thereof, there is a clear limit to both his power and to that of Inanna.

In addition to the observations of limits to the power of Inanna and Dumuzi[d], Sonik (2012:391) also avers that she violates not only the boundaries of the netherworld, but also other boundaries as well. These boundaries include cultural and gender boundaries. Westenholz (2009:233) adds that in some settings Inanna/Ishtar can be observed as a beautiful goddess of love during daylight hours who can also transform herself into a bearded goddess of war by night.

Another portrayal of Inanna/Ishtar is in the accounts of her festivals. In the festivals of Inanna, one of the major themes in most every event is sexual activity. Gwendolyn Leick (2008:130) shares that the followers of Inanna believed that sex was to be enjoyed by both humans and gods. Leick shares that the followers of Ishtar would offer prayers and incantations and that they "asked for satisfaction in love, within or without the marriage bed, to cure impotence and to bestow sex appeal. The gods themselves were subject to the power of erotic desire that was conceptualized as a divine force in its own right."

Leick (2008:127) further demonstrates the obsession with sex that captivated the followers of Inanna. She describes the words of a hymn where Inanna's devotees were engaged in revelry that included "music, plentiful offerings of beer and food, and the setting up of a special bedchamber in the palace." She also shares that the king of the jurisdiction "addressed as Dumuzi-Ushumgalana, enters this chamber to make love to Inanna, who then declares him to be 'her beloved' and a lavish banquet follows. These rites are said to be performed 'in order for her to determine the fate of all the countries,' for the king 'to enjoy a pleasant reign,' to 'decree him a good fate.'"

Adding to the information supplied by Leick, Philip Jones (2003:291) offers further detail between the relationship between Inanna and the king:

> According to a number of literary texts, kings from the late third and early second millennia-and perhaps even earlier-consummated a ritual union with Inana, the goddess of love and war. Given the literary nature of our evidence, this ceremony may have been only an intellectual construct, rather than an event in real life. Irrespective of this, however, it remains a

major source, not only for early Mesopotamian religious thought in general, but ideas of kingship in particular.

Continuing with the theme of the sexual union between Inanna and kings, Jones (2003:292) describes the festival surrounding the installation of the king and Inanna's involvement in them. He has obtained this description from an ancient Sumerian hymn (Iddin Dagan A). The subject of the first two sections is the goddess in heaven. She is glorified and compared to an astral body that can be seen in the sky (the sun and the moon). After these opening appellations to Inanna, the subject of the hymn is the other major gods of the pantheon that Inanna is in relationship with. These gods are An, Enlil, and Enki. The next sections of the hymn describe a carnival scene where licentious activity is taking place to include cross-dressing, bondage, and self-mutilation. This occurs under the watchful gaze of Inanna who views all of the revelry from her heavenly perch. Inanna appears to the revelers in their dreams as they sleep. The final scene depicts the consummation of the marriage.

Continuing on the theme of sexuality, Westenholz (Cited by Leick, 2008:127) observes that prostitution by a goddess such as Inanna in the ancient cultural milieu was understood to be a primal force that came from the realm of the divine with particular relevance to Inanna/Ishtar:

> In Inanna/Ishtar is observed contradictory aspects of female sexuality as she is both prostitute and bride, lady of the heavens and the earth, capable of motherly love and transgressive love, a binarity that some commentators relate to her astral embodiment as the planet Venus (Westenholz 2007, p. 345).

In addition to Leick, Tikva Frymer-Kensky (1992:48) shares that normal boundaries do not limit Inanna. She offers that even boundaries such as between humans and the gods or humans and animals do not restrain Inanna as she is portrayed as not only the lover of humans but also of horses. Frymer-Kensky continues:

> But Inanna is no outlaw. Unrestrained "free love" is her domain, but so married, socially-conforming love. Inanna/Ishtar represents and gives patronage to the sexuality of the prostitutes, but as Ishara, one of her names, she is the patron of marital sexuality, to whom the bed of bride and bridegroom is devoted.

Another aspect of Inanna that is related to her cunning and ability to breach sacred boundaries is her ability to deceive and manipulate others for her own purposes. Jean Bottero (1992:237) observes Ishtar's ability to obtain the *me* from Enki. As goddess of Uruk, it was in Inanna's best interest to obtain the *me* for her city as it would make her and also her domain more powerful. Bottero describes the *me* as a category that is not known in our modern world. He defines a *me* as "an entire cultural area, an acquisition of organized and civilized life reduced to an essential feature which sums it up or evokes it." On one occasion Inanna manipulates the god Enki, who holds all of the *me*, to host a banquet for her. During this banquet Inanna gets him drunk and subsequently wrests all of the *me* from Enki. In doing so, Enki is able to retain the *me* for himself. However, because Inanna stole the *me* from Enki, now she has access to the power and benefits of the *me* along with Enki. This incident along with others demonstrates the ability of Inanna to deceive and defraud others in order to further her interests.

In addition to Bottero, Stanley Kramer (1961:67-68) also notes the cunning of Inanna with the theft of the *me* and shares that Enki is not too happy about it. As she makes her get away in her "boat of heaven," Enki sends sea monsters after her but Inanna's servant, Ninshubur, repulses them three different times. Inanna is able to elude the attempts of Enki to sabotage her escape and she arrives at her home city of Erech greeted by her people as a victor with her spoils. The *me* or as Kramer calls them "the divine decrees" are unloaded one by one as the people cheer.

In reference to the Sumerian/Akkadian formulation of the netherworld, Bottero (1992:216) paints a gloomy picture of this underworld as the gods continue to dominate life there. He describes the netherworld as a "dark, silent, and sad cavern where all had to lead a gloomy and torpid existence forever." Bottero further writes that anything positive on earth would be negative in the netherworld. In this world, there was a different pantheon of Gods who were beholden to Ereshkigal the goddess who was in control of the netherworld along with her "terrible" husband Nergal who came along later.

In addition to Bottero, Judy Grahn (2010:64) also discusses the underworld and features the roles of Ereshkigal and Ereshkigal's daughter Nungal. Regarding Nungal, she is known as the midwife of life and death and her temple is located at the edge of the netherworld, "just as the human midwife is stationed at the gateway to the womb." Nungal's most important role is a judge over who lives and who dies among people. Regarding Ereshkigal, Grahn notes that Ereshkigal causes Dumuzi[d] and his sister to die and be reborn every six months, and also is the agent for Inanna's "three days of death."

Augmenting the description of the netherworld given by Bottero and Grahn, Dina Katz (2003:235) offers her opinion on the Sumerian metaphysical composition of humans. Katz offers that the sources she has surveyed indicate that the ancient Sumerians believed that after the body perished, the human experience continued beyond death. During life, the body was composed of both body and soul. Upon death, the soul went to the netherworld where it existed along with other souls of the departed. The souls of those who entered the netherworld were nourished by those relatives who remained on the earth and made offerings on their behalf. Upon death, the individual ceased to be a dualistic entity and remained as one unified soul in the netherworld. The Sumerians believed that this was the actual metaphysical composition of a human being upon death. This belief in the existence of actual dead spirits was confirmed when actual offerings were presented on behalf of a deceased relative by other relatives at the burial and after the burial as well.

In addition to Katz, Jane McIntosh (2005:226) also gives a description regarding the existence of the dead:

> The dead endured a gray and empty existence, their happiness directly related to the quantity and quality of the offerings of food and drink made by their children and grandchildren. Later generations forgot them, and they became part of the general undifferentiated mass of the dead, although there is some suggestion that they were recycled as spirits for new babies.

In summarizing the growth of Inanna's cult, it is observed that she spread to other parts of the Levant from her native Sumer. In Akkad she became known as Istar or Ishtar and gained additional attributes. Inanna/Ishtar then spread to Sidon, Tyre, and Ascalon (Phoenicia). Eventually, a Canaanite form of Inanna/Ishtar is observed in the mention of Ashtoreth and Asherah in the Old Testament. In addition to Ashtoreth and Asherah, Astarte is also observed in the pages of the Old Testament as well (Astarte is translated as Ashtoreth in many versions of the Bible). In addition to Astarte, the husband of Ishtar is listed in the Old Testament as well under the name of Tammuz (aka Dumuzi). Regarding the survey of the literature concerning the soteriology/theology for the cult of Inanna, there is not an abundance of information for us to peruse from antiquity. Prayers are mentioned in the literature but as also seen in the literature, these prayers seem to be related mostly to sexual matters. Moreover, the deceased are "nourished" by the offerings of their living relatives. Relatedly, obsession with sexual matters is also observed in manifestations and descriptions of Inanna to include any manner of deviant behavior as described above.

In relation to the death and "resurrection" of Inanna, it is observed that her death and her reanimation occur in the netherworld itself and not in the realm of the living. It is only when she is re-animated in the netherworld that she goes back to the "land of the living." Additionally, a proxy (actually two) was required for her to be able to stay among the land of the living. This proxy for Inanna ended up being her husband, Dumuzi and Dumuzi's sister, Geshtinanna. Inanna discovered that Dumuzi was unconcerned about her whereabouts when she went missing after she made her descent into the netherworld. With the exposition of the scholarly literature pertaining Inanna/Ishtar having ended, there are many contrasts to be drawn to the character and person of Jesus Christ and to his resurrection.

3.3.3 Exposition of the legend of Romulus and Remus

A brief summary of Romulus and Remus will be given in order to further the analysis of the assertions that Carrier makes regarding the supposed parallels between Romulus/Jesus Christ and to determine whether they are supported by scholarly literature on the topic. As in the case of the preceding mythical gods, background information on the various characters in the legend, the circumstances regarding the birth and rearing of the twins, as well as the death of Romulus will be developed. This exposition will be completed in order to further clarify the actual circumstances of the life, death, and resurrection of Romulus. Also, the apotheosis of Romulus will be explored to ascertain whether the details of this event comport with the claims that Carrier makes regarding Romulus and Jesus Christ.

Regarding the genealogy of Romulus and Remus, Augusto Fraschetti (2005:1-4) shares that the version of the genealogy considered the most accepted is that the rightful king of Alba Longa, Numitor, was wrongfully dispossessed of the throne by Amulius. Securing his place as king, Amulius arranges for the only son of Numitor to die seemingly by accident while he is hunting. After the death of Numitor's only son the only remaining child left is Numitor's daughter Rhea Silva. Amulius then compels Rhea to become a part of the vestal order so that she will not bear any sons. One version of the story has Rhea going to the sacred grove of Mars and subsequently being sexually ravished by the god Mars himself. After his transgression, Mars prophecies that her sons will be men of great valor. Fraschetti also mentions an alternate account where a slave girl belonging to Tarchetuius, king of the Albans is visited by a phallus that miraculously appears to her and couples with her.[93]

In addition to this account, Andrea Carandini (2011:13) also provides other variant accounts of the legend. One account has it that Romulus and Remus were born to a real woman, Acca Larentia and an unknown father who may have been a "late coming Mercury, behind whom probably hid the divine forbear Mars." A fourth version has Numitor taking his daughter as a Vesta priestess in order to maintain the royal hearth that is located at Alba Longa. Carandini (2011:15) shares:

> One day, this sacred hearth sprouted a phallus, also of the god Mars, who proceeded to possess the princess. From this union between the virgin priestess and the god of spring-the name March derives from Mars-a pair of twins were born. The firstborn Remus, who is always named first by the Romans, the second born Romulus, always named second and moreover, called Atellus, that is, the diminutive alter ("other") with respect to a *primus* (Carandini, 2011:36).

Other information Carandini furnishes is that the legend is believed to come from the time of the founding of Rome or not too long after the founding which is believed to be between the middle of the eighth century and the middle of the seventh century BC.[94]

From this point, the most accepted version of the birth of Remus and Romulus shared by Fraschetti (2005:3-4) has it that Amulius had Rhea imprisoned after hearing that she had become pregnant. After she bore the twins, Amulius ordered his shepherds to drown the babies in the Tiber River. However, the babies were placed in baskets and set adrift by the

---

[93] T.P. Wiseman (2004:199) offers the opinion of Licinius that Rhea Silvia was not raped by Mars in the garden. Rather, she was "ravaged" by her uncle Amulius.

[94] Fraschetti (2005:1) shares that Fabius Pictor an early chronicler of Roman history writes that the twins were born to a vestal virgin by the name of Rhea Silva. Even though this was the most popular founding myth of Rome, Fraschetti reports that there were other tales that also circulated about the founding of Rome. One such early legend has Romulus and Remus as sons of Aeneas or of Aeneas' daughter. But because of the early dating of Aeneas, this story has been discounted. However, Sallust still held as late as the first century BC that Aeneas was indeed the father of the twins and founder of the city. Another version of the founding story comes from Callias of Syracuse who posits that a Trojan woman by the name of Rhome had come to Italy, had married a Latin king, and bore him three sons: Rhoms, Telgons, and Romulus. Yet others aver that Romulus was the only son of a woman by the names of Aemilia, who came from the union of Aeneas and Lavinia. Aemilia had married the god Mars.

shepherds who believed that they would drown. A she-wolf, going to drink from the river, hears the cries of the babies, takes them from the water, and suckles them on her teats. After being discovered by the king's herdsman, Faustulus, the twins are brought to his home where his wife, Acca Larentia, suckles them. Acca was believed to be a prostitute as well. In Addition to Fraschetti's account of the birth of Romulus and Remus, Elizabeth Rawson (2014:279) observes that Livy and Cicero disagreed as to the divine parentage of Romulus and Remus when she writes, "Whereas Cicero rejected the divine parentage of Romulus as observed in *De re publica*, Rawson believes that Livy accepted the divine parentage of Romulus." This demonstrates a major difference in the reporting of a major tenet of the Romulan myth between two prominent reporters of the details of the life of Romulus.

Fraschetti (2005:31) then offers several versions of the murder of Remus. Upon discussing the rule of the city and who should take which part of the new city as their own, Remus and Romulus began to disagree about the methodology of how this would be accomplished. As a result of this disagreement over who received what land to build upon, the disagreement turned violent and Remus was either struck down by Romulus himself or one of Romulus's allies by the name of Celer after Remus willfully steps over a wall that Romulus had established. Another account involves Remus and Romulus sharing power for a period of time with Remus outlasting Romulus. Regarding the most well known version of the story, the two prepare a preordained ritual space where they would receive signs about their roles regarding the new city. As a result of seeing more birds in his ritual space, Romulus is shown to have the auspices to found the city with his vision of how Rome should begin.

In addition to the versions of the murder of Remus given by Fraschetti, Livy (2012:1.7) gives a rendition that after Romulus and Remus disputed over the omen of the birds, a heated dispute arose between their supporters. Livy also reports that Remus contemptuously jumped over the wall that was erected by Romulus. In turn, Romulus reportedly struck down Remus and exclaimed, "So shall it be henceforth with every one who leaps over my walls." Ovid's (Naso, 2012a:Bk 4, IX, Kal. 23) version of the slaying of Remus has one of Romulus' men, Celer, striking Remus with a shovel. Ovid explains that Celer, a follower of Romulus, was given orders by Romulus to put any man to death who crosses over the wall. After this order was given to Celer, Remus approaches the wall of Romulus and begins to mock those erecting the wall even as he jumps over it. Just as Remus jumps over the wall, Celer promptly strikes Remus with a shovel resulting in the death of Remus. Romulus buries his brother and the ghost of Remus haunts his foster parents.

In addition to this violent episode with Remus and his followers, Romulus is also involved in plotting a violent crime against the Sabine people. According to Livy (2012:1.9), Romulus attempted to obtain women for his men who did not have a good supply of wives. So Romulus "sent envoys amongst the surrounding nations to ask for alliance and the right of intermarriage on behalf of his new community." This request was sent to his neighbors, the Sabines, among others. After none of the neighboring nations agreed to assist him, Romulus devised a plot in order to lure the Sabine women to a location where they could be kidnapped and raped:

> To secure a favourable place and time for such an attempt, Romulus, disguising his resentment, made elaborate preparations for the celebration of games in honour of "Equestrian Neptune," which he called "the Consualia." He ordered public notice of the spectacle to be given amongst the adjoining cities, and his people supported him in making the celebration as magnificent as their knowledge and resources allowed, so that expectations were raised to the highest pitch. There was a great gathering; people were eager to see the new City, all their nearest neighbours — the people of Caenina, Antemnae, and Crustumerium — were there, and the whole Sabine population came, with their wives and families.

Ovid Naso (2012b:Bk. 1) continues with the execution of the plot against the Sabines and describes that Romulus gave the sign to begin the execution of the operation. He describes how the fierce warriors came upon the women who manifested their fear in different ways. He comments one last time about how the Romans "carry off the women, sweet booty for their beds, and to many of them, terror lends an added charm."

Regarding this violent attack upon the Sabines, Plutarch (2012:ch. 1) opines that Romulus was looking for an opportunity to make war upon his neighbors:

> Some say Romulus himself, being naturally a martial man, and predisposed too, perhaps by certain oracles, to believe the fates had ordained the future growth and greatness of Rome should depend upon the benefit of war, upon these accounts first offered violence to the Sabines, since he took away only thirty virgins, more to give an occasion of war than out of any want of women... They say there were but thirty taken, and from them the Curiae or Fraternities were named; but Valerius Antias says five hundred and twenty-seven, Juba, six hundred and eighty-three virgins.

In addition to these violent crimes perpetrated against individuals or groups of people, Romulus was also lauded as a successful general in battle. Shortly after the crime committed against the Sabines, the Sabines marched against Rome in order to gain vengeance for the dishonoring of their women. Livy (2012:1.10) describes the exploits of Romulus in dealing with this challenge:

> Romulus came upon them with an army, and after a brief encounter taught them that anger is futile without strength. He put them to a hasty flight, and following them up, killed their king and despoiled his body; then after slaying their leader took their city at the first assault. He was no less anxious to display his achievements than he had been great in performing them, so, after leading his victorious army home, he mounted to the Capitol with the spoils of his dead foe borne before him on a frame constructed for the purpose.

Livy (2012:1.15) also shares about another exploit against the army of the Antemnates who had conducted a raid into Roman territory. Romulus surprised this army as they were in the process of their raid and repulsed them. Livy further opines that Romulus was not victorious in his military campaigns because of his ability as a planner. Rather, it was because of the skill and experience of his army that had been battle hardened. Livy discusses another military campaign as well where he routed the enemy sending them back behind the fortifications of their city. After doing this and in revenge of the bloody conflict that had freshly ended, the retreating army of Romulus devastated the fields of his foe. Clearly, Romulus had set Rome on its path to world dominance through aggression and military might.

Concerning the demeanor of Romulus as he gained in fame and success, Jacob Abbott (2015:ch. 13) offers that the leaders of Rome became jealous of his increasing power. These leaders believed that Romulus was growing more and more domineering as time went on and that he was acting like a despot in that he wielded too much authority in his actions. Moreover, as a symbol of this growing pride he began to wear a purple robe when in view of the public.

Regarding the exit of Romulus from this world, Livy (2012:1.16) offers his perspective. He was reviewing his troops at the "Caprae Palus" when a powerful thunderstorm fell upon him with the result that Romulus disappeared from sight and was never seen again on earth. After the foul weather lifted, the royal seat occupied by Romulus was empty and there were those who reported that Romulus had been taken up to heaven by a whirlwind in the storm. Abbott's version of the story that he shares is that Romulus was enveloped in a flame which came down with the lightning and then was taken back up to heaven by the flame. Not long after these happenings the rumor began to spread that Romulus had been murdered and that either his body had been deposited in the lake or it had been cut up by the senators who disposed of the body by concealing pieces of the body under their robes (Abbott, 2015:ch. 13).

Regarding the disappearance of Romulus, Dionysius (2015:136-137) shares that Romulus was killed by his people because he had released, on his own authority, the hostages from Veientes, for showing favoritism towards the older citizens of Rome in opposition to the younger ones, for exercising too much cruelty in a judgment against some Romans accused of brigandage or robbery, and because he had turned into a tyrant as he grew older. Dionysius conveys that the Patricians carried out the murder of Romulus in the senate chambers and carried his body out in pieces under their robes. Subsequent to this, they buried the body. Another version shared by Dionysius is that Romulus was slain by the new citizens in Rome when the storm darkened everything around them.

T.R. Martin (2012:43) shares Livy's perspective that the people of Rome were irritated by the disappearance of Romulus as they believed that the high-ranking officials of the city were to blame for his disappearance. Upon a riot breaking out in the city, one of the prominent citizens proclaimed that he had seen Romulus that very morning after he had descended from the sky. The glorified Romulus instructed the citizen to tell the Romans that they would be a favored people who would one day rule the world and that this would happen by the will of the gods. Romulus continued to tell the person that Rome would one day rule the world and that its citizens should prepare themselves for this eventuality by training to be soldiers. The person reported that after speaking, Romulus mystically returned to the sky and disappeared.

Regarding the epiphany of Romulus, Ovid Naso (2012a:Bk. 2,XIII,17) has a vivid description of his appearance:

> But Julius Proculus was coming from Alba Longa; the moon was shining, and there was no need of a torch, when all of a sudden the hedges on his left shook and trembled. He recoiled and his hair bristled up. It seemed to him that Romulus, fair of aspect, in stature more than human, and clad in a goodly robe, stood there in the middle of the road and said, "Forbid the Quirites to mourn, let them not profane my divinity by their tears. Bid the pious throng bring incense and propitiate the new Quirinus, and bid them cultivate the arts their fathers cultivated, the art of war." So he ordered, and from the other's eyes he vanished into thin air.

In addition to Ovid, Plutarch (2012:ch. 1) offers his perspective on the epiphany of Romulus:

> Things being in this disorder, one, they say, of the patricians, of noble family and approved good character, and a faithful and familiar friend of Romulus himself, having come with him from Alba, Julius Proculus by name, presented himself in the forum; and, taking a most sacred oath, protested before them all, that, as he was travelling on the road, he had seen Romulus coming to meet him, looking taller and comelier than ever, dressed in shining and flaming armour...But farewell; and tell the Romans, that, by the exercise of temperance and fortitude, they shall attain the height of human power; we will be to you the propitious god Quirinus[95].

Anne Gosling (2002:56-59) shares the perspective of Cicero who believes that the account of the apotheosis of Romulus was told by Julius Proculus at the behest of the senate in order to divert the attention of the people away from the senators. Moreover, she notes that Scipio believed that the deification, as demonstrated through the account of the apotheosis, was a real event that proved the deity of Romulus.[96] Another example of one who endorsed the apotheosis of Romulus and did not believe that Romulus was murdered was Livy. In bringing out the various aspects of the death, apotheosis, and epiphany of Romulus, it is clear that there is a divergence of views.

In this summary of the life, death, apotheosis, and epiphany of Romulus, not only does Romulus and the narrative of his life possess mythical characteristics, especially in his earlier life, but there are also many substantive differences in the accounts of Romulus that have been brought forth by the various authors cited. Moreover, in the demeanor of Romulus as observed with his interactions with others, he is an aggressive

---

[95] Dionysius' (2015:142) version of the speech of Romulus to Proculus upon his epiphany is as follows, "Julius, announce to the Romans from me, that the genius to whom I was allotted at my birth is conducting me to the gods, now that I have finished my mortal life, and that I am Quirinus;" In this passage, Plutarch writes that upon the epiphany of Romulus to Julius Proculus, Plutarch (2012:ch.1) describes Romulus as an "apparition."

[96] In contrast to his opinion regarding the apotheosis of Romulus is Cicero's view that Romulus was in fact divine: "For let us concede to the common opinion of men, especially as it is not only well established, but also wisely recorded by our ancestors, that those who have deserved well of us on account of our common interest, be deemed not only to have possessed a divine genius, but also a divine origin" (Cicero, 1829:Book II).

leader/person who is not afraid to employ violence on behalf of his personal and civil interests. This is not only observed in the slaying of his brother Remus, but also in his military campaigns. Furthermore, in regard to the kidnapping and rape of the Sabine women, Romulus is also observed to be deceitful and violent. Concerning his disappearance and epiphany, the accounts diverge widely on the circumstances of this event. Furthermore, the alleged witness to the epiphany does not tell us whether Romulus appeared to him in a body or some other sort of emanation. It is also noted that the primary sources for the aforementioned accounts of the life of Romulus are neither eyewitnesses to the events they describe nor do they mention the source of their information or how reliable the information is. Additionally, it is probative to note that Romulus achieved great power and worldly success as the ruler of Rome.

3.3.4 Exposition of the legend of Zalmoxis

As in the case of the other mythical/legendary figures, a summary will be provided from scholarly literature in order to establish whether the information provided by Carrier is in agreement with the information coming from the scholarly literature on Zalmoxis (variant spellings include Salmoxis and Zamolxis). In conducting the research on Zalmoxis, it is noted that there were not many ancient sources to draw from. These sources included Ovid, Strabo, Herodotus, and Plato. However, these sources did not have an abundance of information to utilize in the study.

Plato (2015:10-11) only gives scant reference to "Zamolxis" in his *Charmides*. In his dialogue with Charmides, he discusses his experiences that he had with one of the Thracian physicians in the service of the Thracian king Zamolxis who Plato states are so adept that they can even confer immortality. A particular Thracian physician educated Plato on how to use "the charm" in order to help others in the return of the "vital heat." In his dialogue with Charmides, Plato discusses from the viewpoint of this physician the necessity to treat the head and the rest of the body if someone is having problems with his eyes. So, it would be an error to merely be concerned for only the eyes when to cure the eyes, one would need treatment for the head and the rest of the body as well.

Furthermore, Plato (2015:10) offers an analogy given by the Thracian physician in regard to spiritual things giving insight into the metaphysical perspective of the cult of Zalmoxis. The physician stated:

> That as you ought not to attempt to cure the eyes without the head, or the head without the body, so neither ought you to attempt to cure the body

without the soul; and this is the reason why the cure of many diseases is unknown to the physicians of Hellas, because they are ignorant of the whole, which ought to be studied also; for the part can never be well unless the whole is well.

Continuing with this analogy, the physician said that all good and evil in the body actually originates in the soul and transfers to the body (the head, the eyes, etc.). Moreover, if one is allowed to apply the Thracian charm to the soul, then the body will be positively affected. However, Plato further explained that the Thracian physician related that if a person possesses the quality of temperance then the person would have no need of the Thracian charm from Zamolxis or any other person (Plato, 2015:7-11,14).

In addition to Plato, Herodotus (2014: 249-250) relates what his Greek sources have told him about the Getae of Thrace and their god, "Salmoxis." He characterizes them as the best citizens who are not only brave but also law-abiding as well. They believe that they will not die, but that those who die will be received by the god Salmoxis and would go to a place where they would have many good things and live forever. Of this belief in immortality of the Getae, Herodotus writes, "And their belief in immortality is of this kind, that is to say, they hold that they do not die, but that he who is killed goes to Salmoxis, a divinity, whom some of them call "Gebeleizis." Herodotus also relates that "Salmoxis" was a man who was formerly the slave of Pythagoras who lived in Samos. After being released by Pythagoras, he obtained a considerable amount of fame and fortune once he returned to his home. Upon returning home, he built a hall where he entertained the chief men of the Getae.

Giving more information on the origin of Salmoxis, Herodotus (2014:250) offers that he received his information from "the Hellenes who dwell about the Hellespont and the Pontus" that Salmoxis was a slave belonging to Pythagoras. At some point, Salmoxis became free, became wealthy, and ended up returning to his native Thrace where he began sharing his philosophy with the Thracians. He would prepare meals for the most eminent of the Thracian men. When addressing these men, Salmoxis informed them that neither he nor them, nor any of their descendants would die. Rather, they would be received in a place where they would live forever and have all good things.

Even as he was teaching his philosophy to the Thracians, Salmoxis was busy preparing an underground, hidden chamber. Herodotus (2014:250) further reports that after the chamber had been completed, then Salmoxis, began living in the chamber out of the view of the Thracians. Upon losing contact with Salmoxis and believing that he was dead, the Thracians mourned him. After having not had any contact with the Thracians for three years, in the fourth year, Salmoxis reappeared to them. Based on what seemed to be a miraculous reappearance of Salmoxis from the dead, the Thracians gave credence to the teachings of Salmoxis as they believed that he returned from the dead.[97]

He also writes about two of the rituals performed by the Getae. One ritual is the human sacrifice of a messenger every five years and the other is the shooting of arrows when a thunderstorm is overhead. Regarding the human Sacrifice Herodotus (2014:249-250) offers:

> ...and at intervals of four years they send one of themselves, whomsoever the lot may select, as a messenger to Salmoxis, charging him with such requests as they have to make on each occasion; and they send him thus: — certain of them who are appointed for this have three javelins, and others meanwhile take hold on both sides of him who is being sent to Salmoxis, both by his hands and his feet, and first they swing him up, then throw him into the air so as to fall upon the spear-points: and if when he is pierced through he is killed, they think that the god is favourable to them; but if he is not killed, they find fault with the messenger himself, calling him a worthless man, and then having found fault with him they send another: and they give him the charge beforehand, while he is yet alive.

As previously mentioned and in addition to sending a messenger to Salmoxis, the Getae also have a custom where in the midst of a thunderstorm, they shoot arrows into the clouds and make threats towards the gods as they believe that there is no other god save Salmoxis. In his final comments regarding Salmoxis, he is ambivalent as to whether Salmoxis actually really built an underground chamber, or whether he was an actual person or just an indigenous deity to the Thracians. However, Herodotus states that if he were a real person, he believes that he would have lived before Pythagoras.

Regarding the mention of Zamolxis in his writings, Ovid Naso (2012: Bk. 15, Fables Four, Five, and Six) only has a small bit of information. In his discussion about a certain king Numa who some claimed was the student of Pythagoras, Ovid avers that Numa lived over a century after Pythagoras. Ovid further relates regarding Numa that he wanted the people to believe that the laws that he created and disseminated to the people

---

[97] W.S. Greenwalt (2015:345) opines that Zalmoxis, a mortal, supposedly knew death (at least the Getae believed so) and was resurrected which allowed him to deliver his message about the afterlife (like Orpheus). Insofar as Orpheus can be considered a hero, Zalmoxis must also be characterized as one.

were based upon consultations with someone who had the immortal, divine nature, as was the case with past leaders who were believed to have consulted with the gods. Ovid offers that Zamolxis, when he was amongst the Scythians, wanted them to believe that what he was promulgating to them had its genesis from his "Attendant genius or spirit." Ovid was of the opinion that Zamolxis pretended to have this divine connection that gave him the information for his teachings.

Adding to Herodotus and Ovid, Strabo (1892:456-457) mentions that not only had Zamolxis served Pythagoras, but that he had also gathered "astronomical knowledge" as well as some other knowledge from the Egyptians among whom he travelled. Strabo also affirms that Zamolxis would make astronomical predictions and was also able to convince the king of the Getae to allow him "to unite him [Zamolxis] in the government, as an organ of the will of the gods".[98] Furthermore, Strabo reports that at first, he became a priest for the people but was then later esteemed as a god. Upon reaching god status, he dwelt in caverns and rarely communicated with anyone save the king and those appointed to be his assistants. This custom of having a deity or god aid him in the administration of government continues to this day among the Getae. Strabo adds that the mountain where Zamolxis dwelt was still considered in his day to be sacred along with the river that flows by the mountain. In addition to Zamolxis, Strabo elucidates that in his day, the precept espoused by Zamolxis to abstain from foods derived from animals was still in effect among the Getae.

Explaining the significance of occultation and the meaning behind caves in mythical literature, Mircea Eliade (1972:28-29) gives examples of these mythical elements in the ancient Christian legend of the wise men that would climb a mountain every year in order to await the mystical reappearance of a star. This reappearance comes in several forms to include that of a little child as well as a bright light topped by a Star whose brightness exceeds the brightness of the sun. Moreover, Eliade also points out that the religious significance is not because it is dark. Rather, it is because the cave is totally separated from the rest of the world and

---

[98] On this point, Culianu and Poghirc (2005:9928) offer, "Zalmoxis probably taught immortality for valiant warriors. He was worshiped in a grotto, which might have played an important part in the initiation of priests and warriors. A chief priest, his representative in the grotto, was considered a prophet, and he gained such influence in political matters that the state of Burebista could be properly called a theocracy."

also because it was viewed as "an *imago mundi* or a universe in miniature."⁹⁹

Konstantin Rabadjiev (2015:451-453) shares that not only were the nobility eligible for eternal life by virtue of their standing in life, but that other Thracians were also able to enter eternal life by brave death during battle and also by lot every five years. If chosen by lot, the Thracian man would be dispatched to Salmoxis. Rabadjiev also posits that the existence of pits, hearths, and mounds related to the worship of Zalmoxis is also good archaeological evidence that the Getae communicated with their dead as evinced in the account of the messengers being dispatched to Zalmoxis as observed in Herodotus. According to Rabadjiev, these rites of Zalmoxis or as Rabadjiev terms them "rites of passage" are performed at the entrance of tombs. Rabadjiev offers the structural design of the Thracian tomb to support his thesis that the tomb was also considered as an exit point. The tomb's entrance contained a dromos or open area that led to the interior of the tomb. Inside the tomb was the dead body along with the horse of the occupant of the tomb. The horse lay in the antechamber that was located in front area of the tomb.

Yulia Ustinova (2002:267, 281) shares that Strabo listed Zalmoxis as a "seer who uttered god's orders and messages to mortals not only when alive but also after their death." Additionally, Celsus has Zalmoxis on a list of mortals who died yet still received worship after their deaths. In addition to being included among those humans who became deities, Zalmoxis is noted with two other persons for their "exceptional mode of existence: still alive, they descended below the earth, and continued their involvement in the life of mortals, remaining invisible to human eyes." This emphasis on the priest of Zalmoxis residing in subterranean chambers continued in subsequent generations. Only certain individuals would come into contact with the priest such as the king and several other helpers.

Furthermore, Ustinova (2002:280) posits that in their worship of Zalmoxis, the Thracians considered the high priest-king the substitute for Zalmoxis on earth. Ustinova also avers that the cult of Zalmoxis had a belief in not only a blissful afterlife, but also certain initiatory rites. Usti-

---

[99] In addition to the Thracians, Eliade also reports that another ancient Greek writer, Hellanicus, informs us that the neighbors of the Thracians, the Terizoi and the Krobyzi, also believe that they do not die and that their souls go to the god Zalmoxis upon their death. Eliade (1972:31) also points out that these two groups believe that the dead return after being implored to do so by loved ones and relatives who offer sacrifices on their behalf that enables them to return.

nova mentions that Hermippos of Smyrna relates an account of Pythagoras' descent and subsequent life in an underground chamber in similarity to the account of Zalmoxis. He allegedly received the latest current events from his mother who would visit him while he resided in the underground chamber. After a while, Pythagoras appeared before his countrymen and claimed that he had just been in Hades. His emaciated body was used as evidence to convince those within his hearing that what he said was true.

Daniela Sorea (2013:34) offers that Zalmoxis may have been a shaman in accord with the shamans of legendary Greek tradition. Sorea offers the description of Eliade regarding ascetics who lived along the banks of the Danube River as described by both Strabo and Josephus. These ascetics are believed by some to have practiced the use of hemp smoke to facilitate "ecstatic trances," to have had astronomical preoccupations, and also to have had their sanctuaries located within mountain caves. This information provided by Strabo, Josephus, and offered by Eliade has encouraged Sorea to "support the hypothesis of the perpetuation as Zalmoxian of some shamanistic practices previous to Zalmoxis' worship." Related to the origins of the Zalmoxian cult as it moved through the ages Sorea (2013:35) writes:

> Zalmoxis' worship, the Getian god, has been destined, ever since the beginning, for instructed people. This status diminished its chances of survival as it prevented its descent into the rural environment and in folklore. Furthermore, Zalmoxis' religion, by its eschatological dimension, by the enhancement of the initiations, of the asceticism and of the mystery-type erudition could be easily taken over by Christianity. However, the tradition of the solitary and chaste ascetics, revered as saints and heavenly-mystery connoisseurs, survived in the Romanian cultural field.

In addition to Sorea, Michael Cosmopoulos (2003:172) offers a link between other religious figures, to include Zalmoxis, and their emphasis of gaining access to the eternal world through their association with the subterranean world:

> Trophonius, Zalmoxis and Pythagoras then, according to independent traditions, possessed a cave of similar nature, a privileged place where any individual could gain more than momentary access to the world beyond and to divine knowledge of all things, visible and invisible, past, present and future. The connection between revelation and chthonic sites was widespread: Epimenides, for example, possessed universal knowledge thanks to a fifty-seven year sleep in a cavern.

In the religion of Thrace, Bianchi, et al. (1971:231) recognize the Getae and the Dacians regarding their influence on Greek religious thought. They observe that Orpheus who is closely associated with the "Greek mystical consciousness" was reputed to be Thracian, the charms that were intended to cure the soul as mentioned in Plato's Charmides were Thracian (from Zalmoxis), and the immortalization of the human soul that is observed in Greek religious writings was believed to have been inherited from the Thracians.

In Summary, it is not known whether the real person of Zalmoxis ever existed. Strabo offers his observations as to a priest who was believed to be the successor to Zalmoxis. Thus, the information to substantiate the existence of Zalmoxis as a real person has not been confirmed. It is noted from the sources that Zalmoxis, if he existed, aligned himself with the king as his spiritual advisor and oracle. Moreover, in the rites of the cult of Zalmoxis, there was the practice of human sacrifice in their dispatching of a messenger to Zalmoxis. Concerning its soteriology, the cult of Zalmoxis put forward that its followers were able to enter eternal life by virtue of their status as noblemen, by lot every five years, or by dying valiantly in battle.

Also, there has been no Zalmoxian doctrine offered that represents that Zalmoxis died in order to bring acceptance before God and assurance for eternal life to the Getae. Nor has there been any showing that the risen body of Zalmoxis was observed or that it represented the first of the resurrected bodies that guarantees the resurrection of all adherents of the cult of Zalmoxis. Rather, it seems that Zalmoxis endorsed the immortality of the soul and provided proof to them of his ability to defeat death when he hid himself from the view of the Getae for three years.

Moreover, it has been offered that the religious services and other sacred rites were performed in caves as points of connection with their god, that they believed in the immortality of the soul, and their worship most likely had shamanistic qualities as well. Regarding the occultation and epiphany of Zalmoxis, the accounts coming from the ancient sources do not even assert that Zalmoxis died and came back to life. Rather, as mentioned above, the sources report that Zalmoxis convinced the Getae that he traveled to Hades even though he had actually built a subterranean cave in which he resided unbeknownst to them and that he reappeared to the Getae after three years of absence from them.

3.4 Cross-examination of Carrier by scholarly literature

3.4.1 Cross-examination: The resurrection of Jesus Christ coming from mystery religions

In his writings on comparative religion, Hans Schoeps (1968:10-37) notes that all religions have certain basic similarities that they all share. One of these basic elements that Schoeps identifies is common to all religions is that "they move men to the depths of their beings, because religious feeling is rooted in the core of human existence." Other elements that Schoeps notes are a sense of holiness, notions of taboo or "something marked out as forbidden," gift offerings, sacramental offerings, expiatory offerings, prayers, and public rituals.

Developing the expiatory offering as common to religions, Schoeps (1968:33) observes that this offering is made on behalf of a person so that the person does not have to undergo punishment for violating the ordinances of the god. An animal sacrificed instead of the devotee and that suffers in the place of the devotee summarizes the meaning of an expiatory offering. However, Schoeps notices there is a difference in this concept when it comes to Christianity. Instead of a man making a sacrifice in order to appease the deity, in the Christian formulation of the expiatory offering, Jesus Christ is "sacrificed for the redemption of the sins of all men. 'The blood of Jesus his Son cleanses us from all sin' (1 John 1:7)." Therefore, the normal function of this offering is altered. Instead of a man making an offering to appease the deity, the Deity (Jesus Christ) is making an offering on behalf of the man in order to make restitution for the offense of the man. The man merely need join in relationship and covenant with Jesus Christ in order to receive the benefits of the expiatory offering of Jesus Christ.

In addition to expiatory offerings Schoeps (1968:37) also discusses the public rituals as having "as many components and modes of expression as there are religions and sects." Schoeps also notes that these public rituals are dramatic demonstrations to the exaltation of the god and the relationship afforded the devotee to the god. Moreover, these rituals are limited to specific "sacred places and times."

In relation to the parallels that Carrier observes, as Hans Schoeps has noted, there will be similarities in all religions to include ways in which the devotee will attempt to avoid punishment from the deity. Also, there will be many ways in which the devotee will publicly display worship and veneration to their god through various rites and ceremonies. As Schoeps' work on comparative religions is applied to Carrier's claim of Christianity borrowing from preceding pagan religions, there is an important matter that should be investigated. Do the aforementioned basic similarities between religions necessarily point to a causal connection between Christianity and preceding pagan cults? Another germane consideration on this topic is that there are differences in the pagan cults that Carrier offers above as examples from which Christianity borrowed from. If this is the case, then how can these cults with different elements within them all be a source for Christianity when they all diverge in their practices and core dogma?

Regarding a possible connection between Pauline Christianity and the mystery cults, Jonathan Smith (1990:142-43) gives his opinion:

> Most of the 'mystery cults' and the non-Pauline forms of Christian tradition have more in common with each other...The entire enterprise of comparison between the 'mystery' cults and early Christianities needs to be looked at again. Nor is this all. The question is not merely one of a revised taxonomy, urgent as that may be, but of interests. The history of the comparative venture reviewed in these chapters has been the history of an enterprise undertaken in bad faith...The protestant hegemony over the enterprise of comparing the religions of Late Antiquity and Early Christianities has been an affair of mythic conception and ritual practice from the outset.

In this paragraph, Smith rails against those who would compare the earlier pagan religions to Christianity. In no uncertain terms, his research indicates that there is no basis whatsoever to formulate a close connection between Christianity and these earlier "mysteries."[100] In mentioning the undertaking of such comparisons, Smith uses irony to make his point as he refers to the endeavor to make such comparisons "an affair of mythic conception."

In responding to Carrier's claims that the resurrection stories of the pre-existing dying and rising gods contributed to the resurrection account of Jesus Christ, there are a number of scholars who take issue with this assertion. S. Angus (1928:258-59) offers his analysis of mystery reli-

---

[100] Smith (1990:108) further opines, "it is, to put matters bluntly, poor method to compare and contrast a richly nuanced and historically complex understanding of Pauline Christology with a conglomerate of 'mystery texts' treated as if they were historically and ideologically simple and interchangeable; to treat the former as developmental and the latter as frozen."

gions preceding Christianity. He states that the Greek and Roman religions succumbed easily to the mystery religions. However, regarding Judaism and Christianity Angus states, "there was one religion of the earlier political type which did not yield to the Mysteries, but entered the lists against them. The religion of Israel was for six centuries, from the days of Jeremiah to Ezekiel to the triumph of Pauline Christianity..."

In addition to this perspective on the mystery religions and Christianity, Angus (1928:278) gives evidence for the syncretistic aspect of the mysteries as opposed to the uncompromising views of Judaism and Christianity. Angus offers that in the religious and cultural milieu of the mysteries, there were different gods who deemed it acceptable to be located in the same temple with a priest officiating on behalf of all of the different gods. Therefore, one man could owe allegiance to a variety of different gods from different regions of the world. He further recognizes that polytheism encouraged this sort of religious tolerance. However regarding the Jews and the Christians, Angus writes:

> The Jews stood aloof. Their uncompromising monotheism and the Law rendered them conspicuously intolerant as compared with the adherents of the Mystery-Religions. They would accept no compromise on the question of the imperial cult, Sabbath-keeping, or on such rites as appeared essential to the integrity of their faith (Angus, 1928:278).
>
> Christianity intensified the intolerance of the parent faith and sternly set its face against the tolerance in religious affairs which commenced with the Persians, was first made popular by Alexander, and became settled policy of the Roman Empire. It frowned upon the hospitality of the competing cults. Christianity stands proudly aloof from the throng of the *thiasi*... (Angus, 1928:279).
>
> To those who, according to the religious conceptions of the time, were seeking mediators, it [Christianity] declared 'there is one God; also one mediator between God and man, Christ Jesus' (1928:278).

Everett Ferguson (2003:297-298) also observes a demarcation line between the mystery cults and Christianity even though he observes some minor borrowing from the pagans in some Christian symbols. Moreover, Ferguson observes that some of the mystery cults may have adopted ideas from Christianity as well. Notwithstanding the observation of minor borrowing between the two, Ferguson notes:

> Nevertheless, there is very little evidence for much Christian indebtedness in the first century, and especially in Palestine. Hence, the search for pagan influences in early Christianity has focused on Hellenistic Christianity and

especially on Paul as channels through which pagan ideas reached a religion that began on Jewish soil. This too has failed to be substantiated.

Specifically regarding the resurrection, Ferguson (2003:298) opines that the mystery religions are observed more to be associated with the agricultural cycle. However, Ferguson even doubts this comparison by the time of the proliferation of the mystery cults as the Roman urban culture had dimmed the bond of the people with the soil. Seeing the contrast between Christianity and the mystery religions Ferguson offers, "But insofar as the paganism offered 'dying and rising gods,' these gods are a world apart from Christ's resurrection, which was presented as a one-time historical event, neither a repeated feature of nature nor a myth of the past."

In addition to Ferguson, Carl Clemen (1912:194-95) offers his opinion regarding the mystery cults and their influence on Christian resurrection. Clemen is specifically responding to a theory that other religions influenced Christianity through the mediating influence of Judaism:

> The idea that these religions could have had a direct influence, that the festivals (say) in the cult of Attis and of Osiris could without any intermediary have produced the tradition of the death and resurrection of Jesus, whether at this definite time or any time, is absolutely inconceivable, in view of the antiquity of the tradition.

In very emphatic terms, Brian Metzger (1968:13) denies a linkage between the mystery cults and Christianity, generally. He makes a contrast between the mythical aspect of the mystery deities who were ephemeral entities of an ancient, past and Christianity:

> The divine being, whom the Christian worshiped as Lord, was known as a real Person on earth only a short time before the earliest documents of the New Testament were written. From the earliest times the Christian creed included the affirmation that Jesus was crucified under Pontius Pilate. On the other hand, Plutarch thinks it necessary to warn the priestess Clea against believing that 'any of these tales [concerning Isis and Osiris] actually happened in the manner in which they are related.'

Writing specifically regarding the resurrection, Metzger does not see any link between the dying and rising gods of the mystery cults and the death and resurrection of Jesus Christ. Metzger lists the differences he observes between the two. In the accounts of the mystery cult gods, the gods do not freely give up their lives but only under compulsion. In contrast to these gods is the self-sacrificing nature of Jesus Christ who freely accepted death on behalf of others.

Metzger (1968:18) also observes another major difference in the triumphant proclamation of the death and resurrection of Jesus Christ:

> Christianity *is sui generis* in its triumphant note affirming that even on the Cross Jesus exercised his kingly rule (*Dominus regnat ex ligno*). Contrary to this exultant mood (which has been called the *gaudium cruces*), the pagan devotees mourn and lament in sympathy with a god who has unfortunately suffered something imposed on him. As Nock points out, 'In the Christian commemoration the only element of mourning is the thought that *men* have betrayed and murdered Jesus. His death is itself triumph.'

Metzger (1968:24) also points out that the Mystery cults and Christianity are different in their views regarding their respective philosophies of history. He goes on to explain how the dying and rising gods of the Mysteries are symbolic of the cyclical/recurring nature of the planting and harvest seasons that repeat every year. This stands in contrast to the resurrection of Jesus Christ whose death and resurrection is "once and for all."

From his investigation into the supposed causal connection between pagan religions and the Christianity regarding the resurrection of Jesus Christ, Metzger (1968:24) concludes that a high amount of caution should be utilized when making comparisons between them. Furthermore, he concludes that the "central doctrines and rites of the primitive Church appear to lack genetic continuity with those of antecedent and contemporary pagan cults." Supporting the aforementioned view, Metzger (1968:7) offers that "the early Palestinian Church was composed of Christians from a Jewish background, whose generally strict monotheism and traditional intolerance of syncretism must have militated against wholesale borrowing from pagan cults."

Additionally, regarding the lack of proliferation of the mystery cults into Palestine, Metzger (1968:8fn.) also offers:

> According to the map prepared by Nicola Turchi (in his *Le religioni misteriosofiche del mondo antico* [Rome, 1923], showing the diffusion of the Mysteries of Cybele, dea Syria, Isis, Mithra, Orpheus-Dionysis, and Samothrace in the Roman Empire, the only cult which penetrated Palestine proper was the Isiac cult...It is significant that in an early second century invocation to Isis (P. Oxy. 1380) containing a detailed list of places at which Isis was worshiped (67 places in Egypt, and 55 outside Egypt), the only place within Palestine that is mentioned (lines 94f.) is Strato's Tower, the site of the Pales-

tinian coast just south of Syria chosen by Herod the Great for the building of Caesarea, the capital of Roman Palestine.

In his analysis of the connection between dying and rising gods and Jesus Christ, Bart Ehrman (2012:224), a self-proclaimed agnostic, cites some significant problems that he has with the concept of a "hand-off" from mystery cults to Christianity. In addition to Ehrman's view that early Christians did not believe that Jesus Christ was the Son of God, Ehrman posits:

> First, there are serious doubts about whether there were in fact dying-rising gods in the pagan world, and if there were, whether they were anything like the dying-rising Jesus... Can anyone cite a single source of any kind that clearly indicates that people in rural Palestine say, in the days of Peter and James, worshipped a pagan god who died and rose again? You can trust me, if there *was* a source like that, it would be talked about by everyone interested in early Christianity. It doesn't exist...But there is an even larger problem. Even if-a very big *if*-there was an idea among some pre-Christian peoples of a god who died and arose, there is nothing like the Christian belief in Jesus's resurrection. That's not the same thing.

In addition to his refutation of the linkage between dying and rising gods and Jesus Christ, Ehrman (2012:225-226) also offers that Jesus Christ's resurrection did not come from a deity only being reanimated or restored to life. It was tied to an eschatological event where God would come and gain a more visible role in ruling the earth. As the vanquisher of evil, the victory of Jesus would be apparent when his followers would arise from the dead. In addition to this opinion, Ehrman offers another opinion that there is no "*prima facie* evidence that the death and resurrection of Jesus is a mythological construct, drawing on the myths and rites of the dying and rising gods of the surrounding world."

In his thoughts on the topic of comparisons between Jesus Christ and pagan gods that "preceded" him, John Reynolds (2009:252) shares the trend of atheist or agnostic groups to assert that a god enfleshed (he mentions specifically Osiris and Dionysus) was not unique to Christianity. Moreover, he avers that similarities between Jesus Christ and other pagan gods are merely on a general level or just mere coincidence. Reynolds further posits:

> In none of the myths that predate Christianity does God himself, Creator of the cosmos, become flesh and dwell among humankind. Jesus Christ did not just claim to be *a* god (he was a Jew, after all) but *the* god. This God was

all powerful, all knowing and eternally existent. There was nothing like him in the Greek or Roman pantheon.

3.4.2 Cross-examination: Resurrection of Jesus Christ coming from Osiris/Inanna

Specifically regarding the Osirian myth and a supposed connection to Paul the Apostle, Norman Perrin (2007:17-18) offers his perspective on the subject. Perrin states that there are scholars, such as Bostock, who observe parallels with Osiris and the Pauline resurrection body when Paul associates the resurrection body with a germinating seed (1 Cor. 15:36-49) as the germinating seed motif is part of the Osirian description of renewal of life. Perrin also explains the claim of some scholars that Jesus Christ and Osiris both offer redemption and eternal life to humanity. Because the reanimation of Osiris comes long before the resurrection of Jesus Christ, then it could be argued that the Osirian myth did contribute to the resurrection of Jesus Christ. However, Perrin observes that there are several questions that are germane to the discussion: 1) Are isolated comparisons between Paul's perspective on the resurrection of Jesus Christ and the Osirian myth enough to claim dependence of the former upon the latter? 2) Does this comparison also apply to a more general overall comparison of Paul's theology with that of the Osirian myth?

Regarding the difference between the soteriology of the Osirian myth and Christianity, Perrin (2007:125) writes:

> The christological, covenantal, and eschatological significance of resurrection in the *corpus Paulinum* highlights a fundamental disjunction with the Osirian mythology. Whereas Paul pinned his hopes on certain historical *realia*, the person of Christ and the covenants, there was no comparable basis for hope among the followers of Osiris. Nor do we find in Osirianism anything analogous to the theodicean logic that underpins Paul's Christology and eschatology. By any account, Osiris was a cruel god who discharged his duties as tormentor quite apart from any ethical considerations, either on his part or on the part of the deceased.

In addition to the observation that the individual Christian has a covenant guaranteed by Jesus, this is contrasted to the lack of any covenant with Osiris or any other assurance given to his followers. Perrin (2007:126) also observes that Osiris is never observed as a mediator in any of the Osirian mythical literature as is Jesus Christ in the New Testament. Moreover, Perrin offers that not only are their roles in relation to their followers different, but Osiris can be described as an "anti-mediator" where instead of being an advocate, Osiris is an adversary. Perrin also observes a stark contrast with the eschatological perspectives between Osiris and Jesus Christ. Whereas the follower of Osiris was content to transfer his existence as it was in his earthly life to his eternal life, the Christian has the opposite hope that he will be with Jesus Christ which is "better by far" (Phil. 1:23, NIV).

Regarding Osiris and Jesus Christ, George Nagel (cited by Metzger, 1968:19fn.) observes profound differences between the two. One problem that Nagel notices is that there are many references to battles that are waged on behalf of Osiris that are included in the myth. However, in reference to the actual death and resurrection of Osiris, "they are always quite reticent and give us no more than mere allusions." In addition to the criticism by Nagel, other criticisms of Osiris by Metzger include his opinion that the Osirian cult should be categorized not as a mystery cult but rather mainly as a funerary service for the newly departed. Another concern of Metzger regarding the resurrection of Osiris is that in one version of it, Osiris is reassembled by magic and after this is reinstated to the realm of the dead, not to the land of the living. Metzger (1968:21) believes that this should not be considered as a resurrection at all as he was not restored to life, but consigned to the netherworld. Echoing Metzger, Ferguson (2003:298) opines, "There is nothing in the myth of Osiris that could be called a resurrection: the god became ruler over the dead, not the living."

Adding her perspective on the resurrection of Osiris, Mary Jo Sharp (2009) also offers that Osiris was revived through the efforts of his sister bride Isis by breathing, piecing him back together again, or reciting a spell over him. Regarding the metaphysical aspect of the reanimation of Osiris, she also informs of the opinion of T.N.D. Mettinger who pointed out that Osiris was never fully restored but that he survived in the realm of the dead only. Also, the followers of Osiris hope to survive death and be granted eternal life as well. In obtaining eternal life, the followers of Osiris had to rely upon their good works.

Edwin Yamauchi (1974) also offers his perspective on Osiris in relation to comparing his "resurrection" with that of Jesus Christ. He observes that not only did the followers of Osiris in the time of Plutarch (1st and 2nd centuries A.D.) believe that they could attain life after death by identification with Osiris, but so did those ancient Egyptians during the 2nd millennia B.C. Yamauchi also avers that it would be a serious mistake to equate the Osirian mythical view of the afterlife with that of the Hebrew-Christian formulation. He bases this opinion on several necessary conditions: 1) Mummification of the body 2) Nourishment for the decedent provided each day in the form of food and drink or else symbolically provided by magical drawings on the walls of the tomb 3) Magical texts or spells needed to be included within the coffin. Another unusual aspect of the Osirian formulation was that it involved the *ka* and the *ba* that would hover over the mummified body.[101]

In addition to Osiris, Edwin Yamauchi (1974) offers the Mesopotamian/Egyptian view of the afterlife. In relation to the myth of Inanna/Ishtar and Osiris, Yamauchi posits:

> If the Resurrection of Christ can be investigated as a historical question, one may inquire about the ancient concepts of the afterlife at the time of Jesus and ask whether the Resurrection of Christ was a doctrine that arose from contemporary beliefs.

S.N. Kramer (cited by Yamauchi,1974) further offers the *Descent of Inanna (Ishtar)* to demonstrate that in the story of the death and "resurrection" of Inanna/Ishtar, instead of the popular view that Inanna/Ishtar rescued Dumuzi from death, the actuality of the scenario was that Inanna/Ishtar actually caused Dumuzi to be her substitute so that she could reassume her life in the "land of the living." Kramer's perspective also demonstrates the pessimistic view of the afterlife as portrayed in the words of Ishtar when she tells the gatekeeper that she will "raise up the dead...so that the dead will outnumber the living." Kramer then exclaims, "A calamity and not a hope!"

3.4.3 Cross-Examination: Resurrection of Jesus Christ from Romulus

In reference to the apotheosis and epiphany of Romulus, N.T. Wright (2003:76-77) discusses the religious milieu before and around the life of Jesus Christ in relation to Romulus and those persons who allegedly have been seen after their deaths. He first mentions the story of Romulus and how he had appeared to Julius Proculus after his mysterious disappearance. He then mentions others who were allegedly seen after their deaths

---

[101] Yamauchi (1974) offers the opinion of Roland de Vaux that Osiris could never be an inspiration for the resurrected Christ: "What is meant of Osiris being 'raised to life'? Simply that, thanks to the ministrations of Isis, he is able to lead a life beyond the tomb which is an almost perfect replica of earthly existence. But he will never again come among the living and will reign only over the dead.... This revived god is in reality a 'mummy' god" [The Bible and the Ancient Near East, 1971, p. 236].

to include Aristeas, Cleomedes, and Hercules. According to Wright, an important thing to stress is that in that era, no one believed that these stories proved that there was an actual resurrection of the person observed. Moreover, these incidents have no bearing on the early Christian belief in the resurrection of Jesus Christ.

Along with Wright, Deborah Prince (2012:27, 30) also observes that the Romulan legend is not supported by strong evidence. In her essay, Prince quickly analyzes the evidence for the Romulan legend and shows that there were concerns about the credibility of the story when it was first heard and when the story was told. She then offers another story of another women from antiquity, Philinnion, who had met with a young man at night after she had been buried. According to the ancient source, several witnesses allegedly witnessed the meeting between the two.[102] So there is better attestation for this story than there is for the apotheosis and epiphany of the Romulan legend. She then continues with the difference in the quality and amount of evidence that is included within the Lucan account of the resurrection of Jesus Christ.

On the theme of the good evidence supporting the Lucan resurrection account, Prince (2012:30) writes:

> Luke recognizes and responds to the incredulous and wondering nature of his readers, ancient and modern, and composes a narrative of Jesus' resurrection that works at many levels. The multiple appearances of Jesus, as well as the appearance of two angelic figures, provide the opportunity for a growing number of witnesses to testify to the facts of Jesus' resurrection. His corpse is not in its tomb, he has been seen alive, his identity has been established, and his presence proven to be more than that of a spirit. And the significance of these facts has been established through the more reliable ancient witness of scripture. The accumulating testimony has led Jesus' disciples to certainty in Jesus' resurrection.

Prince draws a contrast between the strength of the evidence for the Romulan legend and the Lucan resurrection account.

---

[102] Phlegon of Tralles, *Book of Marvels*. For more information on this ancient text see William Hansen, Phlegon of Tralles Book of Marvels (Exeter, England: University of Exeter, 1996).

3.4.4 Cross-examination: Resurrection of Jesus Christ coming from Zalmoxis

In regard to Zalmoxis and his occultation/return to the Getae, Dan Dana (1999/2000: 286-88) offers an apologetic argument from the perspective of the early church leader, Origen. Dana shows in his essay that the opinion of the early Christians towards Zalmoxis was mostly favorable because of his beginnings as a slave and because of his asceticism. However, Origen attacked the idea that the resurrection of Jesus Christ somehow issued as a result of Christian borrowing from the cult of Zalmoxis. Origen was countering a heated polemic against the resurrection of Jesus Christ from Celsus, a Greek writer. Regarding the perspective of Celsus on the resurrection of Jesus Christ, Dana (1990/2000:286-88) writes:

> Celsus compares Jesus with gods or heroes known as owners of oracles: 'After this he [Celsus] thinks that because we worship the man who was arrested and died, we behave like the Getae who reverence Zalmoxis'...Here Celsus recalled all those heroes or remarkable figures [to include Zalmoxis] known for their attempts to win over death (but only mythical accounts for Celsus) for compromising the similar attempt of Jesus. But for Origen, on the one hand, the reality of suffering and the bodily death, on the other Easter experiences of the disciples, are doubtless: 'Jesus was crucified before all the Jews and in the eyes of all the people was down from the cross' and hid not like heroes of the legends for reappearing then unexpectedly.

3.4.5 Cross-examination: Christian baptism coming from pagan religions

Regarding Carrier's claim that Christian baptism was derived from pagan baptismal rites (in support of his claim regarding pagan resurrections and Christian resurrection) (3.2.2), Hans Schoeps responds to this claim. Writing decades before Carrier reasserts this contention, Schoeps (1961:61) posits:

> Paul found, rooted in the primitive church, along with the thought of the new covenant, the idea of baptism as a rite of initiation...., I feel that it is impossible to decide whether the transformation of baptism on the lines of Hellenistic cult mysteries, into a real dying together with Christ (Rom. 6:3) was due to the creative thought of Paul or whether it was only an adoption of a custom already practiced in Hellenistic communities (Bultmann).

In addition to the skepticism of Schoeps, Everett Ferguson (2003:298) also has serious objections to the view offered by Carrier. Regarding Christian baptism and a possible parallel with the pagan initiatory rites, Ferguson offers that there are no actual similarities between Christian baptism and these rites involving water. In the mystery cults, the water was applied as a "preliminary purification" and not as an initiatory rite in itself. The way in which the two operated is totally different. Whereas the benefit of the pagan ritual was effectual by the performing of it (*ex opera operato*), the benefit of Christian baptism was a gift given, by grace, from God to the recipient. Even though Ferguson recognized that some Christians were stumbling as a result of influence from the mysteries (1 Corinthians 10), he denies that the church itself had succumbed to its influences. Additionally, another distinction that Ferguson makes is that Christian baptism was for all converts. In contrast to Christian baptism, the mystery cult rites of purification were only for the inner circle of followers.

In addition to Schoeps and Ferguson, A.D. Nock (1938:76-77) offers his perspective on Christian baptism as well as the Eucharist in relation to the mystery religions that were functioning during the time of the ministry of Paul, the Apostle. He affirms that Paul and the believers were exposed to these pagan belief systems and Nock gives evidence of this from Paul's interactions with some of the Christian communities. Nock (1938:77) further offers:

> Since however, Jewish eschatological presuppositions were certainly the starting-point of Paul's Christianity, and since his theology and sacramentalism can be explained in terms of them, we are bound to prefer that explanation. The differences between Pauline and Hellenistic sacramentalism as a substantial entity in the thought of the time is not warranted by the existing evidence...In any case, Paul's unconscious presuppositions and instincts remained Jewish.

In his exposition on baptism, Carrier Cites the *Metamorphoses* (or The Golden Asse) of Apulieus where in this fictional story, he, Lucius, is turned into an ass. However, he regains his status as a man again and is led through an initiation into the cult of Isis (3.2.1). According to Carrier, the main character, Lucius, is baptized and this is a symbolic death and resurrection for him. Carrier uses this account as evidence for his contention that the Christian resurrection account is a myth that was fabricated with the assistance of pre-existing mythical religious cults. In addition to this statement, Carrier (2013:Ch. 2) also discusses a "pre-Christian" papyrus fragment that he also avers has evidence of baptism preceding that of the early Christians.

However, in the passage Carrier refers to (*The Metamorphoses*) regarding the aforementioned initiation of Lucius, the passage reveals that the ritual of purification by washing and sprinkling was performed ten days before the actual initiation itself. From reading the passage, it is clear that the ritual purification is separate from the actual secret initiation that Lucius only tells us very little about. Speaking of the priest who goes by the name of Mythra, Lucius gives a short description of the purification ritual: "Then he [Mythra the priest] brought me to the next basin accompanied with all the religious sort, and demanding pardon of the goddesse, washed me and purified my body, according to the custome [sic]" (Apulieus, 2014:Ch. 48).

In addition to this purification bath, Lucius also informs that there will be a ten-day period of prayer and fasting before the beginning of the actual initiation. As the narrative of the story continues, Lucius only partly describes the actual initiation itself because it is a secret initiation. However, even though he does not describe the initiation itself, he describes his experiences of the gods who are "both celestiall and infernall [sic]" whom he worshipped. He also describes his astral journey where he approached the gates of hell and also observed the sun to shine at midnight. After the initiation ceremony had finished, then he was dressed elaborately as the celebrant of a feast where the other celebrants marveled at his appearance (Apulieus, 2014:Ch. 48).

In examining this passage that Carrier relies upon, it is also noted again that Lucius, the fictional character, states that the initiation itself is secret and that the bath experienced by Lucius was merely a purification rite performed before the actual initiation itself. By virtue of the initiation being secret, there is no knowledge of what rites were performed. Additionally, Carrier refers to a pre-Christian papyrus that allegedly describes a pagan baptism prior to the establishment of baptism in the early Christian church (3.2.1). Carrier gleaned this information from a text entitled, *Corresponding Sense: Paul, Dialectic, & Gadamer* by B.W.R. Pearson.

In this text, Pearson (2001:326-329) refers to a Papyrus text written in 152 BCE from Apollonius, an official at the Serapeum in Memphis to Ptolemaeus and is regarding the activities of the latter where the former Apollonius is venting his anger over some unknown circumstance. Pearson states that there is controversy among scholars over what the text says and he writes, "Depending on the way this papyrus is restored and translated, it may indicate that not only baptism *existed* in the Isis Serapis cult (at least in Egypt), but that the link between death and life that we have seen in Apulieus was also made at a much earlier date" (Pearson, 2001:325). In the first part of the sentence, Pearson has scant information to make his conclusion. He has two variables in his statement. "Depending on the way this papyrus is restored and translated" and that "it may indicate" are instructive as to the strength of the information that he provides as evidence. This will be examined further in section 3.9.1. Also, in similarity to Carrier, Pearson assumes that there was a baptism during the initiation of Lucius when, in fact, Lucius does not say this was the case. Again, the only possible reference to baptism in the *Metamorphoses* is the purification bath that has already been mentioned, but again, this ritual is not part of the actual initiation itself and it is not known what rites were performed in this secret initiation.

3.4.6 Cross-examination: Carrier's thesis based upon a logical fallacy

In supporting his thesis that Jesus Christ was not a historical person, Carrier makes causal correlations between pre-existing pagan myths and the resurrection of Jesus Christ to show that the resurrection of Jesus Christ was developed from these pre-exiting pagan myths. Does Carrier make this correlation based upon facts or proof or does he base his thesis on supposed correlations between the two by virtue of one preceding the other in time? A brief survey of college professors explaining the related logical fallacies of false cause and *post hoc ergo propter hoc* is included below.

Bradley Dowden (internet Encyclopedia of Philosophy) discusses various logical fallacies in a web page outlining these fallacies. In one section of the page, Dowden discusses *post hoc (post hoc ergo propter hoc)* fallacies. In this sort of logical fallacy, that is a form of a false cause fallacy, the *post hoc* fallacy supposes that an event A that occurred in time before event B, is a cause for event B. Dowden further avers that correlations are often good evidence for a causal nexus. However, the fallacy occurs when these correlations are hastily drawn without the proper investigation to ensure the causal connection. Dowden (Dowden: Internet Encyclopedia of Philosophy) then provides an example of the *post hoc* fallacy:

> I ate in the Ethiopian restaurant three days ago and now I've just gotten food poisoning. The only other time I've eaten in an Ethiopian restaurant I also got food poisoning, but that time I got sick a week later. My eating in those kinds of restaurant is causing my food poisoning.

Objection Two: The Gospel Accounts of the Resurrection of Jesus ... 185

It is known that the effects of food poisoning occur shortly after the food is consumed. In this example of a fallacy, it would be important to eliminate other causes before zeroing in on this one cause.

Also writing on "false cause" informal fallacies, Rick Grush (Lecture 14: False cause) characterizes this sort of fallacy. It is when a conclusion is made that A is the cause of B when the only proof that has been offered is that there is a correlation amongst A and B. Grush furnishes two examples of the false cause fallacy:

> During the past two months, every time the cheerleaders have worn blue ribbons, the basketball team has won. So if we want to keep winning, they had better continue to wear blue ribbons...Every time Jerome Bettis carries more than 30 times, the Steelers win. So all Cowher has to do to keep the Steelers winning is to give the ball to Bettis at least 30 times a game.

This fallacy is committed when one concludes that A causes B, when in fact all that has been shown is a correlation between A and B. In these examples given by Grush, a previous activity (the wearing of blue ribbons and the amount of times Bettis carried the football) was thought to have brought about a successful outcome (the basketball team wins and the Steelers win the football game). In relation to Carrier's thesis, to conclude that Christianity assumed the practices of other religions that antedated it by offering supposed correlations between the two is based on logically fallacious reasoning.

In addition to Grush and Dowden, Bruce Murray (Murray, Fallacies in arguments or how arguments go wrong) also writes on the topic of logical fallacies and gives further information about the false cause fallacy. In elucidating upon the false cause fallacy, Murray writes:

> False-cause arguments make unjustified claims about the causes of behavior. This happens frequently in evaluating empirical claims in the social sciences. With the best of intentions, people provide correlational evidence to argue about a cause. A correlation simply means that two kinds of behavior are found together. For example, we know children who voluntarily read a lot score better on reading achievement tests. Can we conclude that we can raise reading scores by getting children to read more? The correlation between voluntary reading and achievement is not enough to support this claim. It may be that children read more because they are good readers.

Murray's comments are probative to this discussion, as merely correlations between two different sets of data do not prove that one is the cause of the other. Therefore, supposed similarities between pagan religions and Christianity do not prove that the practices of one group influenced the other.

In Carrier's claims regarding the connections between pre-existing pagan gods and Jesus Christ, he asserts as proof of this connection that they all antedated Christianity:

> The similarity remains: the death and resurrection of Osiris was clearly believed to make it possible for those ritually sharing in that death and resurrection through baptism to have their sins remitted. That belief predates Christianity (Carrier, 2009: ch. 2).
>
> The dying-and-rising son (sometimes daughter) of god 'mytheme' originated in the ancient Near East over a thousand years before Christianity…The earliest documented examples are the cult of Inanna and Dumuzi (also known as Ishtar and Tammuz) (Carrier, 2014:247).
>
> Another God who submitted to being murdered in order to triumph was the well-revered Roman national deity Romulus, whose death and resurrection was celebrated in annual public ceremonies in Rome since before Christian times (Carrier, 2009, ch. 1).
>
> We must be consistent: claiming the disciples stole the body is as much a proof of a resurrection-belief as claiming Zalmoxis pretended to be dead. Again, none of this entails or implies that Christians "borrowed" from Zalmoxis cult the idea of an incarnated, dying, and rising god promising eternal life through a sacred act of drinking at a meal. But it does entail that those elements of Christianity were not new, but had been elements of other cults long before (and possibly still in their day) (Carrier, 2009:ch. 3).

In comparing the aforementioned claims of Carrier to the above referenced literature on false cause and *post hoc ergo propter hoc* fallacies, it appears that Carrier does use fallacious logic (false cause and *post hoc ergo propter hoc*) when he makes causal connections between pagan myths and Christianity. Instead of mentioning the fact that the pagan cults antedate Christianity and then mentioning certain supposed correlations, Carrier should offer specific and relevant evidence to prove the "pass down" from these mythical cults to Christianity.

3.5 Evidence against Carrier's claim: New Testament scriptures reference Jewish soteriology and eschatology

In addressing the contentions of Carrier, it is a worthwhile endeavor to conduct a brief survey of select New Testament texts to investigate whether the New Testament references pre-existing mystery cults or whether they indicate a different starting point. In the following examination of scriptures regarding Jesus Christ and his work of salvation for humanity, it is observed that the frame of reference for Christian soteriology comes from the Old Testament with its substitutionary soteriology centering on the shedding of the blood of animals sacrifice as a propitiation and atonement for sin. Jesus Christ is observed to be the substitutionary sacrifice to atone for the sins of humanity.

In the New Testament scriptures, Jesus is referred to by various authors of the New Testament Scriptures as the "Lamb of God." In Acts 8:32, 33, the disciple Philip encountered an Ethiopian eunuch who was in his chariot reading from the Book of Isaiah (53:7, 8):

> He was led like a sheep to the slaughter, and as a lamb before its shearer is silent, so he did not open his mouth. In his humiliation he was deprived of justice. Who can speak of his descendants? For his life was taken from the earth (NIV).

In his exposition on this scripture, John Gill (2003:35) includes a statement of "Jewish doctors" that "the morning daily sacrifice made atonement for the iniquities done in the night; and the evening sacrifice, made atonement for the iniquities that were by day." In referencing these verses in Acts, Gill posits that these sacrifices were typical of Jesus Christ. He further evinces that the sacrificial lambs of the Jews were without any noticeable defects and were sacrificed for the children of Israel only. Even so, Jesus Christ is the mystical sacrifice performed once and for all for the "Israel of God which now includes both Jews and Gentiles." This once and for all sacrifice of Jesus Christ mentioned here in the New Testament, has its origins in the sacrificial system of the Jewish faith.

In addition to the comparison of Jesus as the Lamb of God coming from the Jewish sacrificial system, Darrell Bock (2012:187) notices that there are references in Acts that link the resurrection of Jesus Christ to Old Testament Scriptures. In Acts 2:25-31, Peter refers to Psalm 16:8-11, where David proclaims that God will not let his "faithful one see decay (v. 9)" and that there are "eternal pleasures" at the right hand of God (v. 11). In this passage from Acts, Peter makes a correlation between these Old Testament Scriptures as they refer to the death and resurrection of Jesus Christ, that God had raised him from death to life, and that Peter was a witness to this fact (vv. 25-31). Additionally in Acts (13:22-23), Bock (2012, 187:193) also observes the proclamation of the Messiah coming through the lineage of David and that this promise of a Messiah comes through the resurrection of Jesus Christ. Further mention of the resurrection in Acts comes from Acts 15:16 which refers to the assurance that God will rebuild the "Davidic booth" as mentioned in Amos 9:11. This analogy points to the resurrection of Jesus as the starting point for the restoration of Israel by God.

Moreover, another way in which the resurrection of Jesus Christ is observed is in the usage of the title "Son of Man" which is prevalent throughout the Synoptic Gospels. The title Son of Man refers to the eschatological Messiah who is described in Dan. 7:13-14, and who "received authority from the ancient of Days over the kingdom" (Bock, 2012:193). Bock also observes that the Son of Man, who rides on the clouds thereby proving his deity, is mentioned in the Old Testament as well (Exod. 14:20; 34:5; Num. 10:34; Ps. 104:3; Isa. 19:1). In that Jesus referred to himself as the eschatological Son of Man, the implication is that he would arise from the dead in order to fulfill this future role.

In continuing on the theme of Jesus as the Lamb of God within the New Testament Scriptures, T.R. Schreiner (2003:86) describes how Peter clearly instructs that the redemption of the believer with the blood of Jesus Christ "hearkens back to the sacrificial cultus in the Old Testament, where blood was necessary for atonement. The Old Testament imagery continues when Christ is compared to a lamb "without blemish or defect." Schreiner also observes that "early Christians saw Passover, the suffering Servant, and the sacrificial system as fulfilled in the sacrifice of Christ as God's sinless lamb" (Schreiner, 2003:87).

Another perspective on Jesus as the Lamb of God observed in the New Testament comes from Craig Keener (2000:186-187). He observes the prominent use of the title "lamb of God" in John's Book of Revelation. He states that John is sad because there is no one who could open the scroll and the contents therein. An onlooker, seeing John weeping, tells him not to weep anymore because there is someone who can open the scrolls and the man states the titles of this person as "the Lion of the tribe of Judah, the Root of David and that he has triumphed (Rev. 5:1-6)."

In this imagery, Keener (2000:186-187) observes the Jewish influence on this passage in that "The image of the Lion from Judah comes from Genesis 49:9-10, which Jewish people usually applied to the Davidic Messiah (4 Ezra 12:31-32). Also, The 'Root of David' is the Messiah who comes from the truncated house of David (Isa 11:1) anointed by the Spirit (11:2) and appointed to rule all nations with peace (11:3-10; Jer. 23:5; 33:15)." Moreover, Keener observes the paradox of the Christian faith where Jesus conquered by his death and not by force. In this formulation, the conquering lion is actually a lamb. Keener further reflects that the Jewish texts use the imagery of a lion for courage and power but also more specifically for the Messiah.

Regarding John's representation of the victorious Jesus as the sacrificial lamb, Keener (2000:186-187) posits:

> Most significantly, this for John, this is a *slaughtered* lamb, a sacrificial lamb. Plagues will fall on the disobedient world (Rev. 6-16), but just as the blood of the Passover lamb delivered Israel from the climactic plague (Ex. 12:23), so Jesus' blood will protect his people during God's judgments on humanity (Rev. 7:3). Jesus' victory is like a new exodus (5:9-10; 15:3), and Jesus himself is the new Lamb (1 Cor. 5:7).

Also observing the Old Testament imagery of the Paschal Lamb in Jesus Christ, Dorothy Lee (2011:28) writes about John's usage of the term "Lamb of God" as well as allusions in his Gospel to the Passover supper. To this end, she avers:

The Passover allusions are preceded in the opening chapter of the Gospel by the momentous declaration of John The Baptist: "Behold the Lamb of God" (1:29,35). In the Old Testament, the use of "lamb" mostly occurs in relation to Passover, which is generally regarded as the primary referent of the Johannine metaphor... Alongside paschal imagery, the image of the Suffering Servant of Isaiah 53:7 is a likely dimension of the symbolism, with its overtones of suffering on behalf of Israel, an association shared with the paschal lamb (Lee, 2011:15-16).... Incarnation, crucifixion, sacrifice, Eucharist: these unfold as the true significance of Passover and cult, the symbolic framework in which the new emerges from the chrysalis of the old.

Even as Lee offers the Paschal lamb imagery of Jesus in John's Gospel, she also expresses renewed life coming from seeming death in the use of the phrase "new emerges from the chrysalis of the old" which points to resurrection.

Regarding the Christian church as the New Israel, D.A. Hagner (2002:110) observes this as one of the main themes of the Book of Hebrews. He further instructs that Judaism finds its fulfillment in Christianity and brings the former "realities" to their conclusions. Not that Christianity no longer recognizes the old. Rather, Christianity takes the old up and brings the old to its "divinely intended purpose" and is "the rightful perpetuation of the old."

In addition to fulfilling the Jewish covenant of God with the Jews, Hagner (2002:114) mentions the role of Jesus as a high priest (an allusion to Ps. 110:4) "who has ascended to heaven, where he sits at the right hand of God (an allusion to Ps 110:1; 1:3, 13; 4:14), and there "serves in the sanctuary the true tabernacle set up by the Lord, not by man (v. 2). Further elucidating this priestly role of Jesus, Hagner offers that the word "serves" refers to someone who is performing in the role of a priest. On Jesus as our high priest, Hagner (2002:110) submits:

> In view here is not an actual sanctuary in heaven in which Jesus offers his own blood (cf. 9:11-12). The language is not to be taken literally. Rather, it is a way of speaking that affirms the ultimate importance, efficacy, and finality of Christ's sacrificial death on the cross as the fulfillment of the sacrifices of the tabernacle/temple ... Mercy and forgiveness depend finally on the death of Jesus as the one effectual sacrifice toward which all previous sacrifices pointed.

Another allusion to the Old Testament concerning the death and resurrection of Jesus Christ is the incident where Moses raised the bronze serpent in the wilderness in order to stop the plague of the venomous snakes that had infested Israel (mentioned in Numbers 21:8). Referring to the use of the account of Moses lifting up a bronze serpent to heal those who had been bitten by the venomous snakes that is included in John 3:14, John Gill (2003:88) states:

> Moreover, this serpent Moses made, and was ordered to make, was but *one*, though the fiery serpents, with which the Israelites were bitten, were many; so there is but one Mediator between God and man; but one Savior, in whom alone is salvation, and in no other, even Jesus Christ. To which may be added the *situation* in which this serpent was put; it was set by Moses on a pole; it was lifted up on high, that every one in the camp of Israel might see it; and may point out the ascension of Christ into heaven, and His exaltation at God's right hand there, as some think.

In addition to the Old Testament account of Moses and the Serpent in the Wilderness, J.M. Boice (2001:220-221) observes the Old Testament narrative of Jonah and the whale in the New Testament related to Jesus, his death, and resurrection (Matt. 12:38-41). He states that eventually Jesus did give them the sign of Jonah, not only to those who he was speaking to but also to the entire world when he died and rose again. He further opines:

> No one can read that [Matt. 12:38-41] today without understanding at once that it is a prophecy of Jesus' resurrection. It is an excellent preaching text for Easter Sunday... The Pharisees had asked Jesus for a sign, and Jesus had

given one, though it was a sign that would not be seen by them until the close of his earthly ministry and his return to heaven.

In regard to the Old Testament soteriology of the sacrifice of animals and their blood as propitiation for the sins of the Israelites, M.J. Erickson (2007:824) observes that Jesus had a "powerful conviction that his life and death constituted a fulfillment of Old Testament prophecies." Erickson mentions that Jesus clearly spoke of his own life and death as a fulfillment of Old Testament Scriptures to include Isaiah 53. Erickson mentions that this belief can be observed in Luke 22:37 where Jesus quotes this chapter (53:12). In so doing, he identifies himself as the "suffering servant" mentioned in Isaiah. Furthermore, Erickson sees further identification of this theme in Mark 8:31.

In reference to the last supper and its connection to the Old Testament and Jewish tradition, R.H. Stein (1992:541) observes that the last supper recalls the Passover meal as a "type of the messianic banquet." On this note, Stein offers, "Even as among their Jewish contemporaries, the Passover awakened hopes and longings for the coming of the messianic banquet, so even more should the Lord's Supper cause Luke's readers to look not only backward to their Lord's death but forward to his return."

Yet another Old Testament concept displayed within the New Testament is the concept of covenant relationship formed between God and Israel. To that end, H.A. Kent (1972:43) discusses this Jewish concept of covenant as observed in Acts 3:25. Kent shares that this covenantal relationship began with Abraham and the other forefathers. Also, the prophets predicted the coming of the Messiah. In this regard, Kent continues:

> In their scripture was the promise made to Abraham that his seed would bring blessing to all the earth, and Peter declares that Jesus, the descendant of Abraham, was the particular Seed in whom the promised blessing would come. It was to the Jewish nation first of all, and specifically the generation by these hearers at Solomon's porch that God had raised up Jesus.

In addition to Kent, R.A. Rayburn (2007:301) also observes the presence of the Old Testament covenant in the New Testament. Rayburn offers the new covenant that Jeremiah writes about coming in the future (Jer. 31:31-34). He also observes this new covenant as having "strong affinities with other prophetic texts" that relate the victory of God as well as the consummation of God's kingdom in this world.[103] Further delineating his

---

[103] (cf. Isa. 11:6-9; 54:111-15; 59:20-21; Jer. 32-36-41; 33:14-26; Ezek. 16:59-63). The term is found six times in the New Testament (1 Cor. 11:25; 2 Cor. 3:6; Heb. 8:8;

views regarding the covenants in the Old Testament and the New Testament, Rayburn continues that instead of looking at the covenants in both the Old Testament and the New Testament separately, one should look at them together where the new covenant is inclusive of all believers in Jesus Christ, not just believers from Israel.

In addition to the aforementioned authors, J.R. Edwards observes a linkage between the Resurrection of Jesus Christ and the Old Testament. Edwards (2002:368-369) writes:

> To evince that resurrection from the dead is taught or at least assumed in the Torah, Jesus quotes Exod. 3:6, which falls within the Torah accepted by the Sadducees...Jesus, who accepted as axiomatic that the patriarchs and prophets were still alive (Matt. 8:11; Luke 16:22-25; John 8:56), argues that the promises of God are made not to the dead but to the living.

Also observing the resurrection of Jesus Christ from the dead in the Old Testament account of the sacrifice of Isaac, D.A. Hagner observes a nexus between Hebrews 11 and the offering of Isaac by Abraham as observed in Genesis 22:1-14. Hagner (2002:150) observes that when Abraham "received him [Isaac] back," it may have been a "deliberate attempt to parallel Isaac's deliverance with the resurrection of Jesus Christ...Thus figuratively speaking, Isaac, like Christ, was received back from the dead."

In his commentary on Acts, K.O. Gangel (1998:46) offers Peter's testimony about how the beggar at the temple gate in Jerusalem was healed. As the onlookers gasped with astonishment at the healing of this man, Peter chides them about their reaction. In his sermonette following this healing, Peter succinctly connects the forefathers of the Jewish faith to Jesus Christ, his death, and resurrection. In his comments on these verses, Gangel (1998:46-47) posits:

> The gospel rests in history so Peter began there. As a Jew speaking to Jews, he invoked the revered names of Abraham, Isaac, and Jacob. He had no interest in abstract theology, nor did he bother (with this audience) to develop an elaborate introduction, as we shall see later with both Stephen and Paul...We dare not miss the last five words of the verse-we are witnesses of this...we will find these early preachers moving as rapidly as they can to the fact and meaning of the resurrection.

9:15; 12:24; and the disputed reading in Luke 22:20) though the idea of a new covenant is present elsewhere (cf. Rom. 11:27; Gal. 4:21-31).

In observing both the motif of the resurrection and the Old Testament integrated into the writings of Luke, Joshua Jipp (2010:270-271), concentrates on the psalms and observes parallels with the "Suffering anointed one." Jipp recognizes in Luke's writings the usage of the psalms. In particular, when discussing this confluence of sources on the resurrection, he mentions the perspective of J. Ross Wagner who posits that in Acts 4:11, Luke "explicitly" connects Psalm 118 with the death and resurrection of Jesus.[104] Also, observing this nexus in Acts 4:11, Jipp further comments, "What Jesus had declared cryptically in Luke 20:17 is herein proclaimed by the apostles with clarity and boldness." So, the resurrected Jesus Christ, as he spoke to the travelers on the Emmaus Road about the rejection of the Messiah and his subsequent entrance into glory, spoke from Psalm 118 and Peter references Psalm 118 in Acts 4:11 to describe the risen Jesus Christ in his defense before the Jewish officials. Jipp further notes, "At the core of Acts 4 (and Psalm 118) is the motif of reversal. As interpreted by the early Christians, Ps. 118:22 not only portrays the death of the Messiah but also looks forward to his resurrection."

Another Gospel passage that is identified with the Old Testament and also the resurrection of Jesus Christ is located in Mark's Gospel. In Mark 12:18-27, James Mays (2006:45) sees eternal life for humanity as expressed through the risen Jesus Christ. In this passage, the Sadducees are questioning Jesus in attempts to discredit him. They bring up the issue of levirate marriage to draw Jesus out regarding his opinion on the resurrection of the dead. In response to their questioning, Jesus brings out that in God's interaction with Moses in the burning bush, God states that He "is" the God of Abraham, Isaac, and Jacob. Therefore, the "righteous dead" still exist. In his perspective on this passage, Mays (2006:45) writes:

> Jesus use of God's word of self-identification to Moses as a witness to the resurrection shows that a text of Holy Scripture may be read in more than one way. The cited passage does not name the resurrection as its subject. But if the interpreter knows that God of the Fathers is the God who raises the dead, then the plain language of the text can be understood in a fuller sense. Resurrection is not read into the text, but the text is read in the light of the resurrection. Reading texts in their typical fuller sense practices a hermeneutic of the unity of Holy Scripture. Such a hermeneutic is a feature of the content and composition of the books of the New Testament and many of the Old.

---

[104] On this topic, see Sanders, J.A. A hermeneutic fabric: Psalm 118 in Luke's entrance narrative (In Luke and Scripture: the function of sacred tradition in Luke-Acts Evans, C.A. and Sanders J. A. eds.; Minneapolis: Fortress, 1993) 140-53.

3.6 Evidence against Carrier's claim: Paul's emphasis on the resurrection comes from the Old Testament

In addition to the literature of scholars regarding the motif of the resurrection in the New Testament being present in the Old Testament, it is also probative to conduct a survey of scholarly literature in order to determine whether there is any link between the Old Testament and Paul's resurrection theology as Carrier has made parallels between Paul's "version" of the resurrection of Jesus Christ and the pagan mysteries (3.2.1). Specifically, Carrier points to the Pauline baptismal formulation as well as the Pauline view of resurrection as being similar with what is observed in the pagan mystery cults. In particular, Carrier notices a parallel between the resurrection of Osiris and the resurrection of Jesus as relayed by Paul in his writings.

Showing that Paul is using the Old Testament as a referent to his discussion of the renewal of the covenant in Romans chapters nine and ten, N.T. Wright (2012:327) describes Pauls' perspective on this topic. Wright observes that Paul hearkens back to Deuteronomy 30 in its proclamation of the covenant renewal that will be "Near you, on your lips and in your heart (Deut. 30:14)." Wright further discusses that for Paul, his main emphasis regarding the law is that it reveals the Messiah. On this topic, he further offers:

> It is Christos who, in his resurrection and lordship, is 'on your lips and in your heart'. So far from this being (as many have imagined) an odd, awkward Midrash which makes an obscure text dance on its hind legs to an unfamiliar Pauline tune, it is, I suggest, exactly the right text at the right moment in the narrative of Romans 9 and 10. Paul has, in a measure, retold the Pentateuchal story, from Genesis to Deuteronomy, via Exodus and with a hint of Leviticus. The quotation from Joel 2.32 (3.5 LXX) in verse 13 rounds off the point, indicating that he is indeed thinking of the ultimate, eschatological renewal of the covenant.

Further explaining this relationship of the Old Testament in the Pauline covenant renewal in Romans, Wright (2012:327-328) further explains that quotations from the Old Testament (Romans 10: 8,9) that Paul uses in his covenant renewal material in Romans should be taken not only with consideration of its original larger context, but also of:

> ...the still larger context which is the implicit narrative presupposed by many second-Temple Jews; and then of the Pauline context, which is never simply an exposition of 'doctrine' or 'ethics,' supported by detached proof-texts, but always, rather, a fresh telling of Israel's story in the light of its shocking messianic fulfillment and the covenant renewal brought about by the Spirit.

In his discussion of 1 Corinthians 15:20-28, Wright (2003:334) also observes several Old Testament themes beneath the surface of this passage. Not only does Paul observe the Old Testament accounts of creation and the fall, but he also observes that Psalm 8 as expressly referenced in verse 27. Additionally, he observes that this verse is also associated with Psalm 110 as well as "Echoes of Daniel." Wright sees this use of these accounts not as just passing allusions to the Old Testament. Rather in these passages, Wright (2003:337-338) observes:

> The purpose is that in his renewed, resurrected human life he can be and do, for humankind and all creation, what neither humankind nor creation could do for themselves. That is the theology of the one true God, of humankind and of creation which, rooted at every point in the Old Testament, is reaffirmed in this treatment of the resurrection of those who belonged to the Messiah.

In addition to these observations, Wright (2003:372) also makes summary conclusions as he looks back at the theme of resurrection included in 1 and 2 Corinthians. He asserts that the origins of Paul's constellation of writings on the resurrection come from the Jewish perspective, not the pagan one. Moreover, Wright places Paul in the camp of the Jews of his day, and also with the Pharisees amongst others. Wright accedes Paul believed in the physical and bodily resurrection in the future of all those who truly believe in the one true God. Paul also averred that God would complete this task of resurrection by the power of the Holy Spirit that is already conducting preparations with those who belong to the Messiah.

In agreeing with Wright regarding the primacy of the Old Testament in Pauline theology, Christoph Stenschke affirms that the "gospel which Paul proclaims" cannot be understood apart from its Davidic origin. Speaking of Jesus Christ, Stenschke (2012:361) posits that the divine future ruler of the Gentiles comes from the "root of Jesse, the father of David (Rom. 15:12)." He further notices that David was mentioned in Romans 1:3 as well. With these references to the lineage of David as observed in the Old Testament, Stenschke (2012:361-362) further offers:

The references to David and Jesse serve as far more than a mere reference to Jewish tradition. The gospel which Paul proclaims cannot be understood apart from its Davidic origin. Rom. 1:3 and 15:12 form an important *inclusio* around the main corpus of the letter. Jesus as the son of David, is the one appointed to rule the peoples, not Rome.

Moreover, Stenschke offers the perspective of J.T. Harrison (cited by Stenschke, 2012:362) that God had appointed Paul to call the Gentiles "to obedience under the rule of the root of Jesse" and that in opposition to Roman rule, Paul declared:

> ...that Christ was the 'Son of God in power' by virtue of his resurrection and asserted that, as the eschatological Deliverer, he would return from the heavenly Zion to save national Israel (Rom. 1:1-6; 11:26f; 15:12; 16:25f). In all of this, the binding authority of the prophetic Scriptures [of Israel] regarding the Messianic hope is heavily underscored for his Roman auditors.

In reference to the Pauline perspective on the resurrection coming from the Jewish perspective, Markus Cromhout (2011:37) posits:

> For Paul, Jesus' life, death and resurrection was grounded in Israelite tradition (Gal 4:4; Rom 1:2-3, 15:8, 12; 1 Cor 5:7; 19:1-4). Paul specifically says that Jesus, the Messiah of Israel died for our sins/was buried/was raised "according to the scriptures" (1 Cor 5:3). Even his own calling as apostle (Gal 1:15-16 with Jer 1:5 LXX and Isa 49:1, 6 LXX) and the present life of the congregations (Gal 4:21-31) were interpreted from the vantage point of Israelite tradition. Viewed from this perspective we can say it made sense within the Israelite cycle of meaning.

Although Cromhout (2011:44) observes that Paul's resurrection theology is rooted in the Israelite cycle of meaning, he further observes that the resurrection of Jesus and its implications goes "beyond anything that is culturally specific." His experiences with the risen Jesus Christ transformed Paul's view of the resurrection that was rooted in the Jewish perspective on resurrection.

In discussing the resurrection in relation to Paul's perspective, W.D. Davies (1948:303) finds that Paul is totally pharisaic in his formulation of the resurrection that is contained in 1 Corinthians 15 where Paul discusses the matter in detail. This finding is of importance as there are those who would contend that this is a veiled reference to the god Osiris who was associated with the grain cycle of Egypt. Moreover, Davies asserts that the Pauline expression of a grain of corn falling into the ground and his accompanying exposition on the resurrection is fully in line with pharisaic doctrine on the resurrection. On this particular point, Davies (1948:305) offers:

> Making a comparison of this Pauline passage with rabbinical beliefs in the resurrection Rabbi Eliezer stated 'All the dead will arise at the resurrection of the dead, dressed in their shrouds. Know thou that this is the case. Come and see from (the analogy of) the one who plants (seed) in the earth. He plants naked (seeds) and they arise covered with many coverings; and the people who descend into the earth dressed (with their garments), will they not rise up dressed with their garments)?'(Pirke de Rabbi Eliezer, XXXIII, p. 245.).

Also focusing in on 1 Corinthians 15, Nicholas Lunn (2014:531) observes Jewish influence in Paul's writing on the resurrection. In verse 20, Lunn notes Paul's use of the phrase "first fruits" in relation to Jesus Christ and also in relation to those who have fallen asleep. Lunn observes that the priest that waved the sheaf of first fruits before the Lord was symbolic of the assurance that there would be a future harvest. Lunn believes this is why Paul refers to the First Fruits festival in the Old Testament. It is because the resurrection of Christ does the same thing for those who believe in his name. Jesus Christ assures that his children will "spring forth" again in resurrection.

In addition to the observation of the use of "first fruits" 1 Corinthians 15, Lunn (2014:533) also asserts that there is a nexus between 1 Corinthians 15 and the creation narrative:

> We also note that in this same chapter of 1 Corinthians 15 there is unmistakable evidence that in constructing his response to the resurrection issue Paul has been considering the Genesis creation narrative. In vv. 39–41 he lists the various elements created on Days 4–6 (Gen 1:14–27) in exact reverse order (men, animals, birds, fish, heavenly bodies). Since he definitely had these other days of creation in mind, it is extremely plausible that he was also contemplating Day 3 in the context of the same discussion... we find a typological reading of the third day of creation, as proposed, to be an eminently suitable figure of resurrection, especially of Christ's resurrection, which is the concern of Paul's statement "raised on the third day according to the Scriptures."

3.7 Evidence against Carrier's claim: Paul and idolatry

In noting Paul's stance on Idolatry in the New Testament, Jerry Hwang (2011:577-580) also observes a reference to Exodus 32:6 and its prohibition of Idol worship in 1 Corinthians 10:7. Before focusing on 32:6, Hwang first analyzes the incident of the worship of the golden calf in Exodus chapter thirty-two. After centering in on this chapter of Exodus and exploring the detail and the implications to Israel regarding the worship of the golden image of the calf, Hwang focuses on verse six and in particular the last portion of that verse which is quoted in 1 Corinthians 10:7.

In Hwang's (2011:580) opinion, this point in the narrative (v. 6) is where the disobedience of Israel is at its most flagrant and where obedience to God is at its very minimum. Hwang discusses how instead of Yahweh being the focus of worship in their offerings as was the case in Exodus chapter twenty-four, now the golden calf has taken the place of Yahweh as the recipient of Israel's ritual offerings. Moreover, the language that is utilized in Exodus chapter twenty-four refers to a ritual meal that is eaten on behalf of Yahweh as well. However, in Exodus thirty-two, this meal is again eaten by the Israelites save the object of veneration, Yahweh, has been replaced by the Egyptian idol. Hwang summarizes the rejection of Yahweh by Israel offering the perspective of Durham (cited by Hwang, 2011:581) who avers that "The celebrating of an obligating relationship in Exodus 24 becomes in Exodus 32 an orgy of the desertion of responsibility."

In his concluding remarks on this topic, Hwang (2011:587) observes that Paul utilizes Exodus 32:6 as a "subtle, and yet devastating and well-crafted argument against the carnality of the Corinthians." Moreover, Hwang shows a parallel between the Israelites and the Corinthians in that both felt no guilt as they feasted in an unrighteous manner, yet still pretended to live under God's covenant. In observing the teaching of Paul against any association with idolatry as noted by Hwang, it is odd for one to assert that Paul would engage in merging his theology on the resurrection of Jesus Christ with formulations of the resurrection from pagan cults.

E.I. Still (2004:37, 37fn), in offering his opinion on Paul's relationship to idolatry, concludes upon his reading of 1 Corinthians chapter ten that Paul is unequivocal in his charge to the Corinthian church to abstain from idolatry. He points out that Paul reminds the Corinthians of their covenantal bond with Jesus Christ (v. 16) and also adjures them not to take up the practice of idolatry with their pagan friends (v. 20). He further points out that impending judgment (v. 22) is mentioned after Paul's command to flee from idolatry (v. 14).

In his paper on the topic of eating food sacrificed to Idols as discussed in 1 Corinthians chapter eight, J. Fotopoulos (2002: 613fn, 618) writes that Paul is utilizing the experiences of the Israelites in their history with idol worship as an example for the Corinthians to take heed of. The Israelites, in similarity with the Corinthians, had received food sacrificed to idols, and had sinned by eating food polluted in the use of idol worship just as the Corinthians were doing. Further noting Paul's dialogue with an unknown interlocutor that Fotopoulos dubs as "the strong," Fotopoulos points out Paul's refutation of the position of "the strong." The position of this group is that eating food sacrificed to idols is permissible because the pagan gods they represent do not even exist in reality (v. 5). However, Paul's opinion is clear in a thematically related passage to 1 Corinthians chapter eight (1 Cor. 10:19-22) that these pagan gods are, in fact, demons. Therefore any consumption of food used in the worship of demons is in fact idolatry.

In an earlier Paper on the subject of Paul and Idol worship, Fotopoulos (2002:168) describes the fusion of the "Law-free gospel" with the "Christified Torah" as observed in 1 Corinthians 9:21 and Galatians 6:2:

> Thus, once Paul's Law-free gospel is understood properly, that is without the putative Pauline repudiation of every behavioral regulation of Torah as a simplistic *a priori* assumption of Paul's missionary teaching, proper interpretation of the apostle's position on idol-food consumption should not begin with the premise that "'All things are permissible.'" Rather, Paul's position on idol-food functions as a Christified Torah precept prohibiting sacrificial food consumption as idolatry because of the exclusive Christian devotion due to God the Father, the Lord Jesus Christ, and the Spirit.

In the observations of Fotopoulos on 1 Corinthians chapter eight is observed not only Paul's reliance upon the Jewish religious perspective, but also demonstrating a perspective that is not amenable to the syncretism of Christianity with surrounding pagan cults. Therefore, in these observations we observe in Paul not only a strong association with the traditional Jewish teachings against idolatry but also unwillingness to assimilate pagan customs into Christianity.

3.8 Evidence against Carrier's claim: The Old Testament and idolatry

In his article on Idolatry, P.C. Craigie (2007:588-589) discusses idolatry and the prohibitions within the Bible condemning this practice. Craigie points out that the Hebrew religion as observed in the Old Testament tolerated no practice of idolatry within the Hebrew religion for the most part. Craigie further discusses there were two types of idolatry that were prohibited by the Ten Commandments: 1) The prohibition of worshipping another god that was not Yahweh (Exodus 20:3) 2) The worship of Yahweh in the form of an image (Exodus 20:4-6). Craigie sees the second of these prohibitions as integral to Hebrew dogma. Regarding this worship of God in an image, Craigie points out that the person who worships in this way relegates God to being merely another manifestation of the physical world that nullifies the transcendent nature of Jehovah. Craigie further observes that in spite of the Old Testament prohibitions against the worship of idols, this worship was a problem that remained with the Jews throughout their history. Craigie observes that the denunciation of idols is a common theme in both the pentateuchal and prophetical books of the Old Testament.

Regarding idolatry in the Jewish faith, Millard Erickson (2007:348-349) observes that since ancient times, the Hebrew religion has been strictly monotheistic even as the Jewish faith is observed to be today. Erickson then refers to Exodus 20:2-3 where the commandment to "have no other gods before me" is located. In the history of the nation of Israel from the early days of the patriarchs, God showed his faithfulness and his "unique reality." Because of this, He was entitled to Israel's unwavering devotion. Moreover, Erickson points out that polytheism is rejected outright by the Jewish faith and this exclusion of the worship of any other god is observed throughout the pages of the Old Testament. Moreover, Erickson submits that the conclusion drawn throughout the Old Testament is that there is no other deity save the God of Abraham, Isaac, and Jacob (Exod. 3:13-15). Further scriptural support for the rejection of Idolatry comes from the *Shema* (Deut. 6:4) that emphasizes "the unique, unmatched deity of Jehovah" (Erickson, 2007:349). In addition to the unity or oneness of God as observed in the *Shema* is the commandment to love Jehovah "with all your heart, mind, and soul (v. 5)."

On the prohibitions against idolatry, Erickson (2007:349) writes:

> In positive terms God's people are told: 'Fear the Lord your God, serve him only and take your oaths in his name (Deut. 6:13).' In negative terms they

are told: 'Do not follow other gods, the gods of the peoples around you (v. 14).' God is clearly one God precluding the possibility that any of the gods of the surrounding peoples could be real and thereby worthy of service and devotion (Exod. 15:11; Zech. 14:9).

In addition to the prohibition against idol worship in the Old Testament, Erickson (2007:349) also notices this same prohibition in the pages of the New Testament as well. Specifically, he observes that Paul emphasizes this prohibition in 1 Corinthians 8:4, 6. In these verses and in similarity to the Mosaic Law, Paul brings out the oneness of God as the main reason to abstain from idol worship. In further offering evidence for the belief of Paul in the unity or oneness of God, Erickson also offers 1 Timothy 2:5-6 where Paul refers to Jesus Christ as the one mediator between God and man.

Adding to the perspective of Erickson on idol worship, Yitzhaq Feder (2013:258) offers his analysis on idolatry as observed in several key passages of the Old Testament. In his comments on Exodus 20:2-5, Feder sees the mention of "foreign gods" and "idols" as reducing down to the worship of other gods. According to Feder, the major point that needs to be made is that whether it is the worship of idols or the worship of foreign gods, only the worship of Yahweh is acceptable. Feder further speaks of this passage as supporting not only being separate from other people groups but also not worshipping any other god other than Yahweh. Therefore, just as Yahweh is an "anti-god" that is separate from other gods, the Israelites are to be separate from other peoples.

Feder (2013:264) also notes in Exodus chapter twenty the prohibition of making gold/silver idols is contrasted with the positive command for sacrifices to Yahweh to be conducted only on earthen altars. In this rejection of opulence, Feder sees that Yahweh is not concerned with worldly opulence as his dwelling is truly in heaven. In addition to Exodus 20, Feder (2013:261) also observes these earlier prohibitions against idol worship present in Hosea's invective against idol worship (4:4-19; 5:1-15; 11:2b; 13:1-4) to include the account of Hosea's unfaithful wife.

In discussing Deuteronomy chapter four, Feder (2013:267) observes the central theme as Israel's special relationship with God as that which produced the prohibition against idol worship. Moreover, he sees within the prohibitions of the Decalogue a depiction of idolatry as "a foreign practice that constitutes infidelity to Yhwh [sic], such that the violation of this commandment is tantamount to a denial of Israel's distinctiveness" (Feder, 2013:267). Not only does Israel's idolatry cause injury to its relationship with God, but it also lessens its distinctiveness as God's chosen nation.

Not only is the disapproval of the worship of foreign gods and idols codified in the OT, but so is the worship of "other gods" as well. As delineated in section 3.3.2, it is known that the Inanna/Ishtar cult had spread into the regions surrounding Israel in the name of the Astartes of the Levantine region. In addition to Inanna/Ishtar spreading to these areas, it was also noted that Ashtoreth of the Canaanites was also another goddess considered to be the Canaanite form of Astarte and thus, Inanna/Ishtar.[105]

Astarte/Ashtoreth is observed in the Old Testament a total of eight times.[106] In these verses, when the Israelites engage in Astarte/Ashtoreth worship, it always follows that this activity is characterized as Israel forsaking God and/or arousing God's anger. In Judges 2: 16-17, God establishes judges who lead Israel against foreign raiders. However, the Israelites would not listen to these judges and they continued to "prostitute" themselves to other gods. In Judges 10:1-6, the passage relates that the Israelites "did evil in the eyes of the Lord" when they again began to serve the Baals and the Ashtoreths (as well as other local deities). In 1 Samuel chapter seven, after the return of the Ark of the Covenant from the Philistines (vv. 1-6), this passage describes the Israelites "turning back to the Lord." At this juncture, Samuel the prophet instructed the people that if their intent was to restore relationship with God (Yahweh), then they would need to rid themselves of all of the foreign gods that they were worshipping, and specifically mentions the "Ashtoreths." He further admonished the Israelites to serve "the Lord" only (Bible: 2015).

In 1 Kings 11:5-11, there is another mention of Ashtoreth in relation to King Solomon who had married many foreign wives even though God had instructed Israel through his prophets that its men should not intermarry with women from foreign lands. In describing his interaction with Ashtoreth, in v. 5, the passage refers to how Solomon began to follow Ashtoreth, the goddess of the Sidonians and by virtue of this worship of Ashtoreth, "he did evil in the eyes of the Lord (v. 6)." As a result of this "evil," the Lord instructed Solomon that he would wrest the kingdom from out of the hands of his son and give it to one of Solomon's subordi-

---

[105] In the NRSV Bible, Ashtoreth is mentioned as Astarte (cf. Bible Gateway at https://www.biblegateway.com/quicksearch/?quicksearch=Astarte&qs_version=NRSV). Also the NIV Study Bible (Bible, 2015:436fn) has Astarte and Ashtoreth as being synonymous with each other.

[106] Cf. Judges 2:13, 10:6; 1 Samuel 7:1-6, 12:10, 31:10; 1 Kings 11:5, 11:33; 2 Kings 23:13.

Objection Two: The Gospel Accounts of the Resurrection of Jesus ...

nates (v.11). One other mention of Ashtoreth in the Old Testament is 2 Kings chapter twenty-three where there is a description of the purging of foreign altars from the Kingdom of Judah. In his campaign to this end, King Josiah desecrates the sacred high places devoted to the "Ashtoreth, the vile goddess of the Sidonians" as well as other gods. (v. 13). The moniker "vile goddess of the Sidonians" given to Ashtoreth by the author of 2 Kings is very clear regarding the author's impression of the goddess Ashtoreth.

In addition to the Old Testament mentions of Inanna/Ishtar in the form of the syncretized goddess Astarte/Ashtoreth, there is also a mention of a Sumerian/Akkadian mythical figure who is an integral actor in the cult of Inanna/Ishtar. The husband of Inanna/Ishtar, Tammuz (the Akkadian form of Dumuzi), is also observed in the Old Testament as well (Ezekiel 8:14). In this passage, the Lord is showing Ezekiel all of the detestable things that the Israelites were engaged in during his time as a prophet of Israel. Most of these detestable things were religious observances of the Israelites worshipping foreign gods. In verse fourteen, the passage describes the women at the North Gate of the temple, mourning the god Tammuz and notes that this is a detestable act. As observed in the exposition of Inanna, Tammuz (aka Dumuzi), is banished to the netherworld as a result of philandering with prostitutes (one version) while his wife, Inanna was missing in the netherworld.[107] Inanna comes back to earth and the "demons" accompanying her take him and his sister to the netherworld as substitutions for Inanna. Thus, this is the reason why the women are crying at the North gate. They are mourning the mythical pagan god, Tammuz, the husband of Inanna.

In this scene, there are several instances where the Lord is showing the prophet Isaiah things that are being done in secret or in the darkness (vv. 12-13). Even though there is no description of sexual acts in this depiction, the worship of Inanna/Ishtar centered on sexual acts (3.3.2). Therefore, not only is there the forsaking of the Lord with the turning of the Israelites to pagan gods, but there is also the likelihood that they are committing any number of sexual acts in their worship.

These instances of the mention of Inanna/Ishtar and Tammuz in the Old Testament are good evidence regarding the inflexibility of the orthodox Hebrew faith in the Old Testament towards extrinsic influence from pagan cults. Granted, the Israelites were greatly affected by these cults and they received judgment from God for their lack of devotion to Him. However, the doctrine of the orthodox Hebrew religion never changed

---

[107] Cf. 3.3.2.

throughout the Old Testament as evidenced by the aforementioned passages concerning the prohibition from idol worship and also concerning Inanna/Ishtar in her different forms. It has always been an abomination for any Hebrew/Jew to worship any god other than Yahweh. This distinction is probative because Carrier's claim is that pagan syncretism had crept into the Jewish/Christian faiths. Would a devout Jewish author who converted to Christianity accept the claims of a mythical, pagan cult?

3.9 Evidentiary analysis: Carrier's contention in light of accepted principles of evidence

3.9.1 Mystery religions: In general

In making his claim that there were linkages between the resurrection of Jesus Christ and pre-existing pagan cults, Carrier does not offer any evidence based on accepted principles of evidence to support this claim (2.5.2, 2.5.3, 2.5.4). In particular, Carrier offers no relevant evidence based on FRE 401. In showing supposed correlations between the pagan myths and Christianity, he offers no specific evidence coming from antiquity that there was a "pass-down" from these earlier pagan myths to Christianity. Carrier presents no literary sources that provide accounts from eyewitnesses to the association of pagan priests with Jewish or Christian clergyman. Where is the relevant evidence that the Christian or Jewish leaders collaborated together with pagan priests in forming a new syncretistic body of dogma? The only evidence that Carrier offers is from literary sources that describe the activities or belief systems of the various pagan cults. But this information does not rise to the standard of relevant evidence because it does not provide proof of a nexus between these two groups. After all, that is the claim of Carrier; that the resurrection of Jesus Christ was derived from pre-existing pagan myths. Even though Carrier offers information from literary sources of supposed correlations between the two, he does not offer evidence that makes this alleged connection "more or less probable" or that "is of consequence in determining the action" (2.5.2).[108]

Related to the lack of evidence based upon FRE 401, Carrier also does not offer evidence that is based upon FRE 602 (2.5.4) as the information that he provides does not come from historical witnesses who would have observed with their own senses conferences of these aforemen-

---

[108] Cf. 2.5.2 regarding further discussion of relevant evidence in relation to the point at issue.

tioned groups (pagan cults, Judaism, and Christianity) where Jews or Christians adopted pagan rites or teachings into official dogma. Rather, he assumes that this is the case because of the supposed correlations that he and others observe between these groups. Also, he does not offer any facts that are undergirded by proof (FRE 104(b)) to prove his claims. Furthermore, he does not show that the New Testament authors were dishonest, possessed bad character, or had any motives to present false testimony (FRE 607 and FRE 608).

In similarity to FRE 602, federal jury instructions that provide guidance to juries on the evidence they have received also bring clarity to the issue under discussion. In section 2.6.2, FPJI 1.06 relates that evidence can be broken down into two forms of evidence, direct and circumstantial evidence. A description of both of these forms of evidence is given. Does Carrier have a witness from antiquity that directly observed the pass down from the mystery religions to Christianity? Does he provide circumstantial evidence to support his claims?

3.9.2 Christian baptism influenced by pagan baptism

Carrier offers information that Pauline baptism has parallels with pagan baptism (3.2.1). However, this information comes from a fictional account and also a disputed papyrus that "may have" been referring to a pagan baptism. In the first instance, a fictional account bearing witness to a baptism is not a witness in accord with FRE 602, or in accord with FPJI 1.06. Moreover, the fictional witness did not even describe a pagan baptism but only described a purification bath before the secret initiation rite where according to Carrier, the initiation revealed a parallel to Christianity. However, the account does not describe any initiation aping Christian baptism. Rather, the brief description is one of an astral, mystical journey where he is awed at the deities and their environs.

3.9.3 Paul Influenced by the mystery cults

Relatedly, Carrier does not offer in his own writings or in the literature of others any witnesses who observed Paul conferring with and accepting the views of pagan priests or scholars. Rather, as we have seen, Paul denounces associating with pagan religious devotees or their religious rites at every turn. Even in doing so, on several occasions, Paul refers to Old Testament passages in order to buttress his claims against engaging in the worship of other gods/idols.

In addition to the aforementioned evidential problems, it is observed that the central data that Carrier relies upon to support his thesis are supposed correlations between the two and the fact that the mystery cults specifically cited above (Osiris, Inanna, Romulus, Zalmoxis) as examples of cults that antedated Christianity (3.2). As has been noted, relying upon mere correlations without establishing a proven nexus between two events is based on logically fallacious reasoning (e.g. false cause, *post hoc ergo propter hoc*). Just because a group antedated another one does not mean that the earlier group in some way shaped the ideas of the following group.

Additionally, on the point of correlations between religions, it is observed that there are going to be some correlations between all religions (3.4.1). There will be various forms in which the religious devotee seeks to obtain divine approval to include various rituals, initiation rites, sacramental meals, and sacraments of expiation/identification. Just because two groups may generally have these forms of religious expression in common does not mean that one necessarily issues from another or that one has contributed to the other. Again, to prove this properly, one would need evidence of an actual nexus coming from accepted principles of evidence.

3.9.4 Osiris

In moving to an evidentiary analysis of Carrier's claims regarding Osiris and Jesus Christ, the aforementioned evidential problems and logical fallacies apply to this mystery cult as there are no instances that Carrier provides of a "hand off" between Osirian devotees and the early Christians (contra 1.06 direct evidence from a historical witness, *FRE* 602). Even though Carrier does ostensibly utilize scholarly literature and the New Testament as sources for his theories, these sources are not considered to be relevant evidence (*FRE* 401) because he offers no evidence of a linkage between Osirian devotees and early Christians. Furthermore, Carrier misconstrues the data coming from the resurrection narratives and also from the scholarly literature review. Because of his inaccurate use of this data, Carrier does not make conclusions that are based upon facts undergirded by proof (contra *FRE* 104(b)).

Moreover, Carrier's contention of parallels to the resurrection of Jesus Christ and the raising from the dead of Osiris opens up the evidential issue that if there are parallels observed in the death and resurrection accounts of both groups, then there should also be other markers in both that point to a common origin in other aspects such as accounts of the deities of each group, soteriology and metaphysical composition of the dead, etc. Furthermore, just because the myth of Osiris comes before the resurrection of Jesus Christ with the addition of supposed correlations does not mean that the myth of Osiris influenced early Christianity. However, what is observed after the cross-examination of Carrier's claims and the exposition of the Osirian myth is a list of contrasts, not correlations as Carrier alleges.

The first major contrast observed is that the Osirian cult is based on a religious myth whereas the Christian religion is based on a historical account of an actual person who is rooted in space-time history. In other words, there are no witnesses from ancient Egyptian history that Carrier has offered that actually witnessed the real Osiris. Carrier agrees with this contention (3.2.3) but ignores the evidence based upon accepted principles of evidence that confirm the reality of Jesus Christ as a person who lived, died, and was observed after his death by a chorus of historical witnesses (2.8) in accord with the aforementioned accepted principles of evidence (FRE 401, FRE 104(b), FRE 602, FPJI 1.06-historical direct evidence/circumstantial or indirect evidence, FPJI 1.07 (5) corroboration).

Another contrast brought out in the cross-examination from scholarly literature is that Jesus Christ knew of his impending death and willingly accepted it. In contrast to this, Osiris was tricked by co-conspirators who brought about his death. In addition to the willingness to die, the death of Osiris itself is contrasted to that of Jesus Christ where he was drown in a casket. It was only after his drowning, and after his body was reclaimed and hidden by the goddess Isis that his body was found by Seth and cut up into pieces. In response to the scattered body pieces of Osiris, Isis reclaimed them and magically put them back together again with the help of Anubis and Thoth. However, the phallus was missing from the corpse of Osiris but that was recreated magically. While dead, Isis was able to make Osiris copulate and as a result of this sexual act with a dead Osiris, she was able to conceive a son. After the son grew to be a man who sought to avenge his father's death, a pantheon of gods convened and rendered judgment that Osiris could be raised to "life" in the underworld as king of the netherworld.

In contrast to this, Jesus Christ died by crucifixion because he answered "I am" when the high priest asked the question, "Are you the Messiah, the Son of the Blessed One (Mark 14:61-64)?" In contrast to the motivation behind the "legally" sanctioned murder of Jesus Christ, the motivation behind the unsanctioned murder of Osiris was that Osiris had unknowingly committed adultery with Nephthys, the wife of his murderer and brother Seth. Furthermore, Jesus Christ did not commit adultery nor did he have sex with a woman, have a wife, nor did he physically sire a child. Moreover, a pantheon of gods did not render the judgment that Jesus Christ was worthy to become king of the netherworld. Nor did Jesus Christ need assistance from any other gods (as with Osiris, Anubis, and Thoth) to reclaim his physical body.

Additionally, several contrasts are observed between the resurrection of Jesus Christ and the translation of Osiris. One of these contrasts is that Jesus Christ died and then was raised in an actual body that could actually be seen by other humans, could be touched by other humans, and who spoke in a manner where he could be heard by the human ear. Additionally, the resurrected Jesus Christ could not only prepare meals, but also consume them as well. In contrast to this, Osiris was raised from physical death to the netherworld, the realm of the dead. He no longer walked upon the earth as a normal person but after his "translation" he never assumed his body again in the land of the living. Moreover, his body had been mummified before he was raised from the dead (3.3.1). So, there is a profound difference between Osiris and Jesus Christ in the metaphysical aspect of their "translations." Jesus Christ arose to immortal life in a restored body whereas Osiris was translated from a mummified body to a non-corporeal existence in the netherworld.

In other aspects of the origin and early life of Osiris as compared with Jesus Christ, there is a marked contrast as well. Whereas Osiris was born from the union of two parents who were gods, Jesus was born from a virgin and the implanting of the divine seed into Mary (there was no sexual intercourse involved). Moreover, as Osiris grew, he was considered as royalty and became powerful by virtue of his parentage. He also married his sister, Isis, with whom he had sexual intercourse with inside the womb. He was Osiris, king of Egypt. In contrast to Osiris, Jesus Christ had a humble existence being born to a non-regal family, had no personal effects to speak of, and had no symbols of earthly power or prestige. He did not marry nor did he have sexual intercourse with anyone. Moreover, the public ministry of Jesus was concerned with helping those who were in need both physically and spiritually. In essence, his earthly life was concerned with serving others in every way whereas in contrast, Osiris was the ruler of a mighty nation with all the trappings of power, prestige, and fame (one "cross-examining" scholar indicated that Osiris was cruel- 3.4.2). Moreover, E.A Budge also offered that Osiris ordered the sacrifice of many and also entombed persons as living sacrifices (3.4.2).

In reference to the contrasts between the soteriology of the Osirian myth and Christianity, an obvious contrast is that for the Osirian devotee there is no personal relationship with Osiris that transforms the believer.

Rather, identification with Osiris is just a vehicle in which to obtain eternal life. It has been shown that Osiris was the guarantor of the vegetation and inundation processes of the Nile. Also, it was brought out in the exposition and the cross examination of Carrier that Osiris was more of a funerary god than a deity who was relevant to the daily life of his devotees (3.3.1). Moreover, the requisite magical incantations that must be recited in addition to the judgment process of Ma'at determine who enters the netherworld. In Osirian soteriology, one must be presented before a tribunal of gods in the netherworld and one's life must be weighed as in a scale. If the good deeds outweigh the bad and you have said or possess the right incantations, then you enter the netherworld. If you do not, then you will be exterminated. In this soteriological framework, the achievement of eternal life is based upon the actions of the devotee.

In contradistinction to the Osirian soteriological framework, Christianity stresses identification with Jesus Christ in order to obtain eternal life. By the salvific atonement on the cross and the subsequent resurrection of Jesus Christ from the dead, the Christian is assured of eternal life due to relationship/identification with Jesus Christ. Therefore in juxtaposition to the Osirian formulation, acceptance by God does not come through the activity of the adherent but rather by the sacrificial work of Jesus Christ. Thus, the two soteriological systems stand in total contrast to each other. Moreover, in the Christian formulation of judgment, the arbiter of eternal destiny is not a tribunal of various gods. Rather, it is Jesus Christ himself who will judge each and every person.

3.9.5 Inanna/Ishtar

In assessing the strength of the evidence for a nexus between the cult of Inanna/Ishtar and Christianity, again, Carrier has not offered any relevant evidence (FRE 401) based on accepted principles of evidence. There are no witnesses that he offers from antiquity who observed a "hand off" to the Christians (FRE 602 and FPJI 1.06). Thus, there is no corroboration of sources to strengthen the data offered by Carrier (FPJI 1.07). Again, he cites the antedating of Inanna's cult before Christianity as partial proof for his contention. Based on this methodology of using this sort of data as proof for his claim, the aforementioned fallacious reasoning also applies to Carrier's claims regarding Inanna.

In the exposition of the Inanna myth, Carrier offers correlations in the method of death and resurrection between Inanna and Jesus Christ. However, after analyzing the myth of Inanna/Ishtar, these correlations are not observed. Rather, observed are many contrasts not only between the death and resurrection of Inanna/Jesus Christ, but also other aspects of their lives to include the formation of the narratives.

As with the Osirian myth, the cult of Inanna is a religious cult that is based upon a myth. Carrier does not contend that Inanna was an actual person. Rather, he is using this myth to demonstrate that Jesus Christ is a mythical character and that the mythical character of Jesus Christ was based upon other myths that came before it. However, as detailed in section 2.5.2, there are ample historical witnesses that speak of the resurrection of Jesus Christ being an actual event in history. As assessed previously, the testimony of these witnesses is bolstered by accepted principles of evidence.

Regarding her death and resurrection, Carrier stated that Inanna was "hung on a nail" and then arose after three days aping the death and resurrection of Jesus Christ. However, the cross examination by scholarly literature as well as the exposition of the Inanna myth brought out that Inanna was already in the netherworld when her sister, Ereshkigal, caused her death by magical means. It was also brought out that there was a theory propounded that Ereshkigal struck her dead because Inanna was trying to usurp her position as the Queen of the netherworld. It is noted that Inanna was already in the realm of the dead when she was dealt this deathblow. After Inanna had died again (as she was currently in the netherworld), Ereshkigal hung her on a hook on the wall (or some versions state that her corpse was hung on a pole). In total contrast to the death of Inanna, Jesus Christ was not murdered by magical means in the underworld. Rather, his unjust death by crucifixion and entombment were public, occurred at a certain place and time, and were witnessed by many to include an eyewitness who wrote about it (John).

Regarding the time period between the death and "resurrection" of Inanna, after Ninshubur did not see Inanna appear at the right time, based upon a predetermined plan, Inanna's faithful steed began to notify all of the gods and relatives of Inanna that she was missing. Something bad occurred to her while she was in the netherworld. Carrier asserts that this was all accomplished in three days in similarity to Jesus Christ. However, it was brought out in the cross-examination by scholarly literature that the pre-determined time for Ninshubur to start notifying Inanna's friends and relatives about Inanna's missing status would have been three days. Therefore the time from Inanna's death to her resurrection would have been longer than three days as it would have taken Ninshubur longer to visit the relatives and then allow for the magically created imps of Enki to travel back to the netherworld.

Regarding the way in which Inanna was raised to renewed life, the god (and relative) Enki, sent messengers to entreat Ereshkigal to permit Inanna to be raised from her death by magical means. After Ereshkigal granted approval, this was accomplished by two imp-like beings that sprinkle their life giving concoctions on Inanna. Also, the Anunna (another council of gods) allow her to return to "the land of the living" but two galla escort her back. Upon re-emerging from the realm of the dead, Inanna goes back to the "land of the living" to seek for a substitute so that she can remain "alive." She finds her husband Dumuzi/Tammuz and indicates to her underworld escorts that he and his sister, Geshtinanna, are to be her substitute as she was released from the underworld with the proviso that she had to find someone to take her place in the underworld.

In total contrast to the method in which Inanna was raised from the dead, in gaining immortal life for others, Jesus Christ did not need to rely upon any magical potions, a council of gods to allow him to return to life, nor did he need a substitute to enable him to resurrect from the dead. In contradistinction to Inanna, he was the substitute that enabled all others to gain eternal life.

Regarding the metaphysical aspects of the death and resurrection of Jesus Christ, he did not die in the underworld but died in Jerusalem in Judea in the first century. When he died, neither was he extinguished like Inanna in the netherworld. Rather, he still existed in sheol/paradise until he eventually arose from the dead three days later and inhabited the same body, although "glorified." When he ascended to heaven, he remained in the "spiritual" body that he reassumed.

In regard to her origin, a number of different gods are proposed as her father even though Enki is a prominent candidate to be her father. Moreover, Inanna has various titles to include the celestial courtesan, the divine prostitute, and the patroness of free love. In having sexual intercourse with the king, the rule of the king was legitimized by Inanna. As observed in the exposition of Inanna she presided at feast and festivals where sexual liberties of every type were engaged in to include bestiality, transgenderism, bondage, and self-mutilation. However, she is also observed as the patroness of marital fidelity as well. Not only is she described as a prostitute, but also one who has maternal qualities. Furthermore, manifestations of Inanna can change from that of a beautiful goddess during the day and then upon nightfall, a bearded masculine goddess of war. Moreover, she is described as being deceitful and having the ability to manipulate others to suit her own selfish needs.

In total contrast to the life of Inanna, Jesus Christ was born of a virgin and lived a life of total self-sacrifice. He was not engaged or preoccupied with sexual activities of any sort. Rather, he taught that having sex with someone else other than your spouse was wrongful conduct (Matt. 19:9). Neither was he concerned about manipulating others for his own gain but was devoted to not only serving others but also doing the will of the one who sent him (God, the Father) to the end of enduring a cruel death, again, not for some sort of selfish gain. Rather, he died and resurrected from the dead for the gain of all others so that all who believed on him would have eternal life. Also, in contrast to Inanna, some of the titles ascribed to Jesus Christ are Son of Man (Matt. 9:6), Lamb of God (John 1:29), Messiah (Matt. 16:16), I Am (John 8:58), Lion of Judah (Rev. 5:5), Bread of Life (John 6:35), the True Vine (John 15:1), the Son of the Living God (Matt. 16:16), the Word (John 1:14), Counselor (Is. 9:6), and Prince of Peace (Is. 9:6).

In relation to differences in their soteriological formulations, there is not a clear-cut soteriology regarding the cult of Inanna as it was a mystery cult. There is mention of prayer to Inanna in order to aid a devotee in sexual matters. There is also mention of sacrifices on behalf of relatives who are living in the underworld so the departed dead could have sustenance. But other than that, there is no known mention for any soteriological framework for followers of Inanna. Restated another way, there is no known way in which the death and reinstatement to life of Inanna inures to the benefit of her followers. Rather as mentioned before, she even needed a substitute for herself in order for her reinstatement to life. As in the comparison with Osiris to Jesus Christ, there is a marked distinction between Inanna and Jesus Christ that overshadows any supposed correlations that Carrier offers. Moreover, after cross-examination and after comparing the exposition of the Inanna myth to Carrier's alleged correlations, this claim does not appear to be well supported by the evidence as evinced by the numerous contrasts listed above (*FRE* 104(b)- 2.5.3; FPJI 1.05- 2.6.4).

3.9.6 Romulus

In regard to the Romulan legend, it runs into the same problems both evidentially and logically as the aforementioned mystery cults (*FRE* 401, *FRE* 104(b), *FRE* 602, FPJI 1.06; 2.5 and 2.6). In addition to these accepted principles that the Romulan legend lacks, another problem is that FPJI contained within section 1.07 of the U.S. District Court of Appeals gives criteria of how to judge the credibility of a witness. In criterion number five, it mentions the importance of corroboration in strengthening the weight of the evidence. As will be seen below, the "Romulan Epiphany," has no cor-

Objection Two: The Gospel Accounts of the Resurrection of Jesus ... 213

roboration through other witnesses to buttress the offered testimony of Julius Proculus (we do not even know if he is a real person).

In regard to his legendary status, there is a possibility that Romulus may have existed even though there are none who have written that they knew of Romulus from their own experiences. Rather, there are accounts that have been written where others have stated a general timeframe and location for him. However, regarding the key elements of his death and alleged resurrection from the dead, there are no witnesses from antiquity that write about these events. Rather, there is an account that has been handed down with no real traceable chain of transmission.

Also, troubling is that there are so many varying accounts from the Romulan legend as shown in its exposition. Therefore, there is no evidence of his existence, nor is there any evidence of the circumstances of his death and alleged resurrection from a historical witness. Therefore, the data about Romulus does not meet the standards of evidence given by rule 602 and 401, and FPJI sections 1.06 and 1.07. as there is no known historical witness who has observed any events that is mentioned within the corpus of the Romulan legend. Moreover, the facts that Carrier offers are not undergirded by proof (FRE 104(b)) as what he offers as comparisons between Romulus and Jesus Christ do not fit the New Testament resurrection narratives or the scholarly literature review. In contradistinction to the Romulan legend, the life, death and resurrection of Jesus Christ comes from data that is supported by accepted principles of evidence (2.5 and 2.6)

Concerning the supposed correlations between Jesus Christ and Romulus, there are many contrasts in the accounts of their lives on earth. Regarding the details of the life of Romulus, as grandson to a king, he came from a royal lineage. However, his mother was forced to become a vestal virgin by another man who aimed to be the king of Alba Longa and was working to unseat her father. After becoming a vestal virgin there are two accounts as to how Romulus and his twin brother Remus were born. She was either raped by the god Mars or she sexually copulated with a magic phallus that appeared to her. After birth, Romulus reportedly lived a humble life attended by mythical characters until he grew to be a man. Upon founding the city of Rome, either Romulus or one of his men murdered his twin brother Remus. After becoming the undisputed leader of Rome, he was engaged in many wars and also organized the mass kidnapping/rape of the Sabine women. It was also noted in the exposition of Romulus that he wore a purple robe to accentuate his position as ruler of Rome and was believed to have become despotic towards the end of his life.

In contrast to this, Jesus Christ lived a life that was not characterized by conquest, trickery, or violence. Nor did he live a life that was filled with the pomp and circumstance of a conqueror nor did he engage in deceit or plan mass crimes as is the case with Romulus. Neither did he aspire to worldly position or wealth nor is there any evidence that he planned or carried out the murder of any person. Rather, he willingly allowed himself to be murdered on behalf of others. Moreover, while he lived he modeled and taught others to live purely and in service to others.

Regarding the circumstances surrounding the occultation and alleged apotheosis/epiphany of Romulus, there are numerous variations to this story. Two of the most popular variations are that he was speaking to the people of Rome when a sudden dark cloud with accompanying thunder and lightning enveloped him. When the storm cleared away, Romulus was no longer present. Another popular account has that he was murdered at the hands of Roman senators and that pieces of his body were carried out under the folds of their garments and discarded. Thus, we have two accounts of his disappearance that do not mesh with one another and no real evidence he died other than accounts passed down by non-witnesses whose sources were distantly removed from the action of the account. Also, there was only one person, Julius Proculus, who is alleged to have briefly observed the epiphany of Romulus not knowing whether it was even the actual body of Romulus or just a vision of him. Therefore as noted above, there was no corroboration of this one witness (FPJI 1.07 criterion number 5). As part of this epiphany, the proclamation of Romulus to Julius Proculus was about the greatness of Rome.

As stated previously, in complete contrast to Romulus, there is the confirmation of the life, death, and resurrection of Jesus Christ and this confirmation is based upon accepted principles of evidence (2.5 and 2.6). In contrast to Romulus, there is historical testimony that Jesus Christ died. This is corroborated by an eyewitness account of his crucifixion (John) and other accounts from interviews of witnesses who were there (Matthew, Mark, and Luke). Also differing greatly from the Romulan legend, was the number of persons who witnessed the resurrected Jesus Christ after his known death (over 500; 1 Cor. 15:6). Also diverging from the Romulan legend, the post-resurrection proclamation of Jesus Christ was not about the glory of a particular earthly kingdom. Rather, it was about guidance through life, relationship with God, and a future hope of eternal life. In regard to soteriology, there is not a clear teaching of how a devotee of Quirinus would receive eternal life.[109]

3.9.7 Zalmoxis

Regarding Zalmoxis and a supposed connection between his cult and Christianity, Carrier again offers no relevant evidence based upon FRE 401 that shows any causal connection. Moreover, Carrier does not offer any historical witnesses who observed with their senses (FRE 602 as well as FPJI 1.06) this hand-off of rituals or rites from the Getae to the Christians. In addition to these evidentiary deficiencies, the facts that Carrier utilizes are not supported by proof, as the facts he relies upon do not cohere with the New Testament resurrection accounts and the scholarly literature review (contra FRE 104(b)). Furthermore, Carrier only offers supposed correlations between Christianity and the Zalmoxis cult of the Getae. Was there a clan of Thracians who resided in Jerusalem during the first century and were adherents of the Zalmoxis cult? Was anyone writing about the influence of the Zalmoxis cult upon the Christians in the first century of the church? Carrier has not presented any evidence to answer these questions (contra FRE 401; 2.5).

As was the case with the other gods previously treated, in response to Carrier's claims of correlations between Zalmoxis and Jesus Christ, there are a number of contrasts that become apparent after the cross-examination of Carrier's claims and the exposition of the Zalmoxis cult. As noted in the analysis of the other gods, it is unknown whether Zalmoxis ever really existed. Herodotus doubted his existence and all of the sources that mention Zalmoxis are far removed from the time that he may have lived.

In regard to the occultation and apotheosis of Zalmoxis, it is apparent that he did not die when he was not observed for three years as the report from Herodotus informs us of the subterranean chamber that he built to deceive the Getae. One of the elements in a resurrection is that you have to have a death as one of the elements showing that there was a resurrection. The account of Herodotus reveals that he did not die but rather hid himself from the view of the Getae. In relation to other aspects of the Zalmoxis cult, every five years, a messenger from the Getae would be dispatched to Zalmoxis (human sacrifice). Concerning its soteriology,

---

[109] Regarding the importance of eternal life, Corneliu Constantineanu (2010:57) offers, "in the first-century world, religion was not perceived primarily as a search for the 'salvation of the soul' into eternal life..."

it appears that if one lived a good life or was courageous in battle, one was eligible to go to heaven and be with Zalmoxis.

In contrast to Zalmoxis as stated in the analysis of the aforementioned gods and their cults, the life, death, and resurrection of Jesus Christ were confirmed by witnesses who were contemporaneous with him and who wrote about him. Furthermore, there was no need to send messengers to Jesus Christ via human sacrifice because Jesus Christ left the Holy Spirit of God to dwell with his followers (John 14:26,15:26). Also, the occultation of Zalmoxis for three years where he secreted himself in a subterranean chamber stands in contrast to Jesus Christ. Jesus Christ remained in the grave until he arose from the dead three days later as the guarantor of eternal life for those who would come into relationship with him. Furthermore, there was no deception or trickery on behalf of Jesus Christ to make his followers believe that he had died and risen from the dead.

In addition to these contrasts, Jesus Christ did not make alliances with or become an official priest for any ruler as observed in the exposition of Zalmoxis. Rather, he eschewed earthly power in his life of service and self-sacrifice. Moreover, Jesus Christ did not seclude himself in caves as part of his ministry as did Zalmoxis. Rather, he was often among the people healing them of physical ailments and teaching them about a life devoted to God through him. Also, Jesus Christ did not demand that a "messenger" be dispatched to him every five years (human sacrifice). Rather, he willingly sacrificed his life on behalf of humanity so they could be reconciled to God. Moreover, there is no mention of Zalmoxis sacrificing himself on behalf of his followers.

3.9.8 New Testament writers influenced by pagan mystery cults

In regard to the evidence presented by Carrier's claim that the writers of the New Testament were influenced by pagan myths, it has been shown that the resurrection as described in the New Testament had its roots in the Old Testament as indicated by the allusions in the New Testament referring to Old Testament scriptures. Jesus Christ also referred to the Old Testament on several occasions when alluding to his impending death and resurrection from the dead. In addition to this, there are scriptures that refer to the resurrection from the dead that are in the Old Testament as well as those that point to a future Messiah.

In reference to the assimilation of pagan rituals into the Christian religion, it was shown that there are prohibitions against the worship of

Idols in the Old Testament. The practice of worshipping idols was often referred to as "detestable" in the Old Testament. If the worship of idols was not condoned, then why would the Hebrew authors of the New Testament blend aspects of pagan myths into their writings? Where in the Old or New Testament is the worship of idols (pagan gods) tolerated? The prohibitions against idolatry are observed in the New Testament not only in the gospels but also in the writings of Paul. This is probative to the discussion as Carrier mentions that Paul's writings introduce pagan principles regarding the resurrection. However, when surveying Paul's writings in the New Testament, Paul discusses that Christians should not be engaged in the worship of idols in any way to include eating meat sacrificed to idols. So, if Paul was against the worship of pagan gods, then why would Paul introduce pagan ideas into his literature? Furthermore, Paul discusses the resurrection of Jesus Christ from the framework provided by the Old Testament that does not tolerate the worship of idols. Thus, these scriptures coming from the Old and New Testaments prohibiting idol worship are circumstantial evidence (FPJI 1.06) that neither Paul nor any other New Testament authors developed their ideas for the resurrection of Jesus Christ from pagan cults. Moreover, this evidence (no idol worship condoned) is relevant (FRE 401) and is supported by facts based on proof from both Old and New Testament scriptures (FRE 104(b)).

3.10 Summary

In chapter three, a survey was completed as to the claim of Carrier that pre-existing pagan and mythical cults influenced the Christian formulation of the resurrection of Jesus Christ as observed in the New Testament. In his literature, Carrier has cited a number of these gods as possible examples. Specifically, Carrier's writings on four of these gods (Osiris, Inanna, Romulus, and Zalmoxis) were examined in detail. Carrier supported his thesis by referring to supposed correlations between the "dying and rising gods" of the mystery cults and the resurrection of Jesus Christ. Additionally, he supported his thesis by also noting that these dying and rising gods antedated Christianity. According to Carrier, if there are similarities between these pagan cults and Christianity and if they pre-existed Christianity, then an inference can be drawn that Christianity was influenced by them.

After reporting and examining material from Carrier's literature on the topic, an exposition of mystery religions was conducted. After this general survey was completed, a specific inquiry into four of these gods (Osiris, Inanna, Romulus, Zalmoxis) was undertaken. In addition to conducting an exposition of these four cults, a cross-examination of Carrier's claim by use of scholarly literature was also conducted. After this cross-examination of Carrier's claim, evidence was offered against his claim. This evidence came from scripture references within both the Old and New Testaments.

Subsequent to these literature surveys, an evidential analysis by accepted principles of evidence was completed. The results of this analysis revealed that Carrier's claim that the resurrection of Jesus Christ was influenced by pagan mythical cults did not meet the standard of relevant evidence as propounded by rule 401 of the *FRE*. Moreover, the data he supplied did not meet the requirements of *FRE* 602 and FPJI 1.06 (and in some instances FPJI 1.07), as evidence should be from the personal knowledge of a witness. Carrier's historical witnesses did not provide evidence of an actual nexus between the "resurrections" of pagan gods and the resurrection of Jesus Christ. Moreover, Carrier's facts were not supported by proof (contra *FRE* 104(b)) as they did not correspond with the scholarly literature or the New Testament resurrection narrative.

In addition to these problems with his evidence, it was shown that Carrier's claim was also based on logically fallacious reasoning, as mere alleged correlations and chronological priority do not equate to causality. Rather, causality should be proven by a thorough examination of the evidence. Additionally, the cross-examination of Carrier's material supporting his thesis by scholarly literature and the exposition of the four mystery cults weakened the correlations that he claimed were present between Christianity and mystery religions (contra *FRE* 104(b)). Moreover, relevant evidence (*FRE* 401) coming from the Old and New Testaments revealed that Old Testament scriptures (the influence of Judaism) framed the Christian formulation of the resurrection (affirmed by *FRE* 104(b) and FPJI 1.06-circumstantial evidence). Also introduced to rebut Carrier's claim was evidence that pagan idol worship was expressly forbidden in both the Old and New Testaments. Specifically, references from Paul's writing revealed that Judaism framed his perspectives on the resurrection and the worship of pagan gods.

Chapter Four

Objection Three: The Disciples Hallucinated the Risen Jesus Christ

4.1 Introduction

Although Carrier is a mythicist scholar, he argues, rhetorically, that the disciples hallucinated the risen Jesus Christ. In coming to this position, Carrier argues that there could be several different explanations for the experiences that the disciples had as listed in the different accounts of the resurrection in the New Testament. In his writings on the encounters of the disciples with the risen Jesus Christ, Carrier posits hypnagogic, hypnopompic, bereavement, and schizophrenic hallucinations as possible reasons for these experiences. Other possible reasons Carrier submits for the reports of the disciples are fatigue, deprivation, and guilt could have triggered hallucinations of Jesus Christ.

In addition to explicating Carrier's perspective on these appearances, pertinent scholarly literature coming from the discipline of psychology will be offered in order to determine if the different sorts of hallucinations mentioned by Carrier could possibly match the reports of the encounters included within the Gospel resurrection narratives. In keeping with this aim, an exposition of scholarly literature on hypnagogic, hypnopompic, bereavement, and schizophrenic hallucinations will be conducted. Moreover, the scholarly literature on hallucinations will be further examined to see if exhaustion and guilt are possible causes. In addition to these inquiries, it is also probative to examine other types of hallucinations to determine if other sorts of hallucinatory phenomena could qualify for what the disciples experienced. Hallucinatory activity is also known to come from those who suffer from post-traumatic stress disorder (PTSD), hallucinogenic drug use, epilepsy, Charles Bonnet Syndrome, Parkinson's Disease, and Alzheimer's Disease[110].

After the exposition on the various forms of hallucinations has been conducted, Carrier's claims will also be cross-examined by the scholarly

---

[110] Parkinson's Disease and Alzheimer's Disease will not be examined as these are diseases that are normally associated with the elderly and no serious scholar contends that the disciples were elderly men.

literature on the various forms of hallucinations to determine if the experiences of the disciples were in accord with any known forms of hallucinations. Moreover, other scholarly literature authored by Christian apologists and scholars will also be offered to further cross-examine Carrier's contention. After these analyses have been conducted, evidence that the disciples were not hallucinating will be offered. The evidences supporting the position that the disciples had real encounters with the risen Jesus Christ are: 1) the corroborative nature of these experiences from multiple sources who experienced the risen Jesus 2) most of the disciples who had post-resurrection encounters with Jesus Christ died as martyrs. After the aforementioned examinations are conducted, Carrier's claim of hallucinating disciples will be compared to the aforementioned accepted principles of evidence to determine if his claim is in accord with them.

4.2 Carrier's Claim: PRA were hallucinations

4.2.1 PRA: Hypnagogic/Hypnopompic hallucinations

In his web-based series, *Why I Don't Buy the Resurrection* and included within the chapter entitled, *Rebutting Lesser Arguments*, Carrier (2006g) mentions that hypnagogic hallucinations are commonplace occurrences today and that many visions reported from antiquity were most likely to occur in the afternoon when it was customary for Mediterranean people of that day to enjoy a mid-afternoon nap. However, even as he offers hypnagogia as a possible explanation for these experiences, he also offers the possibilities of prolonged fasting as well as sleep deprivation as causes of hallucinatory experiences:

> But consider also that having such visions and voices do not require one to be insane: hypnagogic hallucinations are an ordinary occurrence for everyone, and it has been observed that visions in antiquity were most common in the early afternoon, the time all Mediterranean cultures enjoyed a post-meal siesta, and they become extremely likely after prolonged periods of fasting or sleep deprivation (such as going 40 days and 40 nights with little food or sleep in a mesmerizing desert landscape). Any manner of delusions could arise from such experiences.

In further discussing the phenomena of visions in antiquity and their presence within the New Testament, Carrier (2006d) offers that there are many examples of hypnagogic hallucinations and other associated phe-

Objection Three: The Disciples Hallucinated the Risen Jesus Christ 221

nomena located within the Book of Acts (7:55-56, 10:1-7, 11:5-14, 12:6-11, 16:9-10, 22:17-21). After mentioning this, Carrier also notes that many of the appearances of Jesus appeared at dawn, which he claims is the time when hypnagogia is most prevalent.[111] However again, even after offering these explanations, Carrier also offers several other possibilities to account for the experiences of the risen Jesus Christ such as physical/psychological distress, darkness, stirred hopes, and a need for reassurance.

In additional discussion regarding hypnagogia as a potential cause for the hallucinations of the risen Jesus Christ, Carrier (2005a:ch. 5) mentions a personal encounter that he believes he experienced when he was in a hypnagogic state:

> Indeed, I would have to include myself in their numbers. In addition to a vivid Taoist mystical experience of an obviously hallucinatory nature, there was a night when I fought with a demon trying to crush my chest-the experience felt absolutely real, and I was certainly awake, probably in a hypnagogic state. I could see and feel the demon sitting on me, preventing me from breathing, but when I "punched" it, it vanished. It is all the more remarkable that I have never believed in demons, and the creature I saw did not resemble anything I had ever seen or imagined before. So what was it? Supernatural encounter or hallucination? You decide.

Carrier uses his own mystical experience of a demonic creature sitting on his chest as an example of a hypnagogic hallucination. In this experience, Carrier notes that he had never imagined such a creature before nor did he believe in the existence of demons. A relevant area of inquiry in his example of the demonic creature sitting on his chest would be to investigate what a hypnagogic hallucination is and whether any of the PRA were similar to this hallucination in any sense.

Continuing his conversation regarding the real possibility that the disciples hallucinated the risen Jesus Christ, Carrier (2005a:ch.5) again mentions the likelihood of hypnagogic hallucinations as a cause for the appearances of the risen Jesus Christ. However, in this instance, Carrier

---

[111] According to the scholarly literature, hypnagogia would be the state when someone is transitioning to sleep. Hypnopompia would be the state where one is transitioning from sleep to being awake. Thus, most people would be more likely to be waking up than going to sleep at dawn. It would be more likely that a hypnopompic experience would be one to be experienced at dawn as hypnopompia is associated more with the time when one wakes up rather than a particular time in the day (cf. 4.3.1).

suggests that there were a number of conditions present that would cause the disciples to have hallucinations. Among the other conditions he lists as contributing factors are being recently bereaved of Jesus Christ after his crucifixion, anxiety-filled circumstances, social influence, suggestion, and a cultural predisposition to hallucinate. He summarizes that with all of these listed factors combined you could not have a better environment for the occurrence of a hallucination unless you added to this combination of conditions a hypnagogic or trance state in the mix which he states could have been induced by "fasting, fatigue, marathon praying, and other ascetic activities."

Going from a general discussion about the hallucination prone disciples and then focusing on Paul, Carrier (2005a:ch. 5) offers reasons for Paul's experience with the risen Jesus Christ:

> "Why Paul?" He wasn't among the disciples and experienced Jesus much later than they did. So what brought about his revelation? We can never really know for sure-Paul tells us precious little. But I can hypothesize four conjoining factors: guilt at persecuting a people he came to admire; subsequent disgust with fellow persecuting Pharisees; and persuasion (beginning to see what the Christians were seeing in scripture, and to worry about his own salvation); coupled with the right physical circumstances (like heat and fatigue on a long, desolate road), could have induced a convincing ecstatic event.

In offering reasons why Paul might have experienced the risen Jesus Christ, Carrier offers the reason of fatigue as one of the possibilities for causing the hallucination. He further posits that fatigue (that could have induced a hypnagogic hallucination) in combination with other factors likely caused Paul to have these experiences with the risen Jesus Christ. A relevant matter to research in regard to hypnagogia is whether a hallucination of this sort can account for Paul's experience with the risen Jesus Christ.

In *Not the Impossible Faith: Why Christianity Didn't Need a Miracle to Succeed*, Carrier (2009:ch. 10) again lists various sorts of possible causes for the PRA of Jesus. In this list of possible causes, Carrier also briefly mentions hypnopompia as a possibility for those who experienced the PRA of Jesus Christ:

> But there are many opportunities even for normal people to enter the same kind of hallucinatory state, especially in religious and vision-oriented cultures: from fasting, fatigue, sleep deprivation, and other ascetic behaviors (such as extended periods of mantric prayer), to ordinary dreaming

and hypnagogic or hypnopompic events (a common hallucinatory state experienced by normal people between waking and sleep).

In similarity to hypnagogia, it will also be probative to determine the nature of hypnopompic hallucinations and whether these sorts of hallucinations could be what the disciples experienced.

4.2.2 PRA: Bereavement/Grief hallucinations

In addition to offering hypnagogic and hypnopompic hallucinations as possible causes for the experiences of the disciples with the resurrected Jesus Christ, Carrier (1999, 2005) also suggests "bereavement hallucinations" as a possibility. Carrier makes reference to a study conducted by Slade and Bentall where they conclude those who have had hallucinations in antiquity were, as a rule, not stigmatized by their culture after their hallucinations became known. Moreover, Carrier notes that these sorts of hallucinations have been legitimized by certain cultures:

> The authors [Slade and Bentall] also found that "hallucinations involving bereavement" are common--and, for example, visits by the dead to the bereaved are culturally accepted as genuine in Hopi Indian culture (p. 86-88). Finally, they found evidence that hallucination plays a role in reducing, and this anxiety-relieving property in turn has a reinforcing effect on the believability and frequency of hallucination (p. 108).

Not only does Carrier evince that bereavement hallucinations have been accepted as legitimate throughout history, he also offers that these sorts of hallucinations are important in reducing the anxiety of the bereaved.

Carrier (1999, 2005) continues to focus on bereavement hallucinations as a possible cause for the disciple's experiences with the risen Jesus Christ. He provides another list of factors that he believes made the disciples prime candidates for hallucinations:

> These two factors fit the situation of the disciples after the crucifixion incredibly well. They were primed for hallucination by their bereavement, their anxiety-filled circumstances (John 20:19), their cultural predisposition to see and believe things that confirmed their deepest expectations in religious terms, and the opportunities for social influence and suggestion (as one or two individuals prepare the rest for the possibility that Jesus is risen)...

Included within Carrier's list of causal contributing factors are bereavement hallucinations as well as the anxiety that would develop after the loss of Jesus Christ to death by crucifixion. Along with mentioning these factors, Carrier also mentions that they were predisposed to have hallucinations in order to confirm their deep religious expectations and also to gain influence within the community. An analysis of the relevant resurrection narratives would be helpful to determine if the eleven remaining disciples and Paul were expecting Jesus Christ to rise from the dead.

Carrier (2009: ch. 10) makes another assertion endorsing a bereavement hallucination as a good theory of what the disciples encountered:

> All of this, as well as the confusion and grief of losing a beloved leader and the resulting crisis of faith (which often leads people to latch onto anything to restore meaning and hope), more than establishes the "emotional excitement" requirement for hallucination.

Carrier mentions that being bereaved of a beloved leader fulfilled the requirement for emotional excitement. A relevant question to ask at this juncture; is emotional excitement one of the criteria that causes bereavement hallucinations?

Carrier (2006c) continues his discussion on encounters with the dead by mentioning that it was a frequent occurrence that many people from antiquity claimed to make contact with their gods or deceased heroes. Additionally, he offers that scientists have discovered various causes for these mystical experiences. He shares that some of the causes for bereavement hallucinations are psychological, cultural, and neurophysiological in nature. However, Carrier notes that scientists have not uncovered a supernatural explanation for these encounters with deceased heroes or gods.

Concerning Paul and his encounter with the resurrected Jesus Christ, Carrier (2006d) opines that Paul merely references a vision in 1 Corinthians 15:8. In this passage, Paul does not discuss encountering a revived corpse. Carrier continues that many other people in the Bible had visions as well to include Stephen:

> I think it is almost certain that many people, such as Stephen (cf. Section IV of Probability of Survival vs. Miracle), had visions. People still do. People had visions of almost every god in antiquity, and still have visions of many gods and beings now, as well as of the deceased, among other bizarre things (cf. Robin Lane Fox, *Pagans and Christians*, for the ancient cultural context of this kind of thing).

Carrier believes that visions of the deceased that still occur today are in similarity to what Paul experienced during his Damascus Road experience. Is there any evidence coming from scripture that Paul's encounter with Jesus Christ was more than just a vision?

4.2.3 PRA: Schizophrenic hallucinations

In addition to the aforementioned forms of hallucinations, Carrier (2010:305) also asserts that schizophrenic hallucinations are a viable option for the PRA that the disciples and others experienced. In supporting this contention, Carrier offers that there have been many groups of people who have observed hallucinations together and that these sorts of hallucinations can be induced by ecstatic trance experiences. He further offers that many of the early Christians were "trancers" and "hallucinators" and that this is proven by the fact that many Christians prophesied and spoke in tongues (2 Cor. 12 and 1 Cor. 14:26-30). Carrier then offers, "In fact, functional schizotypes are prone to congregating into cults like this and just as prone to this kind of hallucinatory behavior."

Further expositing on his opinion that those who experienced the risen Jesus Christ may have hallucinated, Carrier (1995, 2005) offers that these persons may possibly be a sort of person who is for the most part well adjusted and functional, yet can have visionary experiences:

> Claridge McCreery, in "A Study of Hallucination in Normal Subjects" (*Personality and Individual Differences* 2.5; November, 1996: pp. 739-747) found that there is a kind of 'happy schizotype' who is "a relatively well-adjusted person who is functional despite, and in some cases even because of, his or her anomalous perceptual experiences."... It is entirely possible that cultural support led schizophrenics into comfortable situations where their visions were channeled into "appropriate" religious contexts.

Carrier (1999, 2005) continues his thought on "happy schizotypes" and suggests that these type of people would be the ones who originated make believe miracle stories (to include the resurrection of Jesus Christ) and that the hearers of these reports would believe them to be credible reports of real happenings. Carrier also submits that these types of visionary persons would gravitate to religious groups, in order to become associated with "miracle workers." In Carrier's estimation, this is why so many of the entourage of Jesus had hallucinatory experiences. It is because they were composed of a high percentage of "happy schizotypes" and schizophrenics. Moreover, these types of persons would feel welcome in this environment that is conducive to persons having hallucinatory experiences. In turn, the disciples would share their hallucinatory experiences with others. Those who accepted the hallucinatory encounters of the disciples would be either "hallucinators" themselves or those who also believe that these hallucinations were positive experiences (Carrier, 2005a:187-88).

4.2.4 PRA: Hallucination caused by guilt

Another possible cause offered by Carrier for the hallucinations of those who encountered the post-resurrection Jesus Christ is intense feelings of guilt.[112] In particular, Carrier (2005b) singles out Paul as someone whose guilt over his persecution of the early Christian church, who he later came to admire, would bring on this sort of hallucination. He also mentions Paul's disgust with the Pharisees and their persecuting ways as another possible cause related to experienced guilt.

In more detail regarding Paul, Carrier (2010:307-08) provides additional data regarding the possible cause of Paul's revelation of Jesus Christ being a hallucination caused by guilt. He begins by suggesting that the odds would be pretty good for at least one of the many Jews opposed to the Christian church to come over to the Christian side from Judaism. He again offers that Paul could have become enamored with the early Christian church and that the cognitive dissonance he felt after personally doing so much harm to this group would cause him to have a hallucination thereby relieving the stress induced by his cognitive dissonance. This stress would not only be the catalyst for his hallucinations, but it would also be the stimulus for Paul joining the Christian church. Furthermore, Paul would feel an obligation to perform penance for what he had done to the church. So, out of obligation to repay the Christian church for the wrongs that he had committed against it, he would promote its moral and social reforms.

---

[112] Carrier (2006f) offers the massacre at Jonestown as an example of those who had the motivation to provide an extraordinary account of what happened which may have partially been motivated by guilt: "I offer the case of Jonestown: several survivors have, in order to preserve their faith that Jim Jones was good and divine, concocted stories of secret government hit squads, and still today stick by their "eye-witness" accounts of groups of soldiers firing machineguns into the crowds, despite overwhelming evidence that only a few dozen were killed by firearms (and they only by single pistol-shot to the head each), the other 900 by suicidal doses of poisoned punch. For example, see Michael Meiers, *Was Jonestown a CIA Medical Experiment? A Review of the Evidence*, published by Mellon Press, which also published four other books by Jonestown survivors, all with bizarre "eyewitness" accounts justifying their participation in, and one might think, guilt-ridden survival of, the Jonestown disaster (see Note 6)."

Carrier (2010: 307-08) continues his discussion of Paul's hallucinations in relation to his supposed cognitive dissonance:

> But the hardships involved suggest he had a genuine passion for the moral and social mission of the early Christians or even its apocalyptic convictions. And whether he fabricated his way into a mission for the greater good, or his natural tendency to hallucinate constructed the experience he needed to persuade him to find such a way out of his torment, entirely natural causes of his conversion can be imagined without proposing anything extraordinary.

Carrier offers that Paul could have either fabricated his encounter with Jesus Christ due to seeing the nobility in the Christian cause or again suggests that he could have hallucinated him in order to rid himself of guilt.

One other variant that Carrier (2006d) offers related to Paul's possible feelings of guilt as a cause for his hallucination of the risen Jesus Christ is that Paul could have possibly observed a naturally occurring light which could have caused him to have an emotional reaction thereby causing a hallucination to occur. Carrier further opines that he could envision a scenario where Paul may have been trying to save the Christians from the Romans. Moreover, this possible mission could have had its emotional genesis coming from Paul's guilt over what he had done to the Christians and also because of his admiration for them as well.

4.2.5   PRA: Hallucinations from fatigue/seizures

One final category of hallucination that Carrier mentions as a possible cause for those who had post-resurrection encounters with the risen Jesus Christ is physically induced hallucinations. One such physical state that Carrier offers for consideration is fatigue. Along with other factors mentioned previously in this section, Carrier (2005a:ch. 5) writes that "coupled with the right physical circumstances (like heat and fatigue on a long, desolate road), could have induced a convincing ecstatic event..." Carrier (2009:ch. 10) also links the physical state of fatigue or sleep deprivation to hypnopompic or hypnagogic hallucinations.

In addition to fatigue, another physical factor that Carrier (2006d) briefly lists as a possible cause in relation to Paul's encounter with the risen Jesus Christ is that Paul could have been having a seizure event:

> Moreover, this particular encounter in Acts has all the earmarks of something like a seizure-induced hallucination: Paul alone sees a flash of light, collapses, hears voices, and goes blind for a short period. An embolism is

sufficient to cause or explain all of this...Paul gives other accounts of his vision, which claim that others saw it, too. Doesn't this suggest a genuine vision from God? First of all, there is still never any mention of Jesus appearing in the flesh. Rather, all that appears is a light from heaven (*phôs ek tou ouranou*, 9.3; *ek tou ouranou...phôs*, 22.6; *ouranothen...phôs*, 26.13). So even if several saw the light, it can still have a natural explanation, from lightning to a reflection from a distant object, or even a simple ray of sunlight peaking through a cloud, any of which could also have induced a seizure or affected Paul emotionally, causing an hallucination (or inspiration).

In this description, Carrier not only offers that a seizure could have been produced as a result of observing a light flash (seeming to refer to an epileptic seizure), but also that another brain event (an embolism) could have also been a possible cause for a hallucination as well. Could Paul's Damascus Road experience be related to a seizure caused by physical factors?

4.3 Exposition of scholarly literature on hallucinations

4.3.1 Hypnagogic/Hypnopompic hallucinations

The exposition of scholarly literature on these two particular types of hallucinations is germane to the central inquiry of this project. Does Carrier provide evidence consistent with the aforementioned accepted principles of evidence that any of the PRA of Jesus Christ were hypnagogic or hypnopompic hallucinations? Regarding hypnagogic/hypnapompic hallucinations, Carrier has proposed these sorts of hallucinations were good candidates for what the disciples had experienced (4.2.1). In that he has proposed these sorts of hallucinations as possibilities for the PRA of Jesus Christ, then it is probative to research what the composition of these hallucinations are, the conditions in which they occur, and making contrasts/comparisons with the experience of the disciples as contained within the New Testament.

4.3.1.1 Hypnagogic hallucinations

In giving a definition for hypnagogic experiences, Andreas Mavromatis (1987:3) describes it as follows:

Hypnagogic experiences are commonly defined as hallucinatory and quasi-hallucinatory events taking place in the intermediate state between wakefulness and sleep. The term 'hypnagogic' (from the Greek *hypnos*=sleep, and agogeus=conductor, leader) was introduced into the literature by Maury who used it with specific reference to the presleep or sleep onset phenomena. Other terms suggested for these occurrences include 'presomnal or anthyhypnic sensations', 'visions of half sleep', 'oneiragogic images', 'phantasmata', and 'faces in the dark'.[113]

Mavromitis (1987:81) informs that the most common type of hynagogia is the visual modality and that common features of this modality are "eternality, autonomy, clarity of detail, brevity of duration, vividness of colour, and the sense of reality they impart in the subject." Other qualities of hypnagogia that can be observed by those who experience them are minuteness in size of the hallucination as well as the opposite state as well. Another aspect that Mavromitis brings out is that hypnagogic images differ from images that we observe daily. Hypnagogic images are "more vivid, sharp, and detailed, and they do not blend with ordinary images when attempts to inject them with the latter are made." In addition to these characteristics of hypnagogic images, Mavromitis also lists the different classifications of these images. These images include formless images, designs, faces, figures, animate and inanimate objects, nature scenes, scenes with people, print, and writing.

In addition to these visual hallucinations, auditory phenomena are also observed by those experiencing hypnagogia to "include the hearing of crashing noises, one's name being called, a doorbell ringing, neologisms, irrelevant sentences containing unrecognizable names, pompous nonsense, quotations, references to spoken conversations, music, etc. Not only are there visual and auditory hallucinations associated with hypnagogic hallucinations, but other hypnagogic experiences include somesthetic, kinesthetic, tactile, thermal, gustatory, and olfactory experiences. Other sensory experiences of hypnagogia include myoclonic jerks, falling, being

---

[113] Mavromatis (1987: 231) points out that hypnagogic imagery can also turn into a dream state. In addition to this observation Mavromitis also informs that there are links between hypnagogia and forms of meditation where the participant is able to relax and upon reaching a meditative state can experience a state of satori or mystical enlightenment. Common experiences of both meditation and hypnagogia include unusual sensations, the feeling of being 'chemically' linked with the world, being unable to describe these experiences, and "temporal immediacy." In addition to these commonalities between hypnagogia and meditation, Mavromitis also lists a link between hypnagogia and "psi states" such as telepathy, clairvoyance, clairaudience, psychometry, and ecsomatosis.

touched, the sense of heat and cold, and a number of tastes and smells. Another hypnagogic experience while falling asleep that was noted was nonsensical statements (Mavromatis, 1987:81).

Peter McKellar (1989:88) gives additional detail regarding hypnagogic imagery. In 1861, Alfred Maury gave Hypnagogia its name and also notes that Aristotle mentions hypnagogic experiences. McKellar observes that Aristotle recognized the tendency of this pre-sleep state experience to produce not only fear but also anxiety in the young people of his day. McKellar writes that the most frequently observed manifestations of hypnagogia are auditory hallucinations where someone may hear an assortment of sounds such as voices, music, and other auditory noises. He also notes that oftentimes, hypnagogic imagery will commence without warning.

In continuing his description of hypnagogia McKellar (1989:92) notes that there is great variance in the content of hypnagogic imagery. One image may be that of a landscape whereas another maybe from the viewpoint of looking through a slit in a curtain that is described as a misty cloud. McKellar describes these images as "surprising" to the one experiencing them and also that they are spontaneous in nature. Moreover, the one having the experience describes them as one they watch as a spectator. McKellar also uses F.E. Leaning's (cited by McKellar, 1989:92) research into hypnagogic imagery. Leaning recognizes five different categories for hypnagogic images: 1) formless light charged clouds that float between the eye and eyelid 2) Faces (some kind but others frightening) 3) Designs and objects 4) Landscapes 5) Scenes.[114]

In speaking to his patients and also gleaning from his own personal experience with hypnagogic imagery, McKellar (1989:108) states that a common impression that those who experience it have is that it is just another part of life. It is viewed as "an interesting variant of normal mental life." McKellar also describes how Mary Shelley and Stevenson's Jekyl-Hyde novel were influenced by this imagery. McKellar also identifies a famous German scientist who had hypnagogic images that he utilized in his theorizing of chemical compounds (Benzene).

---

[114] Another hypnagogic image described by McKellar (1989:110) is a polyopic manifestation of many images, in one instance, a group of pink cockatoos on a table talking to each other. Yet another manifestation of hypnagogic images is labeled hypnagogic synaesthesias. These images are experienced in synchronization with sounds heard by the person viewing the images. McKellar was familiar with one of these sorts of images. He describes hearing of a bubblelike figure that ran in rhythm to the music of Bolero.

Objection Three: The Disciples Hallucinated the Risen Jesus Christ

Another quality of hypnagogic imagery mentioned by McKellar (1989:110-11) is that the various manifestations of the imagery are autonomous. They come and go randomly without the aid of the one experiencing them. However, McKellar has interviewed subjects who were able to insert themselves into the action once the action of the drama commenced. However, the subject or patient was not able to determine the action but could alter certain details once it had begun. Another patient discussed the ability to influence his imagery. This patient would think that he wanted the shape of a cloud to change and it would. However, he could not determine the new shape of the cloud.

Andre Aleman and Frank Laroi (2008:40-41) advise that the term hallucination was first used in 1572 but described them as related to "ghostes and spirits walking by night [sic]." Most of the time hypnagogia and hypnopompia are observed in those suffering from sleep-related disorders to include narcolepsy, cataplexy, sleep paralysis, and excessive daytime sleepiness. In addition to this information Aleman and Laroi also report that there are high incidences of hypnagogia in the general population. Ohaya and others report that 37% of the general population stated that they had experienced hypnagogic hallucinations and that 12% of the general population had experienced hypnopompic hallucinations.

Moreover, regarding the emotional impact of hypnagogic imagery, Aleman and Laroi report the findings of Cheyne Newby-Clark, & Rueffer (cited by Aleman, A. & Laroi, F., 2008:18) that reveal the most common emotional reaction to these hallucinations is fear. Ohayan (cited by Aleman, A. & Laroi, F., 2008:18) reported that approximately half of his respondents registered the emotion of fear after experiencing hypnagogia or hypnopompia. In addition to these surveys, Laroi and Van der Linden (cited by Aleman, A. & Laroi, F., 2008:18) reported the respondents to their study registered mostly negative reactions as well.

Ghazi Asaad (1990:98) offers additional information on hypnagogic hallucinations. Regarding this variety of mental imagery, Asaad writes:

> In hypnagogic hallucinations, the person experiencing it is usually aware that the experience is unreal. These hallucinations are normally vivid and often terrifying in nature. West (1975) has hypothesized that as one goes from wakefulness to a sleep state, the awareness of the environment is decreased and the cortical arousal is high. This disparity between these two factors may be the reason this type of hallucination is experienced. The reverse cycle of returning to wakefulness from sleep is believed to trigger hypnopompic hallucinations.

J. Allen Hobson (2002:153) introduces hypnagogic hallucinations as "visuomotor sensations at sleep onset." He further explains that if the subject is still awake or if he is aroused by dreamlike images, then his experiences are in this category. In further explaining hypnagogic imagery, Hobson (2002:154-55) explains the process by which hypnagogic imagery manifests itself by making analogy to someone who encounters an open door upon arriving at home. When this occurs, a person is immediately aroused and his senses are more alert. The first reaction to such circumstances is to believe that an intruder has entered your house. This fear would increase if noises were heard coming from the second story of the home. In this sort of scenario, one's imagination may very well increase the anxiety of the person that encounters the open door as he may revert to scenarios from movies that he has viewed. After investigating, it is realized that the cleaning lady merely left the door and a window upstairs open. But because of your heightened internal state of awareness and because of your imagination, you had an unrealistic perception of what was going on inside the house. Hobson states that as you are going to sleep, the internal stimuli of your dream consciousness temporarily overwhelms the external stimuli causing the dream images to intrude into your wakefulness thereby causing the hallucinations.

Regarding hypnagogic hallucinations, Oliver Sacks (2012:208) mentions that they are not like "true" hallucinations in that they are not "felt as real and are not projected into external space." However, they are related to other hallucinations because they are "involuntary, uncontrollable, autonomous; they may have preternatural colors and detail and may undergo rapid and bizarre transformations unlike those of normal mental imagery." Sacks further describes the hypnagogic hallucinations that his patients have had as being random, having no real pattern, and being composed of an infinite variety of constantly alternating patterns and forms. They are also fleeting in nature and are more like flashes than dreamlike episodes.

In addition to these qualities of hypnagogic hallucinations, Sacks (2012:206) explains there are other manifestations than just colors. There are an endless variety of symptoms to include, auditory hallucinations of persons speaking or music playing. Another sort of hallucination that is common in these sorts of experiences is the observance of faces that appear before the subject. In his studies of those who hallucinated faces, Sacks finds that there are different ways in how faces are visualized. He reports that some faces come out of a misty background and then disappear, some faces are ugly, but then others are pleasant. There may even be a clustering of faces as well. Concerning visualized faces, Sacks offers that these faces are very often clearly defined, but unrecognizable. As with the other manifestations of these sorts of hallucinations, the faces have no real meaning along with the other meaningless images that cascade through the consciousness of the one hallucinating.

4.3.1.2 Hypnopompic hallucinations

Ghazi Asaad (1990:98) provides a brief description of hypnopompia as a word derived from the Greek Word "hypnos" rendered as sleep and the Greek word "pompe" which means "going away." F.W.H. Myers (cited by McKellar, 1989:101) named hypnopompic imagery after he distinguished this type of imagery from the hypnagogic variety. An example of one such type of hypnopompic image is the hallucination of already being up and in the process of getting ready for work. Another experience noted by McKellar is a woman "picking her way through a mass of crabs on the carpet." She finally reached the light switch and turned it on to reassure herself that the crabs were merely a hallucination. McKellar also uses the term "false wakings" as synonymous with hypnopompia. McKellar advises of the differing emotions that are experienced during hypnagogic and hypnopompic imagery. Emotions that McKellar identifies are interest, amusement, anxiety, surprise, and anger. He also describes feelings of guilt that he has had for not rescuing an imaginary Siamese fish (McKellar, 1989:107).

J. Allen Hobson (2002:137) discusses hypnopompic hallucinations and states that they are a continuation of the dream state as a person transitions from dreaming to waking. These hallucinations merely continue the dreaming process into the period of wakefulness. To lend credence to this proposition, Hobson offers that most people have had unusual experiences upon waking to include sleepwalking, a vivid dream where there is exciting activity, or even being unable to move upon arousing from sleep.

In comparing hypnopompic and hypnagogic imagery, Hobson (2002:137) notes that hypnopompic hallucinations may be more terrifying than hypnagogic imagery. Hobson further offers that hypnopompic hallucinations can be more terrifying when a person is trying to wean himself off anti-depressants and other psychoactive drugs that interrelate with the brain. He further shares that some of these patients dread the idea of awakening because the post-sleep hallucinations can be so severe. Hobson gives an example of a hypnopompic hallucination experienced by one of his patients who, upon waking, experienced a large alligator snapping at her from under her bed.

Oliver Sacks (2012:210-217) observes that there is a difference between hypnagogic and hypnopompic hallucinations. Whereas hypnagogic hallucinations "proceed quietly and fleetingly," hypnopompic hallucinations "are often seen with open eyes, in bright illumination; they are frequently projected into external space and seem to be totally solid and real" (Sacks, 2012:210). These hallucinations have several different effects upon those who experience them. They can be pleasurable, terrifying, or benign. They also do not last long because they occur as one is waking from sleep. In some instances, an image from the dream can linger in a hallucination but then it quickly disappears. Even though the one experiencing this hallucination knows that it is a hallucination, they report that the vivid images will remain in their memory for many years because of how vivid the images were. Not only can this form of hallucination be visual but it can manifest with the other senses as well.

4.3.2 Schizophrenic hallucinations

The exposition of scholarly literature on schizophrenic hallucinations is necessary in order to analyze whether Carrier's claim of hallucinating disciples is in accord with accepted principles of evidence. What are schizophrenic hallucinations and how do they present in someone suffering from them? In what mode are they experienced? Were, the disciples schizophrenic or did they possess schizotypal personalities as Carrier has posited? As Carrier alleges, did the disciples just make up the PRA of Jesus Christ because of their mental disorders/instabilities (4.2.3)? Did groups of schizophrenics or those with schizotypal personalities all congregate together in groups and then fabricate stories as alleged by Carrier (4.2.3)?

Regarding the first known mentions of schizophrenia, the authors (Begley *et al.*, 2002) of an article in the magazine *Newsweek* entitled "The Schizophrenic Mind" describe the origins of schizophrenia along with its attendant symptoms. The authors supply that Emil Kraeplin first described the symptoms of schizophrenia in the 1890s and that it is characterized by not being able to discern reality from imagination. The article reports that one percent of Americans have schizophrenia with the figure remaining constant throughout the years.

Regarding a description or definition of schizophrenia,[115] Christopher Frith (1992:4-5) supplies information regarding the symptoms of schizophrenia:

---

[115] K. Newman-Taylor and S. Sambrook (2013, 266) define schizophrenia as: "A diagnosis of mental disorder characterized by auditory hallucinations, paranoid or

In order for the patient to be diagnosed as schizophrenic the patient must report particular kinds of bizarre experiences and beliefs. Many of the symptoms involve hearing voices (hallucinations). These voices are described as, "discussing my actions", "talking to me," "repeating my thoughts." Commonly found bizarre beliefs (delusions) are that "others can read my thoughts," "that alien forces are controlling my actions," "that "famous people are communicating with me," "that my actions somehow affect world events."

Frith (1992:5-6) further explains that schizophrenia can be diagnosed because of the symptoms and the signs observed in the subject. Moreover, Frith offers that schizophrenia can be ascertained from talking with the subject about the symptoms and from observing the signs of schizophrenia in the patient. As schizophrenia becomes more serious, the unusual beliefs and experiences will no longer be prominent with mainly the "negative" aspects of the disease remaining. If a patient is observed in the later stages of the disease, then research into the earlier stages where the symptoms are present is needed to confirm the diagnosis. Frith further explains that anywhere from 30 to 50 percent of the cases will reach a chronic/deteriorated state after the first two to five years of manifesting the disease even though serious manifestations of bizarre behavior can still occur from time to time.

In reference to the diagnosis of Schizophrenia, Paul Bennett (2011:159) explains there are a number of symptoms that signal the onset of Schizophrenia in a person. If a person possesses two or more of these symptoms, then the person likely has schizophrenia. These symptoms include a person having delusions, hallucinations, disorganized speech, grossly disorganized or catatonic behavior, and negative symptoms to include flattened mood, alogia or avolition. If any of these symptoms are severe enough, then just displaying only one can lead to a Schizophrenia diagnosis. A severe symptom could be if a person is having hallucinations of a "voice keeping up a running commentary on the person's behavior or thoughts, or involve two or more voices conversing with each other."

In paranoid schizophrenia, Begley *et al.* (2002) inform that the sufferer becomes convinced that someone is out to get them and is divorced from reality as the disease manifests in the patient. They experience voices and images that are only occurring inside their minds and they believe

---

bizarre delusions, and disorganized speech and behavior, and associated with significant social or occupational impairment. The diagnosis is controversial and its value in predicting aetiology and course of the disorder and effectiveness of treatments has been questioned".

what they are experiencing is occurring in the real, external world. Begley *et al.* also give several examples of schizophrenia sufferers to include those who act on commands to kill as well as a man who barricades himself inside his house and positions makeshift noise alarms at key entrance points to alert him if someone is trying to enter his home. In conducting research on these behaviors, scans were completed of the brains of schizophrenia sufferers that revealed that the auditory cortex and other parts of the brain that control memories (hippocampus) and emotions (amygdala) display intense activity levels. This leads researchers to surmise that the symptoms must arise as a result of physical abnormalities in the brain that deceive the sufferer into believing that the voices and other stimuli being experienced in the brain are real.[116]

Frith (1992:68) offers that only twenty percent of schizophrenia sufferers reported other than audio hallucinations to include visual, tactile, or internal sensations. He further reports that most schizophrenic patients believe these hallucinations are real. Frith gives an instance of the persistent belief in the reality of hallucinations by the schizophrenic patient coming from Evelyn Waugh's novel, *The Ordeal of Gilbert Pinfold*.[117]

Frith (1992:68-69) describes one set of theories of "schizophrenic hallucination origination" as coming from a misperception of an external stimulus. He further observes these theories coming from abnormal cognitive processes underlying the perception of the external stimulus. He gives an example of someone hearing running water (stimulus A) but instead of hearing running water, the subject hears a baby crying (stimulus B). Another possibility for a schizophrenic hallucination from input ex-

---

[116] M. Gates and R. Ancill (1994:266) share the findings of their research regarding the neural basis for auditory hallucinations. They report that there is much interest in studying this type of phenomena because of its close link with Schizophrenia. They also share that "auditory hallucinations may occur due to pathology in perception and memory systems in the temporal lobe." The authors continue that "the auditory association cortex projects widely to other systems, including the amygdala and hippocampus; therefore, pathological phenomena could occur due to a disruption in any part of this network of systems" (Gates & Ancill, 1994:246).

[117] In this novel, Waugh's main character, Gilbert Pinfold has the following experience: "For a long time, two hours perhaps, Mr. Pinfold lay in his bunk listening. He was albeit to hear quite distinctly not only what was said in his immediate vicinity, but elsewhere. He had the light on, now, in his cabin and as he gazed at the complex of tubes and wires that ran across his ceiling, he realized that they must form some sort of general junction in the system of communication. Through some trick or fault or wartime survival everything spoken in the executive quarters of the ship was transmitted to him" (Waugh, 1957:78).

ternal to the schizophrenic patient is that the patient becomes confused due to several auditory stimuli occurring at the same time. The patient may not be able to delineate between the two sounds. They are too similar to the patient. Due to the confusion of hearing several aural stimuli at once, noisy environments may exacerbate the problem for the schizophrenia sufferer. However, Frith observes that if a schizophrenia sufferer has this problem, then the noise problem is coming from the nervous system of the patient.

Another possible explanation for the confusion with the schizophrenic patient suggested by Frith (1992:69-70) is the patient has a problem interpreting a noise that they have heard. If a woman has a fear of being inattentive to a baby, then she may perceive any number of noises to be the cry of a baby. Similarly, Frith also suggests that schizophrenic hallucinations may be due to some disorder of bias as the hallucinations often mirror the beliefs and obsessions of the patient. At the end of his analysis, Frith shares that he does not believe that the misperception of external stimulus accounts for schizophrenic hallucinations. Frith (1992:76) also "assumes" from his work with schizophrenic hallucinations that some auditory hallucinations are based on inner speech from the patient that the patient believes is coming from an external source.

In *Visual Hallucinations in the Psychosis Spectrum and Comparative Information From Neurodegenerative Disorders and Eye Disease*, the authors (Waters et al., 2014: S236) discuss visual hallucinations related to psychosis.[118] Their research indicates that VHs possess the physical characteristics of real perceptions. Physical characteristics they observe in VHs of this type are that they are life-sized, solid, detailed, and are projected into the external world. They also indicate that these VHs can be either colorful or black and white, and can possess three-dimensional forms that include shadow and depth as well as distinct edges. VHs are also frequently known to be dynamic or can also be static with the content of the VH sometimes changing in size.

---

[118] The authors provide a description of psychotic disorders from the American Academy of Child & Adolescent Psychiatry: Glossary of Symptoms and Illnesses (cited by Waters *et al.*, 2014, S242): "Psychotic disorders include severe mental disorders which are characterized by extreme impairment of a person's ability to think clearly, respond emotionally, communicate effectively, understand reality, and behave appropriately. Psychotic symptoms can be seen in teenagers with a number of serious mental illnesses, such as depression, bipolar disorder (manic-depression), schizophrenia, and with some forms of alcohol and drug abuse. Psychotic symptoms interfere with a person's daily functioning and can be quite debilitating. Psychotic symptoms include delusions and hallucinations."

Regarding the sense of reality experienced by the psychotic patient, the aforementioned authors (Waters *et al.*, 2014:S237) share that the images are perceived by the patient to be "real in a concrete sense." As evidence of this subjective reality experienced by most patients, activity related to the hallucination such as swinging at the image or moving toward the vision or even trying to keep them safe from the hallucination is often observed. The authors also note that the psychotic patient has no control over the content and the form the VH takes. Moreover, the authors indicate that when the VH manifests itself, the patients are surprised and cannot change what is being portrayed in the VH.

The authors (Waters *et al.*, 2014:S237) further supply information relating to the onset and triggering events for VHs in psychotic patients. The onset of VHs in psychiatric patients has been associated with tiredness, stress, loneliness, and relationship problems. Other causes of VHs in these patients include negative emotions, and heightened levels of anxiety. Reactions reported by the authors are pleasure, reassurance, happiness, and indifference. VHs can also cause negative reactions such as sadness, fright, and hopelessness. One reaction of patients to a hallucination is they believe they must act upon something suggested in the VH or they will face some sort of punishment if they do not act in accord with the VH. The authors are sure to point out these reactions are in direct contrast with hallucinations caused by organic conditions as the sufferers of these conditions know that the hallucination(s) they are experiencing is not real. Regarding their beliefs about their VH, psychotic patients frequently associate the source of their VHs as being supernatural in origin and they feel the compunction to act on the message of the VH in order to preserve their wellbeing (physical/psychological).

> One other important point brought up by the aforementioned authors (Waters, *et al.*, 2014: S236) is in regard to "multi-modal" hallucinations or those that include more than one type of sensory perception (e.g. visual, audio, tactile, etc.). The authors' research reveals that combinations of audio and visual hallucinations occur in up to 84% of schizophrenia patients. However, regarding this audio/visual combination of hallucinatory activity, the authors (Waters, *et al.*, 2014, S237) are careful to point out the following:
>
> It is important to note, however, that "simultaneous" (or "fused") auditory and VHs are not a frequent occurrence. In most cases, they are experienced at different times (e.g., an auditory hallucination one day and a VH the next). Furthermore, when simultaneous auditory/VHs do occur, they are typically unrelated (e.g., seeing the devil while hearing the voice of a relative inside one's head), suggesting that the mechanisms for auditory

and VHs in these disorders must be partly independent, though with some overlap.

Regarding the term schizotypy, N.J. Holt et al. (2008:1) report that it is a term that comes from "schizophrenic genotype" and those having this as part of their personality makeup make them more vulnerable to contracting schizophrenia. However, Holt et al. also advise that in the professional literature, there are two distinct approaches to the topic of schizotypy. One group advocates that a person located on the schizotypy scale means that one will most likely in the future end up suffering from schizophrenia. The other school of thought rejects the notion that schizotypy is indicative of future psychopathology and should be viewed as a "personality continuum upon which all people vary." With this second methodology, schizotypy is afforded a neutral status in relation to mental health. However, this methodology recognizes that interaction with "risk (e.g. stress) and protective variables (e.g. supportive social networks)" will lead either to healthy (creativity) or unhealthy (psychosis) outcomes (Holt et al., 2008:1-2). In that Carrier commented on the possibility of the disciples and early Christians possessing a "happy schizotypal" personality that led to them be prone to experience hallucinations, (4.2.3) it is probative to include information on this type of personality.

Additional information supplied by Holt *et al.* (2008:2) analyzed differences in schizotype clusters with related factors. In their study, these authors share several factors that comprise a "happy" or "benign" schizotypy personality. Holt *et al.* list four factors with the most prominent factor being unusual experiences. The items listed under the category of unusual experiences include "magical or religious beliefs, altered sensations and perceptions of one's own body and the world, déjà vu, jamais vu, auditory hallucinations and pseudo-hallucinations. In addition to these qualities, another factor observed in schizotypal subjects are cognitive disorganization that is characterized by introvertive anhedonia, and impulsive non-conformity. However, a happy schizotypal personality is one that is well adjusted, believes in the paranormal and scores high on tests measuring creativity (Holt et al., 2008:10).

In an article on the Mayo Clinic (2016) website, the symptoms for schizotypal personality disorder are included, compared and contrasted with schizophrenia. One contrast that is brought out between schizotypal personality disorder and schizophrenia is that those who have the former condition may experience brief psychotic episodes to include delusions or hallucinations. However, these symptoms are not as "frequent, prolonged, or intense as in schizophrenia." In addition to this contrast with schizophrenia, differences between distorted perceptions and reality can be made known to schizotypal disorder sufferers whereas those suffering from schizophrenia do not have the ability to distinguish between what is delusional and what is reality.

4.3.3 Bereavement/Grief hallucinations

Carrier has written much advocating that the disciples experienced hallucinations as a result of the tragic loss of their beloved leader, Jesus Christ. Because of the emotional trauma of losing someone so important to them, the disciples could have hallucinated the risen Jesus Christ. This frequently reported phenomenon of the bereaved receiving visits from the recently departed seems to be believable upon a surface analysis. However, does an inquiry into this version of Carrier's bereavement hallucination supposition match up with the results of an examination of the resurrection narratives by accepted principles of evidence? Do the findings of this analysis comport with the scholarly literature on bereavement/grief hallucinations? A survey of this literature is needed to determine whether there are solid correlations between what the disciples experienced as recorded in the New Testament resurrection narratives and bereavement hallucinations.

In describing bereavement/grief hallucinations Castelnovo *et al.* (2015:266) define post-bereavement hallucinatory experiences (PBHE) as "abnormal sensory experiences that are frequently reported by bereaved individuals without a history of mental disorder. Given current uncertainty over the continuum of psychotic experiences in the general population, whether or not they should be considered pathological remains unclear." In addition to this definition, Castelnovo *et al.* (2015:267) share that in the *Diagnostic and Statistical Manual of Mental Disorders* (DSM-5), there is a diagnosis listed for "persistent complex bereavement disorder" that is "characterized by severe and persistent grief and mourning reactions." One of the features listed for this bereavement disorder is hallucinations of the decedent's presence. Castelnovo *et al.* also explain that the presence of this disorder in the general population is estimated to be between 2.4%-4.8%.

However, not all of those reported to have the disorder actually hallucinate their deceased relative.

In their research on bereavement hallucinations, Epstein et al. (2006:255) reference a 1971 study conducted by Rees that registered nearly half of a sampling of bereaved persons as having experienced sensory hallucinations on a regular basis up to ten years after the death of their loved one. Their conclusion is that a large number of the bereaved do not cut off their emotional ties with their deceased loved one for many years. Epstein et al. continue their survey regarding bereavement hallucinations and offer the findings of Shuchter and Zisook (1993) whose research revealed that contact with the deceased by the bereaved occur quite frequently and in various forms to include sensing, talking with, dreaming of, and reminding themselves of the decedent. Moreover, the frequency with which those who were bereaved had contact with the deceased did not lessen over time after the passing of the decedent. The duration of the contact with both examples given are of interest due to the long duration reported by the researchers.

N.P. Field and C. Filanosky (2010: 3-4) report that a bereaved person who has a hallucination of a deceased relation misconstrues an internal source of information as coming from an external source. These hallucinations are often reported as occurring in an environment of diminished sensory capability where the one experiencing the hallucination or illusion has a greater opportunity to misjudge what he is seeing (e.g. lying in bed at night). They further elucidate that hallucinations and illusions of a decedent by the bereaved is indicative of a failure to properly process the grief related to the death of the loved one. Field and Filanosky also share that increased usage of externalized continuing bonds (i.e. hallucinations and/or illusions) with the deceased relation by the bereaved will occur if the cause of death involves the violent loss of the decedent (e.g. by accident, suicide, and homicide). Moreover, they offer that if the hallucination experienced by the bereaved is traumatic in nature, it is most likely due to the trauma of what the bereaved experienced if they were present when the decedent died and the failure to properly integrate the loss. The findings of these studies are useful in comparing the experiences of those interviewed with the resurrection narratives included within the New Testament.

M. Sanger (2009:70) reports on sensing or feeling the presence of loved ones after they have died. Sanger gives an example of a woman who continues to communicate with her deceased mother on a weekly basis after she died. Many would view this sort of communication as hallucinatory or failing to sever the relationship bond in a healthy way. Sanger is curious if this sort of activity is pathological or if this sort of continuing communication should be considered a normal part of the grieving process.

Sanger (2009:70-73) shares the study of Davis and Smith (1977) that found 40% of Americans felt at least one time as if they were really communicating with someone who had died. A study that was conducted a little earlier than that of Davis and Smith treated a similar topic. Sanger reports that Kalish and Reynolds (1977) queried bereaved persons to determine if they had ever felt the presence or experienced any deceased person they knew after they had died. The results of this study were broken down into percentages by race with 55% of African-Americans, 54% of Mexican-Americans, 38% of Anglo-Americans, and 29% of Japanese-Americans answering in the affirmative. Sanger also notes that the only type of post-bereavement phenomenon that has a negative connotation implied is bereavement hallucinations. However, the usage of the phrase "continuing bonds" by many professional psychologists signals a shift where having a bereavement hallucination is no longer viewed negatively. Sanger offers that this shift is significant progress in removing the stigma from those who experience bereavement hallucinations.

In their survey of the research of other psychologists in relation to the bereaved experiencing their deceased relations, Keen *et al.* report on the trends coming from these various research projects. They share the findings of Rees (1971) (cited by Keen *et al.*, 2013:388) regarding the most common experiences reported by the bereaved. Rees reported that of the 293 widows that he interviewed, 137 of them had PBHE with feeling the presence of the deceased (39%) leading the list followed by seeing (14%), hearing (13%), and speaking (13%) to the decedent. They continue with their survey by sharing the research of Olson *et al.* (cited by Keen *et al.*, 2013:399) (1985) who interviewed 46 widows. They found that 28 (61%) of these widows had "sense of presence" experiences.[119] The most frequently experienced phenomenon was seeing the decedent (48%) followed by auditory hallucination (30%). Other hallucinations reported were feeling the presence of the decedent (20%), touching (13%), and talking (11%) with the decedent. Moreover, Keen *et al.* reported the findings of other research projects as well.[120]

---

[119] From (Steffen and Coyle 2011:580), "Sense-of-presence experiences can be defined as the nonmaterial quasisensory subjective but (experienced as) veridical feeling of presence of the deceased (Bennett & Bennett, 2000; Datson & Marwit, 1997) which tends to occur unexpectedly (e.g., Conant, 1996) and is generally perceived as comforting (e.g., Parkes, 1970; Sormanti & August, 1997), pleasant (Grimby, 1998), and helpful or positive (e.g., Chan *et al.*, 2005; LaGrand, 1997). Sometimes, though, sense-of-presence experiences are perceived as negative."

[120] Keen *et al.* (2013:390) also report on the factor that makes having a sense-of-presence experience more or less likely: "Studies have explored the factors that made having a sense-of-presence experience more or less likely. Simon-Buller, Christopherson, and Jones (1989) carried out a quantitative study that analyzed

In summarizing their survey of the various research findings of the aforementioned psychologists, Keen *et al.* (2013:390) share that from approximately half to three-quarters of the bereaved respondents reported having a sense-of-presence hallucination even though the research was conducted in different areas of the world and spanned four decades. The general findings of these surveys indicate that the most common form of these experiences was to feel that the decedent was nearby. In relation to actually experiencing the decedent with one's senses, their survey revealed less agreement here with a general trend of seeing the decedent as the most common form of hallucination followed by hearing a sound related to them.

Additional sensory experiences reported by Keen *et al.* (2013:390) were having an olfactory hallucination where perfume or aftershave products were smelled. Further sensory experiences with the deceased included feeling the weight of the decedent on the bed or sensing the touch of the decedent. Furthermore, they report the findings of several researchers who found that some of the participants in their studies experienced the deceased in a combination of sensory modalities at the same time. In these contacts with the deceased, it appears that most of these contacts are of a brief duration and mostly in one mode. The experience of the decedent in multiple modes has been reported but is rare according to this report.

> Regarding the Japanese and the way in which the bereaved interrelate to their deceased relatives, Keen *et al.* (2013:394) note the difference between how the Japanese view their contact with the dead as contrasted with the Western perspective on contact with the dead:
> Yamamoto *et al.* (1969) interviewed 20 widows in Japan and reported that 90% (n 1/4 18) of them reported sensing the presence of the deceased at the family altar where ancestor worship takes place. Additionally, 50% (n1/410) also reported either seeing their dead husbands, or hearing his voice or footsteps. The authors described how Japanese religious culture means that ancestors are worshipped and believed to be contactable after death and that it is seen as a normal cultural aspect to continue a relationship with the deceased through the family altar…Yamamoto *et al.* (1969) suggest that religious beliefs were a helpful aspect of coping and that none

---

42 variables to explore to what extent they could predict that someone would sense the presence of the deceased. They found that the variable most predictive of this was their religious orientation. People who identified themselves as more liberal (rather than conservative) in their religious orientation were more likely to experience the phenomenon."

of the widows were concerned about having their experiences because ancestor worship at the family altar is an accepted cultural practice in Japan.

The widespread, continuing contact with dead relatives, along with the acceptance of contact with the dead of the Japanese bereaved with their dead relatives is contrasted with the Western attitude towards experiencing their dead where there is less acceptance of PBHEs. What is probative regarding this study is the duration of the relationship between the bereaved and their deceased relations that seems to span most of the lives of the bereaved.

Susan Kwilecki (2011:221) surveys the scholarly literature on PBHEs and observes a shift in the view of these hallucinations. Kwilecki observes that in the past, PBHEs were considered a process in which the bereaved severed ties with the deceased. However, Kwilecki reports that the new trend is for the one mourning to continue the relationship past death with the recently departed loved one. This relationship is sustained through an ever-changing mental representation. Kwilecki offers that a growing body of literature on the subject shares this sentiment. This is relevant to the topic at hand as it shows the on-going or sustained nature of the relationship of the bereaved with the decedent.

Oliver Sacks (2012:209) mentions the prevalence of bereavement hallucinations in various world cultures and offers an example coming from English literature with Shakespeare's *Hamlet* and *Macbeth*. In *Hamlet*, Hamlet's father appears to him after his death and in *Macbeth* several characters see ghosts, daggers hanging in midair, and the blood of the departed king. Sacks (2012:231-36) offers several examples of persons not only dreaming about their recently departed loved ones but also hallucinating about them as well. He offers instances from his own life where he often dreamt about his parents and three brothers who preceded him in death. He also discusses the occurrence of illusions where he believed that he had seen his mother on repeated occasions after her death. However, this illusion was based on seeing persons who had similar characteristics as his mother.

Other bereavement hallucinations that Sacks (2012:209) offers as examples are people hearing the voice of a loved one, seeing the face of a departed friend suspended in midair smiling, or a recently departed relative jogging by their house in his favorite pair of yellow running shorts. In all of these circumstances, Sacks ascribes these occurrences to persons who are responding to their grief of experiencing a profound loss. In one instance, Sacks shares an example of a man who experienced his father in his bedroom upon waking. His father was wearing a familiar outfit and was sitting in his bedroom. The recently departed father communicated to his son that everything was fine. Upon getting out of his bed, the son reported that his father was no longer there. These examples given by Sacks reveal the fleeting nature of many bereavement hallucinations. In these sample cases, the hallucinations are very brief encounters lasting only for seconds.

4.3.4 Seizure related hallucinations

Could Paul's experience with the risen Jesus Christ be as a result of an embolism or seizure? This is one of many theories that Carrier uses to suggest that the followers of Jesus hallucinated when they experienced the risen Jesus Christ (4.2.5). Does Paul's Damascus Road experience, as observed in several places in the New Testament (Acts 9; Acts 26; 1 Corinthians 15) match up with what Carrier propounds?

In relation to hallucinations as a result of epileptic seizures, Elliott *et al.* (2009: 162) report that hallucinations, illusions, and delusions in epilepsy are "as a result of localized or network based neuronal epileptic activity that can be investigated especially using intracranial stereoelectroencephalography". Furthermore, they report that from a neurological perspective there is not much reason to differentiate between these various modalities (from a brain perspective) as a result of the "physiological overlap" of these phenomena. Continuing their explanation of the relationship between hallucinations and the brain, Elliott *et al.* (2009:163) submit that through many years of testing and research, it has been determined that hallucinations occur as a result of "the activation of a localised [sic] group of neurones [sic] which can be investigated by cerebral recording and cerebral stimulation."

Regarding hallucinations from an organic perspective, Elliott *et al.* (2009:164) further explain that organic hallucinations where a percept occurs without a stimulus happen as a result of a physiological brain disorder/disease. In essence, there is a local disturbance in the brain that causes a perceptual response. Due to this disturbance, an epileptic discharge in the brain can result in a hallucinatory, delusional, or "illusional" event. They further relate that Robert Penfield discovered the correlation between brain states and hallucinatory activity in 1938. Penfield was conducting brain surgery on epileptic patients. He would electronically stimulate the temporal lobe of these patients. Penfield reported that they would have two types of responses he categorized as "experiential and interpretive mental phenomena" (Elliott *et al.*, 2009:165). The experiential phenomena were described as representations of "mental events from the patients' personal past" that could be very vivid and could result in a "unified subjective experience" as a result of the integration of several elements (perception memory, affect) (Elliott et al., 2009:165).[121]

Elliott et al. mention the work of several researchers who conducted various studies. One of these studies was conducted by Taylor et al. who reported that occipital seizures resulted in various hallucinatory phenomena.[122] Another study conducted by Mallard et al. (cited by Elliott, 2009:168) show that various types of seizures experienced by epilepsy patients come from different brain structures.[123] Mohammed et al. (cited by Elliott, 2009:168) conducted research centering on auditory hallucinations being experienced by six children. He utilized a magnetoencephalography (MEG) to chart the brain activity while the children were experiencing the hallucinations.[124] Still more research has reported

---

[121] Gloor (1990) (cited by Elliott et al., 2009:165) "summarises [sic] the key features of 'experiential responses' as follows: (a) there may be a vivid or intrusive recall of a past event; (b) there is a feeling of familiarity or reminiscence (déjà vu, deja vécu); (c) the characteristic sensation of dreaminess; (d) the patient is said to be always aware of the incongruity and illusory nature of the experience; (e) affective states such as fear, sadness, guilt, anger or sexual excitement are common; (f) these responses typically lack certain features such as forward motion in time (with the exception possibly of musical hallucinations) and scenes do not evolve; and (g) auditory hallucinations are said to be almost entirely without semantic content (i.e., they lack coherent meaning)."

[122] According to Taylor et al. (2003) (cited by Elliott et al., 2009:169), "elementary hallucinations were divided into positive (simply shaped flashes of colour or light, phosphenes) and negative (scotoma, hemianopia, amaurosis) manifestations. Simple illusions may also occur where objects may appear to change in size (macropsia and micropsia), shape (metamorphopsia), or lose colour (achromatopsia). Panayiotopoulos (1999) provides a qualitative analysis of visual symptoms in 9 patients with idiopathic occipital epilepsy with visual hallucinations (IOEVH). He found that elementary ictal visual hallucinations comprised mostly multiple bright coloured spots, circles, or balls lasting for between 5 and 30 s, although in one patient up to 10 min. Taylor also reports that "Ictal complex visual hallucinations tend to last a few seconds to minutes with the patient retaining insight into the unreality of the experience" (Taylor et al., 2003).

[123] This study showed different areas of the brain related to hallucinatory activity: Heschl's gyrus for primary auditory hallucinations, more extended and lateral parts of the superior temporal gyrus for complex auditory hallucinations and basal — temporal gyri and temporo-occipital junction for complex visual hallucinations (Bancaud and Talairach, 1993) (cited by Elliott et al., 2009: 168).

[124] As reported by Mohammed et al. (2006) (cited by Elliott et al., 2009a: 168), "Three patients had elementary hallucinations, one had a complex hallucination and two had both complex and elementary hallucinations. Sounds heard included stampeding elephants, unbearable and buzzing sounds as well as rushing water.

correlations between epileptic seizures and parts of the brain. Taylor et al. (cited by Elliott et al., 2009a) show that hallucinations of the occipito-temporal cortex causes a hallucination coming from this region of the brain to be not only more complex but also more colorful. Additionally, Lance and Smee (cited by Elliott et al., 2009:169) indicate that the aforementioned type of hallucination is often associated with parieto-occipital lesions and also lesions located on the temporal lobe of the brain (David et al., 1945).

Another sort of hallucination mentioned by Elliott et al. (2009:169) associated with epilepsy include palinopsia[125] which has been identified to come from the right posterior cerebral region and autoscopia which may come from seizures of the occipito-temporal junction zone. Autoscopia is described as rare and where persons "perceive mirror images of themselves of normal size, shape and density, they may be in situations from their past or performing complex tasks (Sveinbjornsdottir and Duncan, 1993; Dewhurst and Pearson, 1955; Ionasescu, 1960)" (cited by Elliott et al., 2009, 169). One final summary statement regarding hallucinatory phenomena in epileptic states comes from a second paper (Elliott et al., 2009b:183). They offer that hallucinatory states coming from epileptic activity are "indistinguishable from those in the primary psychoses" with the exception that often accompanying epilepsy are additional features of confusion or altered awareness.

Asheim Hansen and Eylert Brodtkorb (2003:667) discuss various hallucinatory activity related to epilepsy. One point that these authors share,

---

Two patients complained of amplification of sound whilst another at age eleven heard friend's voices talking about him. All 6 patients demonstrated clustered MEG spike sources in the superior temporal gyrus; two had scattered spikes in the superior temporal gyrus as well as clustered MEG spike sources in the left inferior and middle frontal gyri or parieto-occipital region."

[125] Gersztenkorn and Lee (2015:60) define and give examples of palinopsia: "A palinoptic scene consists of a short, stereotyped action sequence that continuously replays for several minutes (e.g., a patient views a person throwing a ball and then sees the same scene repeated many times). The palinoptic image or scene may occur immediately following the stimulus or may be delayed. Hallucinatory palinopsia can also refer to seeing an object or physical feature that is superimposed onto other objects or people in the same context for a few minutes. For example, a patient sees a man with a beard and then observes a beard on every subsequent person viewed. Another example might be seeing a person wearing distinctive shoes and then the same footwear is observed on every other person. Hallucinatory palinoptic afterimages are a dysfunction of visual memory and are caused by seizures or cortical lesions, such as neoplasms, infarctions, and abscesses."

among others, is the affect of fear is the predominant characteristic of "experiential" seizures. Hansen and Brodtkorb also discuss the occurrences of "ecstatic seizures"[126] that are mostly characterized by pleasurable feelings. Moreover, some of these "ecstatic seizures" contain religious imagery as well.[127]

In their report on hallucinations and other phenomena that occur during seizure activity, Kasper, *et al.* write that oftentimes it is difficult to make a delineation between hallucinations, delusions, and illusions. However, they note that if a patient is able give an account of "a stereotyped, specific subjective symptom, whether designated a 'feeling,' 'sensation,' perception,' or 'experience' from his or her seizures, it is classified as an 'ictal symptom' (Kasper et al., 2010:14). Kasper *et al.* further state that when an ictal symptom manifests itself, it is known as an epileptic aura. Moreover, they also note that these auras include many hallucinations from different classifications. In further discussing epileptic auras, Kasper *et al.* are quick to point out that these auras are not some-

---

[126] In reference to the various emotional correlations between epilepsy and their related hallucinations, Hansen and Brodtkorb (2003:667) share, "It has been known since the late 19th century that 'psychic' phenomena can be part of epileptic seizures...The semiology of these seizures typically combines elements of perception, memory and affect. Although fear by far is the most common affective symptom, several patients experiencing varying degrees of pleasure during partial seizures have been described. Of 100 patients with emotional symptoms as part of a seizure, only 7 described pleasure. However, in another series of 52 such patients as many as 12 reported pleasurable emotions."

[127] Hansen and Brodtkorb offer an example of an ecstatic seizure from an epilepsy patient: "The attacks started in her late twenties. 'I had an intense sensation in my stomach as if I were a teenager helplessly in love. Sometimes I heard voices, enjoyable and frightening at the same time.' These sensations invariably were followed by anxiety and fear accompanied by shuddering and an urge to swallow. They often occurred during relaxation after deep concentration. She is an artist and when having an attack at the end of a performance in a church, she imagined the voice to come from God. This episode was terrifying. She considers herself an agnostic and feared for her mental health" (Hansen & Brodtkorb, 2003:669); "There is little doubt that the Russian writer Fyodor Dostoevsky experienced emotions of ecstatic or pleasant quality during his epileptic seizures and 'Dostoevsky epilepsy' is being used as a synonym to epilepsy with such seizures" (Hansen and Brodtkorb, 2003:667); Regarding particular religious themes within these seizures. Hansen and Brodtkorb aver, "Nevertheless, particular religious interests were not present in our four patients with 'supernatural' ictal phenomena. They lived in a secular culture and none were regular church attendants. However, at least two of them seemed to be particularly attracted to mysticism" (Hansen & Brodtkorb, 2003:672).

thing that precedes the seizure itself. Rather it is to be considered as part of the seizure event.[128] Kasper *et al.*, also advise on the sorts of sounds which may indicate that an epileptic patient is having an auditory hallucination. Sounds that one may hear include a tone, sound, or noise. These hallucinations are believed to come from the "primary acoustic cortex within Heschl's gyri. Further symptoms of auditory hallucinations are "ear-plugging, hearing quiet voices very loud, or vice versa, and echoing effects also occur" (Kasper *et al.*, 2010:17). Moreover, Kasper *et al.* also offer that the more complex of the auditory hallucinations (hearing words, speech, voices, talking people, melodies, music) appear to relate with auditory association cortices (Kasper *et al.*, 2010:17).[129]

Oliver Sacks (2012:155-159), discusses epileptic hallucinations and offers several examples of them. The types of hallucinations observed by epilepsy sufferers are of varying sorts. There are the variety of epileptic hallucinations that are simple in nature and are composed of various shapes, colors, and patterns. There are also more complex seizures that can take the form of familiar forms or persons. One sufferer reported inkblot spots that morphed into her mother. Another patient reported that a glass that she saw multiplied into numerous glasses in her total field of vision. However in these seizures, the person was not convinced that the glasses were in fact real. Sacks gives several examples of persons whose lives have been impacted by these seizures. One such example was when one of his patients who had experienced an ecstatic hallucination as a result of a seizure had reported that it was like he was in a happy dream that he had just awoken from. Sacks (2012:160-63) ends his comments on this type of hallucination stating that even though epileptic seizures have a neural basis in the brain, there is no explanation for the meanings, emotions, and values that people place on their hallucinatory effects.

---

[128] "Ictal symptoms including delusions seem to be quite rare, but might be underrated because they are not reported or are misclassified as psychotic. True ictal psychosis as part of a single isolated seizure is a rare event. Rather, psychotic symptoms relate to seizure clustering and the postictal state. However, delusional content may characterize ictal semiology in individual patients" (Kasper *et al.*, 2010:20).

[129] "Hearing voices during a partial seizure almost never takes the form of commanding or threatening voices talking in the third person" (Kasper *et al.*, 2010:18).

4.3.5 Charles Bonnet syndrome

Even though Carrier does not specifically offer CBS as a possible explanation for the PRA of Jesus Christ, it is still probative to analyze this sort of seizure related condition. After all, Carrier's general theory is that the disciples hallucinated the risen Jesus Christ. Thus, it is helpful to analyze CBS to see if it aligns with the experiences of the disciples.

Nair *et al.* (2015:204) list the effects of CBS, its causes, and its origin. They describe CBS as:

> ...a rare clinical condition that encompasses three clinical features: complex visual hallucinations, ocular pathology causing visual deterioration, and preserved cognitive status. Common associated ocular pathologies include age-related macular degeneration, glaucoma, and cataracts. While symptoms of CBS could herald the onset of dementia in the elderly, patients are often neurologically normal. Furthermore, an intraocular cause alone may not necessarily lead to CBS; a lesion anywhere in the visual pathway can be associated with the syndrome.

Nair *et al.* (2015:206) continue that CBS was named by de Morsier, who studied the writings of Charles Bonnet who had written extensively about the experience of his grandfather, Charles Lullin, and the hallucinations that Lullin experienced as he aged. They also share certain risk factors of CBS to include being over 64 years old, being socially isolated, having low cognitive function, having a history of stroke, as well as poor bilateral acuity.

Nair *et al.* (2015:206) also explains that criteria for CBS include the following: 1) the presence of formed and complex hallucinations 2) persistent or repetitive hallucinations 3) full or partial retention of insight 4) the absence of delusions 5) the absence of hallucinations in other sensory modalities. Additionally, it is known that those who suffer from CBS know that the hallucinations that they experience are not real and that the hallucinations they experience fit in with the visual background of what they would normally experience. Regarding the pathophysiology of CBS, Nair *et al.* (2015:206) report that this is largely unknown. However, there are many theories of how the VHs become manifest to the CBS sufferer. One popular explanation is that CBS lesions located within the visual pathway lead to the broadcast of abnormal signals that travel to the visual cortex. Thus, when the abnormal signals are added to the already existing visual signals, this causes the hallucinatory activity. An alternate theory explains that serious visual impairment "leads to the production of *de novo* images from the visual cortex thus causing the visual hallucinations" (Nair *et al.*, 2015:206). This theory, known as the sensory deprivation/phantom vision theory, offers that this syndrome is likened to someone who is missing a limb having sensations that the limb is still attached.

There is a third option that has been posited for CBS that is known as the neuromatrix theory. This theory, explained by Nair *et al.* (2015:206) proposes that the neuromatrix, the network of neurons in the brain, is capable of manufacturing phantom images. This image or pattern broadcast by the neuromatrix will seem to the subject to have a personal affective tone as well as "cognitive meaning." Other possible causes for CBS related hallucinations Include "impaired cerebral perfusion, social isolation, and other psychological factors." Ocular conditions that are observed to be the largest contributors to CBS are age-related macular degeneration and glaucoma. In addition to these ocular disorders, other common eye syndromes include cataracts, diabetic retinopathy, corneal opacity, and retinal detachment among others. In concluding their remarks on CBS, Nair *et al.* explain that even though the visual impairment is manifested, it is much more likely that a CBS sufferer will contact a psychiatrist first as they may think that they are suffering from mental illness instead of CBS (Nair, 2015:206-207).

Dominic ffytche (2010:218) refers to CBS as "the association of visual hallucinations and eye or visual pathway disease." Ffytche shares that much of Bonnet's research contributed to what would be later known as the cognitive sciences. Further work that he did in this regard was to develop a "neuroanatomical account of the conscious mind." Bonnet also offered that vibrations of certain nerve fibers would cause visual perceptions and other sensory experiences to include hallucinations. He based his conclusions on observing his visually impaired grandfather who would hallucinate from time to time.

Dominic ffytche (2010:218-220) describes the onset and effects of CBS. He states that the onset of CBS comes following a period of diminished eyesight. Hallucinations that are associated with CBS will occur in a series and can last anywhere from seconds to minutes in duration. However, after a period of experiencing these hallucinations, they will eventually diminish in time. He further describes the hallucinations as being silent, set in the external world, and that the patient does not have control over these hallucinations. He further explains that the patients who have CBS feel as though they are spectators watching an ongoing event. Even though CBS sufferers may not be able to see at all, their hallucinations will be in great detail. In time the patients realize the images they are viewing are not real. However, when they are experiencing the hallucinatory images, the patients are sometimes uncertain as whether these experiences are real or not. Ffytche also explains the images caused by these hallucinations vary widely from colors, shapes, patterns, grids, and tapestries, etc. to complex imagery such as distorted faces, letter strings, branching forms, and vehicles. Other hallucinations observed were multiple copies of the same object as well as objects that move along with the movement of their eyes. Ffytche further explains that the seeing of something that is not there is similar to viewing something that is there. The only difference is that there is not any external visual input for those experiencing hallucinations.

Adam Zeman (2002:232) discusses the work of Dominic ffytche whose research revealed that there are increased areas of activity around several brain regions to include the fusiform gyri in those CBS patents that were having hallucinations. This was discovered upon conducting functional imaging of the brains of CBS sufferers. The conclusion that Zeman makes with these observations is that the brain itself with no external stimuli can be the source of visual experiences that appear to the one experiencing them to be real when in actuality the visual images are being generated from inside the brain. Related work confirming the findings of ffytche comes from research with musical hallucinations where electrical activity is observed coming from parts of the brain that normally function when external auditory stimuli is heard.

In relation to hallucinations that are experienced as a result of visual difficulties, Zeman (2002:230-231) describes two separate incidents where someone was having unusual visual experiences. In one case a man encountered many unusual visual hallucinations for a period of five days. Zeman describes these hallucinations as starting out simply with noticing that oncoming cars at night all had their right head lights out. As the man entered the hospital after continuing visual difficulties, he began to experience still more hallucinations to include colored numbers and letters that floated into view, and that all of the patients that he observed in the hospital had plastic tubing that was coming out of their mouths and then connected to their ears. After experiencing these visual oddities Zeman also described this subject as visually transferring seagulls that he observed outside into the hospital and they were everywhere. They were resting on people's shoulders and heads, setting on the rims of glasses, etc. This was only the beginning of a barrage of images that continued to manifest themselves to him. They finally ceased after five days. It was determined that the man had experienced a stroke that had caused him to have visual difficulties. His temporary visual difficulties led to the CBS related hallucinations that he experienced.

In addition to ffytche, and Zeman, Waters *et al.* (2014:S233) briefly discuss CBS in relation to other debilitating eye diseases. Waters *et al.* explain that VHs occur as part of varied and different psychiatric and organic disorders. Also, they further discuss that hallucinations in age related eye disease occur in between 10% and 60% with the complexity of the VH linked to the severity of the visual loss. Waters *et al.* also share that the most common visual disorder that leads to VHs is macular degeneration.

In the case of hallucinations related to CBS, Oliver Sacks (2012:5-7) offers that the patient with diminished eyesight uses hallucinations as a mechanism to compensate for their blindness. In descriptions provided by Sacks, the patients quite often report the hallucinations are pleasing even though they can also experience frightful visions as well. In the case of CBS, Sacks reports that the sufferers know they are hallucinating. This is also the case with Parkinson's Disease patients who know the hallucinations are not real, ignore the hallucinations, and are generally not frightened by them.

4.3.6 Drug induced hallucinations

Carrier did not offer drug-induced hallucinations as a possible cause for the PRA of Jesus Christ. But it is probative to investigate drug-related hallucinations as Carrier has generally alleged that the disciples hallucinated the risen Jesus Christ. So, because of Carrier's overall claim, it is beneficial to examine drug related hallucinations in order to see if this explanation of the PRA of Jesus Christ could account for what the disciples experienced.

Regarding the hallucinations caused by the use of hallucinogenic drugs, Nicolas Langlitz (2013:83-89) provides his own personal experiences as a researcher of hallucinogenic drugs. Langlitz describes his participation in a Swiss hallucinogen research project where he was a test subject. He would ingest substances and the neuropsychopharmacologists had wired him with electrodes in order to monitor his brain activity after ingestion of the drug under study. His participation began in the summer of 2005. Langlitz describes his hallucinations once he ingested psilocybin. His first hallucinogenic encounter had him in a large cave covered with geometric patterns. He also reported whirring noises in stereo. However, Langlitz stated that he knew that they were pseudo-hallucinations that were not present there in the laboratory.

Langlitz (2013: 89-90) also noted that when he spoke to the research staff by way of intercom, this allowed him to surface from his hallucinogenic world. He further stated that this illusory world seemed bizarre and alien. He did not feel comfortable in this environment. Not only did Langlitz report colorful geometric objects, but he also reported many facial images that would flash before him while he was in this state. Langlitz reported that he was able to keep in communication with the research staff to tell them what he was experiencing throughout the experience.

In addition to his own experiences, Langlitz (2013:109-110) also describes the experiences of other researchers who ingested LSD and measured the affects. The two researchers who ingested LSD had different reactions. While one researcher experienced only mild hallucinations, the other test subject became fearful during the "trip" and sensed himself becoming smaller and the EEG chamber becoming larger and larger. Moreover, random images that were being shown on a video screen made the second researcher very fearful. At one point an extra staff person was called in to reassure the subject that everything was going to be alright. Langlitz reported that things could get out of control while experiencing psilocybin.

In addition to his reaction to other hallucinogenic drugs, Langlitz (2013:139) also reports how a test subject reacts to mescaline. This subject reported that he had disturbances of perception, illusions, psychomotor inhibitions, alteration in time perception, and auditory/visual hallucinations. It was believed that these reactions were similar to the symptoms of schizophrenia. Langlitz also cites Karl Jaspers who discusses the "radical privacy of mental states" and related this to the experience of mescaline and the study of schizophrenia. Those who experienced mescaline and were treating those with schizophrenia now had a better idea about what schizophrenia sufferers go through.

In similarity to Nicolas Langlitz, Heinrich Kluver (1969:14-15) shares the experiences of others when they ingested various forms of mescaline. Kluver shares the work of Beringer in his experimental use of "mescal buttons" that was conducted at the Psychiatric Clinic in Heidelberg. Two experimenters reported visual hallucinations of rings that were constructed of fine steel wire and all rotating clockwise. Also, these rings were arranged with smaller circles becoming larger circles. The researchers further reported that the wires were bright, however the spaces between the wires were also luminescent as well but appeared to be brighter than the wires themselves. In one case, as the "vision" progressed, a violet hue was cast upon the scene. This portrayal of the concentric wires then began to move around the field of vision. In addition to this panorama of glowing and multi-colored wires, one experimenter also observed a beautiful mosaic dome with different colors. The scene turned into many geometric figures. The psychedelic journey continued with the appearance of a palace decorated with rare tapestries and motionless women who were present. The "vision" ended with the observance of the outlines of crocodiles, and other lizards that did not elicit fear in the experimenter. Also, observed in this stage of the "vision" were human intestines, parts of abdomens, and also parts of a pregnant human uterus.

Kluver (1969:20) shares the experiences of other mescal experimenters. H. Ellis describes his experiences with three different types of visions when experiencing the effects of mescal. In the first stage of visions "the visions never resembled familiar objects; they were extremely definite, but yet always novel; they were constantly approaching, and yet constantly eluding, the semblance of known things." Another mescal experimenter, Rouhier, describes a second type of vision as being of familiar things such as fences, objects, and landscapes. "Monstrous forms, fabulous landscapes, etc" characterize visions of the third order.

Kluver (1969:66-67) offers other traits of mescaline addictions. He states most mescaline hallucinations are "formed" as opposed to some hallucinations that may be characterized as dusty. Kluver also describes the presence of geometric forms to include checkerboards, spirals, grating, lattices, tunnels, funnels, and cobwebs to name some of them. In addition to these geometric forms found in mescaline hallucinations, there are also similar forms observed in hypnagogic hallucinations as well. One of the visual phenomena recorded by those who use mescaline is the "indescribableness" of these hallucinatory experiences.

Phillip Wiebe (1997:208) explains the difference between hallucinations of the drug-induced type in comparison to those of the schizophrenic variety. His survey of Irving Feinberg's work (cited by Wiebe 1997:208) reveals the difference between the hallucinations of schizophrenics and drug users are four in nature. The first difference is that schizophrenic hallucinations appear suddenly whereas those from drug induced experiences occur slowly with the hallucinations manifesting from simple to more complex. Other differences include schizophrenics having hallucinations because of emotional need/delusional preoccupation whereas drug induced hallucinations develop without these influences. Third, schizophrenics hallucinate with their eyes open whereas drug users normally have their hallucinations in dark environments (mescaline and LSD). The final contrast between schizophrenic and drug induced hallucinations is that schizophrenic hallucinations are usually superimposed over their environment whereas a drug induced hallucination usually distorts the existing world.

In addition to the above data given by the aforementioned scholars relating to hallucinations and certain hallucinogenic drugs, Asaad offers additional insight into drug related hallucinations. Asaad (1990:54-55) gives an example of a tactile hallucination from drug use where the one hallucinating experiences the sensation of bugs crawling up their skin. Asaad refers to those who ingest psychedelic drugs and that they oftentimes experience "synthetic hallucinations," where the one hallucinating is likely to visualize colorful hallucinations and may even hear a loud noise along with the visual experiences.

Another manifestation offered by Asaad (1990:54-55) is that auditory hallucinations will be prominent along with a bright light. In those who are long-time users of hallucinogenic drugs, flashbacks often occur where prior experiences are randomly relived. Asaad also advises that in most cases, the patients are usually aware of the unreality of their hallucinations, even though there are some who are delusional who believe that these experiences are real. In the case of the delusional patient who believes the hallucinations are real, Asaad mentions that it is hard to distinguish the delusional hallucinator from one who suffers from schizophrenia. Some patients may be visibly distressed whereas another patient may be relaxed and enjoying the experience. Asaad also points out that it is important to know that a certain drug will not always produce the same experience in a person every time.

In relation to the ingestion of various types of drugs, Asaad (1990:59) reports that visual hallucinations frequently occur especially when in a dark environment or when the eyes are shut. Hallucinatory reactions to drugs normally depend on the personal traits of the one experiencing the hallucination, the dose, the mood of the person ingesting the drug, and also the physical setting of where the drug was ingested. Another aspect of hallucinatory activity observed by Aleman and Laroi (2008:68-69) is that persistent use of cocaine can result in *cocaine psychosis*, which is described by them as a "sub-acute delirious state characterized by auditory hallucinations with persecutory content." Furthermore, one other aspect that Aleman and Laroi bring out is that illicit drug use over a long time period is the main reason for one to experience hallucinations where there are no other problems present in the individual experiencing them.

4.3.7 Post-traumatic stress disorder related hallucinations

Could PTSD related hallucinations account for the encounter the disciples had after the death of Jesus Christ? Were the disciples traumatized by the violent death of their leader? Was this trauma so severe that it caused the disciples to hallucinate their leader subsequent to his burial? Analyzing the hallucinations related to PTSD is beneficial in order to investigate Carrier's overall claim that the disciples hallucinated the risen Jesus Christ.

A definition for post-traumatic stress disorder is given by the National Institute of Mental Health (NIMH) (2016) as "a disorder that develops in some people who have seen or lived through a shocking, scary, or dangerous event." The article further posits that it is a natural reaction to display fear in the wake of a traumatic incident. Most people will recover from the natural impulse (flight or fight) after reacting to trauma they are exposed to. However, those who continue to grapple with what they experienced may be diagnosed with PTSD. A characteristic of PTSD is that people who suffer from it may feel frightened or stressed at a time when they are not in any danger.

The NIMH article (2016) further explains that not all traumatized persons will be afflicted with PTSD and that within three months of the trauma experienced, symptoms will begin even though sometimes the symptoms will not develop until years later. Even though the symptoms of some people may only last for a short duration, PTSD symptoms may last for many years. The symptoms for PTSD must last for at least one month in order to be categorized as a PTSD sufferer. The article includes a list of symptoms for PTSD to include: 1) one re-experiencing symptom 2) at least one avoidance symptom 3) at least two arousal and reactivity symptoms 4) at least two cognition and mood symptoms.

In addition to the definition of PTSD supplied by the National Institute for Health, Aleman and Laroi (2008:50) elucidate on the hallucinatory activity that often troubles sufferers of Post Traumatic Stress Disorder. This is a syndrome that develops in people who have experienced an extremely traumatic stressor that causes a reaction of "intense fear, helplessness or horror." One of the signs that someone has undergone PTSD is that the person will try to avoid the stimuli that is reminiscent of the original stressful event, will demonstrate numbness in their emotional responses, will demonstrate increased arousal, and will have flashbacks from the original traumatic event. These flashbacks are multi-modal and are experienced as intrusive recollections, and can be auditory, visual, tactile, and/or olfactory in nature. In addition to these qualities, Aleman and Laroi share that there are many similarities between PTSD and schizophrenia.

In addition to Aleman and Laroi, A.M. Arens (2015:116-118) explains that when someone re-experiences a traumatic event like his friends dying in combat or hearing the cries of those wounded in battle, these experiences are considered to be PTSD and not a psychotic event. Arens also shares the case of an experienced combat veteran, named Karl, who began to experience the symptoms of PTSD to include hallucinations. Some of the hallucinations experienced by Karl were reliving past combat which included observing dead bodies. At first Karl thought these were merely flashbacks but realized that they were not when the hallucinations continued and were not of past battle activities that he participated in personally. Some of the hallucinations he described were of dead bodies or of a Muslim woman dressed in traditional Muslim clothing and were not triggered by "trauma-related cues." In addition to the visual hallucinations, Karl also experienced auditory hallucinations consisting of a baby crying, a drill sergeant yelling, and the voices of yelling soldiers.

4.3.8 Fatigue/Deprivation and guilt related hallucinations

Another claim that Carrier has made regarding the PRA of Jesus Christ is that they have their bases in physiological conditions. Carrier avers that the disciples could have hallucinated the risen Jesus Christ as a result of being fatigued or as a result of sensory deprivation. Are these physical conditions enough to elicit a hallucination? In addition to these physiologically based hallucinations, Carrier also offers an explanation that Paul was conditioned to have a hallucination because of the guilt of his persecutory actions towards Christians. Does the scholarly literature on these topics strengthen or weaken Carrier's position?

Regarding fatigue being a cause for hallucinations, Asaad (1990:106) advises that various types of hallucinations are known to have occurred to perfectly normal people under certain conditions to include sensory deprivation, starvation, severe fatigue, life-threatening stress, grief reactions, and cultural influences. Asaad refers to these hallucinations as mostly pseudohallucinations. Reeve *et al.* (2015:97) also discuss the topic of hallucinations regarding the relationship between schizophrenia and sleep deprivation. In their research, they assert that early studies conducted during the 1950s and 1960s indicate that otherwise healthy individuals who were sleep deprived may eventually experience psychotic like experiences to include hallucinations with these symptoms increasing in severity commensurate with the amount of time spent awake.[130]

---

[130] Reeve *et al.* share several anecdotal accounts coming from a sleep deprived subject: "He saw a fine smoke begin to rise from the floor....as he stared at the floor more closely, fine jets of water appeared to be rising" (Bliss *et al.*, 1959) Also, Reeve *et al.* point out the findings of Koranyi & Lehmann, (1960) (cited by Reeve *et*

Reeve et al. (2015:103) share the findings of a sleep deprivation study where those who participated in a 168 km ultra-marathon were interviewed after an average period of wakefulness that lasted 46 hours and 38 minutes. Of the seventeen volunteers that took part in a survey after the completion of the race, four of them reported having hallucinations during the event. Furthermore, these studies indicate, "experimentally reducing sleep increases psychotic like experiences." Reeve et al. (2015:108) conclude from their survey of sleep deprivation studies that it is "likely that sleep dysfunction among individuals with psychosis is associated with poorer clinical outcomes." In observing the hallucinations of those who experience fatigue, Sacks (2012:160-163) gives the real life example of an exhausted and overheated triathlete who imagines that his mother and sister are standing along the side of the course at a certain location. Upon going up to this area, the athlete realizes that his relatives were not present there at all.

In relation to guilt as a cause for hallucinations, no research could be found that validates the position that guilt in and of itself could be a factor in experiencing a hallucination. However, there is data that confirms that the emotion of guilt can be a result of experiencing a hallucination or that guilt may accompany the actual cause of a hallucination. One example of the former would be a patient who has a hypnagogic hallucination. McKellar (1989:107) shares that his patient experienced various emotions to include guilt and fear as a result of having a hallucination where an imaginary Siamese fish dies.

In addition to these aforementioned examples of guilt in relation to hallucinations, Wells (cited by Keen et al., 2013:391) shares a case study of a woman who experienced a sense of presence of the deceased along with mild depression. In this study, Wells asserts that this sense of presence hallucination was a psychological defense that occurs in the unconscious against guilt and anger at not seeing the deceased for several months before she died due to family conflicts. Furthermore, Elliott et al., (2009:165) express that guilt can be one of the affective emotions that can come as a result of a triggering event along with an auditory hallucination caused by an epileptic seizure. However, in these examples coming from the professional literature, guilt is not a causal factor of a hallucination. Rather,

---

al., 2015:97) who notice a rise in psychotic symptoms in already psychotic patients as a result of sleep deprivation: "Intriguingly, one experimental study found that 100 h of wakefulness was associated with a resurgence or exaggeration of psychotic symptoms in a small sample (n = 6) of inpatients with schizophrenia (Koranyi & Lehmann, 1960)" (Reeve et al., 2015:97).

it is either a by-product of the hallucinatory event (i.e. Siamese fish) or it is experienced along with the hallucination.

4.3.9 Conclusion: Exposition of scholarly literature on hallucinations

As an analysis of scholarly literature has been completed on the various causes of hallucinations, it is now appropriate to cross-examine carrier's hallucination hypothesis by means of the information developed from the scholarly literature review. This cross-examination of Carrier's hallucination hypotheses will ensue in light of the developed and relevant scholarly literature/New Testament resurrection narratives. After this cross-examination has been completed, then the information obtained from the exposition will be used to aid the research project. Additionally, conclusions will be drawn as a result of contrasting and comparing Carrier's claims to the scholarly literature/New Testament resurrection narratives (4.8).

4.4 Cross-examination of Carrier's "hallucinating disciples" by scholarly literature

In a trial, whenever the plaintiff[131] offers a witness who gives evidence in a case, then the defendant[132] is permitted to cross-examine[133] the plaintiff's witness. In this research project, Carrier's data was explicated and

---

[131] The term "plaintiff" is defined by the Glossary of Legal Terms (United States Courts: plaintiff) as "A person or business that files a formal complaint with the court."

[132] The term "defendant" is defined by the Glossary of Legal Terms (United States Courts: defendant) as "An individual (or business) against whom a lawsuit is filed."

[133] The definition of the term "cross-examination" given by *Nolo's Plain-English Law Dictionary* (Cornell University of Law, cross-examination) states, "At trial, the opportunity to question any witness who testifies on behalf of any other party to the lawsuit (in civil cases) or for the prosecution or other codefendants (in criminal cases). The opportunity to cross-examine usually occurs as soon as a witness completes his or her initial testimony, called direct testimony. Cross-examiners attempt to get the witness to say something helpful to their side, or to cast doubt on the witness's testimony by eliciting something that reduces the witness's credibility -- for example, that the witness's eyesight is so poor that she may not have seen an event clearly. When a witness's direct testimony ends up being hostile to the party that called the witness, sometimes that party's lawyer is allowed to cross-examine his own witness."

Objection Three: The Disciples Hallucinated the Risen Jesus Christ 261

then Carrier's data was followed by an exposition of scholarly data on the various forms of hallucinations as well. Now, a cross-examination of Carrier's hallucination hypotheses by scholarly literature and by Christian apologists/theologians is appropriate in order to determine whether Carrier's contentions are in accord with accepted principles of evidence.[134]

4.4.1 Cross-examination: The disciples were hallucinating: In general

In the aforementioned section (4.3), an explication of scholarly literature was conducted on the various forms of hallucinations. In response to the scholarly literature review in combination with Carrier's "hallucinating disciples" claim, it is now relevant to cross-examine the overall notion that the disciples hallucinated the risen Jesus Christ. Therefore, the scholarly literature coming from Christian apologists/scholars included below is offered to conduct this cross-examination.

In countering the claim that the disciples were hallucinating, Gary Habermas concludes from studying research offered by Perry (1959) (cited by Habermas, 2012b:156) on after death communication (ADC) that the resurrection has a great number of witnesses and that the best ADC case cannot compare to the number of witnesses attributed to the resurrection of Jesus Christ. Habermas also offers the opinion of Allison (2005) who is also impressed by the "Strength and diversity of the resurrection appearance traditions." Habermas further opines that ADCs that have been reported through history are in stark contrast to these manifestations of the risen Jesus Christ and that the PRA of Jesus Christ are not akin to the reported ADC in historical literature.

In regard to the way in which Jesus Christ was experienced after his resurrection, Jake O'Connell (2009:92) offers that in line with other religious traditions, if Jesus was experienced as a hallucination by the disciples, then he would have appeared in a glorious form. However, the risen Jesus Christ is nowhere depicted as having a glowing or grand appearance that those viewing him would be in awe of. Instead of this, it is observed that the appearance of Jesus in bodily form is altogether ordinary.

In his contribution to a symposium on the resurrection, Stephen Davis (1997:130-131) discusses the PRA and how Jesus was observed. Was Jesus visualized or was he actually observed in the normal sense of seeing somebody in passing. In arguing against those who believe that Jesus was merely visualized, Davis asserts that the evidence for this perspective is

---

[134] Cf. 4.8 for the evidentiary analysis of Carrier's hallucinating disciples contention.

anemic at best. Davis explains that the rationale behind this position is that Jesus appeared only to believers. However, Davis notes that the disciple Thomas, who did not believe that Jesus Christ had arisen from the dead, was convinced that it was Jesus after he encountered him. This sudden awareness of the risen Jesus Christ was evidenced by his now famous reply, "My Lord and my God (John 20:28)." This is relevant to Carrier's discussion regarding hallucinating disciples as Thomas did not even believe that Jesus Christ had arisen from the dead. So, if Thomas did not believe that the other disciples had seen the risen Jesus Christ already, then how would he be pre-disposed in a group setting to hallucinate the risen Jesus Christ? Thus, there is no explanation from the biblical texts that would give reason for Thomas hallucinating the risen Jesus Christ because of his skepticism against the idea of Jesus Christ arising from the dead.

Referring to the interplay between the subjectivity/objectivity of those who experienced the PRA of Jesus Christ, Anthony Kelly (2008:121) posits:

> Their subjectivity anticipated nothing like what happened, and yet the resurrection event called into existence a new intentional consciousness. And once their subjectivity is constituted through what must have been an extremely surprising event and disorienting experience, it could proceed to explore the objective dimensions of the reality concerned, in line with the Lonerganian axiom, "genuine objectivity is the fruit of authentic subjectivity."[135]

---

[135] Arguing against the merely subjective experience as suggested in the hallucination theory, Kelly (2008:122-123) further comments, "A kind of mental myth is constructed. It may prove useful for polemical purposes, but it remains strangely inapplicable to any familiar experience." Kelly likens this tension between the subjective and objective nature of the resurrection experiences to the genius of the musical compositions of Mozart. Those who are trained in classical music can testify to the objective musical genius inherent within the compositions of Mozart. Yet, there is still the aspect of the subjective experience of this music as one familiarizes oneself with the experience of hearing and appreciating it. This appreciation continues as one generation after the next experience the objective genius of Mozart upon hearing and reading his compositions. In similarity to the objective appreciation of Mozart and his music, those of each succeeding generation will subjectively enjoy Mozart's musical compositions. Kelly further makes analogy to the resurrection with classic literature and art. The objectiveness of classic works of art and literature are akin to the objectivity of the musical genius of Mozart. The objective and subjective experiences of these timeless treasures that still endure with us today are reminiscent of the resurrection of Jesus Christ in its objective/subjective evidence that still remains powerful today.

Objection Three: The Disciples Hallucinated the Risen Jesus Christ

In responding to Gerd Ludemann's view that the disciples were having visions of a risen Jesus Christ, C. Bryan (2011:162-164) does not put much stock into Ludemann's claim. His main reply to "visionary disciples" is that it does not "explain the texts which stubbornly, persistently, and without exception witness to the Easter faith." Furthermore, the explanation that many people in antiquity and people today still have visionary experiences does not explain the PRA. At the worst, offering this as evidence for visionary disciples would be they were hallucinating and at best it would mean they were having a genuine experience of being comforted. However, neither of these explains the texts themselves that assert categorically that Jesus Christ had arisen from the dead and is in total contrast to the "visionary disciples" hypothesis.[136]

Concerning the psychological predisposition to have a hallucination, Habermas (1997:271-272) asserts that hallucinations can often come as a result of one's hopeful expectation[137], but then points out that the disciples were not hopeful at all after all of the events that had recently occurred surrounding the arrest and crucifixion of Jesus Christ. He then mentions that Jesus appeared to many people in different settings. Habermas then offers that anyone who believes that all of these different people/groups were all hallucinating "multiplies the improbable, bordering on naiveté."[138]

---

[136] Another point that Bryan (2011: 169-170) makes against the "visionary disciples" hypothesis is if the disciples had actually only had visionary encounters with the risen Jesus Christ, then why didn't they just say so. The Gospel writers certainly had it within their vocabularies to properly delineate between a physically present Jesus and a spiritually or visually manifested Jesus. If he were merely an apparition, then the authors would have described him in that regard instead of using the language of an actual bodily resurrection.

[137] A hallucination experienced as a result of an expectation of having one by itself was not observed in the survey of scholarly literature completed during this research project.

[138] Habermas (1997:316fn) offers information that he received when corresponding with Gary R. Collins, a clinical psychologist. Regarding hallucinations, Collins avers, "They certainly are not something that can be seen by a group of people. Neither is it possible that one person could somehow induce a hallucination in somebody else. Since an hallucination exists only in this subjective, personal sense, it is obvious that others cannot witness it;" Habermas (1997:317fn) continues to offer reasons why the disciples could not be having group hallucinations as suggested by Carrier: "Then, even if it could be shown that individuals have hallucinated simultaneously, it does not at all follow that these experiences are collective. Since hallucinations are private events peculiar to individuals (see note 41 above), how could they share *exactly the same* subjective visual perception? It is far more likely that the collective phenomena in question are either

Another observation pointed out by Habermas (2015:58) is that the disciples were completely changed as a result of experiencing these appearances of Jesus Christ. He notes that hallucinations do not transform people as eventually, hallucinators can be reasoned with that their hallucinations did not actually occur. Specifically, Habermas shares there are two ways in which most hallucinators are convinced that their experiences could not be real: 1) when others who are present with the hallucinator do not observe what the hallucinator reports 2) when what is observed does not happen normally in human experience. However, he notes that there were groups that observed the risen Jesus Christ. By virtue of these repeated group experiences with Jesus Christ, the aforementioned criteria answer the objections that the risen Jesus Christ was an observed hallucination.

Mike Licona (2010:484) gives his perspective on group hallucinations. In one sense, hallucinations are like dreams in that you cannot share in the same dream as another person. Licona then gives an example where he has a dream where he and his wife go on a vacation to Hawaii. After starting his "Hawaiian vacation" dream, Licona cannot wake up and tell his wife to join his dream so that she can go on vacation with him. He and his wife could both return to sleep and dream of vacations to Hawaii. However, both of them would not have an identical dream. In addition to his vision related comments, Licona (2010:485fn) also makes the observation that when Jesus appeared to all of the disciples at one time, they all experienced the same encounter with Jesus. This can be observed in the various New Testament accounts of the encounters with Jesus by the disciples.

Regarding the evidentiary aspects of the PRA of Jesus Christ, J.W. Montgomery (2002:94) avers that most people are familiar with the states of life and death even though they might not know how the mechanisms of life began or why all humanity must experience death. It is also axiomatic that most people of normal intelligence know how to determine if a person is dead or alive. Therefore, when a man is observed to be crucified, those witnessing or taking part in the crucifixion will know when the subject of the crucifixion is dead. By the same token, if a man is ob-

---

perceptual misrepresentations of physical manifestations...or *individual* hallucinations experienced by some, while others present are not hallucinating." Habermas (1997:316fn) further discusses the perspective of Zusne and Jones who are not even sure that "group hallucinators" are even hallucinating.

served to be eating fish, then he should be classified as alive.[139] Montgomery further (2002:94) offers:

> In Jesus' case, the sequential order is reversed, but that has no epistemological bearing on the weight of evidence required to establish death or life. And if Jesus was dead at point A, and alive again at point B, then resurrection has occurred: *res ipsa loquitor*.[140]

Regarding the theory of the resurrection of Jesus Christ being a vision, N.T. Wright offers (2003:691) that Mary also experienced the risen Jesus Christ. Thus, when she encounters the risen Jesus Christ, it is not as if she merely had a vision. It would not be like Odysseus who had a vision of a bodiless spirit that he could not cling to. Rather, Mary not only observed the empty tomb, but she also saw and clung to the risen Jesus Christ. Therefore, she could be assured that she was not observing an apparition like others may have in ancient times. Additionally, Wright states that this is the case in Luke, John, and Acts where Jesus ate fish with his disciples.

It would be probative at this juncture to offer the analysis of Clay Jones of Biola University who offers a serious blow to all general theories that the disciples could have hallucinated a risen Jesus at the same time. In the fall of 2013 semester of a Biola University class entitled "In defense of the Resurrection," Doctor Jones (2013) gave his opinion on this topic on the class discussion board:

---

[139] Montgomery offers the words of Thomas Sherlock (cited by Montgomery, 2002:93) regarding the evidence for the resurrection: "Suppose you saw a man executed, his Body afterwards wounded by the Executioner, and carry'd and laid in the grave; that after this you shou'd be told, that the Man was come to life again: What wou'd you suspect in this case? Not that the Man had never been dead; for that you saw yourself: But you wou'd suspect whether he was now alive. But wou'd you say, this Case excluded all human Testimony; and that Men could not possibly discern, whether one with whom they convers'd familiarly, was alive or no? Upon what Ground cou'd you say this? A man rising from the Grave is an Object of Sense, and can give the same Evidence of his being alive, as any other Man in the World can give. So that a Resurrection consider'd only as a Fact to be proved by Evidence, is a plain Case; it requires no greater Ability in the Witnesses, that that they be able to distinguish between a Man dead, and a Man alive: A Point, in which I believe every man living thinks himself a Judge" (Montgomery, 2002:93).

[140] *Res Ipsa Loquitor* is a phrase in Latin meaning "the thing speaks for itself." "In tort law, a principle that allows plaintiffs to meet their burden of proof with what is, in effect, circumstantial evidence" (Cornell University Law School Legal Information Institute, *Res Ipsa Loquitor*).

One of the major problems I have with the hallucination theory is that the hallucinations were interlocking. For example, while Thomas was hallucinating Jesus telling him to touch his hands and side the other disciples had to hallucinate Jesus telling Thomas to do that. For another, when Jesus walked off with Peter and John followed them then their hallucinations had to interlock. That's impossible.

Jones rightly observes the impossibility of the intersection of exact and common hallucinations being experienced by each of the disciples. Not only would this be impossible in the example offered by Jones but it would also be impossible in the case of the experience of the five hundred who experienced Jesus. How could the five hundred who experienced the risen Jesus at the same time be hallucinating? The fact that the hallucinations of all five hundred persons were both identical and interlocking would be unexplainable or impossible.

In reference to the probabilities regarding the likelihood that the disciples/women at the tomb hallucinated the risen Jesus, Tim and Lydia McGrew (2009:620) offer their assessment. The women who were there to anoint the dead body of Jesus had no preconditions that would make it likely they would have hallucinations. Moreover, Luke reports they were puzzled when they found out the tomb was empty (Luke 24:4). The McGrews point out this bewilderment is corroborated when Mary Magdalene does not recognize the resurrected Jesus at first when she encounters him (John 20:15). After offering the aforementioned analysis, the McGrew's further offer that the entire group of five women would have to be effected by this hallucination. Because of these factors, the McGrews believe that "the prior probability for a group hallucination under these circumstances is prohibitively low."

In addition to their perspectives on the probability that the women hallucinated the risen Jesus Christ, the McGrews (2009:626) also observe the lack of probability that the disciples hallucinated the risen Jesus Christ. In similarity to Clay Jones, the McGrews aver not only would the hallucinations have to be parallel, they would also have to be integrated as well. They explain that the disciples were not only interacting physically and verbally with one another, but also with Jesus Christ, himself. On this theme they continue:

> The suggestion that their parallel polymodal hallucinations were seamlessly integrated is simply a nonstarter, an event so improbable in natural terms that it would itself very nearly demand a supernatural explanation. Finally, these detailed, parallel, integrated hallucinations must be invoked repeatedly across a period of more than a month during which the disci-

ples were persuaded that they repeatedly interacted with their Lord and master here on earth. And then, abruptly, they stopped. Christ no longer appeared on earth... The sort of complex, repeated, integrated hallucination that would be required to explain even one disciple's testimony and willingness to die for it would represent a serious mental illness.

Groothuis (2011:556-57) also observes that Paul and James show that wish fulfillment could not be a reason for their hallucinations because they were not expectant that Jesus would appear to them after his death. Another observation is that the hallucination theory leads to the fact that the Christian religion is based on "mental illness" and that the disciples quite literally preached a "message of madness." Another point that Groothuis makes about the resurrection of Jesus is that all of these hallucinators could have been easily cured of their "mental disorders" by simply visiting the grave of Jesus Christ. He further offers that both the Jewish and the Roman establishments would have eagerly aided in refuting the resurrection by merely producing the body of Jesus Christ or by taking them to the known gravesite.

Glenn Siniscalchi (2012:729) believes that the form of early Christian church worship is a good apologetic tool and posits that the resurrection of Jesus Christ was the event that initiated the worship of the early church. But how did the disciples know the resurrection of Jesus Christ took place? It took place because of the evidences of the empty tomb and the appearances of Jesus Christ to the disciples. Also, the rite of Christian baptism points to the bodily resurrection of Jesus Christ from the dead. In addition to pointing to the aforementioned worship modalities, Siniscalchi also posits that the new day of worship for the Christians, Sunday, was the day the empty tomb was discovered and where Jesus was observed to be alive. Therefore, the day of worship shifted to Sunday in honor of the resurrection of Jesus Christ.

Another argument made for the historicity of the resurrection of Jesus Christ comes from Michael Welker (2007:466-470) who analyzes the writings of N.T. Wright on the topic. Welker agrees with Wright (cited by Welker, 2007:466) who posits that the combination of the empty tomb and the PRA are "historical bedrock." He also asserts that most New Testament scholars would agree the empty tomb by itself would be a mystery and a tragedy. Also, the appearances of Jesus Christ standing alone would have been classified as hallucinations or visions that were known to have occurred abundantly in the ancient world. Moreover, Welker agrees with the conclusion of Wright that Jesus Christ was witnessed a sufficient number of times in order to counter the claim that he was disembodied in these appearances. However, he notes that Jesus Christ was sufficiently different in his post-resurrection state. Thus, Jesus Christ was not just reanimated to his previous existence. Welker further offers the evidence of the various accounts of the risen Jesus Christ to counter the claim that these appearances were just "fanciful imaginings, self-created fantasies, or psychogenic phenomena in that they stress an intense palpability through hearing, seeing, touching, and eating."

Regarding the discussion of Carrier relating to hallucinations as having the effect of reducing anxiety in the disciples, as noted before, Carrier references the work of Peter Slade and Richard Bentall to make his point (4.2.2). However, Slade and Bentall (1988:108) are more nuanced in their assessment as they expound on hallucinations in relation to anxiety. They note that hallucinating "patients:"

> Are sometimes less disturbed following an episode of hallucination than preceding it. If this is indeed the case, it would suggest that hallucinations may serve a positive function of reducing anxiety. Experimental evidence in support of this hypothesis is limited. On the one hand, a number of treatment studies (described in Chapter 7) have demonstrated that operant conditioning techniques can be used for the *reduction* of hallucinations, suggesting that hallucinations may sometimes be under operant control. On the other hand, Tarrier (1987), in his interview study conducted with hallucinating and deluded schizophrenics, found that 18 out of 25 of his sample reported feeling *more* disturbed after their hallucinations than beforehand...Nor is it the case that an increase or reduction in stress is the only consequence of hallucination that might affect their future occurrence. The functional significance of hallucinations for the hallucinator would therefore seem to be an appropriate area for future research.

In this material from Slade and Bentall, there are several important observations to make regarding Carrier's claim that hallucinations are stress-reducing events. The first observation after reading the material from Slade and Bentall is that the possible "anxiety reducing" effects of hallucinations are not for normal functioning persons. Rather, they are for *patients* or those who are already suffering from mental health issues.[141] So if a normal person has a high level of anxiety, having a halluci-

---

[141] In a chapter entitled *Variables Affecting the Experience of Hallucination*, Slade and Bentall (1988:82-109) are discussing "patients" in this chapter. The variables they discuss and the studies they cite involve mostly schizophrenic/psychotic patients. Carrier leaves this out of his characterization of those who experience a reduction in anxiety as a result of hallucinations (cf. P. 82-109); Moreover, Slade and Bentall (1988:82) urge caution to those who attempt to apply their re-

nation would not bring a reduction in tension. Another salient observation is that data coming from a study conducted by Peter Slade indicates that hallucinations *may* aid in reducing anxiety. Thus, after taking a thorough look at the relevant material from Slade and Bentall, what is clear is this issue has not been resolved and is in need of further research. Moreover, as observed above, Slade and Bentall offer evidence counter to Slade's experimental data. So, Carrier's characterizations of Slade and Bentall's research do not accurately portray what these researchers actually reported about the relationship between anxiety and hallucination.

4.4.2 Cross-examination: Schizophrenic hallucination

After giving Carrier's contentions about the disciples possibly being schizophrenic/schizotypal and the incredible stories about the resurrection of Jesus Christ being disseminated by deluded disciples, the scholarly literature on schizophrenia was examined. Could the disciples have been schizophrenic or could they have been on the schizoptypal scale? In this section, Carrier's contention in this regard will be cross-examined by Christian apologetic authors and scholars.

In their joint paper on hallucinations and the resurrection of Jesus Christ, Bergeron and Habermas (2015:164) aver that the proposed hallucination hypotheses after an analysis of medical and psychiatric literature are 'naïve.' They further state that those who experience hallucinations are sick and that they require care such as "medical and psychosocial support, a structured environment, pharmacological support, and behavioral treatment." Furthermore Bergeron and Habermas write:

> Persons suffering from psychosis in Jesus' time, not having the benefit of modern medical treatment, might well be considered lunatics or demon possessed (e.g. Matt 4:24). They would be unlikely candidates to organize as a group and implement the rapid and historic widespread expansion of the Christian religion during the first century.

---

search results to those other than psychotic patients: "A number of variables have been found to affect the probability that a given individual will hallucinate in a given situation. These variables include environmental events, constitutional factors, and learning effects. Because many of the relevant data have been collected from subjects suffering from psychotic hallucinations, caution may be necessary when attempting to extrapolate findings about these variables to other types of hallucinatory experience (e.g. drug-induced hallucinations)."

4.4.3 Cross-examination: Bereavement hallucinations

The survey of scholarly literature on bereavement hallucinations was given in order to compare this literature to Carrier's contention that the disciples' experiences with Jesus Christ were merely bereavement hallucinations. Included in the section below is a cross-examination of the bereavement hallucination hypothesis by literature from Christian apologists and scholars. Does the bereavement hallucination hypothesis provide a better explanation for the PRA of Jesus Christ than the disciples actually experiencing the risen Jesus Christ in the flesh? Does Carrier's bereavement hallucination hypothesis remain the best explanation of all the data after this cross-examination?

Bergeron and Habermas (2015:167) comment on the theory propounded by Carrier *et al.* that the etiology for the disciples' experiences with the risen Jesus Christ was grief and bereavement (hallucinations). Disagreeing with this assertion, Bergeron and Habermas submit that in the normal process of grieving the loss of a loved one, oftentimes a close relative will have visual appearances of the decedent and that these sorts of grieving encounters are not considered pathologic. Rather they assert that instead of hallucinations these encounters should be referred to as "visions." In referring to these experiences as "visions" and not as hallucinations, there is no "inherent implication of underlying processes."

Specifically mentioning the disciples' encounters as included within the New Testament, Bergeron and Habermas (2015:170) submit:

> Bereavement experiences could have included visions of Jesus, but it definitely would be unexpected that all the disciples would have such visions. Bereavement visions would not have been considered actual or real encounters with a physically living Jesus. Tactile bereavement experiences of the deceased Jesus would have been unlikely and, if experienced, would likely have been considered unpleasant. It is also unlikely that the disciples would have disclosed their bereavement experiences to others, let alone have launched a campaign of widespread public proclamation of Jesus' resurrection based on such illusions of bereavement.

In the aforementioned passage from their paper, Bergeron and Habermas (2015:170) offer that it could be a possibility that some of the disciples had a vision of Jesus. But one reason why they are convinced that the ap-

Objection Three: The Disciples Hallucinated the Risen Jesus Christ

pearances were not hallucinations or visions is because of the ubiquity of these sightings amongst all of the disciples.[142]

In response to an objection by John Hick to the PRA of Jesus Christ to the disciples as veridical encounters, Gerald O'Collins (1997:10) offers counter evidence. Regarding the post-resurrection encounters, John Hick hypothesizes that these encounters could have been "waking versions" of a NDE where those close to death experience a bright light and encounter a shining figure that Christians identify as Jesus Christ. In addition to this contention, Hick then mentions "bereavement sequences" and offers that Jesus Christ may have been vividly present to the early Christians right after the crucifixion of Jesus Christ. In these two suggestions by Hick, O'Collins views them as mere attempts to explain away or "generalize away" anything that points to the unique and authentic nature of the PRA.[143]

O'Collins (1997:10) goes into more detail regarding his opinion on Hick's conjectures. Regarding Hick's objection that the PRA were "waking" NDEs, O'Collins' first point is that the nature of the death and resurrection of Jesus Christ is quite different than someone who dies and is resuscitated back to life. Moreover, O'Collins posits that NDEs happen to individuals and not groups of people. This is relevant because on several occasions, Jesus Christ appeared to groups of people (the disciples on several occasions, and more than 500 at once). So, for Hick's NDE explanation to apply to the PRA of Jesus Christ, then all of the persons in each group that Jesus appeared to would be having a NDE simultaneously. Of course, a group of people having a NDE all at the same time where they encounter Jesus Christ seems to be nearly impossible. He further points

---

[142] Referring to the notion that the disciples saw visions of Jesus, J.D.G. Dunn (1975:132) asks pertinent questions: "Why did they [the disciples] include that it was Jesus *risen from the dead*? Why not visions 'fleshed out' with the apparatus of apocalyptic expectation, coming on the clouds of glory and the like....? Why draw the astonishing conclusion that the *eschatological* resurrection had *already* taken place in the case of a *single individual* separate from and prior to the general resurrection"?

[143] Furthermore, O'Collins (1997:12-13) argues generally against the enterprise of giving explanations on scientific grounds for the resurrection of Jesus or generalizing away the PRA under some other type of naturally occurring phenomena (e.g. Paul being an epileptic or being guilt ridden for his past conduct towards Christians). Rather as Stephen Davis (cited by O'Collins 1997:12-13) points out, the resurrection itself was an entirely singular event so in keeping with the uniqueness of this event, it logically follows that the resurrection events themselves would be unique as well. Therefore accepting flawed analogies of the resurrection appearances does nothing to explain these unique events.

out that there is no evidence that any of the primary witnesses to the resurrected Jesus Christ of the primary witnesses to the risen Jesus Christ such as Paul, Mary Magdalene had NDEs.

In a dialogue between Antony Flew and Gary Habermas that was moderated by John Ankerberg, Flew (Habermas & Flew, 2005:9) submitted that the disciples had hallucinated in similarity to those who have reported losing a loved one. In response to this assertion, Gary Habermas counters by offering that most people who experience this sort of hallucination are either elderly or alone. In addition to making this point, Habermas also offers that seeing a departed loved one after they die does not cause a lifelong transformation.

In a chapter entitled, *Applying resurrection research and closing loopholes*, Habermas (2006:90) summarizes his response to the view that the disciples hallucinated the risen Jesus Christ. He restates that Hallucinations are internal states of consciousness that are experienced only individually and not corporately as a group.[144] Other observations that he makes are that the disciples were not in the proper frame of mind to have hallucinations, the tomb of Jesus should have been occupied with the body of Jesus if the disciples were hallucinating, and that Paul and James, two skeptics, also saw the risen Jesus Christ.

In responding to an assertion by Carrier that there are a number sightings of Jesus Christ today where people claim to talk and have physical contact with Jesus, A.T.E. Loke offers the response of William Lane Craig (cited by Loke, 2009:575-76) that there are no examples of this offered by psychologists today that come anywhere close to the diversity, and multiplicity of the resurrection appearances of Jesus Christ that occurred over a small time period. Loke offers that even if skeptical scholars are able to come up with additional examples, why should these encounters be automatically deemed to be hallucinations. Within the Christian worldview, a central tenet would be that spiritual entities exist. Loke gives as an example of the reported manifestations of demons.

---

[144] Habermas and Licona (2004:106) give an example to show how hallucinations cannot be experienced as a group. They ask you to suppose that you are on a ship that has sailed across the Atlantic Ocean and at some point the ship you are on sinks and you and others are floating in the ocean. After, three days of floating in the water without food, drink, or sleep, one of the survivors sees a large ship on the horizon. However, the man is really hallucinating. Will the other survivors of the sunken ship see the imagined ship on the horizon? Most likely they will not. If the other person who hallucinates influences others to have a hallucination of a ship as well, will all of the hallucinating people observe the same ship to have the same hull number in each of their hallucinations?

Therefore, it is quite possible that what some people report today could be real, "extra-mental" entities. Just because an experience such as this is unusual does not mean that the experience is a hallucination.

Loke (2009:576) continues that the apologist can argue that "based on first epistemological principles, a consistent unity of perceptions over time concerning a single entity that involves multiple sensory routes (seeing, hearing, touching) by different people in a group would strongly suggest that such an entity exists outside of our minds." Loke continues that it is highly unrealistic to assert that numerous persons who observe the same external images and have other physical contact with a "putative entity" have generated these images as a result of their personal, internal causal mechanisms.

William Lane Craig (2000:190-192) counters the claim made by Carrier that, under certain circumstances, it would be within the realm of possibility to trigger a hallucination event where a group of people experience the hallucination together. In response, Craig states that one problem with this theory is that it would not explain the "persistence of causal effects." Craig offers, for instance, that a hallucination would not explain the fact that there were fish that disappeared (after having been eaten) which could be checked well after the "triggering event."[145]

In addition to the other cross-examinations on Carrier's attacks on the PRA of Jesus Christ, Gerald O'Collins (2011:229-230) offers that a comparison of these appearances with the bereavement hallucination research completed by Dewi Rees is not a good one. Collins offers that not only does Jesus appear to individuals but also to groups. There is no data coming from the Rees (1971:37-44) study of bereaved widows that identifies any bereaved groups having contact with a decedent. Regarding this comparison O'Collins writes, "The individual nature of these experiences moves the bereavement analogy away from the resurrection witness of the New Testament, for which appearances of the risen Christ to groups are at least as significant as the appearances to individuals."[146]

---

[145] Cf. John 21:7-15. Certain forms of hallucinations do not have "triggering events (e.g.- Schizophrenic hallucinations, hypnagogic/hypnopompic imagery, etc."

[146] Regarding another facet of the 1971 Rees study of bereaved widows, O'Collins (2011:232-233) points out, "...the question at stake remains: how far can we press the analogy between the experiences of the 293 widows and widowers that Rees studied scientifically 40 years ago and the Easter experiences of Jesus' first followers? Nearly three-quarters of Rees's (232) widows and widowers kept their experience to themselves. By way of contrast, those to whom Jesus appeared quickly passed on their experience to others. After Jesus appeared to him, within hours Peter told the other disciples what had happened (Luke 24:34); this seems

Regarding the paranormal study of apparitions as possible causes of the PRA of Jesus Christ, Glenn Siniscalchi (2014:192-193) shares research that he has conducted on the topic. He has gleaned this information from parapsychologists who gather and share anecdotal reports from the eyewitnesses of apparitions. He first explains the differences between apparitions, mirages, illusions and, also hallucinations. Siniscalchi further offers that one way in which to delineate between an apparition and the other categories such as illusions, and hallucinations is that the apparition will normally communicate new information that was previously unknown to the one experiencing it. Even though many wish to explain this sort of phenomena naturalistically (i.e. hallucination), Siniscalchi offers that in some cases a paranormal explanation such as an apparition makes more sense. Siniscalchi further offers that there is a developed taxonomy of apparitional experiences to include 1) experimental apparitional experience 2) crisis apparitions 3) post-mortem apparitions 4) common ghost apparitions. Siniscalchi posits that as apparitions relate to the study of the PRA of Jesus Christ, the one category that is important to discuss is the third category, post-mortem appearances.

Additionally, Siniscalchi (2014:194-95) offers that there is some difficulty in delineating between hallucinations and apparitional appearances and it is believed by some scholars involved in this research that some post-mortem phenomena thought to be apparitions do appear to be hallucinatory activity. Also, Siniscalchi notes that most of the descriptions of apparitional encounters that are within the relevant literature are not in accord with the PRA. Moreover, Siniscalchi asserts that it is important to offer data on apparitional appearances in addition to hallucinations when discussing the PRA of Jesus Christ. To this end, Siniscalchi offers that data coming from post-mortem apparitional experiences almost always occur indoors. In contrast to this, Siniscalchi offers that the New Testament accounts of the PRA of Jesus Christ are observed to occur both inside and outside. Other contrasts that Siniscalchi observes include: 1) apparitions are not normally observed by groups (2-12%) 2) are not normally observed by their enemies (less than 1%) 3) are not normally able to be touched (2.7% reported that they touched the apparition) 4) those who

---

clearly implied by Luke's narrative. When Jesus met Mary Magdalene, she went at once to bring the good news to the other disciples (John 20:18). According to Matthew, Mary Magdalene and 'the other Mary' immediately ran to tell 'the disciples' the good news of the resurrection that they had received from an 'angel of the Lord,' and this mission was straightaway strengthened when they met the risen Jesus himself" (Matt 28:1-10).

experience these post-mortem apparitions do not believe that these apparitional figures have risen bodily from the dead (less than 1%). However, Siniscalchi notes that the risen Jesus Christ met all these conditions over a short time span. After calculating the odds of the improbability that appearances of Jesus were apparitional in nature, Siniscalchi calculates that the odds that Jesus was an apparition are set at 1:3,800,000.

In dialogue with John Crossan, Wright (2006:35-36) questions Crossan on his view that the PRA of Jesus may have been an apparition:

> You say that we are actually hardwired to have visions of people after they die. And I've heard you there to be aligning yourself with the argument that Gerd Ludemann has put out, that in fact, and this is a well-known phenomenon in the ancient and in the modern world, that after someone you love has died, sometimes even before you know they have died, you can actually see them in the room with you and it's very real and very clear...presumably plenty of other people in the ancient world had visions of people after they had died, and that doesn't mean they're alive again-it means they're dead. That's the point. The ancient pagan writers were very clear about that. That's one of the reasons that you have these meals with the dead at the tomb, not to bring them back again, but actually as a way of making sure that Uncle Joe ain't coming back again...you wouldn't then say, well, this is basically the same thing as somebody being alive again. That's precisely what it isn't.

4.4.4 Cross-examination: PTSD hallucinations

After conducting the review of the scholarly literature on PTSD related hallucinations, it is now appropriate to cross-examine the possibility that the disciples hallucinated the risen Jesus Christ because of the effects of PTSD by use of Christian apologetic/scholarly literature. Specifically dealing with PTSD related hallucinations in relation to its possible connection to the PRA of Jesus Christ, Gerald O'Collins shares his perspective. Responding to Peter Carnley's retort that the disciples would have been more likely to hallucinate because of the emotional intensity surrounding the death of Jesus, O'Collins (2009:98) responds by noticing that Carnley does not rely upon any scientific data or studies to support his assertion that the disciples would be more likely to hallucinate. Moreover, he also avers that the bereaved persons in Rees (1971) studies were only individuals and not groups of persons.

4.4.5 Cross-examination: Fatigue/Deprivation/Guilt hallucinations

The scholarly literature review was completed on these varieties of hallucinations. Does the "fatigue" hypothesis match the data coming from the New Testament resurrection narratives and from the scholarly literature? After examining scholarly literature on hallucinations of the sensory deprivation variety, does this strain of Carrier's hallucination hypothesis cohere with the scholarly literature review and the PRA of Jesus Christ as listed in the New Testament? Moreover, after the scholarly literature review on the relationship between guilt and hallucinations, does Carrier's contention that guilt influenced Paul to have a hallucination of Jesus Christ make the most sense of the data developed? Included below is a cross-examination from the literature of Christian apologists/scholars specifically regarding Carrier's contentions that hallucinations due to fatigue, sensory deprivation, or guilt were causal factors of the experiences of Jesus Christ.

Habermas (2009:41) offers an example of navy seals who have been known to hallucinate under extreme conditions. Seal trainees frequently report hallucinations as they are placed under tremendous deprivation and stress during their training. After experiencing a hallucination and later discussing the hallucination with others, these seals did not believe the hallucination they observed was real. Once they were able to gain relief from their deprivations (to include sleep) and once they were able to talk about the hallucination with their seal mates, they realized that they were hallucinating.

Another cause of hallucinations that Zusne and Jones (2014:119) report is a hallucination that is caused by sensory deprivation. It was learned as a result of behavioral science research conducted in the 1950s and 1960s that it is necessary and important for humans to experience varied sorts of stimulation in order to promote healthy development and growth. The research revealed that if these levels fall below normal levels, then humans will try to produce such stimulation by altering their environment. If humans are not able to achieve this, then they will produce the needed stimulation internally in the form of hallucinations. They report the research on this topic that was conducted in 1957 at McGill University. In this project, those who were deprived of the aforementioned sort of stimulus began to hallucinate. They started off hallucinating "lights, geometric patterns, wallpaper border like designs, as well as more complex visions that came and went spontaneously."

Objection Three: The Disciples Hallucinated the Risen Jesus Christ

Zusne and Jones (2014:120) offer the example of Admiral Richard Byrd who experienced hallucinations during a self-imposed exile in a small space in the "Antarctic polar night." During this time period, he reported seeing hallucinations and experienced what he described as an "oceanic" bond with the universe. Zusne and Jones also point out the experience of Christiane Ritter, another person who intentionally isolated herself. She reported hallucinating monsters, felt as if she was one with the moon, and also observed her past life flash before her. These authors report that those who involuntarily were sequestered at sea also reported experiences similar to those of Byrd and Ritter.

Zusne and Jones (2014:117) also discuss the phenomena of collective hallucinations "where the same hallucination may be experienced by two or more persons." If these are totally subjective events, then how do more than one person synchronize their hallucinatory, subjective experiences with one another? In their discussion of this topic, Zusne and Jones offer that expectation as well as emotional arousal plays an integral part. They further share the single greatest casual factor for this sort of hallucination is the emotional excitement of religious groups.

Another contributing factor Zusne and Jones (2014:117-18) list is that the group must be informed about what they are going to experience before it happens. They also explain that the most common sorts of manifestations of these collective hallucinations are those observed in the sky (e.g. radiant crosses, religious symbols, flying objects, saints). In addition to some of the factors of these hallucinations, there are going to be those who do not see what is reported by the other hallucinators. Zusne and Jones also provide their opinion that these sorts of group hallucinations were more common in the past than in the present milieu because people were more uneducated, and because the populace in these past times were more likely to give supernatural explanations to phenomena that they could not explain.[147]

In reference to the women witnesses to the empty tomb and PRA of Jesus Christ, William Lane Craig (2000:192) surmises that the women witnesses would not have had the guilt that Peter probably had after his denial of Jesus Christ before his crucifixion. Therefore, the women's encounter with Jesus Christ after his resurrection would lessen the explanatory power of the hallucination hypothesis because what he believes to be a causal factor (guilt) would not be present.[148]

---

[147] On this sort of group experience being a group hallucination, cf. section 4.6.1.
[148] The scholarly literature survey completed in this project revealed that guilt in and of itself is not a cause for hallucinations.

Habermas and Licona (2004:107) also discuss that for Paul, it does not appear he was grieving the death of Jesus nor did he have the disposition of others who hallucinate (some sort of trauma). Before, the appearance of Jesus to Paul, it is known that Paul was traveling to Damascus in order to arrest Christians. Therefore, he was zealous to persecute these Christians and thought he was doing God's will. Thus, he was not feeling guilty for the work that he was preparing to do in Damascus.[149]

4.5 Carrier's redirect examination

Upon the first cross-examination of a witness being completed in a federal trial, the plaintiff may again question the witness to clarify anything that the cross-examination of the witness revealed (Cornell University Law School, redirect examination). Additionally, P.J. White (s.a.) explains that redirect examination is "for the purpose of clarifying the direct examination and addressing issues raised in cross-examination." In the context of this project, Carrier has raised specific objections to several Christian apologists/scholars who have objected to his contentions. Therefore, Carrier's rejoinder is included below regarding several different issues brought out during the cross-examination of Carrier's contentions.

4.5.1 Redirect examination: Countering "group hallucinations" cross-examination

Carrier has offered his position in written form in opposition to the arguments of scholars who oppose the hallucinating disciples claim. Because of Habermas's perspective on group hallucinations, Carrier (1999, 2005) criticizes him for it. Carrier complains that Habermas only treats

---

[149] As the Cross-examination of Carrier comes to a close, it is important to emphasize a major methodological problem that Carrier has: Carrier has a number of theories about the PRA of Jesus being various sorts of hallucinations. However, as exhibited throughout chapter four, there are a number of differences between these different sorts of hallucinations. Does Carrier making numerous claims about different types of hallucinations all at once help his overall argument? In essence he claims, "it could have been this type of hallucination or that sort of hallucination." In making so many claims about the PRA of Jesus Christ possibly being multiple sorts of hallucinations, he actually weakens his position. He would be better off to posit just one type of hallucination instead of trying to show that it could have been multiple types. In positing so many theories, he proves none of them.

one book that discusses mass delusions in relation to the resurrection of Jesus Christ and his main critique of this material is included within only one footnote. Carrier opines further that Habermas's arguments "are not very sound" (Carrier, 1999, 2005). He further offers that Habermas only provides one explanation that mass delusions reported by religious devotees are "actual religious visions of the divine and not hallucinations at all." He further avers that Habermas does not provide any real argument for his position and that Habermas is "begging the question" when he merely states his opinion without providing any foundation for it.

In continuing his rejoinder, Carrier (2005a:ch. 5) counters those that say mass hallucinations are improbable. In response to this claim, Carrier asserts that the original appearances to the disciples were "revelatory epiphanies" and compares the appearances to the visitation of the Holy Spirit at Pentecost and also further offers "Paul's ideal of a church enraptured[150] as proof that group hallucinations are possible." Carrier further hypothesizes that the early Christians could be persuaded into believing that they had in fact experienced Jesus Christ when one Christian had such an experience and then persuaded others that they had a similar occurrence.[151] Carrier further continues, "Each would see Christ in his own way, yet all would take this as jointly seeing the same Christ" (Carrier, 2005a:ch.5). Thus, the actual revelation that Christ was raised from the dead took place "in the beginning and was preached by those disciples who had heard it" (Carrier, 2005a:ch.5). In his chapter entitled, *The Burial of Jesus in Light of Jewish Law* Carrier (2005c:ch. 10) varies his explanation of how the disciples may have group hallucinated the risen Jesus Christ from the previous explanation in that he offers that the reported experience of one such disciple could infect the rest of the group of witnesses with the implication that each person's contribution would influence the other witnesses. Carrier further posits that this would account for all of the New Testament narratives of the resurrection being different from one another.

---

[150] Carrier references 1 Cor. 14:23-31 and also 1 Cor. 12:7-10 to support his contention that the disciples could have had a group hallucination of the risen Jesus Christ.

[151] Carrier (2005a:ch. 5) refers to these sorts of experiences as "anchoring" and "memory contamination" when the disciples are engaged in them amongst themselves and as normative "interpretation" and suggestion when an authority figure is involved.

4.5.2 Redirect examination: Disciples were expecting to encounter the risen Jesus Christ

In response to the cross-examination of Carrier's (1999, 2005:ch. 10) claim of hallucinating disciples, several scholars brought up that there was not an expectation or excitement present that would lead the disciples to encounter the risen Jesus Christ. Rather, they were dejected and not anticipating any sort of appearance. In reply to this argument, Carrier (2005c:ch.10) offers that Jesus Christ:

> ...repeatedly predicted and thus created the expectation in others...but we have so little reliable information about any of the mass experiences we simply cannot rule out the possibility that expectation and excitement did not play a factor, and if we cannot rule that out, then we cannot establish a miracle as a necessary explanation.

Carrier (2005c:ch. 10) further submits that the early Christians were desperate as a result of the arrest and crucifixion of Jesus Christ and were looking for meaning and these impulses could have "inspired these reinterpretations, and dreams or visions could have contributed as well. Thus, the second requirement for hallucination, 'expectation,' has adequate support."

Additionally, Carrier (1999, 2005) posits that because of the fact that hallucinations were believed to be real in the milieu surrounding the early Christian church, the disciples would have radical transformations because they would automatically believe that the hallucinations were real:

> One thing I will add: the argument that hallucinations would not inspire radical transformations of character is absurd, since the very nature of hallucinations is such that you rarely know you are hallucinating. Because of its nature, a hallucinated experience will easily be believed real, and will thus have exactly the same effect as a real experience.

4.6 Recross-examination of Carrier

In federal criminal hearings, it is within the discretion of the court to allow a recross-examination after the redirect examination if new matters have been brought up during the redirect examination. In this instance, Carrier's position on the above-mentioned topics takes issue with positions taken by Christian apologists/scholars. Therefore, the writings of Christians/scholars will be presented to counter Carrier's rejoinder (White:s.a.).

4.6.1 Group hallucinations

Regarding Carrier's contention that Jesus Christ could have been hallucinated by a group after his crucifixion, Gary Habermas (2001:3) submits:

> Even if it could be established that groups of people experienced hallucinations, it does not mean that these experiences were therefore collective. If, as most psychologists assert, hallucinations are private, individual events, then how could groups share exactly the same subjective visual perception? Rather, it is much more likely that the phenomena in question are either illusions — perceptual misinterpretations of actual realities — or *individual* hallucinations.

Bergeron and Habermas (2015:162) offer that in the New Testament resurrection accounts, there were no experiences noted that matched up with a group hallucination where there were the appropriate "psychodynamics" present. They also offer that these sorts of hallucinations are not present in any of the peer-reviewed literature on the topic or in the *Diagnostic and Statistical Manual of Mental Disorders*. They further aver, "The concept of collective hallucination is not part of current psychiatric understanding or accepted pathognomy. Collective hallucination as an explanation for the disciples' post-crucifixion group experiences of Jesus is indefensible."[152]

Regarding the viability of an actual group hallucination being experienced by the disciples and other early witnesses, Jack O'Connell (2009:85) offers that in the scenario of a group apparition (e.g. the baby Jesus or Mary), not everyone is able to see the supposed apparition. Moreover, O'Connell notes that in one study conducted by Patrick Walker only 67% of a group where an apparition was believed to be present reported that they saw the apparition while the others present did not. Furthermore, in one other case, Walker reported that only fifty of two thousand actually beheld the supposed apparition.

---

[152] The McGrews explain the improbability of group hallucinations: "The implausibility of such hallucinations or visions for all the witnesses is notable in a special way in the case of James, Jesus' brother, who was not even with the other disciples at the time of the putative PRA. While the problem with their simultaneous experiences lies in part in the need for them all to be interacting with each other and with Jesus as if he were physically present when in fact he was not, the problem with James's conversion is that it would have had to happen, coincidentally, in virtue of a similar experience at about the same time" (McGrew & McGrew, 2009:637fn).

Specifically concerning apparitions of Mary, Walker (cited by O'Connell, 2009:85) noted a correlation between the form of Mary visualized and the background of the visualizer. Therefore, if someone was familiar with the Virgin Mary as "Our Lady of Mount Carmel," they would see her visualized in this motif whereas someone else may visualize Mary from another perspective. He further notes that someone who is expecting to see Mary in a particular way will visualize her from his or her own subjective perspective. Therefore, in a group setting, the apparition will not be viewed objectively but only as one expects the person to appear.[153]

In response to Carrier's comparison of the "Acts chapter two experience" of the disciples as proof that they were having group hallucinations, this comparison would not line up with the data coming from this passage. It is true that there was an "out of the ordinary experience" when the disciples were in the upper room as there was "a sound like the blowing of a violent wind that came from heaven and filled the whole house where they were sitting (v. 2)." Additionally, there were visual manifestations similar to flames of fire that were observed as well. However, there were others that observed these manifestations in addition to the disciples ("God fearing Greeks") who heard the sound of the violent wind and gathered together because of the sound (vv. 5-6)). In addition to hearing the sound and gathering together because of it, many also heard their own languages being spoken by the entourage of the disciples and were curious why the disciples were speaking in their native tongues (of the hearers) (vv. 7-12). In fact, these manifestations and the ensuing curiosity of those who observed these manifestations is what gives Peter his impetus to preach his sermon. It is to explain the outpouring of the Holy Spirit on the disciples that was witnessed by the crowd that had gathered after hearing and observing this phenomenon.

So, there were many non-Christian Jews from other countries who witnessed these audio and visual manifestations. As a result of witnessing

---

[153] O'Connell (2009:88) furnishes an example of what a post-resurrection encounter of Jesus Christ might look like if they were group hallucinations: "By examining the cases above, we can deduce what the resurrection appearances would have looked like if the hallucination hypothesis is correct. The group appearances (although not necessarily the individual appearances): 1) would have been expected; 2) would probably have involved some external signs of extreme stress (e.g. fainting; 3) would have involved Jesus being seen only by some members of the group; 4) would have involved Jesus being seen differently by those who did see him; 5) would not have involved Jesus conducting group conversations. It is clear that in their present form, the resurrection narratives do not characterize the appearances in these ways."

these manifestations, and Peter's speech many of these God fearing Jews (approx. 3000) converted to Christianity that day (vv. 40-41). This instance of mass conversion is also proof of the veridicality of the experience. This was a supernatural event that seemed so convincing to those who witnessed it, that three thousand of those who gathered to further investigate these unusual occurrences converted to Christianity that day.

4.6.2 Disciples expected to see the risen Jesus Christ

Answering the objection that there could be mass hallucinations where there is an air of expectancy, John Johnson (2001:232) gives the opinion that this variety of mass hysteria can be explained by an already existing phenomena such as a bright light (as in the case of the Statue of Mary at Knock), the way in which the light might catch a statue of Mary or image of Mary, etc. He also identifies the "air of miraculous expectancy with which many Catholics visit shrines." Johnson observes that these factors of mass hysteria would not figure into the PRA of the risen Jesus Christ, as those who experienced Him were not "miracle hungry pilgrims."

Johnson (2001:233) further addresses the topic of the expectation of the early Christians who were looking forward to the resurrection. Johnson states that the Christians did not have a preexisting socio-cultural framework where the resurrection would fit comfortably. A risen Messiah was a new concept to the religious world. Johnson shares the perspective of Wolfhart Pannenberg (cited by Johnson, 2001:233) who wrote:

The primitive Christian news about the eschatological resurrection of Jesus- with a temporal interval separating it from the universal resurrection of the dead- is, considered from the point of view of the history of religions, something new, precisely also in the framework of the apocalyptic tradition.

Gerald O'Collins (2009:94) discusses the circumstances surrounding the resurrection appearances and observes that rather than expectantly awaiting for Jesus Christ to appear to them, the mindset of the disciples was in line with the devastating consequences of the preceding days when Jesus was arrested, tortured, and executed. They were not expecting to see Jesus Christ. O'Collins also opines that if Jesus appeared to only one group, then it would be easier to claim that the one group had a visionary experience. However, Jesus Christ appeared to any number of persons in any number of settings. He appeared not only to one group, but others as well and also to individuals alone.

Along with Johnson and O'Collins, Bergeron and Habermas (2015:162) address the mindset of the disciples after the crucifixion of Jesus Christ.

Moreover, they utilize passages from the New Testament as their foundation to make their observation. In regard to the issue of expectancy, Bergeron and Habermas observe that those who have encountered apparitions with others in attendance note that not all persons in these group settings will see the apparition claimed by others. Additionally, they also report that oftentimes, those reporting the observance of an apparition in a group setting will see the apparition differently and will not carry on conversations with the apparition.

In addition to these observations regarding apparitions, Bergeron and Habermas (2015:162) observe that the disciples were not expecting to have any contact with Jesus Christ in bodily form after his crucifixion. They aver that a majority of scholars accept that the New Testament accounts of the resurrection characterize the post-crucifixion disciples as "forlorn" (Lk 24:10-11, 17, 21). They continue that this sort of reaction would be normal after the gruesome death of a beloved friend.

Furthermore, regarding the expectancy of the disciples seeing a risen Jesus Christ, O'Connell (2009:92) offers that if Jesus was expected to return, all of his followers would have reported him in a glorious form. He further offers that by the time of the writing of the Gospels there were no reports of a glorious form of Jesus Christ that were observed:

> However, it is evident that by the time the Gospels were composed there were no stories of glorious resurrection appearances circulating, for the Gospels present us with decidedly non-glorious appearances; Jesus' appearance is quite mundane and ordinary. Yet, I believe it can be shown that if the early church had stories of glorious resurrection appearances, it would have desired to preserve them, and hence such stories should, if they ever existed, appear in the Gospels. That the early church did not preserve stories of glorious appearances indicates that such stories were never there to begin with.

Tim and Lydia McGrew (2009:625) also add to the opinion of the above scholars on the expectancy of the disciples to see the resurrected Jesus Christ. They explain that the disciples were unlike the many devotees who throng to various shrines with the expectation of having a vision. Rather, they were experiencing both fear and grief. Moreover, they observe that there was no expectation of a Messiah who would die and rise again in the Judaism of that day. This is borne out by the skepticism shown by the initial reaction of the report from the women as well as the initial reaction of Thomas when presented with the testimony of the other disciples who had encountered the risen Jesus Christ.

In addition to the aforementioned scholars, Groothuis (2011:556) offers that the disciples had resigned themselves to the fact that Jesus Christ was dead. Therefore, they were shocked when they heard reports that Jesus Christ had arisen from the dead. Also, Groothuis points out that the Jews of that day would not be expecting anyone to rise from the dead. Rather, the Jewish eschatological perspective would be that the resurrection would occur at the end of time with no one being resurrected until the end.

Furthermore, the McGrews (2009:620) mention that the women also had no expectation of seeing Jesus Christ alive after the crucifixion. Rather, their purpose was only to anoint the corpse of Jesus Christ where it laid in the tomb of Joseph of Arimathea. This is also borne out by the reaction of the women when they encountered the empty tomb (Luke 24:4). This observation is also confirmed by the consternation of Mary Magdalene who did not recognize Jesus Christ when she came across him (John 20:15).

4.7 Evidence against Carrier's hallucinating disciples

In section 4.2, Carrier's literature was presented that supported his "hallucination hypothesis." After Carrier's literature was analyzed, then a survey of scholarly literature on the subject of hallucinations was presented which was followed by a cross-examination of Carrier's contention by the literature of Christian apologists/scholars. In this section, evidence against Carrier's specific contention that the disciples hallucinated the PRA of Jesus Christ will be offered. This evidence comes from the New Testament as well as from research conducted regarding the martyrdom of the original disciples. Scholarly literature from Bible commentators regarding the corporeity of Jesus when he was experienced after his death and research conducted on the martyrdom of the disciples will be offered against Carrier's contention. Additional circumstantial evidence against Carrier's claim included in this section are the conversions of both Saul and James who were both at one time nonbelievers in Jesus Christ. In addition to this circumstantial evidence, the corroborative evidence of the empty tomb in conjunction with the PRA will also be offered as confirmation for the corporeity of the PRA of Jesus Christ after his death.

4.7.1 Evidence against the hallucination hypothesis: PRA in bodily form

4.7.1.1 Matthew

Regarding the evidence for the corporeity of Jesus in the Gospel of Matthew, Craig Keener (1999:711-712) points out that all early Christian sources endorse the view that Jesus Christ rose in bodily form from the dead even though there are some scholars who offer unsupported inferences without any foundation for their views. Keener also points out that many of those who see him worship him (1 Cor. 15:5, 7; Matt. 28:9). Keener believes that the aforementioned worshipping of the risen Jesus Christ is good evidence that they not only saw him but also knew his identity as the same Jesus Christ with whom they served prior to the crucifixion. The risen Jesus Christ is no one other than "God Incarnate."

Bible commentator Joseph Benson (1839) references the ninth verse of chapter twenty-eight of Matthew's Gospel to describe how the emotional state of the disciples quickly changed from fear to reverence. This is evidenced by the way in which they positioned themselves as they fell prostrate and embraced his feet. Benson believes that being able to embrace Jesus was granted to these women because "the angel's words having strongly impressed their minds with the notion of his resurrection...might have taken his appearing for an illusion of their own imagination, had he not permitted them to handle him, and convince themselves by the united report of their senses."

John Gill (1746:63) explains that in Matthew 28:9, the disciples were encouraged to approach the man who spoke to them because they recognized his mannerisms and his voice. In similarity to Benson, Gill also observes that not only did they fall prostrate on the ground and worship him, but they also embraced his feet so they could be assured that he was actually alive and no longer dead; that he was not just a phantom or a spirit. They worshipped him because after his death he arose back to life. Thus because of His resurrection, Jesus Christ was the actual Son of God and was the proper object of religious adoration. Also commenting on verse nine and in similarity to Gill, Spence and Joseph offer that Jesus allowed "the women" to touch him in order to "assure themselves of his corporeity by touch as well as sight" (Spence & Joseph, 1961).

4.7.1.2 Luke

Griffith (2000:296) expounds on the evidence within the gospels regarding the resurrection of Jesus Christ. He focuses in on the appearance of Jesus in Luke twenty-four to the two disciples on the road to Emmaus. He observes details of this Lucan account to contain good evidence. He lists that according to the account in Luke, the two who encounter Jesus on the Emmaus Road did not know of the appearance of Jesus to either Peter or to Mary Magdalene. However, these witnesses were able to verify the report of the empty tomb. Moreover, the conversations with the "stranger" occurred in broad daylight under normal conditions.[154]

Griffith (2000: 302-305) further describes the appearance of Jesus Christ to the eleven in Luke chapter 24. He mentions that the eleven were frightened when Jesus appeared to them (v. 37). He also goes over the evidence for the corporeity of Jesus that rebuts the initial fear of the disciples that Jesus was an apparition when he appeared to them. He offers that the recently resurrected Jesus Christ the disciples encountered still bore the marks of crucifixion on his hands, feet, and side, had flesh and bones (vv. 39-40), could be touched (v. 39), and could eat food (v.43).

Regarding the "touchability" of the resurrection body of Jesus Christ, Griffith (2000:304-307) avers that this is strong evidence that the body of Jesus Christ was neither an apparition nor a ghost. Griffith makes this statement after sharing the passage in John where Jesus appears to the disciples a second time when Thomas is present. Griffith avers, "The plain implication is that Jesus ate of both the bread and fish. This is evidence of the factuality of Jesus' resurrection: his resurrected body was seen to ingest food not only one evening in a closed room in Jerusalem, but one morning on an open lake shore in Galilee."

In his commentary on Luke, Bock (1996:615) observes that it is a major challenge to our present day culture to believe that the resurrection of Jesus Christ actually occurred. The empty tomb was not enough to convince the disciples of Jesus that he had arisen. The entire interaction between the two on the Emmaus Road and Jesus is what it took for them to believe that Jesus, in fact, had arisen from the dead. In their discussion before Jesus joined them, they were in despair. However, after encountering Jesus their minds were changed. Jesus did not merely die after be-

---

[154] It is also noted that the risen Jesus Christ was observed not only to walk and talk with these two witnesses, but they also observed him as he entered their dwelling, as he picked up a loaf of bread, gave thanks for it, and broke it in half (cf. Luke 24:13-32).

ing crucified. His interaction with the two men assured them and the other disciples that he was, in fact, alive.

Continuing with his analysis of the resurrection account in Luke, Bock (1996:620) discusses the reports of the resurrected Jesus that continued to come in. Bock discusses how the incidences of contact with the risen Jesus Christ were "stacking up." Because the disciples believe that Jesus may be a spirit or a ghost, they are frightened. In response to this anxiety over the presence of Jesus, Jesus asks them the reason for their dread and doubt of him. Jesus then asks them to not only to look at his hands, his feet, but also to touch them as well. These marks in a body made out of flesh are the evidence that he is the same person that died of crucifixion and that is speaking to them now alive. In addition, Jesus remarks plainly that spirits do not have flesh and bones as he does (v. 39). So, Jesus reassures his disciples that he is no longer dead, but that he is now alive again. In further emphasizing the reality of his resurrection, Jesus asks for something to eat and assures the disciples that he is not a ghost but an actual flesh and blood person (vv. 42-43).

4.7.1.3 John

In discussing the appearance of Jesus Christ to the disciples, the second time, Elmer Towns (2002:207) recognizes the proclamation of Thomas (John 20:28) as the apex of the book of John. Towns further explains this is the case because Thomas gives the "strongest or highest expression of Old Testament deity." After proclaiming his pessimism on the first occasion of the appearance of Jesus Christ to the disciples when he was absent, Thomas is overawed by this encounter with the risen Jesus Christ. In this passage (John 20:26-29), John writes about his observation of the interaction between the risen Jesus Christ and Thomas. After witnessing the body of the risen Jesus Christ to include the nail prints from his crucifixion, Thomas makes the aforementioned proclamation of faith.[155]

Towns (2002:216) further discusses the appearance on the beach, the miraculous catch of fish, and Jesus Christ preparing breakfast for the seven disciples that were present. Towns offers that this appearance to the

---

[155] Regarding the proclamation of Thomas, Craig Keener (2003:1211) offers, "Thomas's very skepticism makes him the ideal proponent of a high Christology by indicating the greatness of the revelation by which he was convinced. Thomas has spoken for the disciples in this Gospel before (11:16), and his revelation elicits the Gospel's climactic Christological confession, 'My Lord and my God' (20:28), which forms an *inclusio* with the prologue (1:1, 18)."

disciples was not in order to reveal himself to them. Rather, it was for them to more fully comprehend the reality of his resurrection. In previous appearances, there were doubts among some who were present. On this occasion, none doubted that it was Jesus Christ in the flesh. For in John 21:12, this experience with the risen Christ is so complete, no one present dared to ask the identity of the honored visitor as they "knew that it was the Lord." In this encounter, there is no doubt that they are speaking and eating with the bodily, risen Jesus Christ.

Gary Burge (2000:562fn) explains that the early church father, Ignatius, believed that the disciples actually touched the body of Jesus Christ. In his book to the church at Smyrna, Ignatius writes:

> For I know and believe that he was in the flesh even after the resurrection; and when he came to Peter and those with him, he said to them: 'take hold of me; handle me and see that I am not a disembodied demon.' And immediately they touched him and believed, being closely united with his flesh and blood.

Burge further insists that John, in his Gospel, is communicating clearly about the reality of the resurrection. Woven throughout the flow of the narrative is the 'power and the certainty of Jesus's life from death' (Burge, 2000:566). The encounters with the risen Jesus Christ are not illusions or fantasies dreamed up by the witnesses in order to allay their anxiety. Peter and John go to the tomb, examine the evidence and are stunned by what they see. Shortly thereafter, Jesus appears (20:20) to the disciples in the upper room and this is no mere phantom that they encounter. He immediately gives evidence that he is not an apparition or a ghost. He is the same man who was nailed to the cross, a real flesh and blood man with visible wounds.

Burge supplies corroboration of the encounter of the disciples with a flesh and blood Jesus Christ by noting that in John's first epistle, John emphatically proclaims that the disciples witnessed the risen Jesus Christ with their own physical senses. This eyewitness perspective is the basis by which the disciples know the details of the risen Jesus Christ are true (1 John 1:1-4). The disciples saw, heard, and touched the risen Jesus Christ. Burge (2000:572) then contrasts the words of John with the perspectives of Marcus Borg and John Dominic Crossan:

> John is trying to affirm the very thing Borg and Crossan deny: This Jesus is not a fantasy but a real man, a resurrected man who can talk and be touched despite the fact that he has been transformed by the power of his resurrection.

4.7.1.4 Acts

Regarding Paul's experience on the road to Damascus (Acts 9), Schnabel (2012:443) discusses the nature of it. He discusses how Paul has an objective seeing and hearing of Jesus Christ and references 1 Corinthians 9:1. Paul has experienced Jesus Christ in his divine splendor and proclaims the same.[156] Adding justification that Paul's experience was veridical, Schnabel also mentions that Paul argues that his apostleship is valid because he had seen the risen Jesus Christ just as the other disciples had a "real encounter" with him. (1 Cor. 15:5-8).

Schnabel (2012:445) continues that Luke's account of Saul's conversion in Acts 9:3-6 was not a psychological, subjective, or mystical experience. This is borne out by the residual effect that the appearance of Jesus Christ to Saul had on his travel companions as "they stood there speechless, because they heard the voice but saw no one (v.7)." The implication from this scenario is that Saul had seen someone who was enveloped in light. Further demonstrating the reality of Saul's encounter with the risen Jesus Christ, Luke describes the after effects of Saul's encounter. On this topic, Schnabel avers (2012:445):

> He gets up from the ground. He cannot see anything despite his eyes being open. He needs his fellow travelers to lead him into Damascus, taking him by the hand. He cannot see for three days, during which he neither eats nor drinks.

The after-effects of Saul's encounter with the risen Jesus Christ are additional proof that his appearance is no mere vision, apparition, or hallucination. If it was merely a subjective event, then Saul would not have any physical symptoms. The description from Saul's encounter with the risen Jesus Christ demonstrates that this event includes both subjective and objective elements.

R.C.H. Lenski (2008:356-357) also avers that any notion that Saul's conversion experience while on the road to Damascus, was other than an authentic encounter with the risen Jesus Christ, is misguided. He discuss-

---

[156] In his assessment of the passages in the Book of Acts that mention Paul's conversion experience, Ben Witherington (1998:310) sees agreement in the essentials of these passages (Acts chapters 9, 22, 26) although there are some differences in the details. Furthermore, Witherington observes that these summaries comport with what is observed in Paul's letters where Paul mentions his conversion (Galatians 1-2; 2 Cor. 3:18, 4:6). The various references to Paul's conversion from the pen of Paul and Luke strengthen the New Testament testimony on this event.

Objection Three: The Disciples Hallucinated the Risen Jesus Christ

es both the objective and subjective nature of the event. He first focuses in on those who were accompanying Saul. Not only did Saul fall prostrate, but so did his squad of "policemen" (Acts 26:4) who were accompanying him to roust the Christians in Damascus. He observes that Saul's assistants must have been totally confused by what they beheld after they observed Saul talking to someone that they could not see. In one description, Saul's companions heard the voice (9:7) and in another description they also saw the light (22:9). Lenski further explains that great attention has been given to Saul's conversion with differing theories abounding about what actually happened. One theorist proposes a sudden thunderstorm that is the genesis of the conversion experience. Another offers that it is a psychological event caused by guilt over his past treatment of Christians. Lenski flatly rejects these explanations.

Moreover, regarding Saul's conversion, Lenski (2008:357-358) writes:

> The vision of Jesus was not something that transpired only in Saul's own soul either as imagined by himself or as wrought in Saul's soul by the Lord...Jesus actually appeared to Saul... Was this man mistaken in regard to what happened on the road to Damascus? Did he labor under psychological delusions and the like? The cause must measure up to the effect. The apostleship of Paul, as it is recorded in the New Testament, cannot be traced to anything that was merely subjective, mistaken, unreal. Luke recorded the realities, and they will ever stand as what they are.

In similarity to Lenski, J.B. Polhill (2009 437-438) also decries various attempts at giving explanations other than what Paul plainly states. These differing explanations include a thunderstorm, a seizure, psychogenic blindness as a result of repressed feelings of guilt, or being convinced by the "correctness of Christian views." Polhill asserts that it is obvious what both Luke and Paul describe:

> What both picture is a *radical conversion* experience. Paul the persecutor was stopped dead in his tracks on the Damascus road. The risen Jesus showed himself to Paul; and with this confirmation that the Christian claims were indeed true, Paul was completely turned from persecutor to witness. Only one category describes Paul's experience, a category not uncommon in Acts. It was a *miracle*, the result of direct divine action.

Even though Saul subjectively encountered Jesus Christ during his Damascus road experience in the content of the Divine message, it is clear that this encounter with the resurrected Jesus Christ was objectively real in every sense.

4.7.1.5 I Corinthians

In regard to the appearance to the 500 at one time (1 Cor. 15:7), Dan Mitchell (2004:213) notes the importance of the Greek verb *ephapax* or "at one time." Mitchell uses the perspective of Murphy-O'Connor, ("Tradition and redaction in 1 Cor. 15:3-7" p. 586) to explain, "there appears to be a conspiracy of silence with regard to this adverb; it is ignored by all the commentaries and studies that I have been able to check. If Paul had merely written 'he [Jesus] appeared[157] to five hundred brethren,' the most natural interpretation would have been to understand it as a reference to a mass vision. Why, then did he need to emphasize this point? The most obvious explanation is that he intended to underline the objectivity of the experience.'"

In conducting a linguistic analysis of the Greek vocabulary utilized in a very early Christological creed contained within 1 Corinthians 15: 3b-6a, 7, Kirk MacGregor (2006:230-31) offers that the Greek word for "raised," εγειρω, in this passage leaves no doubt that the author(s) of the creed considered the resurrection of Jesus Christ to be a grave emptying event. According to MacGregor (2006:230-231), the writers were communicating that the body of Jesus Christ was physically raised. The definition of the aforementioned verb, according to MacGregor is "to cause to stand up from a lying or reclining position with the implication of some degree of previous incapacity."[158] Furthermore, this sort of physical incapacity necessarily refers to the raising of a corpse that was in a prone position to a standing position as a live body.

Moreover, this passage cannot refer to a spiritual formulation regarding the raising of Jesus Christ because a spirit does not lie down or get up. These are physical actions that are described by the verb εγειρω ("raised"). For these reasons, MacGregor (2006:231) believes the Greek vocabulary used here in this passage "demands" that those who authored

---

[157] Craig Blomberg (1994:302) makes a distinction between the usage of the word "ophthe" and "horama" that are used in 1 Cor. 15:5-8: "Eventually a body could have been produced and the disciples' story laid to rest. The verb *ophthe* ("appeared") refers more naturally to an objective reality that the disciples saw rather than to some subjective vision (as might more plausibly be the case with the word *horama*-"vision")."

[158] Edward Goodrick and John Kohlenberger (1999: no. 1586) render εγειρω ("raised") as "to arise, to stand from a prone or sleeping position. From this base meaning, there are several fig. extended meanings: to wake from sleep; to restore from a dead or damaged state: to heal, raise to life; to cause something to exist: raise up (give birth to) a child."

the creed were communicating that Jesus Christ arose bodily from the dead and furthermore, the tomb where he had been laid became vacant after he arose and took on bodily form (MacGregor, 2006:230-31). Based on this analysis, MacGregor asserts that the bodily raising of Jesus Christ is the best conclusion. In addition to this analysis, MacGregor (2006:234) also observes that 1 Corinthians 15:23 implies a bodily raising of Jesus Christ in that Jesus Christ, "the first fruits of the resurrection" ensures the physical raising of his followers from the dead. The analogy used by Paul here in verse twenty-three would break down if Jesus Christ had not risen bodily guaranteeing the physical rising of the saints.

In addition to Mitchell and MacGregor, Rene Lopez (2013:153) also avers that the witnesses to the risen Jesus Christ experienced him as one possessing an actual physical body. They experienced this body with their five senses. However, he offers that the body of Jesus Christ was different in the sense that it cannot be limited by time or spatial limitations. Lopez further notes that Paul teaches in 1 Corinthians chapter fifteen that believers in Jesus Christ will also inhabit spiritual bodies. However, he posits that these spiritual bodies will be "perfectly suited to obey God through the power of the Holy Spirit. But this does not mean that the body is incorporeal." Lopez continues that the testimony in the Gospels as well as Paul's teaching of the resurrection in 1 Corinthians clearly explain that just as Jesus Christ arose in a physical body, so shall all those who are in relationship with him arise in a physical body.

4.7.2 Evidence against the hallucination hypothesis: The eyewitnesses of the PRA experience martyrdom

In his doctoral dissertation, Sean McDowell (2014) has analyzed the evidence for the martyrdom of the disciples/apostles. He has conducted his investigation by analyzing various historical accounts coming from various sources that include passages from the Bible, excerpts from the writings of early Christian church leaders, and other writings coming from various indigenous authors from the regions where the disciples were purported to have ministered in the first century A.D. As the scope of this chapter is to analyze Carrier's views on the hallucinating disciples by accepted principles of evidence, it is probative to conduct a brief evidentiary analysis to determine if there is any evidence to support the claims of the early Christian church that the witnesses to the resurrection were martyred for their faith. If these claims are supported, then they corroborate the resurrection accounts of Jesus Christ in the New Testament (to include the evidence of Christ's bodily PRA) and also provide circumstantial evidence that Jesus Christ arose from the dead.

Regarding the evidence of the martyrdom of the disciples, McDowell (2014:3) writes:

> There is, in fact, reliable historical evidence to trust the ancient and uniform testimony that (1) all the apostles were willing to die for their faith, and (2) a number of them actually did experience martyrdom...In other words, *their* [the disciples] *willingness to face persecution and martyrdom indicates more than any other conceivable course their sincere conviction that, after rising from the dead, Jesus did indeed appear to them.*

In further discussing the persuasiveness of this information, McDowell (2014:3) discusses that the disciples, in essence, being the first witnesses to the resurrection (after the women witnesses) metaphorically signed their testimony of their experiences with the risen Jesus Christ with their own blood. This sort of attestation is good evidence that their convictions were sincerely held. McDowell further asserts that the sacrificial deaths of those disciples who ended up dying for their sincerely held belief in the resurrection gives strength to the veridicality of the resurrection of Jesus Christ. Moreover, as offered in the previous section, the testimony of the disciples/apostles from the resurrection narratives was that Jesus Christ was bodily raised from the dead. Therefore, the martyrdoms of these witnesses of the resurrected Jesus Christ as stated before is good evidence that they encountered the physical, resurrected Jesus Christ rather than a mere, phantom, vision, or hallucination.

4.7.2.1 Evidence for the martyrdom of Paul

McDowell (2014:174) mentions 1 Clement 5:5-7 (otherwise known as his first letter to the Corinthians) (c. AD 95-96)[159] as the first non-canonical book that refers to the martyrdom of the apostle Paul, and also Peter. Even though there are no particulars regarding the details of Paul's mar-

---

[159] Regarding the date for the writing of "First Clement," W.A. Jurgens (1970:7) believes that a more accurate date for this epistle would be circa 80 A.D. The reasons given by Jurgens for this perspective are that those bearing the letter from Clement (Claudius Ephebus and Valerius Vito mentioned in Ch. 64) would most likely be the freed slaves of the Emperor Claudius and his wife Valeria Messalina. He makes an inference based on the age of these couriers who delivered the letter as well as recent calamitous events that are listed in the letter to arrive at the timeframe of 80 A.D. He believes that one of these events could have been the eruption of Mt. Vesuvius which occurred in 79 A.D.

tyrdom, McDowell asserts that the vocabulary and the context of the passages referring to Paul implied the martyrdom of Paul:

> But, to leave the examples of antiquity, let us come to the athletes who are closest to our own time. Consider the noble examples of our own generation. Through jealousy and envy the greatest and most righteous pillars were persecuted, and they persevered even unto death...Through jealousy and strife, Paul showed the way to the prize for endurance. Seven times he was in chains, he was exiled, he was stoned; he became a herald in the East and in the West, and he won splendid reknown [sic.] through his faith. He taught righteousness to all the world, and after reaching the boundaries of the West and giving his testimony before the rulers he passed from the world and was taken up to the holy place. Thus he became our greatest example of persecution (Clement, 1970:7-8).

McDowell (2014:176) also offers another passage from "First Clement" that, in conjunction with the aforementioned passage offered, leads him to believe that Paul was martyred in Rome under Nero: "To these men who lived such holy lives there must be added a multitude of the elect, who suffered terrible indignities and tortures on account of jealousy, and who became shining examples in our midst (Clement, 1970:8)." McDowell (2014:176) explains that the verbiage utilized by Clement is also nearly identical to the account of the Neronian persecution of the Christians by the Roman historian, Tacitus. McDowell shares the opinion of F.F. Bruce who also endorses the Clementine passage as referring to the Neronian persecution of the Christians.[160]

In addition to Clement, McDowell (2014:178) also offers another reference from an early Christian source within the second century, Ignatius, the bishop of the Christian church at Antioch. In *The Letter to the Ephesians*, Ignatius (s.a.(a): ch. 12) discusses his status in relation to the Ephesian church and how he is following the same journey as Paul to death as a martyr:

> I know both who I am, and to whom I write. I am the very insignificant Ignatius, who have my lot with those who are exposed to danger and con-

---

[160] In reference to the martyrdom of Paul at Rome in relation to First Clement, F.F. Bruce (2000:448) avers, "That this is a reference to the persecution of Christians in Rome under Nero is hardly to be doubted: with Clement's 'great multitude' may be compared to Tacitus's almost identical wording. If we took Clement's language *au pied de la lettre* it would imply that Peter and Paul had suffered martyrdom before the persecution which followed the great fire...The most that can safely be said is that Clement bears witness to Paul's death at Rome under Nero."

demnation. But ye have been the objects of mercy, and are established in Christ. I am one delivered over [to death], but the least of all those that have been cut off for the sake of Christ, "from the blood of righteous Abel" to the blood of Ignatius. Ye are initiated into the mysteries of the Gospel with Paul, the holy, the martyred, inasmuch as he was "a chosen vessel;" at whose feet may I be found, and at the feet of the rest of the saints, when I shall attain to Jesus Christ, who is always mindful of you in His prayers.

McDowell (2014:176) explains that Ignatius drafted his *Letter to the Ephesians* to the church in Ephesus as he was on his way to face a martyr's death in Rome and that these letters were his last statements as he travelled to Rome. Moreover, James Aageson (cited by McDowell, 2014:179) observes that Ignatius views himself to be following the same pathway as Paul and sees the Ephesians as a conduit of those slain on behalf of God.[161] Therefore, through discussing his own plight and route to get to Rome, Ignatius informs that Paul travelled a similar route and that Ignatius will have a similar fate as Paul. Even though Ignatius does not mention the mode of execution that Paul experienced, he does intimate that Paul was executed in Rome (McDowell, 2014:180).

In addition to Clement and Ignatius, McDowell (2014:181-184, 190-192) also utilizes the writings of Polycarp, Dionysius of Corinth, Tertullian[162] and Irenaeus[163] as further evidence of the martyrdom of Paul in Rome.

In addition to the writings of these early church fathers, McDowell (2014:155-193) also observes evidence coming from *The Acts of Paul* and *The Martyrdom of Paul*, two second century works, to further buttress his

---

[161] The city of Ephesus of the Roman Empire era was situated north of Antioch and South East of Rome and may likely have been a city Ignatius traveled through to get to Rome. Ancient Antioch was located at present day Antakya, Turkey and ancient Ephesus was located at present day Selcuk, Turkey. It is known that Ignatius paused his journey to Rome (in custody) at the city of Smyrna as he travelled to Troas where he would set sail for Rome (cf. Encyclopaedia Britannica, Antioch, Ephesus, and Saint Ignatius of Antioch).

[162] McDowell (2014:190-93) explains that Tertullian wrote about Paul's beheading and that it occurred in Rome along with the crucifixion of the apostle Peter. McDowell gives the date of Tertullian writing about the martyrdoms of Peter and Paul in the last half of the 2nd century A.D.

[163] Irenaues reports that Matthew had issued a Gospel that he had written while Peter and Paul were ministering in Rome as they laid the foundation of the Christian church. Irenaues further reports, "after their departure, Mark...also handed down to us in writing what had been preached by Peter" (Irenaues, 1970:88). McDowell asserts that this passage does refer to the "departure" or martyrdom of Peter and Paul (McDowell, 2014:183-84).

Objection Three: The Disciples Hallucinated the Risen Jesus Christ

evidence that Paul was martyred in Rome. In addition to these references, McDowell also utilizes several of Paul's epistles (Philippians, 2 Timothy, and Acts) where he implies that he will be executed soon and the probable location of his execution (Phil. 1:13; 1:7,14, 17, 4:22; 2 Tim. 1:16-17; 2 Tim. 2:9; 4:6-8, 6-18, Acts 19:31; 28:17b, 28:31).

In summarizing the strength of evidence for the martyrdom for Paul and the other disciples, McDowell (2014:192-93) utilizes a scale to rate the probability of the historical evidence for each disciple. Regarding Paul being in Rome at the time of his martyrdom, McDowell believes that this scenario has the "highest possible probability." Furthermore, McDowell rates Paul's martyrdom occurring during the reign of Nero as "very probably true." Additionally, McDowell offers that there is no other site of imprisonment for Paul that has been offered as a possibility other than Rome.

4.7.2.2 Evidence for martyrdom of Peter

In his investigation regarding the evidence for the martyrdom of Peter, McDowell (2014:103-104) explains that Peter is the most mentioned apostle in the New Testament, is the first disciple to become a follower of Jesus, and was in the inner circle of Jesus Christ along with the sons of Zebedee, James and John. He further mentions that Peter was in a particularly good position to witness a number of major events relating to Jesus Christ to include the healing of Jairus's daughter (Mark 5:37; Luke 8:51), Jesus Christ in the Garden of Gethsemane (Matt. 26:36-37; Mark 14:32-33), and the Transfiguration (Matt. 17:1-3; Mark 9:2; Luke 9:28-31).[164] He continues that Peter became a forceful spokesman for and leader of the early Christian church.

Regarding the literary evidence for the martyrdom of Peter, McDowell offers through Larry Helyer (cited by McDowell, 2014:107-114) that Peter is connected with Rome along with other cities of the western Diaspora and that he conducted missionary work in cities such areas as Corinth, Antioch of Syria, and also Rome for a period of at least sixteen years or more. McDowell also gives 1 Peter 5:13 as indirect evidence that Peter had resided in Rome where Peter greets the recipients from his location

---

[164] Importantly, Peter was also an eyewitness to the PRA of Jesus Christ as attested to in Matthew 28 (as part of the eleven), Luke 24 (as part of the group of disciples), John 20 and 21 and Acts 2:33. This personal contact of Peter with the risen Jesus Christ in addition to his martyrdom gives powerful circumstantial evidence for the veracity of the resurrection of Jesus Christ.

in "Babylon." McDowell further explains through Richard Bauckham that Babylon was a common way for the early church to refer to Rome. Another Petrine New Testament reference McDowell (2014:120) utilizes as evidence for Peter's martyrdom is his farewell address in 2 Peter 1:12-15 where it is clear that Peter is giving his last testament and that his death looms near.

In similarity to the evidence for Paul, McDowell (2014:111-12, 124-25, 137) also offers the writings of various early church leaders that reveal Peter's ties with Rome as well as mention of his martyrdom there. McDowell offers the writings of Papias who avers that Mark utilized Peter as his main source for his Gospel from Peter's recollections of Jesus Christ and his ministry. This reference to Peter being the source for Mark's Gospel is strengthened by 1 Peter 5:13 which infers that Peter and Mark are together in Rome and also shows their close relationship as Peter mentions Mark as "my son." The writings of Papias about Mark/Peter are not extant but are included within Eusebius's, *The Church's History*. Other early church fathers that write about Peter are Clement,[165] Irenaeus,[166] and Ignatius.[167] In addition to these early Christian writers, McDowell also mentions that *The Acts of Peter (c. A.D. 180), Apocalypse of Peter (c. A.D. 135), The Ascension of Isaiah (A.D. 112-138)*, and several authors who Eusebius mentions in his history all claim that either Peter (along with Paul) founded the church at Rome or that he worked at developing the church there.

---

[165] "Let us set before our eyes the good apostles: Peter, who through unwarranted jealousy suffered not one or two but many toils, and having thus given testimony went to the place of glory that was his due" (Clement, s.a.:7-8).

[166] Cf. 161fn.

[167] McDowell (2014:135) mentions that Ignatius's Letter to the Romans exhibits that Peter (and Paul) was known by the early Roman church and that the church was most likely aware of a tradition relating to Peter's (and Paul's) martyrdom; In his letters, Ignatius mentions both Peter/Paul. Ignatius writes, "Not as Peter and Paul did, do I command you [he bids the Roman church not to interfere in his impending execution]. They were Apostles, and I am a convict. They were free, and even to the present time I am a slave. Yet if I suffer, I shall be the freedman of Jesus Christ, and in him I shall rise up" (Ignatius, s.a.(b):22). Ignatius also writes further on Peter and Paul in relation to martyrdom: "And when he [Jesus Christ] came to those with Peter He said to them: 'Here now, touch me and see that I am not a bodiless ghost.' Immediately, they touched Him and, because of the merging of His flesh and spirit, they believed. For the same reason they [the disciples to include Peter] despised death and in fact were proven superior to death" (Ignatius, s.a. (c): 24).

In summation, McDowell gives the "highest possible probability" that Peter was martyred. Regarding whether Peter was crucified and whether he was in Rome when he was martyred, McDowell assigns that these two criteria were "very probably true." Even though McDowell assents to a Petrine martyrdom in Rome, he is not as sanguine about the possibility of the martyrdom occurring during the reign of Nero as he has assigned the probability of this occurring as "more probable than not."

4.7.2.3 Evidence for the martyrdom of James

In addition to Peter and Paul, McDowell has also conducted an investigation relating to the martyrdoms of both James,[168] the brother of Jesus, and Thomas. We find out through Paul that James also encountered the risen Jesus Christ (1 Cor. 15:7). Regarding James, McDowell (2014:222) rates the evidence that he was executed by stoning as having the "highest possible probability." He utilizes literary evidence gathered from the writings of Josephus[169] (Antiquities 20.197-203), Hegesippus[170] (*Hyponemata* Book 5 as recorded in Eusebius's *Ecclesiastical History*), and Clement of Alexandria[171]

---

[168] Regarding the martyrdom of James, Patrick Hartin (cited by McDowell, 2014:221) avers, "Taking the traditions of Josephus together with those of Hegesippus, Clement, and Eusebius himself, one concludes that there is a basic historical core that testifies to the fact that James did indeed die the death of a Christian martyr."

[169] From Josephus regarding the martyrdom of James: "Festus was now dead, and Albinus was but upon the road; so he assembled the Sanhedrin of Judges, and brought before them the brother of Jesus, who was called Christ whose name was James, and some others, [or some of his companions]; and when he had formed an accusation against them as breakers of the law, he delivered them to be stoned" (Josephus, s.a.:538).

[170] From Eusebius's Ecclesiastical History regarding James: The same writer [Hegesippus] in the seventh book of the same work says in addition this about him, "After the Resurrection the Lord gave the tradition of knowledge to James the Just and John and Peter, these gave it to the other Apostles and the other Apostles to the seventy, of whom Barnabas also was one. Now there were two Jameses, one James the Just, who was thrown down from the pinnacle of the temple and beaten to death with a fuller's club, and the other who was beheaded" (Eusebius, s.a. (c):59).

[171] From Clement of Alexandria regarding the martyrdom of James as reported by Eusebius: "When Paul appealed to Caesar and was sent over to Rome by Festus the Jews were disappointed of the hope in which they had laid their plot against him and turned against James, the brother of the Lord, to whom the throne of the bishopric in Jerusalem had been allotted by the Apostles. The crime which they committed was as follows. They brought him into the midst and demanded

(*Hypotyposes* Book 7 as recorded in Eusebius's *Ecclesiastical History* 2.1-4-5). McDowell also utilizes the *Second Apocalypse of James*[172] (60.15-63.32) as literary evidence as well. McDowell assesses the reliability of the evidence that James died as a Christian martyr as being "very likely true." McDowell also asserts that the probability that James was also thrown off of a high structure of the temple during the stoning process is "more probable than not."

4.7.2.4 Evidence for the martyrdom of Thomas

In offering evidence for the martyrdom of Thomas, McDowell (2014:259-261) begins by noting the boldness of Thomas as someone who is willing to die for Jesus Christ (John 11:8). Not only does McDowell observe this about Thomas, he also observes that Thomas is a prominent figure in the upper room on the occasion of the Last Supper asking Jesus to show the disciples how to get where Jesus is going upon his departure (John 14:5). McDowell is sure to mention Thomas's experience of the risen Jesus Christ in the upper room and his famous confession of faith (John 20:27-28).

---

a denial of the faith in Christ before all the people, but when he, contrary to the expectation of all of them, with a loud voice and with more courage than they had expected, confessed before all the people that our Lord and Saviour Jesus Christ is the son of God, they could no longer endure his testimony, since he was by all men believed to be most righteous because of the height which he had reached in a life of philosophy and religion, and killed him, using anarchy as an opportunity for power since at that moment Festus had died in Judaea, leaving the district without government or procurator" (Eusebius, s.a.(c), 75-76).

[172] The author of the second apocalypse writes about the martyrdom of James the Just, the brother of Jesus Christ: "On that day all the people and the crowd were disturbed, and they showed that they had not been persuaded. And he arose and went forth speaking in this manner. And he entered (again) on that same day and spoke a few hours. And I was with the priests and revealed nothing of the relationship, since all of them were saying with one voice, 'Come, let us stone the Just One.' And they arose, saying, 'Yes, let us kill this man, that he may be taken from our midst. For he will be of no use to us.' And they were there and found him standing beside the columns of the temple beside the mighty corner stone. And they decided to throw him down from the height, and they cast him down...they seized him and struck him as they dragged him upon the ground. They stretched him out and placed a stone on his abdomen. They all placed their feet on him, saying 'You have erred!' Again they raised him up, since he was alive, and made him dig a hole. They made him stand in it. After having covered him up to his abdomen, they stoned him in this manner" (The (second) apocalypse of James: s.a.).

Objection Three: The Disciples Hallucinated the Risen Jesus Christ 301

Regarding the background information on the ministry of Thomas, the Eastern Church has a consistent tradition that Thomas evangelized the country of India. McDowell also utilizes Alphonse Migana (cited by McDowell, 2014:263) who shares this same sentiment showing that Thomas has been consistently listed in this role even though some authors have posited that along with India, Thomas had also ministered in Parthia and in Persia as well. In assessing the literary evidence, McDowell asserts that the evidence is not very clear as some scholars back this Indian perspective whereas other scholars do not. He also shares the sentiment of Frykenburg (cited by McDowell, 2014:264-65) as to the importance of the oral tradition in the Indian culture and how from one generation to the next one, accounts of the family history travelled through history by means of oral tradition, storytelling songs, and also visual media such as inscriptions and manuscripts.

Regarding this oral tradition, McDowell (2014:265) offers that the "Thomas Christians" of today still claim that the apostle Thomas founded them. In one instance, oral tradition by way of a poem, the *Thomma Parvam*, is the instrument that carries this tradition. This poem travelled down through history and then was finally written down in the seventeenth century. McDowell further offers that there are still some "Thomas Christians" today who trace their family involvement in this early Christian church as far back as 80 generations. Although McDowell believes that the tradition of Thomas is rife with legend and mythology, he suggests that this data should not be wholly dismissed and that truth can be extracted from the data.

In supporting that Thomas ministered in India, McDowell (2014:268-69) offers the following sources: 1) *Acts of Thomas*[173] ("At that time we apostles were in Jerusalem…by lot India fell to Jude Thomas also called Didymus") 2) *Teachings of the Apostles* ("India, and all the countries belong-

---

[173] "When the apostle had said these things, Misdaeus considered how he should put him to death; for he was afraid because of the much people that were subject unto him, for many also of the nobles and of them that were in authority believed on him. He took him therefore and went forth out of the city; and armed soldiers also went with him. And the people supposed that the king desired to learn somewhat of him, and they stood still and gave heed. And when they had walked one mile, he delivered him unto four soldiers and an officer, and commanded them to take him into the mountain and there pierce him with spears and put an end to him…And when he had thus prayed he said unto the soldiers: Come hither and accomplish the commandments of him that sent you. And the four came and pierced him with their spears, and he fell down and died" (The acts of Thomas: s.a.).

ing to it and round about it, even to the farthest sea, received the apostles' ordination to the priesthood from Judas Thomas, who was guide and ruler in the church which he had built there") 3) *Hippolytus on the* Twelve (And Thomas preached to the Parthians, Medes, Persians, Hyrcanians, Bactrians, and Magians, and was thrust through in the four members of his body with a pine spear at Calamene, the City of India, and was buried there"), 4) Origen's *Commentary on Genesis, vol.* 3 ("Thomas, according to tradition, was allotted Parthia...") 5) *The Clementine Recognitions* 9.29 ("In short, among the Parthians-is Thomas, who is preaching the Gospel amongst them") 6) *Oration* (33.11) by St. Gregory of Nazianzen (..."Thomas with India" p. 390).[174]

In addition to these references from literary sources, McDowell (2014:281) again offers the tradition of the "St. Thomas Christians" whose oral tradition has Thomas arriving in India around 52 A.D., after ministering in different regions of that area, he is reported to have been martyred for his faith at Coromandel near the "Little Mount." He was buried within a shrine that he had built in the town of Mylapore. The St. Thomas Christian Encyclopedia (cited by McDowell, 2014:281) reports that established tradition has it that many early Indian Christians made pilgrimages to the tomb of Thomas from Malabar, the Near East, and China. Moreover, McDowell offers (2014:284) that a contingent of Portuguese landed in Malabar, India circa 1500 A.D. and found that there was an established Indian Christian church who asserted that Thomas was the founder of their church. Furthermore, the St. Thomas Christians are convinced that they are descended from the ministry of Thomas. McDowell (2014:284) also notes that the tradition of the St. Thomas Christians is independent of the Acts of Thomas thus strengthening the claim that Thomas ministered in India. In conclusion, McDowell assesses the probability of Thomas travelling to India and that he experienced martyrdom as "more probable than not."

4.7.3 Evidence against Carrier's hallucinating disciples: The conversions of James and Saul

In examining the explanatory power of the "Hallucination Hypothesis," William Lane Craig (2008:379) states that the "Hallucination Hypothesis" is again found wanting for the reason that it does not explain why those opposed to the faith became Christians after they experienced the risen Jesus Christ. He offers that James, the younger brother of Jesus, did not

---

[174] cf. McDowell (2014:268-69) for the references for the six sources.

believe that Jesus was the Messiah at one point (Mk. 3:21, 31-35; 6:3. Jn. 7:1-10). However, Craig offers James was a believer in Jesus Christ later as evidenced by Acts 1:14. In this passage, the brothers of Jesus are praying in the upper room along with Mary the mother of Jesus after the Ascension. Craig also notes that James eventually became one of the leaders of the early Christian church in Jerusalem. Moreover, Craig points out that an extra-biblical historian (Josephus) mentions that James, the brother of Jesus, is eventually martyred for his belief that Jesus is the Messiah.

In regard to the unlikely conversion of Paul to the Christian faith, Habermas and Licona (2004:107-109) offer that it does not appear that he was grieving the death of Jesus nor did he have the disposition of others who hallucinate (some sort of trauma). Before the appearance of Jesus to Paul, it is known that Paul was traveling to Damascus in order to arrest Christians. Therefore, he was zealous to persecute these Christians and thought that he was doing God's will. Thus, he was not feeling guilty for the work that he was preparing to do in Damascus. Moreover, Habermas and Licona also offer that the circumstances of Paul's conversion to Jesus Christ are similar to the circumstances present in the conversion of James. It was known that James and other family members of Jesus did not believe that he was the Messiah. Moreover, they believed that Jesus may have even been a little deluded. In similarity to Paul, James, a pious Jewish man, would not have been in the frame of mind to have a hallucination of Jesus after his crucifixion. Moreover, a hallucination would not be powerful enough to change his life.

Adding more data to the evidence coming from the conversion of James and Paul to the Christian faith, Gary Habermas (2001:4) avers that James and Paul would be poor candidates for hallucinating the risen Jesus Christ. This would be the case because, as noted above, James is observed in the New Testament to be an unbeliever during the ministry of Jesus (John 7:5; Mark 3:21). Furthermore, there is no indication that Paul and James had any expectancy to see the risen Jesus Christ. These facts coming from the New Testament are circumstantial evidence that these men did not hallucinate the risen Jesus Christ as skeptics and enemies of the faith would not have a predisposition to hallucinate Him.

Regarding the conversions of James and Paul, Habermas (2015:57) questions why anyone would think their brother was God (especially James who was known to be a skeptic regarding Jesus). Furthermore, Habermas explains that Paul would have no expectancy to see Jesus Christ. Explaining why most scholars are of the opinion that the disciples believed Jesus Christ had arisen from the dead, Habermas (2006:79) makes an important observation. Not only did Paul have a post-resurrection encounter with Jesus Christ himself, but Paul also discussed his experience with Peter and James who told Paul they also had post-resurrection encounters with Jesus Christ as well (1 Cor. 15:3-8; Gal. 1:18-19). Paul's investigation into the post-resurrection experiences of the other apostles corroborates his own encounter with the risen Jesus Christ.

4.7.4 Evidence Against the hallucination hypothesis: The empty tomb in conjunction with the PRA of Jesus Christ

Ben Witherington (2000:137) observes that it was not just the PRA of Jesus Christ that persuaded the disciples that Jesus Christ had arisen from the dead. In addition to the PRA, Witherington asserts that the first Christians also stressed that the actual body of Jesus Christ had arisen. The only explanation for this early belief of the Christian church is not only that something happened to the body of Jesus, but also that Jesus Christ "must have been in personal and visible contact with his followers after Easter" (Witherington, 2000:137). If it was a just a missing body, then it would be reasonable for the followers of Jesus to assume that he had been translated into heaven in similar fashion as Elijah or Enoch. Moreover, the empty tomb alone would lend credence to the theory of grave robbing. Witherington (2000:136-37) concludes his thought by positing that an empty tomb alone would not have led to a belief that Jesus Christ arose from the dead and that "there must have been appearances of the risen Lord to various persons."

As Antony Flew, Gary Habermas, and John Ankerberg discuss the historicity of the resurrection, Ankerberg (cited by Habermas & Flew, 2005:66) mentions what he believes to be a serious problem. Ankerberg opines it would be a serious problem for early Christianity if claims were made that Jesus Christ had been seen alive after his death while Jesus body was still in the tomb. Also included in a chapter titled *Applying resurrection research and closing loopholes*, Gary Habermas (Habermas & Flew, 2005:90) submits that the tomb of Jesus should have been occupied with the body of Jesus if the disciples were hallucinating.

In concert with the perspectives of Habermas and Ankerberg, Christopher Bryan (2011:170) makes a related observation regarding the historicity of the PRA. Bryan questions the "visionary Jesus" theory when he asks a fundamental question:

> Why did the first Christians bring 'resurrection' into their proclamation at all (other as future hope)- unless they genuinely believed that something

had happened that could only be spoken of in this way? And if we concede that, then naturally we must ask just what might have happened that led them to such a conviction-and we are back where we started. These then, are reasons for doubting that the empty tomb and appearance narratives can adequately or properly be understood as parables or metaphors for a visionary experience or a birth of new insight.

In similarity to Bryan's observation, Gerald O'Collins (2009:93) posits, "The discovery of the empty tomb served as a secondary sign, which was ambiguous by itself but which taken with the appearances served to confirm the reality of the resurrection. The gospel stories of one or more women finding Jesus's tomb to be mysteriously open and empty contain a reliable core." O'Collins (cited by Prusak, 2000:78-80) also explains that the PRA of Jesus Christ could be referred to as Christophanies because it was the initiative of the risen Jesus Christ to reveal himself to the faithful. Prusak also mentions that O'Collins notes the importance of the empty tomb with the appearances as the corpse of Jesus Christ had been raised and transformed. This new body observed by the Easter witnesses was not a replacement for the old one. Rather, it was the same body restored.

Glenn Siniscalchi adds to the sentiment of the above scholars when he offers the perspective of William Lane Craig (cited by Siniscalchi, 2012:717). Craig avers that it is important to emphasize the following four facts that need to be reckoned with in regard to the resurrection of Jesus Christ: (1) the burial of Jesus; (2) The discovery of Jesus's empty tomb by a group of women followers; (3) the post-mortem appearances; (4) the disciples' belief in the resurrection despite their predisposition to the contrary.

In emphasizing early Christian worship as an apologetic argument for the veracity of the resurrection, Siniscalchi (2012:729) posits that the resurrection of Jesus Christ was the event that initiated the worship of Jesus Christ by the early church. But how did the disciples know that the resurrection of Jesus Christ took place? It took place because of the evidences of the empty tomb and the appearances of Jesus Christ to the disciples. Additionally, Siniscalchi notes that Christian baptism, an early initiatory rite, points to the bodily resurrection of Jesus Christ from the dead. One other observation by Siniscalchi to this end is that Sunday was the day the empty tomb was discovered and where Jesus was observed to be alive. Therefore, the day of worship shifted to Sunday in honor of the resurrection of Jesus Christ.

In addition to the aforementioned material, Siniscalchi also offers the perspective of Richard Swinburne (cited by Siniscalchi, 2014:371) regarding the evidence for the resurrection coming from both the empty tomb and the PRA. However, Swinburne first establishes *a priori* evidence that the God of the Bible would be the sort of person who is interested in humanity. Thus, seeing the plight of humanity, God would come to the aid of humanity by incarnating himself, enduring crucifixion and death, and raising himself from the dead in order to cure the fallen human condition. After offering this *a priori* evidence for the resurrection, Swinburne also offers the *a posteriori* evidence for the resurrection of Jesus Christ confirming its veracity (empty tomb, PRA, etc.). After providing this evidence, Swinburne concludes that the *a posteriori* evidence matches up better with the aforementioned *a priori* evidence than any other hypothesis.[175]

David Baggett (2009:125) refers to Flew's endorsement of hallucinations as not being the likely explanation for the PRA. He then offers reasons supporting his perspective. One such reason Baggett offers is that the hallucination theory does not properly deal with why the tomb was empty where Jesus body had been placed after his crucifixion. Also, Baggett is also curious as to the reason that the disciples believed there was a resurrection at all. Why did they not just explain the appearances as visions? Along with Baggett, William Proctor (1998:185) also questions the "hallucination hypothesis." Referring to the empty tomb, he reasons that "hallucinations don't make bodies disappear" and that if the hallucinations caused the disciples to stir up trouble because of their hallucinations, "the religious authorities would have moved quickly to pull out the body and end their disruptive behavior" (Proctor, 1998:185). In similarity to Baggett and Proctor, William Lane Craig (2008:397) avers that the explanatory scope of the "Hallucination Hypothesis" is too narrow.[176] This is due to a hallucination being unable to explain the empty tomb, the ap-

---

[175] The terms "*a priori*" and "*a posteriori*" are used primarily to denote the foundations upon which a proposition is known. A given proposition is knowable *a priori* if it can be known independent of any experience other than the experience of learning the language in which the proposition is expressed, whereas a proposition that is knowable *a posteriori* is known on the basis of experience. For example, the proposition that all bachelors are unmarried is *a priori*, and the proposition that it is raining outside now is *a posteriori* (Baehr, J.).

[176] Craig Blomberg (2000:102) offers his opinion regarding Craig's four points for the veridicality of the resurrection and rates Craig's fourth point as his strongest one. Blomberg asserts that the disciples would not have hallucinated about the risen Christ if they had no preconceived notion that he would actually do so from their Jewish perspectives.

pearances, and the disciples' belief that Jesus had been raised from the dead.[177]

Regarding the empty tomb in relation to the PRA, N.T. Wright (2003:686-870) avers that the empty tomb and the PRA are "historically secure." Concerning the early Christian belief of the resurrection, Wright concludes that neither the appearances nor the empty tomb could in themselves generate belief in the resurrected Jesus Christ. If Jesus was observed by certain persons after his death, it would have been surmised that these people claiming these sightings of Jesus were either hallucinating or having visions. Moreover, if the empty tomb stood by itself, people would be sad and would be curious about what happened to the body. However, when you combine both of these evidences, together there is powerful evidence for the belief in the resurrected Jesus Christ. Wright also explains that the empty tomb is the necessary condition for the PRA.

Wright (2003:689) also points out that the empty tomb of Jesus Christ included the grave clothes. In similarity to the empty tomb, these garments also provide additional evidence that convinced the beloved disciple to believe in the resurrected Jesus Christ. No one would have taken the body of Jesus Christ without the wrappings and the grave clothes. If someone removed the body, they would not have removed the grave clothes before taking the body. The point Wright makes here is that it took more for John than just the empty tomb alone to elicit his belief in the risen Jesus Christ.

Regarding the theory of the resurrection of Jesus Christ being a vision, N.T. Wright offers (2003:691) that Mary also experienced the risen Jesus Christ. Thus, when she encounters Jesus after His resurrection, it is not as if she merely had a vision. It would not be like Odysseus who had a vision of a bodiless spirit that he could not cling to. Rather, Mary not only observed the empty tomb, but she also saw and clung to the risen Jesus Christ. Therefore, she could be assured that she was not observing an apparition like others may have in ancient times. Wright states that this is also the case in Luke, John, and Acts where Jesus ate fish with his disciples.

---

[177] Regarding the appearances in combination with the empty tomb, Herbert Casteel (1990:161) offers, "It is clear that Jesus caused the disciples to believe in His bodily resurrection, and if it was only His spirit they saw, then Jesus was deliberately deceiving them. As stated before, in view of his perfect life and teaching, few are willing to believe that Jesus was dishonest. In addition, this theory fails to explain the empty tomb."

As Wright (2003:695-96) builds his argument for the symbiotic relationship of the empty tomb and the PRA of Jesus Christ, he further posits that the empty tomb would be a necessary condition for the early Christian belief that Jesus Christ had arisen from the dead. However as noted before, the empty tomb would still not be able to stand by itself without the resurrection appearances or some other corroborating evidence. Regarding the PRA, Wright observes that they would be more like a necessary supplement to the empty tomb that turns it from an insufficient condition in itself to a sufficient cause of resurrection belief. Lastly on this topic, Wright offers that the empty tomb and the PRA of Jesus Christ together are both a necessary and a sufficient set of circumstances that led to the rise of early Christian belief.[178]

4.8 Evidentiary Analysis: Carrier's Contention in Light of Accepted Principles of Evidence

4.8.1 Evidentiary Analysis: Disciples Were Hallucinating: In General

After evaluating Carrier's claims by accepted principles of evidence (the FRE and FPJI), his contentions are deficient in several important areas. In order for Carrier's claim of hallucinating disciples to meet the standards of accepted principles of evidence, he would need to provide historical witnesses who: 1) observed the disciples in states of consciousness that are in accord with one of the aforementioned known varieties of hallucinations (as noted in the exposition of hallucinations from scholarly literature) 2) observed the disciples to be hallucinating Jesus Christ when he was not physically present. However, Carrier has not provided any historical sources who report either condition. In the following subsections,

---

[178] Regarding Wright's perspective on the explanatory power of the combination of the empty tomb with the PRA of Jesus Christ, William Craig (2006:142) writes, "So the meat of Wright's argument comes with step three, which implies that the hypothesis or the facticity of the empty tomb and postmortem appearances had the explanatory power to account for the origin of belief in Jesus' resurrection. I think that Wright's claim that the discovery of the empty tomb and the postmortem appearances are jointly sufficient to explain the rise of resurrection belief is relatively uncontroversial, given that we are talking about physical appearances, not mere visions. If Jesus' tomb were found empty and he appeared physically alive after his death, then, given the context of his messianic claims, it seems very probable that the disciples would come to believe that God had raised Jesus from the dead."

Objection Three: The Disciples Hallucinated the Risen Jesus Christ   309

a brief analysis will be conducted to determine whether any of Carrier's "hallucinating disciples" contentions have any evidence coming from the aforementioned accepted principles of evidence. Additionally, other hallucination types not mentioned by Carrier will undergo a similar evidentiary examination to determine if they could have been reasonable explanations of what the disciples *et al.* experienced when they encountered the risen Jesus Christ.

4.8.2 Evidentiary analysis: PRA as hypnagogic/hypnopompic hallucinations

Carrier noted that hypnagogic and/or hypnopompic hallucinations could have been what the disciples were experiencing when they encountered the risen Jesus Christ (4.2.1). However, upon cross-examining Carrier's claim and comparing Carrier's contention with the exposition on hypnagogic hallucinations, a major problem is readily observed. Carrier's descriptions of this sort of imagery do not appear to match either the New Testament descriptions of what occurred nor do the descriptions of hypnagogic/hypnapompic hallucinations from the scholarly literature review appear to match the New Testament resurrection accounts.

Carrier mentioned the exhaustion of the disciples plus the fact that some of these appearances of the risen Jesus most likely occurred around either dawn or near the mid-afternoon break. However, the information coming from the New Testament accounts of the PRA do not indicate that either the women were just falling asleep (hypnagogia) nor were they just arising from sleep (hypnopompia). Furthermore, upon examining the exposition of hypnagogia/hypnopompia, the disciples could not have been experiencing hypnagogic or hypnopompic hallucinations.

Regarding hypnagogic hallucinations, he does not support his claim with relevant evidence based upon facts established by proof (*FRE* 401 and *FRE* 104(b)) because this type of hallucination is only fleeting in nature, and is composed mainly of colors, shapes, patterns, words, and faces. In hypnagogia, the images are merely flashes of images or sounds that do not make sense to the one experiencing the hallucinations. So, the disciples having hypnagogic hallucinations of the risen Jesus do not fit the data for several reasons.

First as mentioned above, hypnagogic hallucinations have faces that are unknown to the one hallucinating. Moreover, the faces that are observed are often fanciful in nature and are oftentimes frightening. Secondly, there is no meaning attached to the hallucination as the visual or auditory stimuli experienced are random in nature to the one experiencing the hallucination. An additional problem observed for not only hypnagogic imagery but also for other types of hallucinations (except for the schizophrenic variety) is that the sufferer knows that the hallucination is not veridical (thus a pseudo-hallucination). If the disciples had experienced the risen Jesus Christ because of their hypnagogic state, then the disciples would have known that they were hallucinating at some point whether during or after the hallucinatory experience. Another problem with this strain of Carrier's hypothesis is that it is hard to believe that the disciples were all having hypnagogic hallucinations at the same time when the risen Jesus Christ visited them (4.3.1).

Adding to the information that a hypnagogic hallucination is known to be a pseudohallucination, Mavromitis described that hypnagogic imagery does not blend with the normal background of our dreams or our visual field. Further bolstering the non-realistic aspect of hypnagogic imagery from McKellar is that most of the hallucinations are auditory, surprising, random, and spontaneous. Furthermore, the exposition on hypnagogic imagery from Leaning revealed that the images produced during the hypnagogic state are formless light clouds floating between the eye and the eyelid, faces (some pleasant and some scary), designs and objects, landscapes and scenes.

Continuing on the non-realistic aspect of this type of hallucination, Sacks mentioned in the exposition on hypnagogic imagery that the hallucinations are not "felt as real and are not projected into external space." Moreover, the types of faces listed by Sacks to be visualized are faces that come out of a misty background and then disappear, ugly faces that are most often unrecognizable, and faces visualized that are meaningless to the hallucinator. Sacks listed earlier that the hallucinations his patients reported were random with no real pattern, had an infinite variety of constantly alternating patterns and forms, were fleeting in nature, and were more like flashes than dreams. For Sacks, the theme of meaninglessness was the most prominent theme observed in hypnagogic hallucinations.

Regarding hypnopompic imagery, Sacks observed that the emotion of terror often accompanied these hallucinations, that they are brief, and that in similarity to hypnagogic imagery, hypnopompic hallucinators know that the experience is a hallucination. In addition to McKellar, Hobson identified this sort of hallucination as being an extension of the dream state into the waking state and offered sleepwalking as an example of this sort of hallucination. Moreover, Sacks explained in the exposition that these sorts of hallucinations are brief and that those having them know they are not real (4.3.1).

After this analysis, it is observed that Carrier does not offer any facts that are based on proof (FRE 104(b)) because his examples are not in accord again with the scholarly literature on the topic. Relatedly, Carrier offers no direct/indirect evidence (FPJI 1.06) on this topic except vague allusions from the New Testament that are not accurate portrayals of the New Testament accounts. Moreover, Carrier does not offer a historical witness outside of the New Testament accounts that observed the disciples to be hallucinating (FRE 602) nor does he offer any corroborative evidence to bolster his views (FPJI 1.07(5)). Carrier's contention would be in accord with these accepted principles of evidence if his descriptions comported with the appropriate New Testament accounts/scholarly literature or if he offered the account of an independent witness or witnesses that the disciples were hallucinating upon going to sleep/waking.

4.8.3 Evidentiary analysis: PRA as schizophrenic hallucinations/"happy schizotypal"

In discussing schizophrenic hallucinations as a possible explanation from accepted principles of evidence, as was the case with the aforementioned hypnagogic and hypnopompic hallucinations, it is incumbent upon Carrier to match up the experiences of the disciples from the New Testament resurrection accounts with the scholarly descriptions of schizophrenic hallucinations in order for his evidence to be in accord with FRE 104(b). In looking back at the aforementioned exposition of scholarly literature on this topic, Frith's description of schizophrenic hallucination offers that sufferers of schizophrenia would most likely report hearing voices that would be discussing their actions or talking to them, repeating their thoughts, or that aliens or famous people were communicating with them. It was also brought out that hallucinations of this variety are mostly auditory in nature (only 20% are not auditory in nature). Additionally, another important point that was brought up during the scholarly literature review is that "multi-modal" hallucinations (those that have more that one type of hallucination manifesting at the same time) in schizophrenics would not be experienced as we might normally experience somebody talking to us. In most cases regarding this sort of hallucinatory manifestation, the audio and visual hallucinations experienced by the schizophrenia patient are often experienced at different times or even different days. Another important quality of multi-modal hallucinations to point out is that a patient may be visually hallucinating one thing and experiencing a totally unrelated audio hallucination.

So, for one or more patients to have both an audio hallucination with a visual hallucination would be rare. Thus, the disciples, when they encountered the risen Jesus who was speaking to them while being observed visually, would not be experiencing schizophrenic hallucinations not to mention experiencing them on numerous occasions. Moreover, most schizophrenic hallucinations are auditory in nature (80%). It is not the case with any of the PRA of Jesus that they were only auditory manifestations. Rather they were multimodal experiences consisting of visual, auditory, and tactile experiences to include extended discussions with various persons (4.3.2).

Even after a brief analysis of schizophrenia and its attendant hallucinations, the symptoms do not match with the behavior of the disciples who experienced the risen Jesus Christ as listed in the New Testament resurrection narratives. In examining the list of symptoms for schizophrenia, did the disciples exhibit deluded behavior before the crucifixion of Jesus or when they first experienced the risen Jesus Christ? In examining the evidence from the resurrection narratives, one would have to answer the question negatively. The disciples did not have deluded or grandiose ideas of themselves after the crucifixion of Jesus. Rather, they were hiding and uncertain of their futures as their leader and savior had died as stated in the Gospel accounts (John 20:19).

Furthermore, there is no evidence from the New Testament that the disciples had unusual conversations with themselves in several voices or that they had incoherent speech. Moreover, there are no accounts in the New Testament where the disciples were exhibiting a total lack of feeling or volition. What about the reasonableness that a band of schizophrenic sufferers were gathered by Jesus to be His disciples? If the percentage of schizophrenia sufferers remains constant at one percent of the population, would it be reasonable to believe that Jesus had the ability to "cherry pick" twelve schizophrenic sufferers out of the general population? Additionally, there is no reason to believe the disciples were having schizophrenic related hallucinations for many of the reasons enumerated for other types of hallucinations. Moreover, in paranoid schizophrenia, the sufferer becomes convinced that someone is out to get them and is divorced from reality as the disease manifests in the patient. Sufferers experience voices and images that are only occurring inside their minds even though they believe that what they are experiencing is occurring in the real, external world.

During the cross-examination of Carrier by scholarly literature, Bergeron and Habermas brought out that the disciples could not have been experiencing schizophrenic hallucinations because schizophrenic patients could not begin a worldwide movement. Furthermore, schizophrenic patients would need some sort of care in maintaining themselves to include medical, psychosocial, environmental, and pharmacological support. Moreover, in that era, others would have viewed them as either lunatics or as those who were demon possessed. Carrier's evidence is, ostensibly, in accord with FRE 401 as he draws from the New Testament resurrection narratives and from scholarly literature. However, because of the lack of agreement between Carrier's schizophrenic hallucinations theory with the New Testament resurrection accounts and the scholarly literature, his evidence is not in accord with FRE 104(b) as he misconstrues the New Testament resurrection narratives and scholarly literature. Moreover, there are no historical witnesses that Carrier submits from sources external to the Bible that demonstrate the disciples were schizophrenic patients, *contra* FRE 602, FPJI 1.07(5) and FPJI 1.06.

In regard to the disciples being inclined to hallucinate because they have the "happy schizotypal" personality type, there is an important distinction to note between the "happy schizotypal" person and the schizophrenic patient. As stated earlier in this chapter (4.8.3), one of the characteristics of this personality type is they have pseudo-hallucinations as opposed to hallucinations that are deemed to be authentic experiences by the one having them (delusions). Therefore, the happy schizotypal person understands that his hallucinations are not real occurrences.

Relating this to the present discussion, if the disciples were deluded about an experienced hallucination and believed that the hallucination was real, then this would mean that they would go from being a "happy" or "benign" schizotypal subject who has non-psychopathic schizophrenic tendencies to a "full blown" schizophrenic sufferer because a deluded person who has hallucinations exhibits two of the four traits (delusions and hallucinations) required of schizophrenia. By virtue of being deluded and having hallucinations, the disciples would qualify as having the disorder. If the disciples knew their experiences were non-veridical, then they would not aver that they experienced the risen Jesus Christ because they would know better. Therefore, the "happy schizotypal" personality type theory as propounded by Carrier would not be in accord with the scholarly material nor would it be aligned with the New Testament resurrection accounts. By virtue of this non-conformity, Carrier's theory would not be affirmed by accepted principles of evidence, specifically *FRE*

104(b) as his facts do not match up with the New Testament resurrection accounts or the scholarly literature.[179]

4.8.4 Evidentiary analysis: PRA as bereavement hallucinations

In the cross-examination of Carrier's proposition that the disciples were having bereavement hallucinations when experiencing the risen Jesus Christ, Gerald O'Collins offered that PBHEs and also NDEs occur to individuals only and not to groups of people. Because of the group experiences of the disciples with the risen Jesus Christ, Carrier's theory would not fit these group encounters. In addition to the observation of O'Collins, J.D.G. Dunn submitted that there was no foundation for the disciples to aver that a single individual would arise from the dead before the general resurrection of the dead at the end of time. If the disciples did not experience Jesus in the flesh, then why didn't the disciples just say that this was the case? If he was experienced in merely some sort of visual perception, why didn't they just use verbiage that would have communicated this sort of manifestation?

Another disparity in Carrier's theory is brought out by Habermas who contended that mostly older persons who are lonely have these perceptions and also observes that those who experience the bereavement hallucinations do not have transformations (4.4.3). If this is the case, then Carrier's theory does not match the circumstances of the PRA of Jesus Christ where there were people from a diverse range of ages represented and who were transformed from timid individuals to bold proclaimers of the resurrected Jesus Christ. Another inconsistency that is observed by Glenn Siniscalchi is that in post-mortem appearance experiences, these mostly occur indoors whereas the New Testament accounts of the PRA of Jesus Christ are observed to occur both inside and outside (4.4.3).

---

[179] One important point to note regarding the general topic of hallucinating disciples as it relates to schizophrenic hallucinations is that all of the hallucinations that have been surveyed heretofore mostly consist of hallucinations where the one experiencing them knows they are not real while they are having the hallucination. If a person having a hallucination does think that the hallucination is real when he is having it and persists in this belief, then this person is most likely a schizophrenia sufferer. Thus, if the disciples believed that they had a veridical encounter with the risen Jesus Christ when it was in fact a hallucination, then they were most likely schizophrenia sufferers. But is this a reasonable conclusion to make based on the existing evidence as just discussed in this section?

Objection Three: The Disciples Hallucinated the Risen Jesus Christ 315

Concerning the duration of bereavement experiences coming from the exposition of scholarly literature, the research of Epstein *et al.* reported that PBHEs often occur over many years (4.3.3) which stands in contrast to the limited duration of the PRA of Jesus Christ to the disciples that occurred a little over a month when it ended abruptly. If the experiences of the disciples were hallucinations, then why did they end abruptly for all of the witnesses? Surely, there would have been at least one or more of the disciples who would have continued having these experiences if they were in fact hallucinations. In addition to this information, the scholarly literature review (4.3.3) brought out that the most common forms of hallucinatory phenomenon are VH (48%), auditory hallucinations (30%), touching the deceased (13%), and talking (11%) with the deceased as well.

It should be noted that all of the PRA of Jesus Christ included a combination of all of these sorts of bereavement hallucinations at once to include the least common types of touching and talking to Jesus Christ on almost every occasion.[180] Therefore, it strains credulity to assert that the PRA of Jesus Christ were hallucinations because of all of the diverse hallucinatory events that would be occurring at one time to multiple hallucinators. As observed above in the scholarly literature review, the odds of various hallucinatory activities occurring all at once are infinitesimally small.

In addition to this information, Sacks gives examples of his patients who had mostly very brief encounters with their loved ones to include a smiling face of a loved one suspended in midair, a loved one running past the front of the house in his favorite running shorts, hearing the voice of a loved one (4.3.3). It is observed that Carrier's claims do not cohere with the New Testament resurrection accounts nor are his claims in line with the scholarly literature on the topic of bereavement hallucinations.[181] Be-

---

[180] Paul's encounter with the risen Jesus Christ would be an exception to this statement, as he had no physical contact with Jesus Christ. However, Paul did report observable evidence of the encounter (blindness, hearing a voice, seeing a light, and scales, perhaps scabs formed on eyes).

[181] The death of Jesus could offer a stimulus for a bereavement hallucination the disciples had just lost someone of great importance to them. He had brought them together as a group, had developed a close bond with them, had given them a unified purpose as a group, had been their teacher, and had been their God in bodily form. So, the importance of Jesus to the disciples cannot be minimized. However in the examples offered by Sacks, there is no bereaved person who actually believed that the loved one they had encountered had actually arisen from the dead. Rather, those who experienced their loved one did so in

cause of this divergence between his claims and the aforementioned scholarly literature on bereavement hallucinations, the facts that he offers are not in accord with FRE 104(b) as he does not offer proof for the facts that he offers. Moreover, he does not offer any historical eyewitnesses to substantiate his claims (*FRE* 602, FPJI 1.07(5)-corroborative evidence, and FPJI 1.06-direct evidence).

4.8.5 Evidentiary analysis: PRA as seizure related hallucinations

The exposition of scholarly material regarding seizure related hallucinations showed a divergence between Carrier's claim that Saul's Damascus Road experience was most likely a result of a seizure related hallucination. Elliott *et al.* shared the research of Gloor who described the experiential past hallucinatory phenomenon of seizure sufferers. Those who experience this type of seizure hallucination are said to be aware of the illusory or incongruous nature of the event, notice that the event does not have an element of forward moving time, and that any auditory hallucinations lack semantic content (fn. 119).

In addition to these observations, Sacks noted in the exposition that there are epileptic hallucinations that are of various shapes, colors, and patterns. Sacks describes the more complex seizure hallucinations as including shapes and familiar persons. Sacks also gave an example of inkblot spots that turned into the mother of the patient. However, Sacks noted that the persons experiencing these hallucinations knew that the experience was not a real life event. Sacks also shares the experience of one of his epileptic patients who experienced an ecstatic seizure where the experience was like a happy dream (4.3.3).

Hansen and Brodtkorb shared in the exposition of scholarly literature about four patients who had ecstatic, religious seizures. They noted that the patients who experienced these seizures had no particular religious interests and were not regular church attendees. Even though they had these religious hallucinations, Hansen and Brodtkorb did not report a

---

brief fashion realizing that their loved one was not living again on the earth. Moreover, as in the other forms of hallucinations previously studied, there is no way to account for how the hallucinations were observed at the same time by all of the disciples. Also, the five hundred persons who experienced Jesus at the same time before he ascended would be an insurmountable problem for Carrier's bereavement hypothesis. Is it reasonable to believe that five hundred people were experiencing "bereavement hallucinations" caused by the death of Jesus at the same time?

change in their religious convictions. One other epilepsy patient who was an agnostic reported similar ecstatic seizures throughout a long timespan. In addition to the ecstatic component, these seizures were also mixed with fear and anxiety. Hansen and Brodtkorb did not report that this patient had a change in her religious perspective after these seizure related hallucinations.

One point that is immediately relevant to this argument is that with the onset of the seizure, the aforementioned scholarly reference on ecstatic seizures describes that they are characterized by ecstasy or a sensation of well being or transcendent joy. Certainly this was not the case in the experience of Paul with the blinding lights, and with Jesus, his archrival, accusing him of persecuting Christians (Acts 9). This certainly was not an experience of religious wellbeing or joy for Paul. Rather, Paul must have been terrified after the experience. As mentioned above, there are religious, ecstatic seizure hallucinations that have a mixture of pleasure as well as fear and anxiety. However, there was no aspect of pleasure reported by Paul. Other facts from the encounter also reveal that Paul not only experienced blindness, but also that he had a "scale like" substance fall off his eyes after several days (Acts 9:18). Moreover, those with him did hear a voice but did not see "anyone" (Acts 9:7) but also reported seeing a light (22:9). If Paul was hallucinating, how was it that his travel companions were able to audibly hear "the voice" speaking to Paul and see a light?

Due to the various manifestations related to seizure related hallucinations not matching up with the claim of Carrier and because the seizure patient does understand that seizure related hallucinations are not "real life events," Carrier's facts are not supported by the evidence coming from the scripture describing the PRA of Jesus Christ and the exposition of scholarly material on seizure related hallucinations. Because of the lack of proof for the facts that Carrier utilizes, his facts do not meet the standard set forth in FRE 104(b) as his facts are not supported by proof based on facts. Neither does Carrier utilize any historical witnesses outside of the New Testament resurrection accounts to buttress his claims in the spirit of FRE 602, FPJI 1.06 (direct evidence), and FPJI 1.07(5) (corroborative evidence).

4.8.6 Evidentiary analysis: PRA as hallucinations caused by fatigue/deprivation

In relation to fatigue being a contributing factor to having a hallucination, Asaad offered in the scholarly literature review that those who are fatigued or deprived of sustenance or visual stimulus often hallucinate. However, Asaad refers to these mostly as pseudo-hallucinations (hallucinations that are known by the hallucinator not to be a real life event). In addition to Asaad, Sacks also discussed fatigue related hallucinations in the exposition of scholarly literature and offered a real life example of a triathlete who thought that members of his family were standing along the roadside when he ran past a certain location. After realizing that his family members were not present where he thought they were, he realized that he had a hallucination of them. In the cross-examination from scholarly literature, Gary Habermas offered an example of navy seals hallucinating during their intense training where they are deprived of sleep for many days and are also fatigued by constant physical activity as well. After the hallucinator was able to get some sleep, he realized that what he experienced was a hallucination. In both of these circumstances, the hallucinator understood that he was hallucinating.

Because these sorts of hallucinations are known not to be real, then the data offered by Carrier does not match either the New Testament resurrection narratives nor does it match the exposition of scholarly material. Therefore, Carrier's facts are not supported by proof and are not aligned with *FRE* 104(b). Additionally, there is no eyewitness testimony coming from any historical witness offered by Carrier who wrote that the disciples were fatigued, deprived of sustenance, or lacked the appropriate visual stimulation that would generate a hallucination contra *FRE* 602 and FPJI 1.06 (direct evidence).

4.8.7 Evidentiary analysis: PRA as guilt hallucinations

Carrier asserted that a possible reason for the PRA of Jesus Christ was that the disciples felt guilt, along with other factors, which triggered hallucinations. He also mentioned that one of the factors that led Paul to hallucinate the risen Jesus Christ was guilt. However, in the cross-examination of Carrier's claim by scholarly literature, Habermas and Licona brought out that Paul was not grieving the death of Jesus nor did he have a pre-existing condition that would cause him to hallucinate. Moreover, Paul was also travelling to Damascus to continue the persecution of Christians. Therefore, the circumstances of his life do not reveal that he was struggling with guilt.

Furthermore, when readers are introduced to Paul in Acts 7, he is at the scene of the martyrdom of Stephen tacitly approving of Stephen's stoning by the Jews (v. 58). Additionally, Paul testifies about how he "savagely persecuted the church of God...trying to destroy it (Gal. 1:13)" but then Jesus called him to preach among the Gentiles (vv. 15-16). Along with Paul's testimony in Galatians, his defense before Agrippa also outlines his predisposition to persecute Christians and his ensuing experience with the risen Jesus Christ.[182] Thus, by his own admission Paul did not have feelings of guilt that pre-existed before his encounter with Jesus Christ.

Also brought out in the cross-examination of Carrier's claim is that the women witnesses to the PRA of Jesus Christ did not have feelings of guilt (4.4.5). This supposed guilt of the women witnesses is not mentioned in any of the New Testament resurrection narratives. In addition to this information, the scholarly literature review in this project did not indicate that guilt in and of itself is a cause for hallucinations. Due to the non-conformity of Carrier's claim with the New Testament resurrection narratives as well as the scholarly literature, his facts are not in accord with FRE 104(b) as he does not correctly describe the conditions of Saul or the women witnesses prior to their experiences with the risen Jesus Christ. Additionally, Carrier does not properly describe the relationship between guilt and hallucinations.

4.8.8 Evidentiary analysis: PRA from other forms of hallucinations

Upon analyzing other forms of hallucinations not mentioned by Carrier, it was also noted that these forms of hallucinatory phenomena could not account for the PRA of Jesus Christ as detailed in the New Testament. The scholarly literature describing CBS hallucinations, drug induced hallucinations, and PTSD related hallucinations gave no indication that these sorts of hallucinations could be what the disciples experienced. An important reason for this is due to the fact that all those who experience the above listed hallucinations know that their hallucinations are not real life events either during the event or after it.

---

[182] In Acts 26, before King Agrippa, Paul gives his defense about his belief in Jesus Christ. He outlines how he locked up Christians, cast death sentence votes against them, and constantly tried to get them to blaspheme God. In verse 11, he states that he was "furiously enraged" against them as well. He also details his experience on the road to Damascus where he was going there to continue the persecution of Christians in Damascus until he experienced the risen Jesus Christ who not only appeared to him but also spoke to him (vv. 12-18). From his own testimony, it is evident that Paul felt no guilt for his activities against the Christians.

Regarding CBS hallucinations (4.3.5), these hallucinations accompany visual impairment in the patient, mostly those who are elderly. Therefore, it would not be reasonable to posit that the disciples were all visually impaired patients. In relation to hallucinogenic drug hallucinations (4.3.6), there is no evidence that has been put forward that the disciples ingested these sorts of drugs. In addition to this, there is a progression of hallucinatory experience where the hallucinogenic drug hallucinations go from forms and objects to faces and persons, etc. Thus, the disciples, if they had ingested drugs, would have seen forms and patterns before they encountered the resurrected Jesus Christ. Furthermore, their "trips" would all be individual and subjective in nature. In regard to PTSD related hallucinations (4.3.7), a reminder of the original traumatic event usually triggers these hallucinations and the theme of the hallucination is normally related to the original traumatic event as well. Thus, if any of the disciples experienced PTSD because they observed the flogging and/or crucifixion of Jesus Christ, then they would re-experience the event in some way in the hallucination.

4.8.9 Evidentiary analysis: PRA were bodily in nature

Craig Keener averred that the consistent witness of the New Testament is that Jesus Christ rose bodily from the dead and points out that the worship of Jesus is proof that they knew his identity and that it was the same person they knew to be Jesus Christ during the PRA. The Post-resurrection Jesus Christ is God "Incarnate (1 Cor. 15:5,7; Matt. 28:9)." Joseph Benson also mentioned that the worship of Jesus (Matt. 28:9) reveals that he was in bodily form as the women fell prostrate and clung to his feet. John Gill also observed that the women embraced his feet and also recognized his voice and his mannerisms. This physical handling insured that Jesus was no mere phantom (4.7.1).

Additional confirmation of the physical nature of the PRA of Jesus Christ in Luke came from Norman Griffith who pointed out that in Luke 24, the resurrected body of Jesus Christ that the disciples observed still bore the marks of the crucifixion and that he had flesh and bones (vv. 39-40) could be touched (v. 39), and could eat food (v. 43). Griffith further wrote that Jesus Christ not only was observed to be eating in Luke but also on the shore of a lake in Galilee. Darrell Bock also discussed the convincing nature of the Emmaus Road experience of the risen Jesus Christ to the men who travelled with and watched Jesus break bread. Bock stated that these two travellers were in despair with the death of Jesus and after their encounter, were convinced that He was alive. Moreover, Jesus confirms verbally that he is no mere ghost (v. 39) (4.7.1).

Elmer Towns discussed the testimony of the skeptic, Thomas, that is included in John chapter 20. Thomas is persuaded that Jesus Christ is physically alive after encountering him (John 20:26-29). Speaking of the PRA of Jesus Christ on the beach (John 21), Towns shared the reason that Jesus Christ revealed himself to the disciples was in order for them to fully comprehend the reality of the resurrection. After this encounter with the risen Jesus Christ, there was no doubt that Jesus Christ had arisen from the dead and was present with them in the flesh. Regarding the Gospel of John as it relates to the bodily resurrection of Jesus Christ from the dead, Gary Burge explained that John's resurrection accounts are rife with the certainty that Jesus Christ bodily arose from the dead and militate against any understanding to the contrary. Burge also offers corroboration coming from John's first epistle (1 John 1:1-4) where John affirms that the witnesses of the resurrection experienced Jesus with their physical senses (4.7.1).

In Acts, Schnabel observed the physical effects of Saul's encounter with the risen Jesus Christ in that he goes blind, he does not eat, and his travel companions hear the voice but do not see anyone (4.7.1.4). Furthermore it is noted that Saul (Paul) needs to be led to Damascus because of his blindness. Moreover, it is observed in Acts 26 that Paul is totally convinced of the veridicality of his encounter with the risen Jesus Christ as he makes his defense before Agrippa.

In relation to 1 Corinthians, Dan Mitchell emphasized the use of the Greek verb ephapax or "at one time" as affirming the objectivity of the resurrection (15:7). Mitchell explained if Paul had written that Jesus had "appeared," then the conclusion could be made that Jesus appeared to the 500 in a mass vision. However, because Paul uses "at one time" after "appeared," the most obvious explanation to Mitchell is that it was an objective seeing of Jesus Christ as opposed to a subjective encounter.

In addition to Mitchell, Kirk MacGregor offered that in 1 Corinthians 15:4, the Greek word for "raised," εγειρω, infers that Jesus Christ was bodily raised. He explained that the definition for εγειρω is to cause to stand up from a lying or reclining position after having been previously incapacitated. He further offered that a spirit does not lie down or rise up. Because of the meaning of this word, it is clear that a physical body is inferred from verse 4.

Summarizing the evidence for the bodily resurrection of Jesus, the various New Testament resurrection accounts corroborate the bodily resurrection of Jesus Christ in keeping with FPJI 1.07(5) as the various resurrection accounts are saying/inferring that Jesus Christ was raised bodily from the dead. This evidence from multiple sources strengthens the evidentiary value of the New Testament testimony. Also, this evidence is in accord with FRE 401 and 104(b) as they are relevant to the discussion and because the facts are based upon proof. Moreover, John and Paul were also eyewitnesses to what they report (FPJI 1.06-direct evidence and FRE 602-observe with the senses). Therefore, the evidence coming from the various New Testament resurrection reports are in accord with accepted principles of evidence.

4.8.10 Evidentiary analysis: Disciples martyrdom as circumstantial evidence for PRA

Sean McDowell investigated the reports that most of the disciples were martyred for their faith in Jesus Christ and that he had bodily-resurrected from the dead. McDowell offers good evidence from various writings that all but one of the disciples was martyred for their belief. In this present project, the martyrdoms of four of the New Testament witnesses to the risen Jesus Christ were highlighted. After examining the evidence provided by McDowell, his investigation revealed that James, Paul, Peter, and Thomas were most likely martyred for their faith in Jesus Christ. This faith in Jesus Christ included the belief that Jesus Christ had arisen from the dead in bodily form. The evidence that these four witnesses to the resurrected Jesus Christ willingly faced death for this conviction is in alignment with accepted principles of evidence (FPJI 1.06-circumstantial evidence and FPJI 1.07(5)) where historical witnesses to the resurrection of Jesus Christ willingly faced martyrdom for their belief in what they had witnessed. Moreover, the evidence is in accord with FRE 401 as this evidence is relevant to the discussion of the belief of the disciples that they had encountered Jesus Christ in bodily form. Also, the evidence is in accord with FRE 104(b) because McDowell's facts are based upon historical documents.

4.8.11 Evidentiary analysis: Conversions of James and Saul as circumstantial evidence

Regarding the conversions of Saul and James, Habermas and Licona, as well as Habermas himself commented on the circumstances of their conversions in the context of hallucinating the risen Jesus Christ. Saul and James would not possess any causal factors for hallucinations as they were both devout Jews and resistant to any notion that Jesus Christ was the promised Messiah for the Jews. Moreover, Habermas posited that James was an unbeliever during the ministry of Jesus. Additionally, there was no expectancy in James and Saul to see a risen Jesus Christ. The fact that both of these men were non-believers (one being an enemy of the faith and the other a devout Jew) and that both men eventually came to believe in Jesus Christ after having a post-resurrection encounter with him is good circumstantial evidence (FPJI 1.06-circumstantial evidence). Why would these two men become followers of Jesus Christ when one was a non-believer and brother of Jesus Christ and the other one was an enemy and persecutor of Christians? A reasonable inference to draw is that they both had convincing encounters with the risen Jesus Christ. These facts are in keeping with FRE 104(b) in that there are historical sources that report that James and Paul were non-believers and that they subsequently were leaders of the early Christian church.

This evidence is also in keeping with FRE 401 in that the literary sources from the New Testament are relevant evidence as to the experiences of both James and Saul with the risen Jesus Christ. As observed earlier in this project, Paul himself testified to the aforementioned facts about himself (FPJI 1.06-direct evidence, FRE 602, 1 Cor. 15:8). He also tells us of the experience of James with the risen Jesus Christ when he visited him in Jerusalem (FPJI 1.07(5), 1 Cor. 15:7).

4.8.12 Evidentiary analysis: The PRA of Jesus Christ corroborated by the empty tomb

The PRA of Jesus Christ in conjunction with the empty tomb of Jesus Christ gives confirmation to the notion that Jesus Christ was raised bodily. Ben Witherington offered that there would not have been belief that Jesus Christ had risen from the dead if the only evidence to support it was an empty tomb. Only the combination of the empty tomb along with the PRA of Jesus Christ would cause belief in Jesus Christ to flourish.

Gerald O'Collins also shared that the empty tomb would have been ambiguous by itself. But the empty tomb along with the PRA is strong confirmation of the reality of the bodily resurrection of Jesus Christ. Furthermore, Gerald O'Collins reported that the body of Jesus Christ that was in the tomb was also identified as transformed and raised by the disciples. In addition to O'Collins, David Baggett explained that hallucinations do not make bodies disappear. Furthermore, if the disciples made too much of a buzz about the resurrection of Jesus Christ, the Jewish authorities would just produce the body to end all of the commotion. However, the authorities were never able to produce a body. Along with these two,

William Lane Craig offered that the hallucination hypothesis fails because it cannot explain the empty tomb.

Wright also joined the aforementioned scholars in his agreement with the symbiotic relationship between the empty tomb and the PRA. These two standing alone do not provide enough evidence. However, when both are present they are both a necessary and a sufficient set of circumstances that led to the rise of early Christian belief. Finally, the empty tomb provides corroboration and circumstantial evidence for the notion that Jesus Christ arose bodily from the dead in keeping with FPJI 1.07(5), FPJI 1.06- circumstantial evidence, and *FRE* 104(b) because there are facts that are based upon proof. Also, *FRE* 401 applies because the discussion is relevant to whether the PRA of Jesus Christ consisted of bodily appearances or hallucinations.

4.9 Summary

In chapter four, the claims of Carrier that the PRA of Jesus Christ were hallucinations were developed. Carrier suggested different sorts of hallucinations (bereavement, schizophrenic, seizure related, fatigue related, and deprivation related). In offering the various types of hallucinations as candidates, he utilized New Testament passages to bolster his perspective. He also made reference to scholarly writings in support of his assertions.

After listing Carrier's claims, an exposition of scholarly literature was provided which detailed the different sorts of hallucinations Carrier had listed as possible candidates. In addition to these types, other forms of hallucination (hallucinogenic drug usage, CBS syndrome, PTSD) were explicated in response to Carrier's overall claim that the disciples hallucinated the risen Jesus Christ. It was found that a number of representations Carrier made about various types of hallucinations did not align with the scholarly literature review.

Following the exposition of scholarly literature, a cross-examination coming from scholarly Christian material was conducted. This material was offered in response to the detailed claims made by Carrier throughout the corpus of his writings. The aforementioned scholarly material included the objections of scholars to these or similar claims set forth by Carrier *et al.*

After conducting a cross-examination, an evidentiary presentation was given against Carrier's theory to include providing different New Testament passages that communicated Jesus Christ was experienced in bodily form after his resurrection. In addition to this evidence, circum-

Objection Three: The Disciples Hallucinated the Risen Jesus Christ

stantial evidence coming from the conversions of two skeptics, James and Paul, was offered in that these two opponents to Christianity would not have converted to Christianity if they had not been convinced of the bodily resurrection of Jesus Christ. Other evidence that was presented against Carrier's claims was that four of the central witnesses to the PRA were martyred for their belief in the bodily resurrection of Jesus Christ. Sean McDowell offered evidence for the martyrdom of Peter, Paul, James, and Thomas. All four of these men were witnesses to the resurrected Jesus Christ. These men would not have paid the ultimate sacrifice had they known that Jesus did not arise bodily from the dead (FPJI 1.06-circumstatial evidence). Finally, the corroborative or confirmatory nature of the empty tomb was also explored. Several scholars noted the importance of this confirmatory evidence to the PRA as being essential to the viability of knowing that Jesus Christ had been bodily raised. This evidence was found to be in accord with FRE 401, FRE 104(b), FPJI 1.06-direct evidence, FPJI 1.07(5)-corroborative evidence and FRE 602.

After giving this evidentiary presentation, an evidentiary analysis was completed of the various forms of hallucinations to see if they cohered with accepted principles of evidence. Even though the evidence presented by Carrier appears to be relevant (FRE 401) in the sense that it came from the New Testament resurrection accounts and from scholarly literature, it was evident that Carrier's evidence oftentimes did not conform to either the New Testament resurrection accounts or the scholarly literature. Therefore, many of his claims were not in accord with FRE 104(b) as his facts were not based on proof but oftentimes were based upon either conjecture or a misconstrual of the material from his sources. Moreover, Carrier did not supply any historical eyewitnesses outside of the New Testament narratives for his contentions, contra FRE 602 and FPJI 1.06-direct evidence. In contrast to this, the evidence against Carrier's hallucination hypothesis comes from the New Testament resurrection narratives which are based on a number of accepted principles of evidence to include FRE 401, FRE 104(b), FRE 602, FPJI 1.06 (direct and circumstantial evidence), and FPJI 1.07(5) (corroboration).

CHAPTER FIVE

Summary, Findings, and Conclusion

5.1 Summary

5.1.1 Summary: Accepted principles of evidence

Upon making an initial inquiry into the evidentiary aspects of Carrier's claims, I questioned whether Carrier was properly utilizing accepted principles of evidence regarding the New Testament resurrection narratives. After making preliminary findings, my objective was to distill accepted principles of evidence from established Anglo-American common law tradition, specifically, the FRE and the FPJI, in order to determine whether Carrier's claims against the resurrection narratives of the New Testament are in accord with relevant scholarly literature, the narratives themselves, and upon accepted principles of evidence. As there is such a stark contrast with Carrier's conclusions questioning the veracity of the New Testament resurrection narratives and the holdings of orthodox Christianity that the resurrection of Jesus Christ is a historical event that occurred in space and time, a set of criteria is needed to assist in evaluating these claims and others like them. It was the aim of this research project to propose a fair and workable set of criteria from the aforementioned accepted principles of evidence. These principles have guided Western society for centuries in determining the quality of evidence being evaluated in criminal matters. Did a purported event actually occur? How strong is the evidence to support that it did occur as reported by witnesses? Because of the space-time claims of orthodox Christianity (Jesus Christ lived, died by crucifixion, and arose from dead), these distilled accepted principles of evidence are germane and helpful as criteria to guide a student/investigator in their quest for a firm foundation upon which to make evidentiary evaluations on this and other topics.

In conducting research into the use of accepted principles of evidence as evaluative criteria, it was found that there was a body of literature coming from Christian scholarship (scholars with legal training and experience) that applied accepted principles of evidence to the New Testament. These scholars demonstrated that the New Testament, and specifically the resurrection narratives are in accord with accepted principles of evidence. While focusing on and further distilling these accepted principles of evidence, the project clarified and gave more detail to the existing research of these legal Christian scholars by analyzing/applying the FRE and FPJI. As aforementioned, these legal standards have guided the United States in evidentiary proceedings for decades. Moreover, in applying these accepted principles of evidence to Carrier's writings, the use of these principles was expanded to not only analyze the New Testament resurrection narratives, but also the writings of those who make claims against the resurrection narratives of the New Testament. Even though there are Christian scholars who refute the claims of skeptical scholars by utilizing evidentiary principles on occasion, no actual complete evidentiary analysis of the writings of a skeptical writer's literature was found during the research phase of this project. When the literature was examined related to the present thesis topic, it was found there was a void in evidentiary analyses of skeptical authors. It is believed that filling this important void is one of the major accomplishments of this research project. Not only through the distillation of accepted principles of evidence as evaluative criteria, but also the thorough analysis of a skeptical author's perspective by evidentiary principles.

Summarizing these principles of evidence, the research included a literature survey explicating the relevant *FRE* and FPJI. Included in the *FRE* were explanations of what is considered relevant evidence in federal criminal proceedings (401(b)). Other important principles explained were that the basis of evidence should be predicated upon facts undergirded by proof (104(b)) and that testimony should be based upon the sensory observations of the witness (602). In addition to these evidentiary principles, other essential accepted principles of evidence were explained: (1) how to properly impeach a witness (607 and 608) (2) the illegality of impeaching a witness based on religious affiliation (610) (3) the occasions when it is permissible to utilize hearsay evidence in certain excepted circumstances (802). One such hearsay exception brought out in the *FRE* was the ancient documents exception (803(16)). John W. Montgomery submitted that the Bible would be considered as excepted hearsay evidence because it met the standards included within *FRE* 901b(8).

In addition to the *FRE*, additional principles of how to interpret evidence that are utilized by courts and juries everyday in the United States were offered and explained. As stated above, these principles are contained within the FPJI. In addition to listing and explaining this information, the origin of the FPJI were also explored along with the need for these instructions in providing a basic explanation of how to receive and to interpret evidence. These FPJI explain basic concepts of evidence to include direct evidence (directly observed by the senses) and circumstantial evidence (chain of circumstances that indirectly prove a fact) (U.S. Court of Appeals for the Sixth Circuit, 2014:Section 1.06). Additionally, other foundational evidentiary principles that are included within the FPJI are weighing the evidence (U.S. Court of Appeals for the Sixth Circuit, 2014:Section 1.05) and judging the credibility of the evidence (U.S. Court of Appeals for the Sixth Circuit, 2014:Section 1.07).

5.1.2 Summary: Carrier's contentions

In addition to delineating the relevant FRE and the FPJI for use as evaluative criteria, Carrier's contentions questioning the veracity of the New Testament resurrection accounts were given. In the first contention given, Carrier objected to the veracity of the New Testament resurrection accounts on the grounds that they contradict each other. The second of Carrier's contentions against the New Testament resurrection narratives propounded that antecedent, pagan, and mythical cults were the source of the Christian concept of the resurrection of Jesus Christ. One final contention posited by Carrier was that the disciples were hallucinating the risen Jesus Christ. Carrier offered many different types of hallucinatory syndromes as candidates to explain the disciples' encounters with the risen Jesus Christ.

5.1.3 Summary: New Testament resurrection accounts are contradictory

In reference to Carrier's claim that the resurrection narratives of the Gospels are contradictory, Carrier's specific contentions were listed and detailed. Carrier asserted that these narratives are not even independent as one evangelist copies another evangelist, that the synoptic Gospels contradict each other, and that this group of three Gospels contradict John as well. Specifically, Carrier pointed out the number and activity of the angels at the tomb conflict, there were different women and the activities of the women at the tomb diverge in each Gospel, the PRA of Jesus Christ in each Gospel differ with each other, and the timing of the removal of the stone from the tomb entrance listed in the Gospels are at variance with each other. Additionally, Carrier also alleged that the identities of these authors are unknown and that he believed this supports several of his core beliefs about Christianity; that Jesus Christ is mythical and that the resurrection accounts are unreliable and contradictory. One further claim that Carrier made about the resurrection narratives is that there are embellishments contained within the resurrection narratives.

Regarding Carrier's claim that the resurrection accounts of the Gospels are contradictory, the literature of Christian scholars, apologists, and other sources was utilized to cross-examine Carrier's contentions. In this cross-examination, it was brought out that rarely will accounts from two separate witnesses be identical but will necessarily have to diverge from each other. Moreover, each witness will put their observations through their own grid of interpretation according to what is important to each particular witness. Furthermore, it was brought out that some of the differences are so insignificant that they do not cast doubt on the narratives. Another observation from this class of scholars is that if there was too much agreement between the narratives, then an accusation of collusion would be justified.

In regard to the objection put forth by Carrier pertaining to the number/activity of the angels at the tomb, Christian scholars and apologists observed that just because there is a different number mentioned in one gospel than in another does not mean that they conflict. It could be that one witness only saw one angel and that there was another angel that was present that was either not observed or that was not important to the writing objective of the evangelist. Furthermore, whenever one angel is mentioned, there is no qualifying adverb used to designate *only* one angel. Another point observed in the cross-examination is that John's angels are not developed from Mark's angel. Rather, instead of embellishments, mere differences were observed with no remarkable discrepancies.

In relation to the different women and their activities at the tomb, the literature review revealed that each Gospel author had similar lists of women witnesses. It was also brought out that the minor differences in the lists were as a result of the different sources utilized by the Gospel evangelists as well as their thematic goals. Moreover, it was noted that there was no need for the Gospel authors to be overly complete in their descriptions. Rather, each evangelist would compile the list of women witnesses in a manner they deemed important.

In relation to the cross-examination of Carrier's claims regarding the PRA of Jesus Christ, Christian scholars and apologists responded that these appearances are generally similar even though there are some differences in them. In reply to Carrier's charge of embellishments and dissimilarities, cross-examining scholarly literature noted that it would have been hard to exaggerate or give faulty testimony within the Gospels without those witnesses, many who were most likely still alive, taking issue with the inaccuracies of these narratives. As far as the different locales reported by the evangelists, it was brought out that John unifies the reports by mentioning both locations and that they utilized testimony that best suited their interests. Moreover, even though there are variances within the setting of the PRA of Jesus Christ, this only demonstrates that the authors were reporting on matters of importance to them. Just because one account centers in one area and another narrative describes a second area for other PRA of Jesus Christ does not mean that one account is wrong and another right. Also, a charge of collusion could be made against the evangelists if all of the accounts of the PRA were totally alike. Regarding Carrier's objection to the timing of the removal of the stone, dissenting scholarship affirmed that the Gospels are in general agreement on this topic and that it was moved either just before or at the same time as the arrival of the women at the tomb.

In addition to the above-mentioned cross-examination, an analysis of Carrier's contention of embellishment was also undertaken by examining the definition of the term "contradiction." Upon conducting this analysis, it was brought out that in the several definitions listed for the term "contradiction" that were surveyed, all but one definition had conflicting parts that were inherent within one entity, not conflicting data between two different sets of data. Moreover, for two different sets of data to be contradictory, it must be shown there is no way they can be reconciled. Additionally, the four separate sources would not be contradicting each other if each source was giving its own particular view on a given subject or chose to add or to subtract items from their Gospel. Moreover, in making his case, Carrier actually weakens his own argument as he notes similarities between the accounts of Joseph of Arimathea. Carrier lists several foundational similarities between the Gospel accounts to include Joseph's status as a "Sanhedrist," that he buried Jesus after his death, and that he placed him in a tomb.

Subsequent to the aforementioned cross-examination, evidence of the similarity of the resurrection accounts was given from the viewpoint of Christian scholars. Evidences given for the similarity amongst the Gospel accounts were the prominence of the women as witnesses to the resurrection, the initial doubt of the disciples that Jesus had arisen from the dead, and Joseph of Arimathea's burial of Jesus Christ in a tomb. Concerning the last positive evidence offered, it was brought out that if there were any serious contenders other than Jesus' burial by Joseph of Arimathea, then there would be some record of it in ancient literature. However, there is no known alternate version of where Jesus body had been lain other than in the tomb of Joseph of Arimathea.

In addition to the aforementioned evidentiary analysis, rebuttal evidence was offered to include further evidence for the reliability of the Bible due to its status as an ancient document in compliance with FRE 901b(8). Thus, it would be considered admissible as excepted hearsay in a court of law under the FRE 803(16). Christian scholars also affirmed that the resurrection narratives of the New Testament were either written by eyewitnesses or by those who heard the accounts of the eyewitnesses. In addition to the literature of the Christian apologists and scholars, several historians also echoed the sentiments of these core principles of evidence as they affirmed that the best historical writings are closely aligned to the sensory observations of the writers or facts obtained by someone who is known to have observed a particular historical event.

In addition to the evidentiary analysis of John, further rebuttal evidence was given against Carrier's contention that the Gospel authors are unknown persons. As far as John being a known person, there are many church leaders who acknowledge the Apostle John as the author of the Gospel traditionally associated with his name. Early church leaders to affirm John are Irenaeus, Clement of Alexandria, and Tertullian. In addition to these early church leaders, the *Anti-Marcionite Prologues* and the *Muratorian Fragment* also confirm that John was the author. In relation to Mark's Gospel, literature from Christian scholars and apologists revealed that ancient sources such as Papias, Tertullian, Origen, and Clement of Alexandria affirm Mark as the writer of his Gospel. Moreover it was brought out that Mark is listed in several New Testament Scriptures one of which shows a close association with Peter (1 Peter 5:13).

In regard to Matthew, a scholarly literature review showed that ancient sources such as Papias, Irenaeus, Eusebius, Tertullian, Origen, and Jerome all support one of the twelve disciples, Matthew, as the author of the traditional Gospel according to Matthew. In addition to the gospels of Mark and Matthew, scholarly literature revealed that Luke also has early attestation for being the author of the Gospel that bears his name. Church fathers supporting the authorship of Luke as the author of the Gospel bearing his name include Tertullian and Irenaeus. Along with these church leaders, other ancient evidence comes from the Anti-Marcionite Prologues and the Muratorian Fragment both dating from the second century. In similarity to Mark, there are also passages where Luke is in the company of Paul as Paul writes to the Colossians (4:10,14) and to Philemon (v. 24). Thus, it was shown that there is not only internal evidence as to Luke's identity coming from the New Testament but also external evidence coming from outside the New Testament as well.

5.1.4 Summary: Antecedent dying/rising gods and Jesus Christ

After Carrier's contentions were listed and detailed regarding Christianity borrowing its resurrection story from antecedent dying and rising gods, an exposition of scholarly literature explaining specific pagan/mythical traditions was provided. Regarding the pagan/mythical cults that Carrier claimed supported the development of the Christian concept of the resurrection, four of Carrier's candidates were identified. Scholarly literature on Osiris, the mythical Egyptian king of the netherworld was exposited to determine if he was an earlier deity who had died in similar fashion as Jesus Christ. In addition to Osiris, scholarly literature was offered regarding Inanna, the Mesopotamian goddess, to determine if what Carrier had claimed regarding her death by hanging on a pole and her resurrection from the dead agreed with the literature survey. After the review of Inanna, the writings of scholars familiar with Zalmoxis were investigated and presented to determine if the circumstances of his death and "resurrection" from the dead were analogous with that of Jesus Christ as Zalmoxis allegedly died and then returned from the dead after three years according to Carrier. In similarity to the other aforementioned three deities, the literature from scholars on the Romulan legend was also surveyed.

As mentioned above, a literature survey on the aforementioned four deities was completed. Regarding Osiris, the Egyptian King of the netherworld, it was shown that Osiris and Re teamed up to reinvigorate the *akh* (eternally existing spirit) of a person that was contained within their mummy. The origin of Osiris was also brought out. Osiris was the son of the god Geb and the goddess Nut. While in the womb with his sister and future bride Isis, Osiris had sex with his sister. Eventually the two married. However, as a result of Osiris accidentally having sex with his other sister Nephthys who was the wife of his brother Seth, Seth launched a scheme to have Osiris assassinated which eventually occurred. After his assassination, the body parts of Osiris were scattered across the land of Egypt but were eventually found by his wife, the goddess Isis, who magically put the pieces of his body back together. The body of Osiris was then mummified with the aid of the god Anubis. Upon a meeting of the council of gods from the underworld, it was deemed that Osiris would be allowed to be reanimated in the underworld and have the role and title of King of the netherworld. The literature survey also revealed that one was granted access to the netherworld by possessing the right magical spells and also by a weighing of ones deeds in a balance. There was no relationship with Osiris that assured entry into the netherworld. Rather, upon the entry of a person (with their mummy remaining in the physical world) into the netherworld, Osiris, along with the god Re, would ensure the *akh* of those residing in the netherworld would remain invigorated. Additionally, there were varying accounts of the Osirian myth. Some of them had Osiris as the god who ensured the inundation of the Nile River and as one who would symbolically die when the crops were harvested every year. Moreover, in his nightly journey to team up with Re or Ra the sun god, he would be resurrected anew every night.

Specifically regarding the cross-examination of Carrier's claims about Osiris by Christian scholars, it was noted that Osiris did not really arise from the dead in a human body. Rather, he was reanimated and installed as King of the netherworld after a council of gods voted on the matter. Thus, he was not resurrected to new life on the earth, but consigned to the realm of the dead. Regarding the divergence in the formulation of the after life, it was also brought out that the Osirian version of the afterlife included mummification of the body, nourishment provided to the mummy on a daily basis, and magical spells within the coffin.

Upon conducting a comparison between the Osirian myth and the New Testament accounts of Jesus Christ, numerous contrasts between the two were noted. The contrasts noted were that Osirianism is a myth and Christianity is based on historical accounts, that Jesus Christ knew of his impending death and willingly accepted it, and that Osiris was surprised by his assassination. Moreover, another contrast between the two was the different method used to kill them. In contrast to Osiris, Jesus Christ was not killed because of a lover's quarrel. Rather, Jesus Christ was murdered because of his claim that he was God incarnate. Another contrast observed between Jesus Christ and Osiris is that Jesus Christ was resurrected in an actual body that walked the earth again whereas the body of Osiris was turned into a mummy and Osiris was only allowed to reside in the netherworld. Moreover, Jesus Christ was resurrected to an immortal life in an actual body whereas Osiris was transferred from a mummified body to a non-corporeal existence in the netherworld.

Additional comparisons of the Osirian scholarly literature with the New testament accounts revealed further constrasts: (1) that Osiris was born from parents who were gods whereas Jesus Christ was born of a virgin who did not have sex with any other person. (2) Osiris was considered the great king of Egypt whereas Jesus Christ had no earthly power or possessions to speak of. (3) Osiris had sex with several women whereas Jesus Christ never married. (4) The life and ministry of Jesus Christ was characterized by coming to the aid of others whereas Osiris was known to be a cruel taskmaster. Moreover, devotees of Osiris had no relationship with him. Osiris was merely a god who presided over the inundation process of the Nile/grain harvests and also was a vehicle to maintain one's existence in the netherworld. In addition to a lack of personal relationship with Osiris and his devotees, Osiris had nothing to do with one's entry into the netherworld. One's entry into the netherworld was actually insured by having the right incantations, a mummy, and by a record of doing more good deeds than bad deeds. In contradistinction to Osirianism, a relationship with Jesus Christ is personal and it is through a relationship with him that one is granted entry into heaven. It is through his death on the cross and by his unique resurrection from the dead that insures this access.

Concerning the exposition of the scholarly literature on Inanna/Ishtar, it was observed that Inanna was originally introduced during the Old Babylonian Period in the city of Uruk and that her cult quickly spread to other regions. As time proceeded, Inanna morphed into the Akkadian Ishtar and then was also adopted by other people groups as well. This Levantine goddess was observed to be multifaceted where on the one hand she is a young maiden and lover, and then on another occasion she is described as a rebellious teenager. In other scenarios, Inanna/Ishtar is observed to be a goddess of war and in others a goddess of fertility and love. She is also portrayed as a prostitute, a cross-dresser, self-mutilator and homosexual. Moreover, she is observed as the wife and legitimizer of kings as she will marry and have conjugal relations at festivals to affirm the rule of the aforementioned kings. Over time, Inanna/Ishtar continued to gain various qualities as her cult spread to further regions. Soon, she appeared as Astarte and she also spread to Greece and Rome being known as Aphrodite and Venus, respectively.

In relation to the primary myth of Inanna/Ishtar given by scholarly literature, it begins with Inanna who discusses her future husband with Utu her brother. Utu states that it will be Dumuzi aka Tammuz, the shepherd, and Inanna objects, as she would rather marry a farmer. However, Dumuzi enters the residence of Inanna and they begin a relationship as lovers and they marry. Eventually, Inanna decides that she should attend a marriage in the netherworld where her sister Ereshkigal is queen. Before she prepares, Inanna gives her faithful assistant instructions that if she does not reappear from the netherworld, then she should summon help. As Inanna goes to the netherworld, she is allowed entry. However, her sister Ereshkigal strikes her dead and hangs her naked body on a pole. Upon not returning to her home, her assistant begins to mourn and to notify Inanna's family and the gods that something has gone wrong and that Inanna is in need of assistance. The god Enki responds to Inanna's plea for help and sends creatures to negotiate for Inanna resulting in her magical reanimation. However, she is allowed to leave the netherworld under the condition that she finds a substitute for her. As Inanna returns to her homeland, she seeks out her husband Dumuzi who is not mourning for her and designates that Dumuzi and his sister will be her substitutes in the netherword. The survey further reveals that most of the cult revolves around sexual activity, that those who die lose their bodies, that their souls have a dreary existence in the netherworld, and that the dead in the netherworld are nourished by the offerings of their living relatives.

In regard to the cross-examination of Carrier's claims regarding Inanna/Ishtar, it was observed in the literature survey that it was not Inanna/Ishtar who died as a sacrifice for others. Rather, Inanna/Ishtar needed a substitute for herself so that she could leave the domain of the dead. Furthermore, after investigating the demise and reanimation of Inanna/Ishtar, it is clear that the correlations that Carrier made were not based upon the descriptions contained within the Inanna myth. Rather, Inanna was struck down by her sister Ereshkigal and the time period is unknown between when Inanna died and when she was brought back to life by magical means. Furthermore, she was only being reanimated to life in the netherworld. So, she was only allowed to travel back to the natural world of the earth when she designated her husband Dumuzi also known as Tammuz and his sister as substitutes for her. In contradistinction to Inanna/Ishtar, Jesus Christ did not need the assistance of anyone to arise from the dead. It was by his own power that Jesus Christ arose from the dead. Rather, instead of needing a substitute to arise from the dead, Jesus Christ himself was the substitute for others to obtain eternal life.

Other contrasts that were brought out in the cross-examination and exposition of Inanna are that Inanna was self-absorbed with most of her energies indulging her prurient interests. Moreover, she is known in these accounts as manipulating others in order to satiate her selfish ambitions. In contrast to the descriptions of Inanna/Ishtar, Jesus Christ lived a life of total sacrifice, was not interested in sex but taught that sexual conduct out of wedlock was wrong, and was not interested in selfish gain as his ministry was centered on serving others. This service and sacrifice for others included knowingly enduring a tortuous death by crucifixion. Regarding the contrast in soteriological formulations between Christianity and Inanna/Ishtar's cult, there is no known way explained in which a devotee receives eternal life through a relationship with Inanna/Ishtar.

This is contrasted with Christianity where the follower of Jesus Christ gains salvation and entry into heaven through appropriating the work of Jesus Christ on the cross for oneself.

The exposition, cross-examination, and evidentiary analysis of the scholarly literature on the Romulan legend revealed that Romulus lived a life in contrast to that of Jesus Christ. It was brought out that Romulus was involved in violence and war throughout his entire life (if he existed) beginning with the murder of his brother Remus. Another violent episode Romulus led was the rape of the Sabine women where Roman men forcefully took the Sabine women, raped them, and then took them for their wives. Moreover the general, Romulus, is alleged to have been involved in many bloody battles putting Rome on it's footing as a military world power. In contrast to the general Romulus, Jesus Christ lived a life that was not characterized by conquest or violence rather, sacrifice for others even to death. The literature on Romulus revealed several versions on how Romulus died (being enveloped in a flame from a lightning strike and never being seen again; being murdered by the Roman senators).

Concerning Carrier's thesis that Christianity came from the Romulan legend, the cross-examination from Christian scholars revealed that the evidence for the Romulan legend is anemic at best. Concerning the death, apotheosis, and epiphany of Romulus, it was noted that only one person observed Romulus after his disappearance (as mentioned above, it is not even known how Romulus was murdered/translated) by one person who is not even sure whether he was observing an actual body or just an apparition. In contrast to the Romulan legend, more than five hundred people witnessed Jesus Christ alive after his death at one time and some witnesses touched and spoke with him. Another important point brought out in the exposition is that the Romulan primary sources were not eyewitnesses nor did they share the sources of the information or how reliable the information was.

In regard to the exposition of Zalmoxis from scholarly literature, it was shown that there was scant reference to the deity. Ancient sources that make brief mention of Zalmoxis include Plato, Herodotus, Ovid, and Strabo. In these references to the Thracian god, there is mention of Zalmoxis as it relates to being a king whose physicians are masters in the healing arts. Also discussed were the Getae, a people who believed that they did not die as a result of their god, Zalmoxis. Other detail brought out in the exposition was that Zalmoxis was a slave of Pythagoras who was freed and relocated to his home of Thrace where he became famous and wealthy. Zalmoxis then built a subterranean chamber where he resided out of view for three years. In the fourth year, he came back to the Thracians and told them that he died and came back from the dead. Other details brought out in the exposition were that human sacrifice was among the rites of their worship, that Zalmoxis was a priest who eventually became revered as a conduit to the gods for the Getaen kings, that he was learned in astronomical knowledge, and that he placed special emphasis on caves as a meeting place with the divine. In addition to Carrier's other three candidates, the cross-examination of Carrier's contention regarding Zalmoxis by a Christian scholar revealed the contrast that Jesus died in front of all whereas Zalmoxis merely hid from view and then after being gone from the public eye reappeared unexpectedly.

In regard to any similarity with the death and resurrection of Jesus, there was no similarity observed between the soteriology of Jesus Christ and that of Zalmoxis. In order to obtain eternal life in the cult of Zalmoxis, one had to either be a nobleman, be chosen as the messenger to Zalmoxis (human sacrifice), or die valiantly in battle. Moreover, there was no showing that Zalmoxis died in order to assure eternal life for anyone. Also, there is no report of how Zalmoxis died or that he was seen after his death alive in bodily form except for the above mention of his hiding and reappearance from a subterranean cave.

Another point that was cross-examined was the contention of Carrier that Christian baptism came from pagan baptismal rites. However, the scholarly review of the literature on pagan cults revealed that there were actually no baptisms akin to what Carrier had described. Rather, upon investigating the same sources that Carrier presented, it was clear these sources mentioned purification baths that occurred before a mystery rite, not a baptism. The bath itself was not an initiation rite. Rather, it was a cleansing ritual to prepare for the actual initiation rite that was actually secret in nature (hence the term "mystery"). In conducting an evidentiary examination of the above-mentioned contention that Christian baptism was influenced by pagan baptism, it was shown that Carrier's reliance upon fictional literature, as part of the foundation for his claim, is not based upon *FRE* 602 (testimony from the senses), and FPJI 1.06 (direct evidence).

Furthermore, to assume that a pre-existing entity caused an event preceding it is not proper. Just because event A happened before event B does not mean that event A caused event B to occur. There must be particularized and specific evidence to make a connection between two events. Therefore, supposed causal correlations between two events are not valid just because one event preceded another one. It was brought

Summary, Findings, and Conclusion 339

out that this type of informal logical fallacy is known as a "false cause" fallacy or more specifically, a *post hoc ergo propter hoc* fallacy.

After presenting the scholarly literature and cross-examining Carrier's contention, evidence against Carrier's claim of pre-existing mystery religions influencing Christianity was offered through a literature review. One observation from scholarship brought out that Paul was against idolatry and that Paul referenced Exodus 32:6 as he wrote about his objections to idolatry in 1 Corinthians 10. Furthermore, when Paul discusses the idolatry of his day he states that the food sacrificed to idols is equivalent to actually sacrificing to demons. The Christian scholars observe that Paul relies upon the Jewish perspective and that this perspective is not agreeable to syncretism with the surrounding pagan cults.

In addition to Paul's contempt for idolatry, it was also shown through the literature of Christian scholars that Paul's perspective on the resurrection comes from the Old Testament and not from pagan sources. For instance, both Romans chapters nine and ten demonstrate Paul's reliance upon Deuteronomy chapter thirty and that Paul's main emphasis regarding the law is it reveals the Messiah. Moreover, concerning 1 Corinthians fifteen, allusions to the creation and fall from Genesis as well as influence from the Book of Daniel were also observed. Additionally, a Davidic influence is also reported when Paul proclaims Jesus Christ as the root of Jesse, the father of David. Also, observed was that for Paul, the life, death, and resurrection of Jesus Christ were grounded in the tradition of Israel. Furthermore, for Paul, his view of the resurrection, which was rooted in Judaism, was transformed by his experiences with the risen Jesus Christ. Another scholar noted Paul's usage of the phraseology "first fruits" in regard to the resurrection of Jesus Christ as an allusion to the Old Testament as well.

Another item of evidence against Carrier's contention coming from scholarly literature is that the Old Testament in no way condoned idolatry. It just was not tolerated by the Jewish faith. That is not to say that the Jews were tainted from their worship of other gods because that certainly was the case. However, traditional Judaism and the Old Testament literature summarily reject any form of idol worship as being acceptable. Orthodox Judaism has always been strictly monotheistic. The survey also portrayed that Paul expressly prohibits the worship of idols in 1 Corinthians chapters eight and ten.

An additional line of evidence against Carrier's claim of Christianity adopting its tenets from pagan religions is that the books of the Old Testament expressly reject worship of a form of Inanna/Ishtar. A form of Inanna/Ishtar, Astarte (also known as Ashtoreth), is mentioned with contempt on several different occasions. Furthermore, worshipping Astarte was believed to be a form of prostitution. If the nation of Israel wanted to restore their relationship with Yahweh, then they would need to rid themselves of other gods one of which was Astarte (Inanna/Ishtar). In addition to the mention of Astarte in the Old Testament, Inanna/Ishtar's husband is also mentioned with disapprobation by the Old Testament authors. Yahweh declares the worship of Tammuz (Dumuzi) is detestable. As there is repeated rejection of the worship of other gods in the Old Testament and the rejection of paganism by Paul, the scholarly literature demonstrates that syncretism of other religions into Christianity has not occurred other than minor borrowing.

Further evidence received from the literature review of scholars is that the New Testament Scriptures do not reference any sort of pagan based soteriology or eschatology. Rather, what is observed is a soteriology/eschatology that is linked to Judaism. References in the New Testament speak of Jesus Christ as the Lamb of God whose sacrifice took away the stain of sin. Moreover, the New Testament authors see Jesus, the Messiah, as coming from the lineage of David. Furthermore, this promise is guaranteed by the resurrection of Jesus Christ from the dead. In addition to these other observations of the New Testament authors, the New Testament frequently mentions Jesus Christ as the "Son of Man." This is a term that is utilized in the Old Testament and connotes deity. In that Jesus Christ refers to himself as the "Son of Man," it implies that the "Son of Man" would arise from the dead to fulfill this role. Other imagery noted by the survey of Christian scholars is that of the "Paschal Lamb" that hearkens back to the first Passover. Still more examples of Old Testament imagery utilized by the New Testament authors is Jesus as our high priest, Jesus' resurrection related to Jonah and the whale (sign of Jonah), and the first communion meal given by Jesus as symbolic of Passover.

In cross-examining Carrier's contention regarding the notion that Christianity came from pre-existing mystery religions by scholarly literature, it was brought out that all religions will have similarities to include worship of the deity, prayers, rituals, etc. Therefore, certain general similarities are to be expected amongst all religions. Moreover, it was also brought out in the survey that there is a marked difference between Christianity and other religions as in other religions, the devotee attempts to appease the deity by his actions. However, a person needs only to join in relationship with Jesus Christ in order to receive the benefits of the work of Jesus Christ for humanity.

In commenting on the borrowing of Christianity from the mystery religions, several commentators registered that there was no borrowing from the mystery religions by Christianity. Additionally, they noted that the Jews were unwavering in their devotion to their faith and would not mix with pagan religions. Furthermore, the resilience of early Christianity is also noted as it resisted corruption by these cults. The literature examined also noted that in some instances, it is known that mystery religions borrowed from Christianity in some measure. Moreover, the once and for all death and resurrection of Jesus Christ stands in contradistinction to the repeating dying and rising cycles of the mystery religions. Additionally it was brought out that there was a lack of proliferation of mystery religions in the area of Palestine during the time that Christianity was birthed there. When comparing the soteriology of the mystery religions with Christianity, a marked contrast was observed.

5.1.5 Summary: The disciples hallucinated the risen Jesus Christ

Regarding Carrier's claims that the PRA of Jesus Christ were hallucinations, in his writings, he offered many candidates for the types of hallucination the disciples may have experienced to include hypnagogic/hypnopompic hallucinations, bereavement/grief hallucinations, schizophrenic hallucinations, as well as hallucinations caused by guilt, fatigue, deprivation, and seizures. Other classes of hallucinations that Carrier did not specifically mention but were deemed probative to examine were CBS, drug-induced, and PTSD related hallucinations.

Concerning hypnagogic and hypnopompic hallucinations, Carrier opined that these types of hallucinations are common today. Going back to the timeframe of the ministry of Jesus, Carrier suggested that someone who took an afternoon nap could very well have experienced these sorts of hallucinations. Additionally, he offered many other experiences as possibilities for what the disciples experienced such as fasting, fatigue, sleep deprivation, ordinary dreaming, and mantric prayer. In the exposition of the scholarly literature on hypnagogia, it was shown that these hallucinations are brief, vivid, sharp images, and they do not blend into the background. Other qualities of Hypnagogic images are they can at times be very small/very large, oftentimes are formless, are designs, are faces, can be figures, and can be nature scenes/scenes with people in them. Furthermore, hypnagogic hallucinations can consist of print or writing and can also be auditory in nature. Another quality of hypnagogia listed in the survey is that the one experiencing this type of hallucination knows that it is not real.

The exposition of literature brought out that hypnopompic hallucinations are on the opposite side of the sleep spectrum from hypnagogia with the onset of hallucinations as one is waking up. These hallucinations were described as a transition from the dreaming state into wakefulness. Another difference that was brought out in the exposition was that in contrast to hypnagogia where the images are fleeting, hypnopompic imagery is often observed with eyes open, in illuminated areas, is projected into external space, and seems to be real to the one experiencing it. These hallucinations are also short in duration, can be remembered for many years, and are known by the one experiencing them not to be real.

As mentioned in the exposition for hypnagogic and hypnopompic hallucinations, both these types of hallucinations are unrealistic, short, and do not make sense to the hallucinator. Furthermore, it is known by the hallucinator that these images are not real. Moreover, the witnesses to the resurrection were not going to sleep or awaking from sleep when they experienced the risen Jesus Christ and it makes sense that group experiences of Jesus Christ as mentioned in the New Testament could not be explained by these types of hallucinations. Furthermore, the other qualities of hypnagogic and hypnopompic hallucinations do not comport with the resurrection narratives as well.

Another type of hallucination mentioned by Carrier as a possible contender for what the disciples experienced was bereavement hallucinations. He conjectured that this type of hallucination helped the disciples to reduce their anxiety as well as helped them gain influence in the community. Moreover, Carrier mentioned that many in ancient times claimed to have encountered ancient gods or deceased heroes.

In the literature review of PBHEs, these were often experienced by normally functioning persons who had recently been bereaved. One of the qualities of this type of hallucination is that one will sense the presence of their deceased loved one at some point. Additionally, many of these people will have PBHEs for years on a regular basis. According to the literature, the most common hallucinatory experience is a sense of presence that the deceased is nearby. Following this sense of presence hallucination, a VH of the decedent was the most frequently reported type of hallucination followed by auditory hallucinations, touching, and talking to the defendant. One source reported that multi-modal hallucinations of this variety have been reported but that they are rare. In addition to these manifestations to bereaved loved ones, the frequency of these experiences across geographical boundaries remain constant. Also, these sorts of hallucinations are normally fleeting in nature only lasting seconds in duration.

In addition to these sorts of hallucinations, Carrier also offered schizophrenic hallucinations as a possibility for what the disciples experienced. He offered that early Christians were "hallucinators" and "trancers" and also that "functional schizotypes" are predisposed to gathering in these sorts of groups. Additionally, Carrier also claimed these early Christians were most likely happy schizotypal persons who created these original miracle stories and then disseminated them to others. He then offered that those who surrounded Jesus were composed of these delusional sorts of people.

As Carrier proposed a schizophrenic hallucination as a possible candidate for the PRA of Jesus Christ, a scholarly survey of the literature on schizophrenic hallucinations was conducted. The survey of literature on the topic revealed that this type of hallucination was often characterized by bizarre experiences and beliefs to include auditory/visual hallucinations and delusions. In contrast with the other forms of hallucination, schizophrenic patients believe that the hallucinations they experience are real. Even though auditory hallucinations are observed to be the most prevalent, VHs also occur frequently. One point brought out in the review is that if the schizophrenic patient has auditory hallucinations and VHs at the same time, then they are typically unrelated to each other. Another scenario of patients experiencing both types of hallucinations is they may likely experience auditory hallucinations on one day and then a VH on another day.

Because Carrier suggested the disciples were most likely "happy schizotypal" people, the survey included excerpts regarding those who are categorized as being in this class. One of the factors attributed to happy schizotypes is they have unusual experiences (magical or religious beliefs, hallucinations, etc.). The literature review brought out that those who are considered to have "happy schizotypal" personality disorder would have hallucinations and other psychotic behavior. However, these episodes will be much shorter than in schizophrenic patients. Additionally, they also know that what they experienced was not real in distinction to the schizophrenia sufferer who believes hallucinations and delusions to be real.

Another class of hallucination that Carrier suggested as a possible candidate for the PRA of Jesus Christ was guilt induced hallucinations. He reasoned that Paul harbored intense feelings of guilt as he so doggedly persecuted the early Christian church. He also offered that Peter may have also harbored a guilty conscience after denying Jesus three times. However, after a survey of the scholarly literature on hallucinations was completed, guilt was not found to be a causal factor for hallucinations even though some of those experiencing hallucinations felt guilty in response to having a hallucination. Moreover, it was also pointed out by Christian apologists/scholars that the woman witnesses to the resurrected Jesus Christ were not feeling guilty before their experiences with Him.

Carrier also focused again on Paul and suggested that Paul's PRA of Jesus Christ may very well have been a seizure hallucination that was caused by an external stimulation such as a bright light. Another related claim made by Carrier is that Paul was extremely fatigued which then triggered a hallucination. However, it was brought out in the scholarly literature pertaining to these sorts of hallucinations that those who experience these hallucinations know shortly thereafter they are not real.

Regarding seizure hallucinations, the research coming from scholarly literature revealed that these hallucinations are physiologically based and are as a result of neural malfunctions or other brain disorders. Among the types of seizure related hallucinations that are experienced are flashes of colored light, ordinary objects changing size or shape, bright and colored spots, circles, and balls. In addition to these simple hallucinations, there were other types of hallucinations reported to include familiar forms or persons. Moreover, many people who suffer from this variety of hallucination report the main emotion associated with it is fear. In some instances, these hallucinations are also associated with feelings of ecstasy and may contain religious imagery. The literature review also described auditory hallucinations that come from this type of hallucination to include hearing loud voices, music, and echoes.

Other hallucination classifications discussed by Carrier as a possible explanation for the PRA of Jesus Christ were the categories of fatigue and deprivation related hallucinations. In the literature review for these two classifications, there was material that referred to them as pseudohallucinations. Furthermore, the longer a person goes without sleep, the more severe their hallucination will likely be. After experiencing sleeplessness over a long period of time, hallucinations may be experienced by persons who are normally mentally stable. However, it was brought out in the literature survey that a fatigue hallucination is brief and that the person experiencing it knows at some point what they observed is not real. Moreover, a person lacking sensory stimulation for a long period of time is likely to experience hallucinations due to the brain compensating for the deficit in one's environment. However, there was no positive evidence from the New Testament that the resurrection eyewitnesses were either sleep deprived, suffered from extreme fatigue, believed their experience with Jesus to be a hallucination/vision, or were in a location where they had a lack of sensory stimulation for an extended period of time.

Thus, the prolonged and repeated contact with Jesus Christ could not be fatigue/deprivation related hallucinations.

One of the types of hallucination disorders that Carrier did not mention as a possibility for the PRA of Jesus Christ were VHs stemming from CBS. These hallucinations were explored because of Carrier's overall claim that the disciples hallucinated the risen Jesus Christ. As stated in the scholarly literature review, CBS hallucinations are as a result of the patient losing their eyesight and the brain compensating for the lack of visual stimuli. Images generated by these hallucinations range from colors, shapes, patterns, and grids to distorted faces, letter strings, and vehicles. These VHs are experienced in a series from seconds to minutes in duration. However as time progresses, the frequency of the hallucinations will diminish. Furthermore, after experiencing these hallucinations, the sufferer will realize that the hallucinations are not real. When comparing the scholarly literature concerning CBS hallucinations with the New Testament resurrection accounts, it is obvious these hallucinatory manifestations caused by this syndrome could not account for what the resurrection witnesses experienced.

Another form of hallucination not mentioned by Carrier as a candidate for the PRA of the disciples is drug-induced hallucinations. As described in the scholarly literature on this subject, among the VHs experienced by those who use hallucinogenic drugs are geometric patterns, flashing facial images, the drug user becoming smaller, and emotions of fear. Still other drug-induced hallucinations that have been reported in scholarly literature are checkerboards, squares, grating, lattices, and tunnels. Additional hallucinatory phenomena reported by the survey include tactile hallucinations or bugs crawling under one's skin and also a loud noise that accompanies other VHs. It was also pointed out as in many other forms of hallucinations that most of those having these experiences understand they are not real even though there are those who are delusional during their hallucinatory experience. Although Carrier did not mention this strain of hallucination as a candidate, it is obvious that this sort of hallucination does not comport with the resurrection narratives after merely listing its characteristics.

One other hallucinatory phenomenon listed in the scholarly literature but not by Carrier are PTSD related hallucinations. These hallucinations are commonly known as "flashbacks," are multi-modal, and can include all of the senses. Not only are they re-experiences of previous emotional trauma, but they can also be separate and new episodes of related hallucinatory experiences as well. Moreover, not everyone who lives through a traumatic event will experience PTSD related hallucinations. Other qualities of PTSD hallucinations are they are normally experienced again and again over long periods of time and the re-experiencing of the original trauma is characterized by intense fear. Additionally, it was brought out in the literature review that PTSD related hallucinations are triggered by an event similar to the original trauma and are known by the sufferer not to be real. As pointed out by O'Collins, there is no evidence to support the notion that the disciples were victims of PTSD. Because of the divergence with the aforementioned criteria for a PTSD hallucination, the experiences of the resurrection witnesses with the risen Jesus Christ could not have been PTSD related hallucinations. Reasons supporting this include their limited duration, the lack of experiencing something similar to the original trauma, the experience of the risen Jesus Christ, and the resurrection witnesses believing their encounters were real.

Regarding the cross-examination of Carrier's "hallucinating disciples" contention, it was brought out generally that the resurrected Jesus Christ did not appear in a glorious form. Rather, his post-resurrection appearance was ordinary. Moreover, the literature from Christian scholars revealed that a vision of Jesus Christ does not explain the resurrection narratives that stubbornly persist in claiming that Jesus Christ arose from the dead. If the disciples/women were merely having visions of Jesus Christ, then why didn't they communicate that they were having visions instead of physical encounters? Also, those who were present when the alleged hallucination occurred can talk most hallucinators out of their hallucinations. Additionally, it was brought out by Christian scholars that the hallucinations of the disciples could not be interlocking as hallucinations are subjective experiences.

Continuing with the theme of the cross-examination of Carrier's claim of hallucinating disciples, Carrier's claim that hallucinations of Jesus Christ helped to reduce the stress of the disciples does not cohere with a reference that he used. Rather, the reference cited by Carrier stated that hallucinations could aid "patients." The authors he cited refer to mostly schizophrenic/psychotic patients and not normal people who may have a hallucination. Specifically regarding schizophrenic hallucinations, Christian scholars brought out that those who were schizophrenics would be deemed as demon possessed lunatics. Therefore, because of their condition, they would not be able to organize a group that would be able to have the fast and extensive expansion that occurred in the nascent Christian church.

Concerning the cross-examination of Carrier's contention that the experiences of the risen Jesus Christ were bereavement hallucinations, Christian scholars contended that the literature on bereavement hallucinations supports the notion that these experiences are not hallucinations. Rather, they are non-pathological visions often experienced by grieving relatives. Moreover, it was also brought out that not all of the disciples would have experienced these hallucinations at the same time if they were in fact PBHEs. Also noted in the scholarly literature review is the diversity and number of appearances that occurred over a small timeframe in the resurrection narratives are contrasted with the bereaved who may experience a sensory manifestation of a recently departed loved one for years. Furthermore, it was shown that individuals who report PBHEs never report as a group and they understand their departed loved one is not alive again. One other point brought out by Christian scholarly literature is that comparing the experiences of the risen Jesus Christ with those in the ancient world who had visions of the dead is not a good comparison. In these reports of visions from the past, those envisioned are dead persons. This is in contrast with the resurrected Jesus Christ who is described as being wholly alive.

In response to the cross-examination literature, Carrier countered that the disciples as a group hallucinated the risen Jesus Christ and those early Christians who heard these reports preached them as if they were the truth. Carrier also posits a variant to the aforementioned theory. Carrier suggested that a report of a hallucination/dream of Jesus Christ by one disciple would have infected the rest of the disciples. Furthermore, Carrier offered that the disciples would have had radical transformations because they would have believed that their hallucinations were real.

In response to Carrier's rejoinder, the literature survey of Christian scholars offered that there were no circumstances present that would have provided the proper environment for group hallucinations and that these sorts of hallucinations are not mentioned in the peer-reviewed literature. Other information offered countering the possibility of group hallucinations included that some who were present were not able to verify the apparition. Also in Acts chapter two, there were those present that also observed the unusual signs other than the disciples. These persons, many who were from other countries, were making observations with their senses and could understand the speech of the disciples in their own mother tongue.

Regarding the disciples' having the expectation of seeing the risen Jesus Christ, it was noted that this expectancy was lacking and that the disciples were not prepared to see a risen Messiah. Furthermore, the risen Jesus Christ appeared to more than one group and also to individuals as well. These appearances were ordinary and not spectacular in any way. This lack of expectation was borne out by Thomas who did not believe the report of the disciples until he experienced the risen Jesus Christ himself. Moreover, the disciples believed Jesus Christ to be dead and were shocked when they heard that he had arisen.

In addition to the cross-examination of Carrier's contentions, evidence against Carrier's contentions was also extracted from the literature review as well. Evidence for the corporeity of the risen Jesus Christ was taken from the resurrection narratives. Two types of evidence coming from the Gospels include the reactions of the disciples upon encountering the resurrected Jesus, and evidence of His "touchability" as well. The reactions of the disciples span from fear/unbelief to joy/belief. There are many examples of how the risen Jesus Christ handled food, was able to be grasped, and was visually recognized when encountered. Moreover, the confession of Thomas is a powerful affirmation of the risen Jesus Christ in bodily form due to his skepticism. In Acts, Paul discusses that his encounter with the risen Jesus Christ was valid because he had experienced the risen Jesus Christ just as the other disciples had. Additionally, it was noted that those who accompanied "Saul" also saw the light and heard the voice of Jesus Christ. Moreover, material from the survey also pointed out that the language used to describe Jesus Christ as arisen from the dead demonstrated he was not encountered in some sort of vision. Rather, 1 Corinthians chapter fifteen describes that the risen Jesus Christ was observed "at one time" by 500 persons. Moreover, the wording of certain passages in 1 Corinthians chapter fifteen leaves no doubt that Jesus Christ had physically arisen from the dead.

In addition to this evidence, other evidence was also presented that most of the disciples who were eyewitnesses to the resurrection experienced martyrdom for being followers of Jesus Christ. Evidence was presented that Paul, Peter, James, and Thomas were eventually martyred for their faith. Various sources were offered giving evidence that these four were killed because of their Christian testimony. Sources for the martyrdom of the aforementioned four Christians leaders come from the writings of early church fathers, from New Testament Scripture, and from secular sources that mention these historical characters. In relation to Thomas, there are sources from India that show that he is recognized as the first Christian evangelist in India and that his martyrdom occurred there when four spears were thrust into him by order of Misdaeus. Moreover, the death of James is included within the writings of Josephus *et al.* It is reported that James was thrown off of the temple and that he was stoned after he landed on the ground. Also, it is believed that Peter and Paul were martyred in Rome in the same general timeframe.

Summary, Findings, and Conclusion

Another line of circumstantial evidence developed from the literature survey were the conversions of James and Paul who are both observed in Scripture to be skeptics in regard to Jesus being the Christ. Moreover, as aforementioned earlier, Paul was more than "just opposed" to the early Christian movement before his conversion. He was also an ardent foe of the early Christian church. Furthermore, being the half-brother of Jesus, James would not have believed that his brother was the Messiah unless he had compelling evidence for it. It was also brought out that Paul corroborated his own experience of the risen Jesus Christ with James (and Peter) when he traveled to Jerusalem.

An additional line of circumstantial evidence that was observed in the literature review is the combination of the evidence for the empty tomb with the post-resurrection appearances. The corroborative nature of both lines of evidence strengthens the case for the veracity of the resurrection of Jesus Christ (FPJI 1.07(5); FPJI 1.05 weighing the evidence). If only one of these lines stood alone, then there would be reason to question whether the event of the resurrection of Jesus Christ really occurred in space and time. Moreover, it was observed that the empty tomb is a necessary condition for the PRA of Jesus Christ.

5.2 Evidentiary findings

5.2.1 Evidentiary findings: Contradictory resurrection narratives

In section 2.8.2, an analysis of Carrier's claim of "contradictory resurrection narratives" was conducted by analyzing his writings and comparing them to the exposited accepted principles of evidence, the New Testament resurrection narratives themselves, and also the relevant scholarly literature. After conducting this analysis, it is clear that Carrier falls afoul of many different accepted principles of evidence. One occasion where Carrier ignores FRE 607/608 is when he does not follow the proper procedure when he impeaches the Gospel evangelists by way of contradictory statements. In doing this properly, he would have to impeach each individual writer as to prior inconsistent statements that he had written. But Carrier fails to do this. Rather, he attempts to impeach the Gospel evangelists as a group and this is improper as only differences in the statements of one witness can be brought up later against that same witness.

Additionally, Carrier does not use evidence that is based upon facts that are supported by proof (104(b)) or that are relevant (401) to this inquiry. In addition to the lack of 104(b) and 401 evidence, Carrier also does not provide any direct evidence from historical witnesses (contra FPJI 1.06), any testimony derived from the sensory perceptions of a historical witness (contra FRE 602), and utilizes no corroborative evidence (contra FPJI 1.07(5)) to further strengthen his suppositions. Furthermore, Carrier does not successfully attack the credibility of the Gospel witnesses because he does not prove they have the motive to lie or slant their testimony (contra FRE 607/608). Additionally, in criterion #5 of section 1.07 of the FPJI, it discusses that two honest persons may describe the same event differently. Thus, Carrier's contention of contradictory resurrection narratives falls afoul of all of the above-mentioned principles of evidence.

As the evidentiary analysis continued, it was noted that the Gospel of John is in accord with accepted principles of evidence as John not only writes much of what he observed with his senses (FRE 602) but he is also included within the action of the narrative itself. Other federal rules of evidence that undergird John's written testimony are FRE 401a and 401b as the testimony from the Gospel of John is relevant in determining the matter under discussion and tends to make the conclusion that Jesus Christ had arisen from the dead "more probable." Other principles of evidence that support John's narrative are FRE 104(b) and FRE 602 as it is based on facts observed by his senses (empty tomb, PRA Jesus Christ), and because it is not impeached by the testimony of others (FRE 607 and 608). Moreover, as adduced above, the Book of John could be presented as evidence based on the hearsay exclusion listed in 803(16) and supported by FRE 901b(8).

In addition to the FRE, John's resurrection narrative is also supported by FPJI 1.06 (direct evidence and circumstantial evidence). In addition to the gospel of John, the Gospels of Mark, Luke, and Matthew are also supported by accepted principles of evidence contained within the FRE and FPJI. Mark's Gospel was shown to be in accord with FRE 401 (relevant evidence), and FRE 104b (based on facts undergirded by proof). It would also be supported by FRE 803(16) as it could be considered as excepted testimony as well. In addition to Mark, Matthew's Gospel was shown to be in accord with FRE 401, FRE104b, and FRE 602 (testimony based on sensory perception). As in the case of the all of the Gospels, Matthew was shown to be in accord with FRE 803(16). Luke's Gospel was noted to be in accord with FRE 401, FRE 104(b), FPJI 1.07 (credibility of the witness-corroboration), and with FRE 803(16).

5.2.2 Evidentiary findings: Antecedent dying/rising gods and Jesus Christ

In conducting an evidentiary analysis of Carrier's contention of a linkage between mystery religions and the Christian notion of the resurrection of Jesus Christ, generally, it was noted that Carrier does not offer any relevant evidence (401) to support his claim. Moreover, he offers no historical testimony that there was a pass down from one of these pagan cults to Christianity even though he offers historical writings that describe the beliefs and activities of various pagan cult groups. In addition to a lack of support from *FRE* 401, it is also observed that there is no support from other accepted principles of evidence to include *FRE* 602 (no historical testimony based on the senses), and moreover no evidence from *FRE* 104(b) as there are no facts to support his central thesis, but merely speculation. Furthermore, Carrier does not properly impeach the New Testament witnesses, as he offers no historical testimony they were criminals, were dishonest, or had any motives to falsify their testimony (*FRE* 607 and 608).

Specifically concerning Carrier's contention that Paul himself was influenced by the mystery cults, Carrier offers no historical witnesses (*FRE* 602-sensory observations; FPJI 106-direct evidence) who note Paul conferring with any pagan devotees. Rather, what is observed in Paul's letters is his condemnation of pagan worship. Moreover, it was shown that Carrier relies upon supposed correlations between antecedent pagan cults and Christianity. However, as explained before, relying upon these correlations without specific evidence is based on fallacious reasoning (false cause and *post hoc ergo propter hoc*).

Pertaining to Carrier's specific claim that the Christian conception of the resurrection of Jesus Christ came from the Osirian myth, Carrier's claims fell afoul of several evidentiary principles. Carrier offered no historical witnesses/literature where a "handoff" was observed from Osirian devotees to early Christians (contra *FRE* 602, FPJI 1.06-direct evidence, FPJI 1.07(5)-corroboration) or even any intermingling of the two groups. Because Carrier does not provide evidence of a "handoff" of Osirianism from cultists to the early Christians, the evidence he provides does not qualify as relevant evidence (*contra FRE* 401). Moreover, because he does not properly deal with the related scholarly literature and New Testament resurrection accounts, the fact that he uses are not supported by proof (*contra FRE* 104(b)). Furthermore, an analysis of the Osirian myth revealed mostly contrasts and few valid comparisons with the life, death, and resurrection of Jesus Christ. Because of the lack of actual evidence for his position, little weight should be granted to the evidence that he provides (in accord with FPJI 1.05 weighing the evidence).

Moreover, an evidentiary analysis was also completed on Carrier's claim regarding Christianity borrowing from mystery cults, to include Inanna/Ishtar. In examining Carrier's claim regarding Inanna, it was observed that Carrier did not provide any relevant evidence (*FRE* 401) to substantiate his claim, as he produced no evidence (contra *FRE* 602 and FPJI 1.06) of any followers of Inanna/Ishtar and followers of Jesus Christ meeting. Concerning the evidentiary analysis of the cult of Zalmoxis, Carrier offers no relevant evidence (contra *FRE* 401) that is based upon the observational testimony of any witness (contra *FRE* 602 and FPJI 1.06) that Zalmoxis died and then arose from the dead. Furthermore, Carrier's claims regarding Zalmoxis/Inanna in comparison to Jesus Christ do not align with New Testament Scripture or the exposition of scholarly literature. Therefore, the information that he relies upon to support his claims are not supported by facts undergirded by proof (contra *FRE* 104(b)), and should not be given much weight (contra FPJI 1.05 weighing the evidence).

Additionally, the evidentiary analysis of Carrier's claim regarding Romulus and Jesus Christ showed there was no corroboration of the risen Romulus (contra FPJI 1.07 Criterion number 5), and that there were no historical witnesses who observed a "hand-off" of any Romulan notions of resurrection to early Christians (*FRE* 401,104(b), 602, FPJI 1.06). Furthermore, even though the name of Julius Proculus is mentioned in the Romulan legend, there are no known historical witnesses who give testimony from antiquity regarding the events of the life of Romulus. As mentioned before, there are only various versions of the legend that come to us through writers with no nexus to the actual events of the legends themselves.

5.2.3 Evidentiary findings: The disciples hallucinated the risen Jesus Christ

In addition to the aforementioned analyses, an evidentiary analysis was also completed to determine if Carrier's contention that the disciples hallucinated the risen Jesus Christ was based upon accepted principles of evidence. Regarding hypnagogic/hypnopompic hallucinations, Carrier's contention does not accord with either the resurrection narratives or with descriptions from the scholarly literature. Also, this variety of hallucination is not believed by the hallucinator to be a real event. Because of the incongruity between the materials coming from the scholarly review as well as from the narratives themselves, Carrier's contention is not in

Summary, Findings, and Conclusion

accord with FRE 104(b). Also, Carrier offers no historical direct/indirect evidence or any corroboration for his perspective (*contra* FRE 602, FPJI 1.06-direct/circumstantial evidence and 1.07(5)-corroboration).

In regard to schizophrenic hallucinations, Carrier's claim did not cohere with the literature review on this variety of hallucination nor did it comport with the resurrection narratives as well. Therefore, his evidence is not in accord with FRE 401 even though he purports to accurately handle both the related New Testament Scriptures and the scholarly literature. Also, his claim in this regard is not in accord with FRE 104(b) as he misconstrues both the resurrection narratives and the scholarly literature. Moreover, Carrier offers no witnesses that the disciples were schizophrenic patients (*contra* FRE 602, FPJI 1.07(5) and FPJI 1.06). Furthermore, the evidentiary analysis revealed that Carrier's theory of "happy schizotypal" disciples did not cohere with FRE 104(b) as his facts do not match up with the New Testament accounts/scholarly literature.

Pertaining to the evidentiary analysis of Carrier's contention regarding bereavement hallucinations, it was determined that Carrier's claim did not cohere with FRE 104(b) as he does not provide proof for the facts that he offers and also because he does not inform us of any historical witnesses that he uses (*contra* FRE 602, FPJI 1.07(5), and FPJI 1.06). In regard to seizure related hallucinations, again, because of the lack of proof relating the facts from the resurrection narratives to the scholarly material, his contention is not in accord with the aforementioned accepted principles of evidence (*contra* 104(b), 602, FPJI 1.07(5) and FPJI 1.06). Moreover, Carrier's claim of guilt-ridden witnesses having hallucinations does not correspond with either the scholarly literature or the resurrection narratives. Because of this disparity, his facts do not align with FRE 104(b) as they are not based upon facts undergirded by proof. Furthermore, the scholarly literature review revealed no instances where guilt was the cause of a hallucination.

Regarding the evidence offered against Carrier's contentions, it was noted that this evidence was in alignment with accepted principles of evidence as they matched up with the resurrection narratives and were relevant to the inquiry (FRE 401 and FRE 104(b)). Moreover, this evidence was based upon historical eyewitnesses (PRA of Jesus Christ bodily in nature) and was supported not only by FPJI 1.06 (direct evidence testimony), but also by FRE 602 (testimony based upon the senses). Regarding the evidence that was circumstantial in nature (disciples martyred for their faith in Jesus Christ, the PRA corroborated by the empty tomb, the conversions of James and Saul) this evidence is supported by FPJI 1.06 (circumstantial or indirect evidence) and is also corroborative in nature (FPJI 1.07(5)).

5.3 Research limitations

In utilizing accepted principles of evidence as criteria to measure the quality and strength of evidence, it is noted that these principles of evidence are not always able to determine whether a proposition is in fact true or false. For instance, someone could claim that his or her ancient ancestor was the Frankish king, Charlemagne. It could be that this claim is in fact true even though the person may have only scant evidence at best for this claim. It is also observed that accepted principles of evidence do not assist in making religious truth claims. For example, the proposition "Islam is the right religion for me" cannot be substantiated by accepted principles of evidence as these principles do not apply to subjective matters of value and meaning. However, utilizing accepted principles of evidence could allow an investigator to analyze core historical claims of Islam to determine the level of evidentiary support for them.

Relatedly, another limitation to the above research methodology is that it necessarily involves matters that are tethered to the space-time continuum. Utilizing accepted principles of evidence to analyze experiential claims is not within the parameters of its use. For instance, the statement "I love the experience of driving my 1970 Ford Mustang more than anything else" would not be a proposition that would lend itself to an analysis by accepted principles of evidence because of the lack of objectivity of the claim and also because there is no space-time nexus in the content of the claim. However, utilizing accepted principles of evidence is probative when dealing with a proposition that is alleged to have occurred in space/time or that is connected to space-time events. For instance, even though the proposition "the New Testament resurrection narratives are contradictory" is evaluative in nature and not directly related to a space-time event, the data from the resurrection narratives is related to alleged space-time events. Therefore, because of the indirect connection of the aforementioned proposition to the events of the resurrection, utilizing accepted principles of evidence in investigating this topic is appropriate.

Another limitation observed is that analysis by accepted principles of evidence cannot prove "beyond a reasonable doubt" that a historical event occurred. Because the present research topic is centered on an event that is historical in nature (the resurrection of Jesus Christ) where no actual living witnesses can be interviewed or questioned, this precludes being able to make such a determination. However, the use of accepted principles of evidence is probative in noting whether there is evidentiary support for a historical claim, and also aids in judging the strength as well as the quality of evidence that undergirds a particular historical claim.

In addition to the aforementioned research limitations, there are some scholars who may perceive weakness in the methodology of this research project. Perhaps, the methodology does not consider the whole spectrum of skeptical challenges to the veracity of the resurrection of Jesus Christ. Perhaps, skeptical authors other than Richard Carrier do utilize sound evidentiary concepts in their research? In response to this possible critique of the present research project, it is noted that it was not conducted in order to explore every facet of skeptical challenges on this topic. Therefore, the views of Islamic apologists or those from other atheist/skeptical scholars on the resurrection of Jesus Christ were not fully developed. Rather, the research project was initiated in order to investigate a particular well-known author's perspective and the evidentiary foundations upon which his theses rested. By only investigating one scholar's perspective, it is believed that this limited range of investigation actually increases the ability to explicate these accepted principles of evidence. If the claims of numerous skeptical perspectives were developed in one project, then it would be more difficult to demonstrate the efficacy of the aforementioned principles. Moreover, having such a broad investigative scope would dilute the strength of the research in developing a clearly defined thesis statement pertaining to evidentiary considerations. Even though the focus of the research is limited, it is believed that this narrow evidentiary focus can be expanded in subsequent research.

5.4 Recommendations

1) Further research is needed concerning Carrier's assertion that Mark was written as a myth. Is the Gospel of Mark a myth or was it written with the aim of communicating actual historical events that involved actual persons? When Carrier makes this assertion, does he utilize any accepted principles of evidence in his research on this topic?

2) Another area in which further exploration is needed is regarding Marian apparitions. Concerning these apparitions, are the details of the experience of the apparition identical among the different witnesses in a single event? Have updated interviews been conducted of these witnesses? If so, have their version of the events changed at all?

3) Another area where further research is needed is in regard to the numerous candidates that Carrier offers for the precursor of the resurrected Jesus Christ. Does the fact that Carrier utilizes so many "dying and rising" gods help him or does it actually work against his contention? Are there accepted legal principles that would apply in the instance of offering so many alternate theories?

4) Relatedly, does the fact that Carrier has many candidates for the type of hallucination that the disciples experienced work against his overall contention? It would be helpful to explore whether offering numerous candidates are in accord with accepted principles of evidence.

5) Another recommendation is to expand the use of these accepted principles of evidence to other scholars. There are many authors who have given their opinions on certain aspects of the New Testament books. It would be probative to analyze the writings of these authors by accepted principles of evidence as well in order to gauge the strength of the evidence they rely upon.

6) In addition to utilizing these accepted principles of evidence to analyze the writings of various authors, it would also be a good use of these principles to analyze the key historical claims of other religious systems in order to assess their evidentiary strength.

Bibliography

Abbott, Jacob. 2015. Romulus [Kindle. ed.]. New York City: Palatine Press. Available: http://www.amazon.com

Abogunrin, S.O. 1981. The language and nature of the resurrection of Jesus Christ in the New Testament. Journal Of The Evangelical Theological Society, 24,1:p. 55-65.

Aleman, A. & Laroi, A. 2008. Hallucinations: the science of idiosyncratic perception. Washington: American Psychological Association.

Allen, J.P. 2005. The ancient Egyptian pyramid texts, Manuelian, P.D., *ed*. Translated with an introduction and notes by J.P. Allen. Atlanta: Society of biblical literature.

Amazon.com. Carrier's books. https://www.amazon.com/s/ref=nb_sb_noss?url=search-alias%3Dstripbooks&field-keywords=Richard+Carrier%27s+Books&rh=n%3A283155%2Ck%3ARichard+Carrier%27s+Books. Date of access: 3 January 2017.

Anderson, N. 1973. A lawyer among theologians. London: Hodder and Stoughton.

Anderson, N. 1985. Jesus Christ the witness of history. Downer's Grove: Intervarsity Press.

Angus, S. 1928. The mystery religions and Christianity: a study in the religious background of early Christianity. New York: Charles Scribner's Sons.

Anon. s.a. The Muratorian fragment. (*In* The faith of the early fathers, vol. 1. Translated by William Jurgens. 1970. Collegeville: The Liturgical Press. p. 107-108).

Apulieus, L. 2014. The golden asse [Kindle ed.]. Translated by W. Addington. London: Heritage Illustrated Publishing. Available: http://www.amazon.com

Arens, A. M. 2015. Trauma management therapy for a veteran with co-occurring combat PTSD and hallucinations: A case study. Clinical Case Studies, 14(2):115-128.

Asaad, G. 1990. Hallucinations in clinical psychiatry: a guide for mental health professionals. Brunner/Mazel Publishers: New York.

Assman, J. 2001. The search for god in ancient Egypt. Ithaca: Cornell University Press.

Assman, J. 2005. Death and salvation in ancient Egypt. Translated from the German by D. Lorton. Ithaca: Cornell University Press.

Baehr, J. A priori and a posteriori. (*In* Dowden, J. & Fieser, J., eds. The internet encyclopedia of philosophy). http://www.iep.utm.edu/apriori/#H1 Date of access: 9 June 2016.

Baggett, D. 2009. A conversation with Gary Habermas and Antony Flew: Did the resurrection happen? Downer's Grove: IVP Books.

Bauckham, R. s.a. The women at the tomb: The credibility of their story. http://richardbauckham.co.uk/uploads/Accessible/The%20Women%20&%20the%20Resurrection.pdf Date of access: 22 April 2015.

Bauckham, R. 2006. Jesus and the eyewitnesses-the Gospels as eyewitness testimony. Grand Rapids: William Eerdmans.

Bauckham, R. 2009. The eyewitnesses in the gospel of Mark. Svensk Exegetisk Årsbok, 74:19-39.

Begley, S., Underwood, A., Springen, K., & Gesalman, A. 2002. The schizophrenic mind. (*In* Newsweek 139, no. 10: 44, Academic Search Premier, EBSCOhost. Date of access 13 March 2014).

Bennett, P. 2011. Abnormal and clinical psychology: an introductory textbook. Maidenhead: Open University Press.

Benson, J. 1839. Benson's Commentary, Vol. 4. *http://biblehub.com/commentaries/matthew/28-9.htm*. Date of access: 9 June 2016.

Bergeron, J. & Habermas, G. 2015. The resurrection of Jesus: a clinical review of psychiatric hypotheses for the biblical story of Easter. Irish Theological Quarterly, Vol. 80(2) 157-172.

Bianchi, U., Horewitz, R., & Girardot, K. S. 1971. Dualistic aspects of Thracian religion. History of Religions, 228-233.

Bible. Carson, D.A., ed. 2015. The NIV Zondervan study Bible. Grand Rapids: Zondervan.

Binder, F.W. 1983. Hearsay handbook. 2nd ed. Colorado Springs: Shepard's/McGraw-Hill, 1983.

Black, D.A. & Lea, T.D. 2003. The New Testament: its background and message. Nashville: B & H Academic.

Blomberg, C.L.1994. The NIV application commentary, 1 corinthians, Muck.T., ed. Grand Rapids: Zondervan.

Blomberg, C. L. 2000. The Jesus of history or the Christ of faith. (*In* Copan, P., ed. Will the real Jesus please stand up?: A debate between William Lane Craig and John Dominic Crossan. Grand Rapids: Baker Books. p. 102).

Bock, D. 1996. The NIV application commentary: Luke. Grand Rapids: Zondervan Publishing House.

Bock, D.L. 2012. A theology of Luke and Acts. Grand Rapids: Zondervan.

Boice, J.M. 2001. The gospel of Matthew, volume I, The king and his kingdom: Matthew 1-17. Grand Rapids: Baker Books.

Bottero, J. 1992. Mesopotamia: Writing, reasoning, and the gods. Chicago: The University of Chicago Press.

Brisson, E. C. 2011. Between Text & Sermon: Matthew 28: 1-10. Interpretation, 65(1):72-74.

Brown R.E. 1994. The death of the Messiah: a commentary on the passion narratives in the four gospels, the anchor bible reference library, vol. 2. New York, London, Toronto, Sydney, Auckland: Doubleday.

Bruce, F.F. 1988. The canon of scripture. Downer's Grove: IVP Academic.

Bruce, F.F. 2000. Paul: Apostle of the heart set free. Grand Rapids: William B. Eerdmans Publishing Company.

Bruckberger, R.L. 1965. The history of Jesus Christ. New York: Viking Press.

Bryan, C. 2011. The resurrection of the Messiah. Oxford: Oxford University Press.

Budge, E.A.W. 1934. From fetish to god in ancient Egypt. London: Oxford University Press.

Budge, E.A.W. 2002. Osiris and the Egyptian religion of resurrection. London: Kegan Paul.

Bunson, M. 2012. Encyclopedia of Ancient Egypt. New York: Facts on File, Inc.

Burge, G.M., 2000. The NIV application commentary: John, Muck. T., *ed.* Grand Rapids: Zondervan.

Cambridge Dictionaries Online [Web]. 2015. Contradiction. http://dictionary.cambridge.org/dictionary/english/contradiction Date of access: 5 November 2015.

Carandini. A. 2011. Rome: Day one. Translated by S. Sartarelli. Princeton: Princeton University Press.

Carrier, R. 1999, 2005. Craig's empty tomb & Habermas on Visions. http://infidels.org/library/modern/richard_carrier/indef/4e.html. Date of access: 3 May 2016.

Carrier, R. 2005a. The spiritual body of Christ and the legend of the empty tomb. (*In* Lowder J.J. & Price, R.M., *eds*. The empty tomb: Jesus beyond the grave [Kindle ed]: ch. 5. Prometheus Books: Amherst). Available: http://www.amazon.com

Carrier, R. 2005b. The plausibility of theft. (*In* Lowder J.J. & Price, R.M., *eds*. The empty tomb: Jesus beyond the grave [Kindle ed.]: ch. 9. Prometheus Books: Amherst). Available: http://www.amazon.com

Carrier, R. 2005c. The burial of Jesus in the light of Jewish law. (*In* Lowder J.J. & Price, R.M., *eds*. The empty tomb: Jesus beyond the grave [Kindle ed.]: ch. 5. Prometheus Books: Amherst). Available: http://www.amazon.com

Carrier, R. 2006a. Stephen Davis gets it wrong. http://www.richardcarrier.info/Carrier--ReplyToDavis.html Date of access: 5 June 2015.

Carrier, R. 2006b. The problem of Luke's methods as a historian (*In* Was Christianity too improbable to be false?:7.3). http://infidels.org/library/modern/richard_carrier/improbable/disproof.html#7.3 Date of access: 10 October 2015.

Carrier, R. 2006c. Wanchick's case is insufficient (*In* Naturalism vs. theism: the Carrier-Wanchick debate). http://infidels.org/library/modern/richard_carrier/carrier-wanchick/carrier2.html. Date of access: 15 April 2016.

Carrier, R. 2006d. Why I don't buy the resurrection story: General case for spiritual resurrection. http://infidels.org/library/modern/richard_carrier/resurrection/3.html Date of access: 7 May 2016.

Carrier, R. 2006e. Why I don't buy the resurrection story: Main argument. https://infidels.org/library/modern/richard_carrier/resurrection/lecture.html Date of access: 18 March 2015.

Carrier, R. 2006f. Why I don't buy the resurrection story: probability of survival vs. miracle: assessing the odds. http://infidels.org/library/modern/richard_carrier/resurrection/2.html Date of access: 30 April 2016.

Carrier, R. 2006g. Why I don't buy the resurrection story: rebutting lesser arguments https://infidels.org/library/modern/richard_carrier/resurrection/4.html Date of access: 7 May 2016.

Carrier, R. 2009. Not the impossible faith: Why Christianity didn't need a miracle to succeed [Kindle ed.]. Published by Lulu.com. Available: http://www.amazon.com

Carrier, R. 2010. Why the resurrection is unbelievable. (*In* Loftus, J.W., *ed*. The Christian delusion: why faith fails. Amherst: Prometheus Books. p. 291-315).

Carrier, R. 2013. How not to defend historicity (*In* Price, P & Zindler, F., *eds*. Bart Ehrman and the quest of the historical Jesus of Nazareth [Kindle ed.]: ch.2. Cranford: American Atheist Press).

Carrier, R. 2014a. Hitler, Homer, Bible, Christ: the historical papers of Richard Carrier 1995-2013 [Kindle ed.]. Richmond: Philosophy Press. Available: http://www.amazon.com

Carrier, R. 2014b. On the historicity of Jesus: why we might have reason to doubt [Kindle ed.]. Sheffield: Sheffield University Press. Available: http://www.amazon.com

Carrier, Richard. 2016. Richard Carrier blogs. http://www.richardcarrier.info. Date of access: 3 January 2017.

Carson, D.A. & Moo, D. J. 2005. An Introduction to the New Testament. Grand Rapids: Zondervan.

Casteel, Herbert C. 1990. Beyond a Reasonable Doubt. Joplin: College Press Publishing Company.

Castelnovo, A., Cavallotti, S., Gambini, O., & D'Agostino, A. 2015. Post-bereavement hallucinatory experiences: A critical overview of population and clinical studies. Journal of affective disorders, 186:266-274.

Chalmers, Thomas. 1816. The evidence and authority of the Christian revelation. Hartford: Sheldon and Goodrich. https://archive.org/details/evidenceauthorit01chal Date of access: 23 April 2015.

Cicero, Marcus. 1829. Republic of Cicero [Kindle ed.]. Translated by G.W. Featherstonaugh. New York: G. & C. Carvill. Available: http://www.amazon.com

Clemen, C. 1912. Primitive Christianity and its non-Jewish sources. Translated by R.G. Nisbet. Edinburgh: T. & T. Clark.

Clement. s.a. Letter to the corinthians. (*In* The faith of the early fathers, vol. 1. Translated by William Jurgens. 1970. Collegeville: The Liturgical Press. p. 6-12).

Clifford R. 2004. John Warwick Montgomery's legal apologetic: an apologetic for all seasons. Bonn: Culture and Science Publ.

Clifford, R. & Johnson, P. 2012. The cross is not enough. Grand Rapids: Baker Books.

Cooney, K. M. 2010. Gender transformation in death: a case study of coffins from ramesside period Egypt. Near Eastern Archaeology:224-237.

Colson, Charles. 1996. Loving God. Grand Rapids: Zondervan Publishing House.

Constantineanu, C. 2010. The social significance of reconciliation in Paul's theology: narrative readings in Romans. London: T & T Clark.

Cornell University Law School Legal Information Institute. Cross-examination. https://www.law.cornell.edu/wex/cross-examination Date of access: 2 September 2016.

Cornell University Law School Legal Information Institute. Federal rules of evidence. https://www.law.cornell.edu/rules/fre Date of access: 4 June 2015.

Cornell University Law School Legal Information Institute. FRE 102. https://www.law.cornell.edu/rules/fre/rule_102. 4 June 2015.

Cornell University Law School Legal Information Institute. FRE 104. https://www.law.cornell.edu/rules/fre/rule_104. 4 June 2015.

Cornell University Law School Legal Information Institute. FRE 401. https://www.law.cornell.edu/rules/fre/rule_401. 4 June 2015.

Cornell University Law School Legal Information Institute. FRE 602. https://www.law.cornell.edu/rules/fre/rule_602. 4 June 2015.

Cornell University Law School Legal Information Institute. FRE 607. https://www.law.cornell.edu/rules/fre/rule_607. 4 June 2015.

Cornell University Law School Legal Information Institute. FRE 610. https://www.law.cornell.edu/rules/fre/rule_610. 4 June 2015.

Cornell University Law School Legal Information Institute. FRE 802. https://www.law.cornell.edu/rules/fre/rule_802. 4 June 2015.

Cornell University Law School Legal Information Institute. FRE 803. https://www.law.cornell.edu/rules/fre/rule_803. 4 June 2015.

Cornell University Law School Legal Information Institute. FRE 1004. https://www.law.cornell.edu/rules/fre/rule_1004. 4 June 2015.

Cornell University Law School Legal Information Institute. Redirect examination. https://www.law.cornell.edu/wex/redirect_examination Date of access: 5 September 2016.

Cornell University Law School Legal Information Institute. *Res Ipsa Loquitor.* https://www.law.cornell.edu/wex/res_ipsa_loquitur Date of Access: 6 January 2017.

Cosmopoulos, M.B. 2003. The archaeology and ritual of ancient Greek secret cults. New York: Routledge.

Craig, W. L. 1989. On doubts about the resurrection. Modern Theology, 6(1):53-75.

Craig, W.L. 1997a. The empty tomb of Jesus. (*In* Geivett, R.D. & Habermas, G.R., eds. In defense of miracles. Downer's Grove: IVP Academic).

Craig, W,L. 1997b. John Dominic Crossan on the resurrection of Jesus. (*In* Davis, S., Kendall, D. &

O'Collins, G., *eds*. The resurrection: an interdisciplinary symposium on the resurrection of Jesus. Oxford: Oxford University Press. p. 249-271).

Craig, W.L. 2000. Closing responses (*In* Copan, P. and Tacelli, R.K., *eds*. Jesus' Resurrection: Fact or Figment? A Debate between William Lane Craig and Gerd Lüdemann. Downers Grove: InterVarsity Press. p. 190-192).

Craig, W.L. 2006. Wright and Crossan on the historicity of the resurrection of Jesus (*In* Stewart, R.B., *ed*. The resurrection of Jesus: John Dominic Crossan and N.T. Wright in dialogue. Minneapolis: Fortress Press. 138-148).

Craig, W. L. 2008. Reasonable faith: Christian truth and apologetics. Wheaton: Crossway.

Craigie, P. C. 2007. Idolatry (*In* Elwell, W., *ed*. Evangelical Dictionary of Theology. 2nd ed. Grand Rapids: Baker Academic. 588-589).

Cromhout, M. 2011. Resurrection in Paul as both affirmation and challenge to the Israelite cycle of meaning. Neotestamentica, 45(1):29–48.

Culianu, I.P. & Poghirc, C. 2005. Zalmoxis (*In* Jones, L., *ed*. Encyclopedia of Religion Vol 14, 2nd ed. Detroit: McMillan Reference USA).

Dana, D. 1999/2000. Zalmoxis in Christian context. Ephemeris Napocensis:275-305.

David, R. 1998. The ancient Egyptians: beliefs and practices. Portland: Sussex Academic Press.

Davis, S.T. 1997. "Seeing" the risen Jesus (*In* Davis, S.T., Kendall, D. & O'Collins, G., *eds*. The resurrection: an interdisciplinary symposium on the resurrection of Jesus. New York: Oxford University Press. p. 126-47).

Davies. W.D. 1948. Some rabbinic elements in Pauline theology. London: SPCK.

Dionysius. 2015. The roman antiquities of Dionysius of Halicarnassus [Kindle ed.]. Translated by E. Cary. London: Aeterna Press. Available: http://www.amazon.com

Dowden, B. Fallacies: post hoc. Internet Encyclopedia of Philosophy. http://www.iep.utm.edu/fallacy/#PostHoc Date of access: 29 January 2016.

Doyle, J.M., Dysart J. & Loftis, E. 2013. Eyewitness testimony: civil and criminal, fifth ed. New Providence: Matthew Bender.

Dunand F. & Zivie-Coche, C. 2002. Gods and Men in Egypt: 3000 BCE to 395 CE. Translated by David Lorton. Ithaca: Cornell University Press.

Dunn, J.D.G. 1975 Jesus and the spirit. London: SCM Press.

Dunn, J.D.G. 2003. Jesus remembered. Grand Rapids: William B. Eerdmans.

Ehrman, B. 2012. Did Jesus exist?: The historical problem argument for Jesus of Nazareth [Kindle ed.]. New York: HarperOne.

Eliade, M. 1972. Zalmoxis, the vanishing god: Comparative studies in the religions and folklore of Dacia and Eastern Europe. Chicago: The University of Chicago Press.

Elliott, B., Joyce, E., & Shorvon, S. 2009. Delusions, illusions and hallucinations: 1. elementary phenomena in Epilepsy research:, Vol. 85:162-171.

Elliott, B., Joyce, E., & Shorvon, S. 2009b. Delusions, illusions and hallucinations: 2. Complex phenomena and psychosis. Epilepsy research, Vol. 85:172-186.

Encyclopaedia Britannica. s.a. Antioch: Modern and ancient south-central. http://www.britannica.com/place/Antioch-modern-and-ancient-city-south-central-Turkey Date of access: 14 June 2016.

Encyclopaedia Britannica. s.a. Ephesus: ancient city, Turkey. http://www.britannica.com/place/Ephesus Date of access: 14 June 2016.

Encyclopaedia Britannica. s.a. Saint Ignatius of Antioch: Syrian bishop. http://www.britannica.com/biography/Saint-Ignatius-of-Antioch Date of access: 14 June 2016.

Epstein, R., Kalus, C., & Berger, M. 2006. The continuing bond of the bereaved towards the deceased and adjustment to loss. Mortality, 11(3):253-269.

Erickson, M.J. 2007. Christian Theology, 2nd Ed. Grand Rapids: Baker Academic.

Eusebius. s.a.(a). History of the church, bk. 3, ch. 39. (In The faith of the early fathers, vol. 1. Translated by William Jurgens. 1970. Collegeville: The Liturgical Press. p. 38-39).

Eusebius. s.a.(b). Fragment in Eusebius, History of the church, bk. 6, ch. 14. (In The faith of the early fathers, vol. 1. Translated by WIlliam Jurgens. 1970. Collegeville: The Liturgical Press. p. 188).

Eusebius. s.a.(c) The ecclesiastical history [Kindle ed.]. Translated by K. Lake. London: Aeterna Press. Available at: http://www.amazon.com

Evans, C. A. 2008. The implications of eyewitness tradition. Journal for The Study Of The New Testament, 31(2):211-219.

Ewen, P.B. 1999. Faith on trial. Nashville: Broadman and Holman.

Feder, Y. 2013. The aniconic tradition, Deuteronomy 4, and the politics of Israelite identity. Journal of Biblical Literature, 132(2):251-274.

Ferguson, E. 2003. Backgrounds of early Christianity. Grand Rapids: Wm B. Eerdmans Publishing Co.

ffytche, D.H. 2010. The visual unconscious: perspectives from the Charles Bonnet Syndrome (*In* New horizons in the neuroscience of consciousness. Perry, E., Collerton, D., LeBeau, F., & Ashton H., eds. Amsterdam: John Benjamins Publishing Company. p. 215-226).

Field, N. P., & Filanosky, C. 2010. Continuing Bonds, Risk Factors for Complicated Grief, and Adjustment to Bereavement. Death Studies, 34(1):1-29.

Foster. B.R. 1995. From distant days, myths, tales, and poetry of ancient Mesopotamia. Bethesda: CDL Press.

Fraschetti, A. 2005. The foundation of Rome. Translated by M. Hill & K. Windle. Edinburgh: Edinburgh University Press.

Frith, C.D. 1992. Cognitive neuropsychology of schizophrenia. East Sussex: Lawrence Erlbaum Associates Ltd., Publishers.

Fotopoulos, J. 2002. The rhetorical situation, arrangement, and argumentation of 1 Corinthians 8:1-13: insights into Paul's instructions on idol-food in Greco-Roman context. The Greek Orthodox Theological Review, vol. 47, no. 1-4:165-198.

Fotopoulos, J 2005. Arguments concerning food offered to idols: Corinthian quotations and Pauline refutations in a rhetorical partitio (1 Corinthians 8:1-9). The Catholic Biblical Quarterly, 67(4):611-631.

Frymer-Kensky, T. 1992. In the wake of the goddesses: Women culture, and the biblical transformation of pagan myth. New York: The Free Press.

Gangel, K.O. 1998. Holman New Testament Commentary: Acts, Anders, M.A., *ed.* Nashville: Broadman & Holman.

Gates, M. & Ancill, R. 1994. Exploring hemispheric function using high frequency digital EEG in Schizophrenia: Exploring the spectrum of psychosis Ancill, R.J., Holliday, S., & Higginbotham, J., eds. Chichester: John Wiley and Sons.

Geisler, N. 2007. Resurrection, objections to. (*In* The Baker encyclopedia of Christian apologetics. Grand Rapids: Baker Academic. P. 657-664).

Geisler, N. and Turek, F. 2004. I don't have enough faith to be an atheist. Wheaton: Crossway.

Gersztenkorn, D., & Lee, A. G. 2015. Palinopsia: peeking behind doors of visual perception, visual memory: pathological afterimages split into two categories: hallucinatory, illusory palinopsia. Ophthalmology Times, (7):60.

Gilbert, G. 1754. The law of evidence. Dublin: for Sarah Cotter.

Gill, J. 1746-63. Gill's exposition of the entire Bible [Kindle ed.]. Available: http://www.amazon.com

Gill, J. 2003. An exposition of the gospel according to John. Springfield: Particular Baptist Press.

Gooch, G. & Williams, M. 2007. Evidence in rebuttal. Oxford reference. http://www.oxfordreference.com/view/10.1093/acref/9780192807021.0 01.0001/acref-9780192807021-e-1189. Date of access: 22 June 2015.

Goodrick, E.W. & Kohlenberger J.R. 1999. The strongest niv exhaustive concordance. Grand Rapids: Zondervan.

Gosling, A. 2002. Sending up the founder: Ovid and the apotheosis of Romulus (*In* Acta classica: proceedings of the classical association of South Africa, vol. 45: p. 51-69).

Graham, M.H. & Ohlbaum, E.D. 1997. Courtroom evidence: a teaching commentary. Notre Dame: National Institute for Trial Advocacy.

Grahn, J. 2010. Ecology of the erotic in a myth of Inanna. The International Journal Of Transpersonal Studies, 29(2):58-67.

Greenleaf, S. 1984. The Testimony of the evangelists. Grand Rapids: Baker Book House.

Grenig, J.E., Lee, W.C., & O'Malley K.F. 2000. Federal jury instructions: criminal, 5th edition. St. Paul: West Group.

Greenwalt, W.S. 2015. Thracian and Macedonian kingship. A companion to ancient Thrace, Valeva, J., Nankov, E., & Graninger, D., *eds*. Chichester: John Wiley & Sons, Inc.

Grieve, V. 1991. Your verdict on the empty tomb of Jesus. Bromley: InterVarsity Press.

Griffith, N. 2000. A lawyer looks at the gospels. Enumclaw, Wa.: Winepress Publishing.

Groneberg, B. 2009. The role and function of goddesses in Mesopotamia (*In* Leick, G., *ed*. The Babylonian world New York: Routledge. p. 319-331).

Groothuis, D. 2011. Christian apologetics: a comprehensive case for biblical faith. Downers Grove: IVP Academic.

Grotius, H. 2010. The truth of the Christian religion in six books, book III [Kindle ed.]. Translated by J. Clarke. London: William Baynes. Available: http://www.amazon.com

Grush, R. Lecture 14: False Cause. On Informal Fallacies. http://courses.ucsd.edu/rgrush/podcasts/logic-audio/lecture-14.pdf Date of access: 29 January 2016.

Gutteridge, Jr. D.J. 1975. The defense rests its case. Nashville: Broadman Press.

Gwynne, P. 2000. The fate of Jesus' body: Another decade of debate. Colloquium, 32(1):3-21.

Habermas, G.R. 1997. The resurrection appearances of Jesus (*In* Geivett, R.D. & Habermas, G.R., eds. In defense of miracles: A comprehensive case in history. Downer's Grove: IVP Academic. p. 262-275).

Habermas, G.R. 2001. Explaining away Jesus' resurrection: the recent revival of hallucination theories. Faculty publications and presentations, Paper 107:1-7.

Habermas, G.R. 2006. Mapping the recent trend toward the bodily resurrection appearances of Jesus in light of other prominent critical positions (*In* Stewart, R.B., ed. The resurrection of Jesus: John Dominic Crossan and N.T. Wright in dialogue Minneapolis: Fortress Press. p. 78-92).

Habermas, G. 2009. A conversation with Gary Habermas and Antony Flew: Did the resurrection happen, Baggett, D. *ed.* Downer's Grove: IVP Books.

Habermas, G.R. 2012a. Philosophy of history, miracles, and the resurrection of Jesus. Sagamore Beach: Academx.

Habermas, G. R. 2012b. Resurrection appearances of Jesus as after-death communication: response to Ken Vincent. Faculty Publications and Presentations. Paper 399:149-158. http://digitalcommons.liberty.edu/lts_fac_pubs/399 Date of access: 27 May 2016.

Habermas, G.R. 2015. Evidence for the historical Jesus: is the Jesus of history the Christ of faith? Lynchburg: GaryHabermas.com.

Habermas, G.R. & Flew, A.G.N. 2005. Resurrected?: an atheist and theist dialogue. Lanham: Rowman & Littlefield Publishers, Inc.

Habermas, G.R. & Licona, M.R. 2004. The case for the resurrection of Jesus. Grand Rapids: Kregel Publications.

Hagner, D. A. 2002. Encountering the book of Hebrews: an exposition. Grand Rapids: Baker Academic.

Handley, K. 1999. A lawyer looks at the resurrection. Kategoria, 15:11-21. http://tgc-documents.s3.amazonaws.com/kategoria/kategoria15.pdf

Hansen, B. Å., & Brodtkorb, E. 2003. Partial epilepsy with "ecstatic" seizures. Epilepsy & Behavior, 4(6):667-673.

Harris, S. 2009. The end of faith: Religion, terror, and the future of reason. New York: W.W. Norton.

Hare, T. 1999. Remembering Osiris: number, gender, and the word in ancient Egyptian representational systems. Stanford: Stanford University Press.

Hawes Publications. Adult New York best seller lists. http://www.hawes.com/pastlist.htm Date of access: 29 Oct. 2014.

Heffron, Y. 2013. Inana/Ištar (goddess). Ancient mesopotamian gods and goddesses. http://oracc.museum.upenn.edu/amgg/listofdeities/inanaitar/ Date of access: 17 January 2016.

Hermann, D. 2014. Reading contemporary responses to the resurrection: Metaphorical, historical, and naturalistic. Theophilus: The student journal of the catholic theological union, 1(1):70-84.

Herodotus. 2014. The histories: complete [Kindle ed.]. Radford: Wilder Publications.

Hitchens, C. 2007. God is not great: how religion poisons everything. New York: Hachette Book Group.

Hobson, J.A. 2002. The dream drugstore: chemically altered states of consciousness. Cambridge: The MIT Press.

Hodges, Z.C. 1966. Women and the empty tomb. Bibliotheca Sacra, 123 no 492:301-309.

Holt, N., Simmonds-Moore, C., & Moore, S. 2008. Benign schizotypy: investigating differences between clusters of schizotype on paranormal belief, creativity, intelligence and mental health. http://www.academia.edu/695141/Benign_schizotypy_Investigating_differences

_between_clusters_of_schizotype_on_paranormal_belief_creativity_intelligence_and_mental_health Date of access: 20 May 2016.

Hurowitz, V. A. 2003. The Mesopotamian god image, from womb to tomb. Journal of the American Oriental Society, 123(1):147-157.

Hurtado, L. W. 2013. Resurrection-faith and the 'historical' Jesus. Journal for the study of the historical Jesus, 11(1):35-52.

Hwang, J. 2011. Turning the tables on idol feasts: Paul's use of Exodus 32:6 in 1 Corinthians 10:7. Journal of the Evangelical Theological Society, 54(3):573-587.

Ignatius. s.a. (a). Letter to the Ephesians (*In* Roberts, A. & Donaldson, J., eds. Ante-nicene fathers, volume 1: The apostolic fathers, Justin Martyr, Irenaeus [Kindle ed.]. 2002. Grand Rapids: Christian classics ethereal library. ch. 12. Available: http://www.amazon.com Date of access: 12 June 2016).

Ignatius. s.a. (b) Letter to the philadelphians. (*In* The faith of the early fathers, vol. I. Translated by WIlliam Jurgens. 1970. Collegeville: The Liturgical Press. p. 22-24).

Ignatius. s.a. (c) Letter to the smyrnaens. (*In* The faith of the early fathers, vol. 1. Translated by WIlliam Jurgens. 1970. Collegeville: The Liturgical Press. p. 24-25).

Imwinkelried, E.J. 2015. Evidentiary foundations, ninth edition. New Providence: Matthew Bender.

Irenaeus. s.a. Against heresies. (*In* The faith of the early fathers, vol. 1. Translated by WIlliam Jurgens. 1970. Collegeville: The Liturgical Press. p. 84-104).

Jipp, J.W. 2010. Luke's scriptural suffering messiah: a search for precedent, a search for identity. The Catholic Biblical Quarterly, 72(2):255-274.

Johnson, A. 1965. The historian and historical evidence. Port Washington: Kennikat Press.

Johnson, J. J. 2001. Were the resurrection appearances hallucinations?: Some psychiatric and psychological considerations. Churchman, 115(3):227-238.

Johnson, J. J. 2004. Hans Frei as unlikely apologist for the historicity of the resurrection. Evangelical Quarterly, 76(2):135-151.

Johnson, P. 2008. Juridical apologists 1600-2000 ad: a bio-bibliographic essay. http://www.academia.edu/1183577/_Juridical_Apologists_1600-2000_AD _A_Bio-Bibliographical_Essay_ Date of Access: 11 June 2015.

Jones, C. 2013. Visions, hallucinations, and bereavement. Biola University discussion board. Online course: In Defense of the Resurrection 691. Date of access: 2 April 2013.

Jones, P. 2003. Embracing Inana: legitimation and mediation in the ancient Mesopotamian sacred hymn iddin-dagan a. Journal of the American Oriental Society. 123(2):291-302.

Josephus, F. s.a. The antiquities of the Jews (*In* the works of Josephus: Complete and unabridged Translated by William Whiston. Peabody Ma.: Hendrickson Publishers. p. 537-539).

Joynes, C. E. 2011. The Sound of Silence: Interpreting Mark 16: 1-8 through the Centuries. Interpretation, 65(1):18-29.

Kasper, B.S., Kasper, E.M., Pauli, E., & Stefan, H. 2010. Phenomenology of hallucinations, illusions, and delusions as part of seizure semiology. Epilepsy & Behavior, Volume 18, Issues 1-2, p. 13-23.

Katz, D. 2003. The image of the nether world in the Sumerian sources. Bethesda: CDL Press.

Keen, C., Murray, C., & Payne, S. 2013. Sensing the presence of the deceased: A narrative review. Mental Health, Religion & Culture, 16(4):384-402.

Keener, C.S.1999. A commentary on the gospel of Matthew. Grand Rapids: William B. Eerdmans Publishing Company.

Keener, C.S. 2000. The NIV application commentary: Revelation, Muck. T., *ed*. Grand Rapids: Zondervan.

Keener, C.S. 2003. The gospel of John: a commentary volume II. Peabody: Hendrickson Publishing.

Kelly, A. J. 2008. The resurrection effect: transforming Christian life and thought. Maryknoll: Orbis Books.

Kent, H.A. 1972. Jerusalem to Rome: Studies in the Book of Acts. Grand Rapids: Baker Book House.

Kluver, H. 1969. Mescal and mechanisms of hallucinations. Chicago: The University of Chicago Press.

Kramer, S.N. 1961. Sumerian mythology: a study of spiritual and literary achievement in the third millennium B.C. New York: Harper and Brothers.

Kwilecki, S. 2011. Ghosts, Meaning, and Faith: After-Death Communications in Bereavement Narratives. Death Studies, 35(3):219-243.

Lake, K. 1907. The historical evidence for the resurrection of Jesus Christ. New York: G.P. Putnam.

Langbein, J.H. 1996. Historical foundations of the law of evidence: A View from the Ryder Sources. Columbia Law Review, 5:168-1202. Date of access: 4 June 2015.

Langbein, J.H. 2003. The origins of adversary criminal trial. Oxford: Oxford University Press.

Langlitz, N. 2013. Neuropsychedelia: The revival of hallucinogen research since the decade of the brain. Berkeley: University of California Press.

Lee, D., 2011. Paschal Imagery in the Gospel of John: A Narrative and Symbolic Reading. Pacifica: Australasian Theological Studies, 24(1):13-28.

Leick, G. 2008. Sexuality and religion in Mesopotamia. Religion Compass, 2(2):119-133.

Lenski, R.C.H. 2008. The interpretation of The Acts of the Apostles: 1-14. Minneapolis: Augsburg Fortress.

Licona, M. 2010. The resurrection of Jesus: A new historiographical approach. Downer's Grove: IVP Academic.

Lilley, J. L. 1940. Alleged discrepancies in the gospel accounts of the resurrection. Catholic Biblical Quarterly, 2(2):98-111 Date of access: 25 May 2015.

Livy. 2012. Book 1: the earliest legends [Kindle ed.]. History of Rome (Complete). Oxford: Acheron Press. Available: http://www.amazon.com

Loke, A.T.E., 2009. The resurrection of the son of God: A reduction of the naturalistic alternatives. The Journal of Theological Studies:flp093.

López, R. 2013. The nature of the resurrection body of Jesus and believers. Bibliotheca Sacra, 170(678):143-153.

Lunn, N. 2014. Raised on the third day according to the scriptures: Resurrection typology in the Genesis creation narrative. Journal of Evangelical Theological Society, 57(3):523-535.

Lyons, W. J. 2004. On the life and death of Joseph of Arimathea. https://www.academia.edu/3635453/On_the_Life_and_Death_of_Joseph_of_Arimathea_Journal_for_the_Study_of_the_Historical_Jesus_2_2004_29-53 Date of access: 23 April 2015.

MacGregor, K. R. 2006. 1 Corinthians 15:3b-6a, 7 and the bodily resurrection of Jesus. Journal Of The Evangelical Theological Society, 49(2):225-234.

Martin, T.R. 2012. Ancient Rome: From Romulus to Justinian. New Haven: Yale University Press.

Mauet, T & Wolfson, W.D. 2009. Trial evidence, 4th edition. New York: Aspen.

Mavromatis, A. 1987. Hypnagogia: the unique state of consciousness between wakefulness and sleep. New York: Routledge & Kegan Paul Inc.

Mayo foundation for Medical Education and Research. 2016. Schizotypal personality disorders: symptoms and causes. http://www.mayoclinic.org/diseases-conditions/schizotypal-personality-disorder/symptoms-causes/dxc-20198941 Date of access: 20 May 2016.

Mays, J.L., 2006. "Is This Not Why You Are Wrong?" Exegetical Reflections on Mark 12: 18-27. Interpretation, 60(1):32-46.

McDowell, J. 1981. The resurrection factor. San Bernardino: Here's Life.

McDowell, J. 1999. The new evidence that demands a verdict. Nashville: Thomas Nelson Publishers.

McDowell, S.J. 2014. A historical evaluation of the evidence for the death of the apostles as martyrs for their faith. Louisville: SBTS. (Dissertation-PhD).

McGrew, L. & McGrew, T. 2009. The argument from miracles: a cumulative case for the resurrection of Jesus of Nazareth. (*In* Craig, W.L. & Moreland J.P., *eds*. The Blackwell companion to natural theology. Chichester: Blackwell publishing, p. 593-662).

McIntosh. J. R. 2005. Ancient Mesopotamia: New perspectives. Santa Barbara: ABC-CLIO.

McKellar, P. 1989. Abnormal psychology. New York: Routledge.

Merriam Webster: An Encyclopaedia Britannica Company [Web]. 2015a Contradiction. http://www.merriam-webster.com/dictionary/contradiction Date of access: 23 June 2015.

Merriam Webster: An Encyclopaedia Britannica Company [Web]. 2015b. Contradiction. http://www.merriam-webster.com/dictionary/embellish Date of access: 23 June 2015.

Merriam Webster: An Encyclopaedia Britannica Company [Web]. 2015c. Contradiction. http://www.merriam-webster.com/dictionary/embellishment Date of access: 23 June 2015.

Metzger, B.M. 1968. Historical and literary studies: pagan, Jewish and Christian. Grand Rapids: Wm. B. Eerdmans.

Miller, D. R. 2013. Is there anything new under the (Mediterranean) sun?: expressions of Near Eastern deities in the Graeco-Roman world. Religion & Theology, 20(3-4):345-370.

Miller, S. 2004. They said nothing to anyone: The fear and silence of the women at the empty tomb (Mk 16.1-8). Feminist Theology, 13(1):77-90.

Milligan, W. 1917. The resurrection of our lord. New York: The Macmillan Company. https://archive.org/stream/resurrectionofou00mill#page/48/mode/2up/search/49. Date of access: 25 May 2015.

Mitchell, D. 2004. The book of first Corinthians: Christianity in a hostile culture, Couch, M. & Hindson, E., *eds.* Chattanooga: AMG Publishers.

Montgomery, J. W. 1969. Where is history going? Grand Rapids: Zondervan Publishing House.

Montgomery, J.W. 1983. The Marxist Approach to Human Rights: Analysis and Critique. Simon Greenleaf Law Review, III:155.

Montgomery, J.W. 1986. Human rights and human dignity. Grand Rapids: Zondervan.

Montgomery, J. W. 1975. Law above the law. Minneapolis: Dimension Books.

Montgomery, J.W. 2002. History, law, and Christianity. Calgary: Canadian Institute for Law, Theology, and Public Policy, Inc.

Morison, F. 1993. Who moved the stone? Carlisle: OM Publishing.

Morkot, R. 2010. Divine of body: The remains of Egyptian kings-preservation, reverence, and memory in a world without relics. Past and Present, Supplement 5:37-55.

Mosteller, R.P. 2005. Evidence history, the new trace evidence, and rumblings in the future of proof. Ohio State Journal Of Criminal Law, 2:524-27 Date of access: 3 June 2015.

Murray, B. Fallacies in arguments, or how arguments go wrong. http://www.auburn.edu/~murraba/fallacies.html Date of access: 29 January 2016.

Nair, A. G., Nair, A. G., Shah, B. R., & Gandhi, R. A. 2015. Seeing the unseen: Charles Bonnet syndrome revisited. Psychogeriatrics, 15(3):204-208.

Naso, O. 2012a. Fasti (In complete works of Ovid. Translated by J.G.Frazer.) [Kindle ed.]. East Sussex: Delphi Classics. Available: http://www.amazon.com

Naso, O. 2012b. The art of love (In complete works of Ovid. Translated by J.L. May) [Kindle ed.]. East Sussex: Delphi Classics. Available: http://www.amazon.com

National institute of mental health. 2016. Post traumatic stress disorder. http://www.nimh.nih.gov/health/topics/post-traumatic-stress-disorder-ptsd/index.shtml Date of access : 25 May 2016.

Newman-Taylor, K. & Sambrook, S. 2013. The role of dissociation in psychosis in cognitive and behavioral approaches to the understandment and treatment of dissociation, Kennedy, F., Kennerly, H., & Pearson, D., eds. New York: Routledge.

Nock, A.D. 1938. St. Paul. New York: Harper Brothers Publishers.

Norman, D. J. 2008. Doubt and the resurrection of Jesus. Theological Studies, 69(4): 786-811.

O'Brien, K. S. 2005. Written that you may believe: John 20 and narrative rhetoric. The Catholic Biblical Quarterly, 67(2):284-302.

O'Brien, R. 1999. Astarte in the temple of Venus: an allegory of idolatry. Studies in philology, 96(2):144-158.

O'Collins, G. 1987(a). Jesus risen. New York/Mahwah: Paulist Press.

O'Collins, G. 1987(b). Mary Magdalene as major witness to Jesus' resurrection. Theological Studies, 48(4): 631-646.

O'Collins, G. 1988. Interpreting the resurrection. Mahwah: Paulist Press.

O'Collins, G. 1997. The resurrection: the state of the questions (In Davis, S.T., Kendall, D. & O'Collins G., eds. The resurrection: an interdisciplinary symposium on the resurrection of Jesus. New York: Oxford University Press. p. 5-28).

O'Collins, G. 2009. Christology: A biblical, historical, and systematic study of Jesus, second edition. Oxford: Oxford University Press.

O'Collins, G. 2011. The Resurrection and Bereavement Experiences. Irish Theological Quarterly, 76(3):224-237.

O'Collins, G. 2012. Peter as witness to Easter. Theological Studies, 73(2):263-285.

O'Connell, J.H. 2009. Jesus' resurrection and collective hallucinations. Tyndale Bulletin, 60(1):69-105.

O'Connell, J.H. 2010. The reliability of the resurrection narratives. European Journal of Theology, 19(2):141-152.

O'Connell, J.H. 2012. John versus the Synoptic Gospels on Mary Magdalene's visit to the tomb. Conspectus: The Journal of the South African Theological Seminary, 14:123-131.

Orfield, L.B. 1945. The federal rules of criminal procedure. California Law Review, 33(4), p. 533-99. http://scholarship.law.berkeley.edu/californialawreview/vol33/iss4/4 Date of access: 5 June 2015.

Oxford dictionaries [Web]. 2015. Contradiction. http://www.oxforddictionaries.com/us/definition/american_english/contradiction Date of access: 4 November 2015.

Parsons, E.E. 1967. Witnesses to the resurrection. Grand Rapids: Baker Book House.

Pearson, B.W.R. 2001. Corresponding sense: Paul, dialectic & Gadamer. Leiden, Boston, Koln: Brill.

Perkins, P. 1992. "I have seen the Lord" (John 20:18): women witnesses to the resurrection. Interpretation, 46(1):31-41.

Perrin, N. 2007. On raising Osiris in 1 Corinthians 15. Tyndale Bulletin, 58(1):117-128.

Pinker, A. 2005. Descent of the goddess Ishtar to the netherworld and Nahum II 8. Vetus Testamentum, 55(1):89-100.

Plato. 2015. Charmides [Kindle ed.]. New York: OIA Press. Available: http://www.amazon.com

Plevnik, J. 1987. The eyewitnesses of the risen Jesus in Luke 24. Catholic Biblical Quarterly, 49(1):90-103.

Plutarch. 2012. Isis and Osiris [Kindle ed.]. Oxford: Acheron Press. Available: http://www.amazon.com

Polhill, J.B. 2009. The Acts of the Apostles: Four Centuries of Baptist Interpretation, Barr, B.A., Leonard, B.J., Parsons, M.C., & Weaver, C.D., *eds*. Waco: Baylor University Press.

Prince, D. C. 2012. Resurrecting Certainty in the Gospel of Luke. Leaven, 20(1):25-30.

Proctor, W. 1998. The resurrection report. Nashville: Broadman & Holman Publishers.

Prusak, B. P. 2000. Bodily Resurrection in Catholic Perspectives. Theological Studies, 61(1):64-105.

Rabadjiev, K. 2015. Religion: A companion to ancient Thrace. Valeva, J., Nankov, E., & Graninger, D., *eds*. Chichester: John Wiley & Sons, Inc.

Ramsey A.M. 1969. God, Christ, and the world. London: SCM.

Rawson, E. 2014. Cicero the historian and Cicero the antiquarian (*In* The Roman historical tradition: regal and republic Rome). Oxford: The Oxford University Press.

Rayburn, R.S. 2007. Covenant, New. (*In* Evangelical dictionary of theology, second edition, Elwell, W.A., *ed*. Grand Rapids: Baker Academic. p. 301).

Rees, W.D. 1971. The hallucinations of widowhood. British Medical Journal, 4(5778) 37-44.

Renggli, F. 2002. The sunrise as the birth of a baby: The Prenatal Key to Egyptian Mythology. Journal of Prenatal and Perinatal Psychology and Health, 16:215-236.

Reeve, S., Sheaves, B., & Freeman, D. 2015. The role of sleep dysfunction in the occurrence of delusions and hallucinations: A systematic review. Clinical Psychology Review, 42:96-115.

Reynolds, J.M. 2009. When Athens met Jerusalem: an introduction to classical and Christian thought. Downers Grove: IVP Academic.

Roberson, J.A. 2015. A season in hell (with Apologies to Arthur Rimbaud): The annihilation of the damned in Ancient Egypt. Expedition, Fall:17-23.

Robinson, E. 1993. The resurrection and ascension of our lord. Bibliotheca Sacra, 150(597):9-34.

Sacks, O. 2012. Hallucinations. New York: Alfred A. Knopf.

Sagebeer, J. 1988. The Bible in court. Philadelphia: J.B Lippincott Co.

Salvoni, F. 1961. Modern studies on the resurrection of Jesus. Restoration Quarterly, 5(2):89-99.

Sanders, F. 2015. How God used R.A. Torrey. A short biography as told through his sermons. Chicago: Moody Publishers. http://www.amazon.com/How-God-Used-Torrey-Biography/dp/0802412688/ref=sr_1_2?ie=UTF8&qid=1433881518&sr=8-2&keywords=Fred+sAnders Date of access: 9 June 2015.

Sanger, M. 2009. When clients sense the presence of loved ones who have died. OMEGA-Journal of Death and Dying, 59(1):69-89.

Schnabel, E. 2012. Acts: Exegetical commentary on the New Testament, Arnold, C.E., *ed.* Grand Rapids: Zondervan.

Schoeps, H.J. 1961. Paul the theology of the apostle in the light of Jewish religious history. Translated by H. Knight. Philadelphia: The Westminster Press.

Schoeps, H. 1968. The religions of mankind. Translated by R. Winston & C. Winston. New York: Anchor Books.

Schreiner, T. R. 2003. The New American Commentary, Volume 37: 1,2 Peter, Jude. Nashville: Broadman & Holman.

Schum, D. A. 2003. Evidences and Inferences in Past Events. (*In* Twining, W. and Hampsher-Monk, I., *eds.* Evidence and inference in history and law Evanston: Northwestern University Press. p.11-24).

Setzer, C. 1997. Excellent women: female witness to the resurrection. Journal Of Biblical Literature, 116(2):259-72.

Sherlock T. 1729. The trial of the witnesses of the Resurrection of Jesus, London: J. Roberts.

Sharp, M.J. 2009. Christianity among the myths [Kindle ed.]. The Aeropagus Journal of the apologetics resource center, Vol 9(6). Available: http://www.amazon.com

Siniscalchi, G. B. 2011. Resurrecting Jesus and Jesus' critical historiography: William Lane Craig and Dale Allison in dialogue. The Heythrop Journal, 52(3):362-373.

Siniscalchi, G.B. 2012. Early Christian Worship and the Historical Argument for Jesus' Resurrection. New Blackfriars, 93(1048):710-732.

Siniscalchi, G. B. 2014. On comparing the resurrection appearances with apparitions. Pacifica: Australasian Theological Studies, 27(2):184-205.

Slade, P.D. & Bentall, R.P. 1988. Sensory deception: a scientific analysis of hallucination. Baltimore: The Johns Hopkins University Press.

Smith, J. J. 2006. Resurrection faith today. Landas: Journal of Loyola School of Theology, 20:135-172.

Smith, J. Z. 1990. Drudgery divine: On the comparison of early Christianities and the religions of late antiquity. Chicago: The University of Chicago Press.

Smith, M. 1998. The death of "dying and rising gods" in the biblical world: An update, with special reference to Baal in the Baal cycle. Scandinavian Journal of the Old Testament, 12:2:257-313.

Smith, M. 2008. Osiris and the deceased. (*In* Dieleman, J., & Wendrich, W., eds. UCLA Encyclopedia of Egyptology, Los Angeles. Available: http//scholar ship.org/uc/tem/29r70244 Date of Access: 16 January 2016).

Smith, M. 2009. Traversing eternity: Texts for the afterlife from Ptolemaic Egypt. Oxford: Oxford University Press.

Sonik, K. 2012. Breaching the boundaries of being: Metamorphoses in the Mesopotamian literary texts. Journal Of The American Oriental Society, 132(3):385-393.

Sorea, D. 2013. Two particular expressions of neo-paganism. Bulletin of the Transylvania University of Brasov, Series VII: Social Sciences and Law, (1):29-40.

Spence, H.D.M. & Joseph, S.E. 1961. The pulpit commentary, vol. 15-Matthew. http://biblehub.com/commentaries/matthew/28-9.htm Date of access: 9 June 2016.

Steffen, E. & Coyle, A. 2011. Sense of presence experiences and meaning-making in bereavement: A qualitative analysis. Death Studies, 35:579-609.

Stein, R.H. 1992. The new American commentary volume 24: Luke. Nashville: Broadman Press.

Stenschke, C. W. 2012. Paul's Jewish gospel and the claims of Rome in Paul's epistle to the Romans. Neotestamentica, 46(2):338-378.

Still, E. I. 2004. Divisions over leaders and food offered to idols: The parallel thematic structures of 1 Corinthians 4:6-21 and 8:1-11:1. Tyndale Bulletin, 55(1):17-41.

Stopp, M.T. 1999. Evidence law in the trial process. Albany: West Legal Studies.

Strabo. 1892. The geography of Strabo, vol. I. Translated by H.C. Hamilton & W. Falconer. London: George Bell & Sons.

Strobel, L. 2003. The case for Easter. Grand Rapids: Zondervan.

SuperScholar. The 25 most influential living atheists. http://www.superscho lar.org/features/influential-atheists/. Date of access: 28 Oct. 2014.

Swinburne, R. 2003. The resurrection of God incarnate. Oxford: Clarendon Press.

Tanford, J.A. 1990. The law and psychology of jury instructions. Faculty Publications. Paper 706: 72-111. http://www.repository.law.indiana.edu/facpub/706 Date of Access: 5 June 2015.

Taylor, J.H. 2001. Death and the afterlife in ancient Egypt. Chicago: The University of Chicago Press.

Tenney, M.C. 1963. The reality of the resurrection. New York: Harper and Row Publishers.

The acts of Thomas. s.a. Translated by M.R. James. The gnostic society library: gnostic scriptures and fragments. http://gnosis.org/library/actthom.htm Date of access: 16 June 2016.

Thebestschools.org. 50 top atheists in the world today. http://www.thebestschools.org/blog/2011/12/01/50-top-atheists-in-the-world-today/ Date of access: 28 Oct. 2014.

The (second) apocalypse of James. s.a. Translated by C.W. Hedrick. The Gnostic Society Library: The Nag Hammadi Library. http://gnosis.org/naghamm/2ja.html Date of access: 16 June 2016.

The secular web. http://infidels.org/library/modern/richard_carrier/#debrev Date of access: 29 October 2014.

Theissen, G. & Merz, A. 1998. The historical Jesus: a comprehensive guide. Minneapolis: Fortress Press.

Tidball, D. 2006. Completing the circle the resurrection according to John. Evangelical Review of Theology, 30(2):169-183.

Torrey, R.A. 1922. Is the Bible the inerrant word of God? New York: George H. Doran Company.

Towns, E. 2002. The gospel of John: Believe and live. Couch, M., & Hindson, E. *eds*. Chattanooga: AMG Publishers.

United States Court of Appeals Fifth Circuit Library System. 2012. Pattern jury instructions (criminal cases). http://www.lb5.uscourts.gov/juryinstructions/fifth/crim2012.pdf Date of access: 3 June 2015.

United States Court of Appeals for the Sixth Circuit. 2014. Pattern criminal jury instructions. http://www.ca6.uscourts.gov/internet/crim_jury_insts/pdf/crmpattjur_full.pdf Date of access: 5 June 2015.

United States Courts. Glossary of legal terms: defendant. http://www.uscourts.gov/glossary Date of access 2 September 2016.

United States Courts. Glossary of legal terms: plaintiff. http://www.uscourts.gov/glossary Date of access 2 September 2016.

Ustinova, Y. 2002. Either a daimon, or a hero, or perhaps a god: mythical residents of subterranean chambers. Kernos. Revue internationale et pluridisciplinaire de religion grecque antique, 15(2002):267-288.

Waters, F, Collerton, D, ffytche, D.H., Jardri, R., Pins, D., Dudley, R., Blom, J.D., Mosimann, U.P, Eperjesi, F. Ford, S., Laroi, F. 2014. Visual hallucinations in the psychosis spectrum and comparative information from neurodegenerative disorders and eye disease, Schizophrenia Bulletin, 40(4):S233-S245.

Waugh, E. 1957. The ordeal of Gilbert Pinfold. London: Chapman and Hall.

Welker, M. 2007. Wright on the resurrection. Scottish Journal of Theology, 60, 458-475.

Wenham, D. 1973. The resurrection narratives in Matthew's Gospel, Tyndale Bulletin, 24:21-54.

Wenham, J. 1992. Easter enigma. Grand Rapids: Baker Book House.

Westenholz, J.G. 2009. Inanna and Ishtar- the dimorphic Venus goddesses (*In* The babylonian world, Leick, G., *ed.*). New York: Routledge.

White, P.J. s.a. Examination, cross-examination, and redirect examination. University of North Carolina School of Government. https://www.sog.unc.edu/sites/www.sog.unc.edu/files/course_materials/White_Examination.pdf Date of access: 6 September 2016.

Wiebe, P.H. 1997. Visions of Jesus: direct encounters from the New Testament. New York: Oxford University Press.

Wigmore, J.H. 1913. Select cases on the law of evidence, compiled and edited by John Henry

Wigmore, 2nd edition. Boston: Little, Brown, and Company.

Wilckens, U. 1978. Resurrection: biblical testimony to the resurrection: an historical examination and explanation. Translated by A.M. Stewart. Atlanta: John Knox Press.

Williams, G. 2013. Narrative space, angelic revelation, and the end of Mark's Gospel. Journal for the Study of the New Testament, 35(3):263-284.

Wiseman, T.P. 2004. The myths of Rome. Exeter: The University of Exeter Press.

Witherington III, B. 1998. The acts of the apostles: A socio-rhetorical commentary. Grand Rapids: William B. Eerdmans Publishing Company.

Witherington III, B. 2000. Resurrection redux (*In* Copan, P., *ed.* Will the real Jesus please stand up?: A debate between William Lane Craig and John Dominic Crossan. Grand Rapids: Baker Books. p. 129-146).

Witt, R.E. 1971. Isis in the Graeco-Roman world. Ithaca: New York.

Wolkstein, D. & Kramer, S. 1983. Inanna queen of heaven and earth: Her stories and hymns from Sumer. New York: Harper & Row.

Wright, N.T. 2002. Jesus' resurrection & Christian origins. http://ntwright page.com/Wright_Jesus_Resurrection.htm Date of access: 15 May 2015.

Wright, N.T. 2003. The resurrection of the Son of God. Minneapolis: Fortress Press.

Wright, N.T. 2006. The resurrection: historical event or theological explanation?: Opening statement (In Stewart, R.B., ed. The resurrection of Jesus: John Dominic Crossan and N.T. Wright in dialogue. Minneapolis: Fortress Press. p. 16-47).

Wright, N. T. 2012. Israel's Scriptures in Paul's narrative theology. Theology, 115(5):323-329.

Yamauchi, E.M., 1974. Easter: Myth, Hallucination, or History? http://www.leaderu.com/everystudent/easter/articles/yama.html Date of access: 24 January 2016.

Zeman, A. 2002. Consciousness: A user's guide. New haven: Yale University Press.

Zusne, L. & Jones, W.H. 2014. Anomalistic psychology: A study of magical thinking, second edition. New York: Psychology Press.

www.ingramcontent.com/pod-product-compliance
Lightning Source LLC
Chambersburg PA
CBHW071145300426
44113CB00009B/1093